MARIE

MARIE

A TRUE STORY

PETER MAAS

RANDOM HOUSE
NEW YORK

Library of Congress Cataloging in Publication Data

Maas, Peter, 1929–
Marie, a true story.

1. Pardon—Tennessee. 2. Misconduct in office—
Tennessee. 3. Ragghianti, Marie. 4. Biography—
Tennessee. I. Title.
HV9475.T2M3 1983   364.1'323 [B]   82-42794
ISBN 0-394-51657-5

Manufactured in the United States of America
Typography and binding design by J.K. Lambert
2 4 6 8 9 7 5 3
First Edition

This is for JMM and SJ

Also for Dante, Therese and Ricky

One day I asked Marie how she had managed to hang in, and she said, "Well, you know, I believed in the system and I had to find out if I was right."

PART I

ONE

In the summer, in Nashville, Tennessee, when she was five, her mother would tie a pink ribbon in her hair, and dress her in a white organdy pinafore and white anklets and shiny black Mary Janes, and take her shopping downtown, and strangers would peer down at her and exclaim, "Just look at those big blue eyes, and those cute curls! What's your name, honey?" and she would smile delightedly and say, "Marie! My name's Marie!" That was what she most remembered about being a little girl.

At the age of eight she already displayed a well-developed willfulness. She was furious when her parents had to go on an overnight trip to Chattanooga and left her behind with the Freemans. Mrs. Freeman picked her up in a brand-new Ford sedan, brought her to the Freeman house and said, "All right, Marie, let's get out." She refused. Instead, she slid down in the front seat and started kicking at the dashboard, giving it some really good whacks. Later in the evening she took the sheets from her bed and hid them, and announced that there was no way she could remain in a home where the beds did not have sheets.

By the time she was ten she had read through the Nancy Drew series and otherwise exhausted the resources of the children's wing of the Nashville public library. When she moved on to the adult section, one of the first books to enthrall her was *Crime and Punishment.*

At seventeen, when she was a senior at Seabreeze High in Daytona Beach, Florida, she was elected Miss Daytona Beach in the annual contest sponsored by the Junior Chamber of Commerce, Miss *Nautilus* by the submarine's crew and Miss Seabreeze, the high school beauty queen. In all three contests the runner-up was a girl named Beverly. She also had taken away Beverly's boyfriend, the star halfback on the high school football team. When it got around to writing things in the class yearbook, Beverly wrote that while they'd had their ups and downs, Marie did have a wonderful smile, and Marie thought, Wow, she must really have gritted her teeth on that one.

When she was nineteen, the boy she would marry decked another boy with one punch at a dance in Memphis. All the other boy had done was give her an admiring look, and the next thing she knew he was out cold on the floor. Even though she knew it was wrong, she couldn't help feeling a guilty shiver of excitement at what had happened. She remembered thinking it was kind of romantic.

Then, after they were married, he started to hit her.

She was twenty-five when she fled from him for the last time in 1968. She had three children by then. She was a devout Roman Catholic, and the kids—a boy, a girl and another boy—arrived rapidly, within three years. The younger boy, still an infant, had been critically ill for months with a mysterious lung ailment that had come close to killing him several times. A tracheotomy had been performed and a silver trach tube inserted in his windpipe, but doctors in three different hospitals couldn't figure out what was wrong. Day and night she would have to suction his lungs to keep him from drowning in his own fluids. The doctors had taught her how to do that.

She was broke and survived on handouts. At first she and the kids lived in a rat- and roach-infested apartment in Nashville. The one phobia she had was the fear of little things that crawled in the dark. Maybe five or six times during the night she would have to suction her sick son. She slept in the same room with him and would awake instantly when he started gasping for breath. Each time was a moment of pure horror for her. She knew what was going to happen. When she switched on the light, she would see dozens of roaches and waterbugs scuttling across the floor and up and down the walls and she would have to choke off the rising terror inside her.

But she did it.

At the age of twenty-nine she decided to put herself through Nashville's Vanderbilt University. She had taught herself how to type, and she began typing theses for students in the graduate school. The technical requirements drove her crazy. The margins had to be just so at the top and bottom and on the left and right, and there were precise rules about hyphenation and footnotes, but the money was good—a dollar a page. After mass on Sunday morning she also ran the library at Christ the King Church, which brought in another hundred a month. And on Friday and Saturday nights she put on hot pants and worked as a cocktail waitress at the Villa, a Nashville club. She made more tips than any of the other girls. Some weekends she took home as much as seventy or eighty dollars.

After she graduated from Vanderbilt in 1974, she got a job with the state government. She had always been interested in politics. Her father had been a political reporter. She was a true-blue Democrat, and a new Democratic administration had just been elected.

She was thirty-five when the Governor of Tennessee fired her. It would have been hard not to notice. The Governor publicly called her a liar, a cheat and a thief. He said that she was an embarrassment not only to the State of Tennessee but to him personally.

· 2 ·

Marie Ragghianti was fired on August 3, 1977. She was then chairman of the Board of Pardons and Paroles, the first female to hold that office, one of the highest executive positions ever achieved by a woman in the history of Tennessee politics. She had been on the state payroll in the relatively obscure job of extradition officer for less than a year and a half when the Governor appointed her to the board. And in the corridors of the state capitol up on the hill in Nashville, where the office nameplates of various legislators often include such parenthetical additions as "Buck" or "Jimmy" to reassure visiting constituents that they were still the good old boys they'd always been, a lot of knowing winks passed back and forth about how Marie had got so far so fast.

The governor who hired and fired Marie was Ray Blanton, a three-time former congressman from rural West Tennessee who had every expectation of running for a second term in another year. Blanton stood in the Populist tradition and spoke of his dirt-farm heritage. He liked to remind people that he had made his first cotton crop walking behind a one-row plow and a brace of mules when he was eleven. But the Blanton family business was construction, principally road-building, and in Tennessee, as elsewhere, getting to lay down a highway took plenty of political know-how.

When Blanton ran for the governorship, he supported Equal Employment Opportunity and the Equal Rights Amendment, promising to advance both blacks and women in his administration. It was post-Watergate 1974, and he made a big thing of President Ford's pardon of Richard Nixon. "We are entitled," he said, "to see justice done whether crimes are committed in the streets or in the White House." His Republican opponent, Lamar Alexander, had once worked in the Nixon White House, and Blanton never let anyone forget it. There had been a photograph published that showed Alexander standing next to a seated Nixon. A Blanton campaign poster pictured Blanton in the same pose alongside an empty chair. The line with it said: *This Chair Is Not For Sale.*

Endorsing Ray Blanton, the state's most influential paper, the Nashville *Tennessean,* declared that at a time when unity of purpose was essential for Tennessee, Blanton had demonstrated that he could unify, that he had already brought together factions of the Democratic party that had been split for half a century. *Mr. Blanton is not flamboyant,* the editorial noted. *He is soft-spoken and low-key, careful and deliberate in his responses and he does not tend to leap impulsively into decisions. His quiet style tends to create the impression of needed caution and stability.*

At first nobody seemed to connect Marie's firing with the federal grand jury investigations that had been going on for almost ten months now.

The grand juries—so far there had been two of them—were looking into possible payoffs involving extraditions, paroles and pardons.

The explanation that flew in Nashville, when you came right down to it, was sex, pure and simple. Snide asides had dogged Marie from the moment the Governor broke the news on May 11, 1976, at one of his regular office press conferences, that he was appointing her.

As usual, she was late. The conference was already under way when she was rushed to Blanton's side. The office was packed with reporters and photographers, television cameras and radio mikes. She was thrown by the turnout. Most of the faces were unfamiliar, and she immediately fell back on her old beauty-queen smile. She knew it was a mistake, but she couldn't help herself. It was instinctive. The last time she had been confronted by so many strange faces and cameras, she was walking down a runway carrying an armful of roses while the band played "A Pretty Girl Is Like a Melody."

The smile grew even more fixed when she heard the Governor say, "It is with great pride that I announce the appointment of Marie F. Ragghianti to the State Board of Pardons and Paroles, effective July 1. Being a member of the Board of Pardons and Paroles is one of the most critical posts in state government. It is a tough and often thankless job." Then Blanton revealed that not only was he putting Marie on the board, but he was naming her chairman as well. "I have total confidence in her ability and in the mature judgment she will bring to this most difficult position," he said. "I know Marie Ragghianti will make fair decisions and serve the best interests of the people of Tennessee. I am very grateful that she is accepting this appointment."

The Governor had been uncommonly effusive. None of the reporters said anything. Most of them were men, taking in for the first time her shapely figure, radiant white teeth set against coppery skin, her long, lustrous dark brown hair. Not quite what they were used to seeing on the pardons and paroles board. Marie saw them looking at her, flabbergasted.

That was when one of the female reporters, Drue Smith of the Tennessee Radio Network, stood up. She always asked the first question anyway. In her sixties, she was a ringwise press conference veteran heaped with costume jewelry who dyed her hair varying shades of red, though on St. Patrick's Day she wore a green wig. For this occasion she had on gold lamé boots, and her hair had a pink cotton-candy cast. Old Drue could always be counted on for a zinger.

"Guv-ehnah Blay-anton," she said, working over the syllables in a sweetly malicious, high-pitched drawl, a multi-ringed hand waving vaguely in Marie's direction, "do *you* mean to tell us that *thee-us* heah is the chay-ahman of the Bawd of Pahdons and Paroles?"

"Yes, Drue, I surely do," Blanton replied. The outside corners of Blanton's eyes slanted down in a perpetual squint. He had a quizzical little half-grin that played on the right side of his mouth. You could never really tell whether he was laughing with you, or at you. Or maybe even sneering.

· 3 ·

The first public awareness that Marie was having any problems with the Governor came in a story by Larry Daughtrey, the *Tennessean's* capitol hill correspondent, on March 28, 1977, nine months after she'd been appointed, four months before she was fired. The story made political watchers perk up. If Blanton's administration wanted to leak something important, it invariably worked through Daughtrey.

At the time the administration had a bill in the legislature to re-vamp state criminal justice procedures. The idea ostensibly was to streamline the correctional system, to make it more efficient, especially in regard to prison overpopulation. A provision in the bill called for enlarging the pardons and paroles board from three to five members, the two new ones to be picked by the Governor. Now another wrinkle had been added: the rejiggered board would get to elect its own chairman.

The reason was Marie, Daughtrey was told. Daughtrey's source said the Governor had made a big damn mistake putting her in there in the first place. She was screwing everybody in sight, and she was a drinker to boot. She was, well, unstable. And worse, a troublemaker. The last straw was this bill on sentencing and paroling. Marie, for God's sake, had been on the task force that fashioned the whole legislative package, and suddenly the word was she was doing everything she could to torpedo it. Sure, the Governor could kick her ass out for "good cause." And he had plenty of it. But Ray Blanton wasn't that kind of guy. After all, Marie had had a tough time, divorced and all that, with three kids to support. If she couldn't shape up, the Christian thing was to bump her from policy-making and let her spin out her time as an ordinary member of the board. It was more than fair. She still would have five years left to serve.

The headline read:

BLANTON BILL
COULD OUST
PAROLES CHIEF

In his story, Daughtrey got right to it. "Gov. Ray Blanton's administration," he wrote, "has introduced legislation in the General Assembly
which would probably result in the ouster of Marie Ragghianti as
chairman of the Board of Pardons and Paroles." Administration sources
were quoted as saying that Marie "had expressed her displeasure" with
the bill expanding the board, although its intent was simply to help out
the present members, who had been "overworked" because of crowded
penal conditions. As the *Tennessean* was a family newspaper, Daughtrey left out Marie's alleged love life, but he leaned heavily into the
"constant friction" between her and the Governor's office since her
appointment, and noted that this wasn't the first time she had "been
at odds with the administration" and that the Governor "would like
to replace her as chairman without firing her." It was pro forma in any
story involving pardons and paroles to mention the federal probe into
payoffs, and Daughtrey, pointing out that Blanton had dismissed the
charges as "politically inspired," now reported that the months-old
investigation had been "apparently unproductive."

Daughtrey was pretty certain he was being used to send Marie a
message. On the other hand, his tipster was very tight with Blanton,
and Daughtrey was convinced that the information accurately reflected
what the Governor had in mind. Besides, he had already heard gossip
that Marie was sleeping around and any honeymoon she had ever had
with the administration was over. Still, he felt bad enough to phone
Marie afterward to tell her he was sorry he'd had to write the story—
that it wasn't anything personal—but his sources were too solid to
ignore.

Daughtrey was right about one thing. A message was being delivered. The morning Daughtrey's story appeared, Marie was late for a
breakfast meeting. So she picked up the *Tennessean* on the steps
outside her apartment in suburban southwest Nashville and tossed it
next to her on the front seat of her car. When she hit the first red light,
she happened to glance down and saw the headline on page one. She
tried to read and drive at the same time, and almost ran off the road.
Finally she decided to forget the breakfast meeting, and pulled into a
gas station and sat there mesmerized, poring over the piece. She must

have read it five times as the inbound rush-hour traffic built up past her.

Daughtrey's article caught her completely by surprise. The way things were going, it wasn't as though she had never considered the possibility of being bounced, but she was unprepared for the reality of it, and the timing, and the really sleazy way it was being done. She had known, of course, about plans to make the board bigger, and actually was not against the idea. She hadn't figured, though, that they would use it to run her out. The message was clear: either she got back in line or she was through. But it was equally clear they still did not understand where she stood, or else they wouldn't have gone about it so tortuously. They assumed she would do anything to keep the chairmanship. And as Marie drove on toward downtown Nashville, she sensed that this time, at any rate, they may have overplayed their hand.

Later, when Daughtrey called her, she fought down the impulse to tell him that for all his solid sources, he didn't know the half of it. If she started being specific about one thing, it could lead to another, and then to something she might regret. So when Daughtrey began prodding her for some kind of comment, she stuck to the prepared statement she had written out as soon as she got to her office. The statement said: *It is with regret that I have learned of the administration's reputed intent to remove me from the chairmanship. It has been my objective at all times to uphold the oath of my office. This I shall continue to do, hopefully with the support of the administration.*

Larry Brinton of the Nashville *Banner,* who had been a journalist on the local scene for nearly twenty-five years, had heard all the rumors about Marie. In his den at home he had a whole wall of plaques and scrolls from his professional peers attesting that he was the best investigative reporter in the state.

Rumor A was that Marie had had a hot romance with T. Edward (Eddie) Sisk, the Governor's legal counsel. She had originally worked for Sisk as extradition officer, and he directly represented Blanton in matters before the Board of Pardons and Paroles, but Sisk had dumped her, so the story went, and in her fury she was doing everything she could to sabotage the administration. Rumor B had Marie bedded down with Blanton himself before being jilted. Rumor C said that she had been passed on from Sisk to Blanton with the same results, and had subsequently seduced her way through the political spectrum, stirring up trouble left and right.

Anything was possible, but Brinton didn't buy the scorned-woman theory. He reasoned that Marie was just too good-looking for that. And he discounted the scarlet-woman scenario as well. Brinton's wife was a Catholic who belonged to the same parish as Marie, St. Henry's, and she had told him that Marie was an almost daily communicant at mass. Both Sisk and Blanton were married men, and Marie was divorced, which seemed to make perfectly ominous sense in Bible Belt Nashville. But while it was widely known that Marie was a "divorcée," Brinton also learned from his wife something that not many others were aware of. Marie had obtained an annulment. Brinton didn't quite understand how a woman with three children could have her marriage annulled, but that was beside the point. The point was that anyone who had gone to such pains, who attended mass practically every day, was not likely to hop in and out of bed unless she was bonkers. And Brinton was sure Marie wasn't nuts—maybe a little flaky, but certainly not nuts.

Brinton's attitude was influenced by another notion. In the beginning he had thought Ray Blanton was all right. He had even voted for him. Then he started picking up things here and there, and one night he came home and told his wife that being an investigative reporter in the Blanton era was like a kid getting a free ride in a candy store. Brinton had already won state Associated Press and United Press International awards for his exposé of the administration's rigged bids in the sale of surplus state property.

The trouble was that he couldn't get a handle on Marie. They had met three or four times, always off the record. He remembered the first time, one Saturday morning right before the FBI seized records of the pardons and paroles board—in the coffee shop of the Sheraton Inn, not far from the federal courthouse building named after Senator Estes Kefauver but across town for anybody working on capitol hill. Then someone walked in whom she knew. She ducked down, scared to death, and told Brinton that she was sorry but would he please leave before they were spotted together. For Brinton, it was more mystery. More intrigue worth unraveling.

Eventually she'd given him some damn good stuff. For example, a story about the pressure from the Governor's office to get a parolee a full pardon long before his normal eligibility. The parolee, as it happened, was in the employ of Blanton's former campaign manager. But that was it, always bits and pieces. Brinton had the feeling that Marie was holding back a lot more than she was telling about the federal investigation. He was sure she was involved. But how?

So far, whatever little Marie had told him checked out. You never knew, though. Brinton was confused by Marie. She made him uncomfortable. Usually the motivation of someone who confided in him as she was doing could be measured and put in the mix—revenge, profit, survival. With Marie it was none of the above. Once he asked her point-blank what was going on up at the board, and she replied, "I'm only trying to do my job." Another time he tried needling her. "Hey," he said, "I hear you and Eddie Sisk are getting back together again," and although she had denied there was anything to get back to, if she understood his meaning, she did it without a trace of personal rancor.

Brinton didn't know where she was coming from.

The first tangible backup that the gossip circulating about Marie could have substance appeared in the *Tennessean* some six weeks later, on Friday morning, May 13. Under a three-column head on the front page of the metropolitan-news section.

> Marie Ragghianti, chairman of the State Pardons and Paroles Board, was issued a citation Tuesday night for reckless driving after she left a party for legislators.
> Mrs. Ragghianti was required to take a drunkometer test when she was stopped near Briley Parkway and Vultee Boulevard, but she failed to register .10, the amount of intoxification by law for a DUI arrest, said Lt. Charles Campbell.
> Mrs. Ragghianti, reached in Memphis yesterday, said she felt the officer, Don Heath, "went out of his way in doing" his duty.

An exceptionally alert reader might have noticed that only the *Tennessean,* of all the news media in the city and state, carried the report, that the incident by then was three days old and that the "party for legislators" was one of the biggest political social events of the year, the annual reception of the powerful West Tennessee Democratic legislative caucus.

Why, Marie thought, didn't they come right out and call her the town whore and the town drunk, and get it over with?

Richard Fisher, a DA from East Tennessee who was very active in the statewide association of district attorneys lobbying for tougher criminal justice legislation, was still in Nashville when he read the story. Fisher had attended the reception, and he remembered that if they had wanted to pick up drunks afterward, they could have carted them off by the wheelbarrowful. There was no question in his mind that Marie's arrest had been set up. And it didn't escape his attention that somebody had taken considerable trouble to plant the story.

· 4 ·

In July, two months after Marie's arrest, a special session of the grand jury looking into alleged bribery in pardons and paroles was announced. Marie was one of the witnesses. It would be her second appearance. She had been before another grand jury the previous November.

But people were losing interest in the federal probe. The FBI had made headlines across the state in October '76, when its agents not only subpoenaed records of the pardons and paroles board but had gone right into the state capitol to seize additional files in the legal counsel's office. It was the first time since 1867, following the Civil War, that federal officials had invaded the capitol's precincts, and everyone was agog.

The grand jury hearings started right after the raids. Marie had been summoned along with her two fellow board members, and there were more witnesses as well. Another grand jury, the same one that was being brought into special session now, had held hearings during the winter. But the lack of any pattern among those testifying—a mixed bag of inmates, ex-cons, state officials, politicians, district attorneys, a mayor, assorted businessmen, bankers, law officers, even a local TV personality—made it difficult for reporters, much less the citizenry, to track the action.

From the beginning Blanton railed that the investigation was a "gutter level" attempt to smear his administration, a smear timed to help Republican incumbent Bill Brock against Blanton's candidate, Jim Sasser, in the 1976 U.S. Senate campaign. It was, said the Governor, nothing more than a conspiracy plotted by Brock, U.S. Attorney Charles Anderson, who was a Nixon/Ford holdover appointee, and the Republican Nashville *Banner*. The old Nixon mentality was still alive and well, Blanton cried, and he fired off a telegram to the Department of Justice demanding an investigation of the investigation. Blanton's attack already had begun to work. Anderson said he was dropping out of the case and had asked the Justice Department's public integrity section to take over.

Now the inside word was that the investigation of pardons and paroles in Tennessee would soon be given up entirely, that it had run out of steam. Much of this conjecture was based on the anticlimactic aftermath of the original FBI raids. They had come with startling suddenness, without any of the usual media alerts. And on their heels —within days, in fact—the grand jury was convened; everyone involved was tight-lipped, businesslike—no circus atmosphere here. The expectation was for immediate indictments and swift prosecutions. Then Andy Reich, the young public integrity attorney who had come down from Washington, described the special July session of the grand jury as nothing more than a review of the evidence gathered so far, evidence that would then be taken back to Washington and weighed. Reich couldn't say when or even if there would be indictments.

As far as the public was concerned, there was every reason to believe that Marie was one of the main targets of the grand jury. There were also other theories. One had it that while she may have been mixed up in some monkey business, she was cooperating with the investigation to save herself. Another was that she was cooperating, period.

But it had begun to dawn on certain members of Blanton's administration that there just might be more to it, that maybe she not only was cooperating but was right in the middle of it all.

Then, abruptly, there appeared to be little doubt about Marie's wild ways. Right after midnight on July 31 she was stopped again by the police, and this time she registered a tenth of one percent when she was tested for the amount of alcohol in her blood. It was the bare minimum for a DUI—Driving Under the Influence. But it was enough. The balloonlike bag she was required to breathe into didn't measure the harrowing stress she'd been enduring for weeks that had culminated in this moment. Couldn't explain how and why it had happened. Dear God, she had thought while the blue police lights flashed, what have I done to myself?

THE TENNESSEEAN, *August 1, 1977*

State Pardons and Paroles Board Chairman Marie Ragghianti was arrested early yesterday by Metro police who charged her with driving under the influence of alcohol.

Ms. Ragghianti, who was issued a citation in May for reckless driving, was released on her own recog-

nizance following the 12:50 a.m. arrest, a police report says.

NASHVILLE BANNER, *August 1, 1977*

MRS. RAGGHIANTI FACES
DRUNK DRIVING CHARGE

Nashville's most popular evening news show on Channel 4 led off
with Marie's arrest, devoting better than three minutes to it. As in all
the other media accounts, her previous brush with the law after having
been at a "party for legislators" was now a big part of the story. "A court
date has been set for August twenty-third," the broadcast concluded,
"but prior to that time she is scheduled to appear in court August
twelfth to answer reckless driving charges stemming from her arrest last
May."

The first phone call was from Marie's mother. "Why didn't you tell
me?" she said.

Some friends called and were very kind, but no one made Marie feel
better. There were some unfriendly calls too. An anonymous man said,
"Hey, baby, I got a big, old thing here waitin' on you to chew." A
woman screamed, "Bitch whore!"

Larry Brinton of the *Banner* called. "I see they stuck it to you again,"
Brinton said. "How are you?"

"Okay, I guess," she replied.

Brinton remembered how tiny her voice was. He had called because
he was genuinely sorry for her. But he was a reporter, and he still
suspected there was much more to Marie than was apparent. He felt
the same about the federal probe. And he imagined if she was ever
going to say anything definitive, it would be now. But she didn't. Just
thanked him for his thoughtfulness.

On the face of it, Brinton had to consider the possibility that he was
overestimating Marie, and in his piece he quoted a high administration
source as saying, "It's not a matter of if she's leaving, it's just a matter
of when she's leaving."

She dreaded going to the office Monday morning. When she did, it
wasn't quite what she'd expected. Instead of all the gossipy inquiries
she had braced herself for, her co-workers in state government assidu-

ously avoided eye contact, did not mention her arrest at all. Case closed, next case. It was as though, magically, she had become a nonperson. She thought things like that happened only in China or Russia.

· 5 ·

The Governor had a press conference scheduled for Monday. He was going to New York City to drum up new business for Tennessee, particularly to attract overseas investment in the state. He would be meeting a number of foreign representatives at the United Nations.

But Marie's arrest got all the attention. What was he going to do about her DUI? "I have to see what the ramifications are," said Ray Blanton, reflective, judicious. "I can either relieve her or discipline her, but I won't take any action until the courts have decided on her guilt or innocence."

Yes, he added, he would discuss the situation with some of his people, but in the end he was the only one legally able to make a decision about Marie's future. Then he indulged in a little folksy reminiscing. He recalled he had been asked the same sort of question in his unsuccessful U.S. Senate race against Howard Baker Jr. in 1972. "Many of the Republican White House people were being indicted at that time," he confided, "and my response was exactly the same. I found a newspaper clipping, or my staff did, the other day that said I would not remove anybody until they were proved guilty by the courts."

The Governor felt pretty good about it. He had not only affirmed his devotion to due process, but managed to lump Marie in with Haldeman, Ehrlichman and the rest.

Even as he spoke, Blanton's order was already being carried out to get Marie's resignation, and if it wasn't forthcoming, to draft a letter telling her she was fired.

In Washington two days later, August 3, the assistant director of public information for the Justice Department, summarizing the status of the grand jury hearings into Tennessee pardon, parole, extradition and executive clemency cases, said that a decision to seek indictments would not be reached soon.

"The decision whether to prosecute will be made by Thomas Henderson, the head of the public integrity section," he explained. "If necessary, he will go to the Assistant Attorney General, Benjamin R. Civiletti, and if necessary, it will go to the U.S. Attorney General, Griffin Bell, but I'm not saying this will happen, only that this is how it could happen."

That afternoon Betty Nixon, who worked in Blanton's press office, announced that Marie had been summarily dismissed. In the unlikely event that anyone had forgotten about it, she emphasized that the dismissal had nothing to do with Marie's drunk-driving arrest. She said that a letter citing the Governor's reasons had been dispatched to Marie but officially declined to disclose its contents. Governor Blanton, she added, was still in New York and unavailable for comment.

It was all a charade. The letter had already been leaked. The accusations against Marie were being broadcast on radio and television throughout the state, and reporters were demanding her response, before she ever saw it. The first wire-service bulletins carried the charge that she had "demoralized" the corrections department and "crippled" its procedure for pardons and paroles, committing "gross improprieties" in the process. By nightfall Marie was the talk of Tennessee.

The three-page letter accused her of systematically rifling taxpayer pockets. It said that during a "typical four-month period" she had billed expenses to the state for presiding over at least thirteen Board of Pardons and Paroles meetings during 1976 which in fact she had not attended. *Despite your absences,* the letter said, pinpointing dates and places, *you nevertheless charged the State of Tennessee for travel expenses to and from each of the Board meetings you were allegedly attending, and on August 24 and 25 charged the State two times: once for the meeting of the Board of Pardons and Paroles you were allegedly attending in Tennessee, and once for a meeting of the Annual Congress of Corrections you may or may not have attended in Denver.*

Besides that, it went on, she had billed the state for at least six board meetings in 1976 and 1977 that had not even been scheduled. It further said that her administrative failures had effectively paralyzed the management of the state prison system, and that by "publicly" discussing the board's affairs, especially her votes and the votes of the other members, she had committed a "flagrant violation" of mandated discretion.

But the big charge, the one that created all the headlines, was that Marie had tried to bilk the state out of precisely $7,584.94 in overtime pay:

Members of the Tennessee Board of Pardons and Paroles are not workers on an assembly line who punch in and out on a time clock and receive "time and a half" for every hour worked beyond 40 hours per week. On the contrary, you and the other Board Members are skilled professionals and you are paid $26,000.00 per year by the people of this state and entrusted with an extremely important responsibility to the people of this state. . . . For you to claim some 600 hours of "over-time" at a cost of $7500 to the taxpayers, is a violation of the law, an embarrassment to the Department of Corrections and for me personally, as the one charged under the Constitution and by statute with the ultimate responsibility for the Board of Pardons and Paroles.

It is particularly embarrassing for the Chairman of the Board of Pardons and Paroles, as the one charged with the responsibility for helping individuals convicted of crime to reenter and contribute to society and to begin productive and crime-free lives, to have herself engaged in such gross improprieties.

Pursuant to the powers vested in me by the Constitution of the State of Tennessee and T.C.A. 40-3601, and pursuant to this written notice, I therefore hereby terminate you as a member of the Board, and Chairman immediately.

Sincerely,
Ray Blanton

· 6 ·

While there may have been some who thought the Governor had gone for overkill in firing Marie, nobody doubted that he had plenty of ammunition. Why else would he have laid it all out on paper, in such detail? Ray Blanton wasn't that dumb.

It was odd, though, and it took a while for it to sink in, that one of Blanton's top commissioners had been indicted on corruption charges in rigged-bidding deals and was still on the state payroll. And that Marie's successor in handling extraditions had been indicted for trying to bribe a hearing officer to keep a relative from being hauled off to Georgia and yet remained at work.

But right then, if the administration wanted Marie out of the way, whatever the reasons, the letter sure looked like a haymaker. What neither Blanton nor anyone else could guess at the time was where the haymaker would really land.

Before it was all over, Tennessee's political power structure would be a shambles. Scandals would erupt everywhere. Reputations would be shattered and indictments returned. There would be jail sentences, to say nothing of four violent deaths—three outright murders, one apparent suicide.

The only thing the Blanton administration had not counted on— from Blanton himself down—was that this one woman, essentially alone, who by conventional lights seemed to have everything to lose and nothing to gain, would fight back.

TWO

About an hour before the Governor's Monday press conference when he declared he wasn't going to do anything one way or another about Marie until the courts had rendered a verdict, C. Murray Henderson, the commissioner of corrections, called and asked her to please step into his office.

Marie had this theory that you could tell a lot about a person's psyche by the kind of eggs he ordered. For example, she always had them sunny-side up. And she would observe with interest whether people asked for hard- or soft-boiled eggs or wanted them scrambled. C. Murray Henderson liked his eggs over easy. That was Murray to a T. He wanted smooth surfaces, nothing ruffled. No trouble.

He was old enough to be her father, tall, with iron-gray hair, a lugubrious face mottled a little from too much booze. Marie thought he was distinguished-looking. She first met him when she had been extradition officer, and she respected his dedication and savvy. He was a professional, and his appointment had been widely applauded. For eight years he had been the warden at the Louisiana State Penitentiary and, before that, warden of the main state prison in Nashville. But he was also an old-line bureaucrat. He had been through the political mill, and loyalty was all-important to him. Ray Blanton had put the butter on his bread, and he would never forget it.

One morning more than a year earlier, she had gone to Henderson while he was having breakfast, eggs over easy. She was on the verge of assuming her chairmanship, and she told him she really needed his advice. She had learned of an attempted clemency payoff that involved someone close to the Governor's office. At least, it looked like that. But as soon as she started spelling out what was bothering her, Murray Henderson became visibly irritated and advised her to stop looking for trouble. She had enough to worry about in her new job. He had made her feel incompetent, even a little crazy. After that Marie's admiration for Murray lessened. But she still liked him, and she believed he liked her. They saw things differently, was all.

Henderson's big corner office was right down the hall. That in itself was part of the problem. It dwarfed the one she had. So did the offices of his deputy and assistant commissioners. At first she hadn't cared, but then she found out that it did matter in the perceptions people had of power. Then, too, she quickly discovered that her aims and Murray's aims were professionally antithetic. He wanted to get inmates out of prison so as to avoid riots behind the walls; she had to worry about the communities that received them. Theoretically, the pardons and paroles board was an independent agency. Yet its budget was controlled by the Department of Correction. If Marie wanted a new typewriter, the requisition had to be okayed by corrections. That was why she had begun to fight for the board's financial independence. And she had already gotten an opinion from David Raybin, over in the state attorney general's office, that Sam Lipford and his probation hearing officers should be reporting directly to her instead of to Murray. "What's wrong with her?" Henderson would demand of Lipford. "Why's she so damn bullheaded?"

Going into Henderson's office on Monday, Marie saw how agitated he was. She wondered if it was about the DUI. "Sit down, sit down," he said, waving at her. Then he got up. He walked around the office. "I don't know how to say this," he said. "Well, the Governor called me in the middle of the night. *Last* night. He wants your resignation."

Henderson looked at her unhappily and said, "Of course, this doesn't have anything to do with the incident of your arrest. It's not related to that, of course," and she found herself automatically replying, "Of course." She felt the tears coming, but she forced them back. "It was just cumulative," said C. Murray Henderson, "an accumulation of things."

He finally sat down behind his desk, still fidgety. He was silent for a second. Then he seemed to brighten: she could have another job in the government, they would even fix up the pay, the Governor himself had authorized it. Anywhere so long as it wasn't in corrections or the Department of Public Safety, which included the state's law-enforcement agencies. That got her back up. "Why?" she asked. "Does the Governor consider me a threat to the public safety?"

He ignored the sarcasm. If she wanted, he said, plunging on, he'd get right on the phone to J. N. Doane, the personnel commissioner, to see what was available. She said that if she couldn't keep the job she had, she didn't know whether she cared to be in state government at all. Henderson jumped on that. Yes, he said, the free enterprise system might be preferable. She had her children to support, and there was good money out there. She could be the executive secretary to some statewide organization. Why, he had a cousin who had been with the pharmaceutical people and made thirty thousand a year, and that was fifteen years ago!

She told him she had occasionally speculated about what she could earn in the private sector, and her voice trailed off, thinking this was all so pointless, why was she saying that? So this was how they were going to smooth everything over, she thought. Make it look as if she'd quit on her own. Solve all their problems with her that way. "I haven't done anything wrong," she said. "I'm not resigning."

He looked so mournful. Here he was, she thought, greasing up the guillotine, and she felt sorry for him. "Murray," she said, her voice suddenly husky, "I want you to know this isn't the worst thing that ever happened to me."

· 2 ·

She was born in Chattanooga on June 13, 1942, the first of five children. Right off she'd been so quick. And stubborn. When Marie was barely two and a half, she learned by herself to lace up her white shoes and tie the bows. Her mother, Virginia, remembered exactly when it was, the night she was getting ready to have another baby. Marie's father was away then, with the Marine Corps in the Pacific. Some friends had come by to take Virginia to the hospital, and Marie proudly appeared, her shoes on and tied. Virginia let her show off doing it two or three times before sending her to bed. Marie immediately reappeared in her shoes, and Virginia gave her a smack on the bottom and packed her back to her room. Then just before leaving, feeling a touch remorseful, she went up to kiss her good-night in her sleep. There was a big easy chair in the room that Virginia sat in to read bedtime stories to Marie. Now Marie was in the chair, wide awake in her nightie, arms folded defiantly, the shoes on again and tied.

Marie's mother was third-generation Tennessee Scotch-Irish. Her people had been blacksmiths and stonemasons. Marie's father, Roque Fajardo, who had been born in Cuba, was the son of a professor of Spanish at the University of Chattanooga. Marie never tired of hearing Virginia tell the story of how she first met Roque—in the first grade at Notre Dame parochial school in Chattanooga. How she knew right then and there the adorable, dark-eyed boy joining the class was meant for her. Like a fairy tale, only better, everyone living happily ever after.

They had eloped, Virginia dropping out of Siena, a small, strict Catholic college for girls in Memphis, and Marie thought that had been so romantic. Her father was a newspaperman, first in Knoxville, then Nashville. And Marie's most poignant recollection of growing up in Nashville was how her father would come home from work and walk into the kitchen and kiss her mother by the stove, and how a feeling of warmth, a sense of profound security, would sweep over her.

In the fifties, Marie could sense the exciting, intellectually stimulating lives her parents were leading in Nashville. The house filled with friends. Talk of newspapering. Politics. Early on, Virginia had told her how she and Roque had made a pact that money would never be a consideration as long as they could get by. Happy, productive, satisfying work was what counted.

But suddenly they couldn't get by. Marie was twelve when a tumor was discovered to be wrapped around the base of her mother's spine. The tumor turned out to be benign, but not all of it could be removed despite two operations over the next three years, and there had been subsequent degeneration. The medical bills were enormous, and Roque quit journalism and Nashville and moved to Daytona Beach in Florida to begin a whole new career as executive secretary of Quality Courts United, a national association of hotels and motels.

For Virginia, although she said nothing to Marie, the move brought fear and great guilt, knowing in her heart that Roque had taken the job for the money alone.

For Marie, leaving Nashville at age fifteen, leaving her friends, had been a bit traumatic, but she adapted instantly to the beach life, lying in the sun in the afternoon with the other girls, watching the guys work out with weights. All of a sudden Nashville looked pretty dull. Her father had bought a neat house, just a block from the ocean, bigger than any she'd ever lived in before. True, after a couple of years in Daytona Beach, her mother had started using a cane to get around, but she had domestic help, and her condition hadn't prevented her from giving birth to Marie's youngest sister, Rose Ellen, in the fall of 1960.

Marie didn't have a care in the world then. She started winning beauty contests, one after another. Boys swarmed around her. Her biggest problem was which one to date that night. Sometimes she made two or three dates for the same night, and her parents would end up having to deal with the calls from bewildered swains. Once, there'd been such a brawl between two boys on the street in front of the house that Roque had to call the police.

Roque told her she was becoming a self-centered little snit, spoiled rotten, and that she'd regret it. He said she'd never be as truly popular as her mother because her main attraction was her looks, and the looks weren't going to last forever. The choice, he said, was between being genuine and superficial, and she had better learn the difference.

About the only thing that hadn't gone her way after graduating from Seabreeze High was the fight over where she would go to college. Virginia had pushed for her old school, Siena, but that hope had never gotten off the ground. The golden beach girl was not about to put up with a campus where makeup wasn't allowed and check-in time Saturday night was 11 P.M. Her father said Loyola of New Orleans or Catholic University in Washington, D.C. Her mother was willing to settle for that, but Marie wasn't. She wanted the University of Miami, more sun and fun.

If there was a trait the family shared, it was being obstinate. Roque said, "Well, you won't go where we want, and you can't go where you want." So the upshot, until someone gave in, had been Daytona Beach Junior College. Which wasn't hard to take. It was almost an extension

of Seabreeze High. You could even wear shorts. And she was still queen
bee. A convertible filled with boys came by every morning to pick her
up for classes.

· 3 ·

One morning at the end of May '61, three weeks short of her nine-
teenth birthday, not even the start of final exams for her freshman year
affected Marie's concentration on her mascara. First up was English.
No problem. She was going in with a straight A average. For that
matter, she had begun to accept the need for a more challenging
academic program, even if it meant backing off on Miami U.

Her mother was standing at the door, saying something about her
father. Marie didn't catch it at first, something about being away. The
interruption was annoying. Marie knew he was on a business trip—he
often was—and she didn't want the mascara to clump on her lashes.
"Yes," she said, "when's he coming back?"

"Well, that's just it," she heard her mother say. "Your daddy's not
coming back."

She remembered staring at herself in the mirror, holding up the
mascara wand. "What do you mean, he isn't coming back? Mom, what
are you talking about?"

"When he left, he said he wasn't coming back."

She turned to look at her mother. Her mother's pretty, usually
composed face was contorted with emotion, although her voice seemed
calm enough.

Marie didn't understand, didn't want to understand, what was being
said. She seized on a wild idea. "Is it Quality Courts? Is there some
problem?"

Her mother shook her head and said something about another
woman. "Haven't you ever answered the phone when a woman called
and asked for your father?" Then her mother said that Roque was in
love with another woman and wasn't ever coming back, that he wanted
to marry her.

Marie couldn't think of anything to say, couldn't cope with it at all.
A horn sounded outside, and she walked blindly past her mother.

The tears started as she went out the front door. She heard the boys
chattering in the car, and one of them said, "Hey, Marie—" and
stopped short. She got in without a word. Suddenly nobody was saying
anything. During the twenty-minute ride to the campus, she kept

crying. Once, when she reached up to wipe her eyes and saw the mascara smeared on her handkerchief, the scene in front of the mirror in her room came back to her, and she was revolted by it. She remembered thinking, too, how considerate the guys were, not asking questions, knowing this was not the time.

When they arrived, somebody held the car door open for her. She didn't move. She never did make the English exam. Nor any of the others. Finally, that morning, she got out of the car and wandered around, trying to deal with what her mother had told her. How could it have been going on without her noticing a thing? Was she that self-absorbed, that insensitive? And she decided yes, she must have been. There was no other explanation. She was guilty of the deadly sin of Pride with all of its corollary vanities, and she prayed for God's forgiveness, and for her mother and father, that they would be together again.

The weeks blurred. She would go into her baby sister's room and look at Rosie in her crib. She was such a beautiful baby, and Marie would think of her growing up without a father, and of their mom alone, and the tears would begin sliding down her cheeks once more.

She didn't get into it too deeply with her mother, afraid somehow that would make it worse, although for whom she wasn't certain. Her mother seemed just as glad. But mostly the message she got was to be understanding of her daddy, to love him, not be bitter. Abstractions. It was easier that way.

She privately flogged herself for her own smugness. She began to question how close they all had been, the whole family, what her standards were. Appearances had been what counted, for sure. Her stock rule of thumb before dating a boy was what he looked like, how many girls were after him.

Marie tried to think of some way to alleviate her mother's mute pain, but there was nothing. Then, early in August, it came to her. Right out of the blue. Her mom's fondest dream had been for Marie to follow her to Siena College. Many of the Dominican sisters who had taught Virginia were still there, and she had stayed in regular touch with them. Indeed, two of her closest classmates had become nuns and were on the faculty.

So Marie decided she would go to Siena. Even Catholic University of America would have been paradise compared with Siena. But it didn't matter now. It took her about thirty seconds to make up her mind. It seemed like such a small thing, yet it would be everything.

Virginia was ecstatic when Marie told her. She was on the phone to the college within minutes. And although class registration was over, she was told that an exception would be made for Marie. Virginia Wilcox was remembered with great affection—bright, vivacious, religious, a first-rate tennis player. The ideal Siena woman. It had been a tragedy when she dropped out. Now it would all be put right. Her daughter would pick up where she had left off.

In Daytona Beach, Virginia hadn't been as concerned as Roque that Marie reveled in the attention she was getting. The swarms of boys, of course, could be pretty aggravating. But to her mind it was a lot better than if Marie were going steady. Even though Nashville had been staid by comparison, it had been essentially the same there, Marie in the thick of things, getting the most Valentines, never going through an ugly-duckling stage. Virginia was convinced, moreover, that Marie was a "good girl" in every sense of the word. Along with her grades, there were plenty of reassuring pluses. During the height of her beauty-queen run, for instance, she never chose revealing bathing suits. She didn't drink and hardly ever smoked, either. And there was no pacing at night wondering where she was. She was in on the dot. It seemed as if, Virginia would think, Marie just wanted to be involved—whether it was a big high school dance or a meeting of the Spanish Honor Society.

But if Daytona's resort atmosphere was turning her head, Siena would fix that. Marie's decision to transfer there was heaven-sent, the perfect antidote to Roque's departure.

· 4 ·

The way Marie figured it, she could hardly have done better than Siena in atoning for past vanities. Because she had enrolled late, she was shoehorned into a room with two other girls, plain, retiring little things, from Mississippi and Missouri. She had absolutely nothing in common with them, and they looked at her as though she were from another planet. Despite their meager wardrobes, there still wasn't enough closet space for the clothes she had brought.

Clothes were very important to her. The deal she had made with her parents was that she could do whatever she wanted with the money she earned, and she spent nearly every dime on clothes. She was fifteen when she started working in a Daytona Beach ice cream parlor. Later she gift-wrapped packages in a department store, then sold cosmetics. After she became a beauty queen, the modeling jobs rolled in, fashions, promoting tourism. Right at that moment, while she was stuck on a campus where even Bermuda shorts were considered too risqué, packets of sugar in restaurants all over Florida featured a sexy picture of Marie posing in a bathing suit on a sand dune. She had known that shorts of any kind, slacks as well, were forbidden on the college grounds, but she found out she couldn't wear them around the dorm either. If she put on shorts, it had to be in her room, which was the last place she wanted to be.

The one campus activity she fervently embraced was daily mass, receiving communion, praying incessantly for her father's return. He was in Las Vegas, sitting out the Nevada residential requirements for a divorce. She dispatched letters to him constantly, imploring him to come back. She wrote of her grief at his absence. She reminded him again and again about Rose Ellen. Did he truly mean for her to grow up without him, without the love and security he had given *her?*

Then, at the end of orientation week, the Siena girls were invited to a dance at Christian Brothers College in Memphis. Marie had half a mind not to go, thinking it'd be a bore, but one of the other girls talked her into it.

She turned, and saw him across the dance floor. David Ragghianti. She'd met him in August on a blind date when she'd come up to Memphis with Virginia to see the campus and register. Marie hadn't been at all impressed. He seemed kind of scrawny and shy compared with the extroverted, beefcake types Marie was used to in Daytona Beach. Then, to her surprise, he'd shown up afterward in Daytona, and she took another look. In his swimming trunks, she had to admit, he was terrific, tanned, with a sinewy muscularity that his clothes had disguised.

The beach, he said, was great for keeping in shape for boxing. Boxing? Yeah, he said, he boxed some. Welterweight, amateur. In Memphis he was a champ. *No kidding,* she said. Did that mean he didn't ever lose? "Lose," he said. "What's that?"

At that time of year Daytona Beach never closed up. For a while they

rode along the neon strip of A-1-A, then went to the amusement park
on the boardwalk and took in the rides. Marie felt like a tourist on the
loose, as if it were the first time she had been on the boardwalk. They
moved on to a pier jutting into the Atlantic and danced. He was a
fantastic dancer, much better than she. At last, regretfully, she told him
she had to get home. It was later than she'd ever stayed out. On the
way, the sky started to lighten. Hey, he said, why didn't they stop on
the beach and watch the sun come up? It was a wonderful idea, she
said. All the time she had been living there, she'd never done that. This
guy, she suddenly thought, was making her feel sensations she had
never experienced. Usually she called the shots, thought up things to
do.

The beach was hard-packed. You could drive right on it. She stayed
in the car with him. The sunrise, exploding out of the ocean, was
spectacular, and she wondered why she hadn't thought of doing this
before. They weren't saying anything, not even holding hands, yet she
felt so close to him. What she had once perceived as awkward reticence
she now saw as something touching and vulnerable, mysterious, intriguing.

All at once she heard her mother's voice. Marie turned and saw her
standing a few yards away, resting on her cane. How could she have
possibly known where to look? Virginia was yelling. Marie couldn't
recall ever having heard her raise her voice in front of other people. Her
mother demanded to know what she was doing. She yelled at him too.
What was *he* doing?

He slipped out of the car, whispering that he'd see her in Memphis.
Marie was mortified. Then the anger came. She hadn't done anything
that terrible. Yes, she thought, she would see him in Memphis.

· 5 ·

At Siena, Marie wondered why he hadn't called her. But she sure
wasn't about to try to get in touch with him first. Now, looking at him
across the dance floor, she was astonished. He hadn't said anything
about going to college there, and then she learned that he wasn't, that
he hadn't even made it through Christian Brothers High before being
kicked out. But that didn't seem to keep him from the dances, which
impressed her. The girl who was telling her this couldn't stop looking
at him all the time she was talking; her eyes looked as if they had X's
in them.

Marie saw the stir he caused among the girls, and the boys too. She noticed how when he approached a group of boys, they fell back, as though in awe. They all appeared to know who he was. Maybe it was because of the boxing, she thought. Still, it was confusing to see him move now with such easy grace and confidence, almost arrogantly, remembering how painfully shy he had been with her on their first date, the vulnerability she sensed in him the second time around. The other funny thing was that he was just going on eighteen, more than a year younger than she, younger than most everyone there.

She was certain he had seen her, and she decided to ignore him. She was getting a pretty good rush herself. Let him think about that. And, besides, the truth was he was such a topnotch dancer, she was afraid to suffer by comparison in front of the other students. She couldn't recall ever having been so defensive.

But it worked out even better than she had hoped. Near the end of the dance, he sauntered over to her at last and said, "Hi, baby." Very nonchalant, as if they hadn't been apart at all. "Oh, hi," she said, just as offhandedly, pleased with herself. He offered to drive her back to Siena.

They went by the Pig 'n' Whistle, a drive-in where the teenagers hung out. Everyone called it the Pig. He got quiet again, almost pensive, she thought, and really considerate. Did she have enough ketchup? Was the shake okay?

They got to the dorm an hour past curfew. The sister in charge was livid. Marie was campused for a week. This was no way for the daughter of Virginia Wilcox to behave, the sister said. It didn't bother her. She was used to having her mother invoked as an example of what she should be.

The following Sunday, after she was off restriction, she spent the afternoon at the zoo with him. They were looking at the elephants when suddenly this one elephant lifted its trunk out of a water trough, seemed to take dead aim, and drenched him. Bystanders laughed, and she started to laugh too, then clapped a hand over her mouth. By now Marie had picked up hints about a volatile streak in David, and she didn't know what to expect. But after a second, he began laughing too. Just call him Elephant Boy, he said.

Eventually they ended up at the Pig. It was the kind of drive-in where carhops brought food trays and hooked them on the sides of your doors. When they had finished eating, he took their tray and threw it on the ground before driving away. "What in the world did you do that for?" she exclaimed. He looked at her and grinned. "I don't know," he said. She thought it was hilarious.

Check-in time Sunday nights was nine. She was late again, and campused for another week.

He'd call her two or three days in a row, and then he wouldn't. She would get news of David from one of the other Siena students dating a friend of his. She would hear how he had talked about her, how much he liked her, and she would feel great. Then she'd hear that he had been out with someone else.

It unnerved her, being out of control like this. She'd always been in control. But after a while she didn't care. Just hungered for any tidbit about him she could get.

She kept grimly playing the game, though. Once, after he hadn't called, he told her, "Well, you know, I called three times."

"Three?" she said. "I thought it was four. I got four messages."

"Oh, right. It was four. I forgot about the last one," he said.

During the week at Siena she had to be in by seven-thirty on Mondays and Wednesdays, eight on Tuesdays and Thursdays, ten on Fridays. Out of her first twelve weeks, Marie was campused nine and a half of them. She might as well have been in a convent, she thought.

One of the few times she wasn't campused after a date was when he stood her up. She was so sore that she went out at the last minute with a senior from Christian Brothers who'd been calling her, a big blond guy, smart, headed for graduate study at Harvard. She was bored stiff.

She tried to analyze what it was that drew her to him. She could never pin it down. It was the mystery of him. She sensed a quality locked in him that nobody else did. Only she could unlock and nurture it. She began to feel very protective about him. Being campused all the time gave her imagination a lot of play.

She got a part-time sales job in cosmetics at Goldsmith's department store right by Siena. Marie did it to earn spending money, but that way they could also meet for lunch sometimes, or she could steal a couple of hours in the afternoon to be with him.

Students from other colleges worked there too. It turned out he had quite a reputation among them. This one boy from Memphis State was just astounded when she said whom she was seeing. Couldn't understand what a girl like her saw in him. She got all sorts of feedback. What a ladykiller he was, and how he ran with a real rough crowd.

It left her baffled. None of it added up. When he was with her, he was always so withdrawn and respectful. She was used to fending off fellows with their hearts on their sleeves. Yet this alleged ladykiller hadn't even tried to kiss her, as if he had placed her on some kind of pedestal, she remembered thinking.

In her head, he began to get mixed up with her father. She would swing from one to the other. Yearning to see him. Yearning to get her daddy back.

· 6 ·

Toward the end of September Marie wrote Roque in Las Vegas and demanded to know if her prayers for his return to Virginia were useless. About the same time her mother's birthday was coming up. Virginia had sold the house in Daytona Beach and moved back to Nashville. Marie sent her a card along with a note that she was having a mass said for her.

A week later Virginia's letter arrived. *Dear Ree,* it began, *I received your beautiful card and words, and I want you to know that all our prayers have been answered. Your mass was heard because your father has come home.*

It was, Marie thought, a miracle. It sealed forever her conviction in the power of prayer.

After that, she concentrated on this mysterious boy. It drove her crazy sometimes trying to comprehend David—always that blank expression.

One Sunday afternoon, edgy over being campused, she sat down with a notebook and pen and tried to list any evidence that he cared for her. But except for his calls she couldn't think of a thing. There was nothing else to indicate his interest. No overt signs of affection. No endearing words. No flowers. Nothing you'd expect. However, she was sure he did care for her. She was absolutely certain of it.

On their next date they went to a fair. He had amazing coordination, and she left with an armful of toy animals and dolls he had won pitching baseballs, tossing hoops. He had just said something that made her laugh when he looked at her intently and suddenly said he needed her. She was the one person who could make somebody of him, save him from himself.

The intensity in his face startled her. She had been right all along, she thought. He does need help, and she would help him. She wanted to reach out to him. But the moment was gone as quickly as it had come. When she started to speak, he walked away.

At the Thanksgiving recess he told her he loved her. And really kissed her for the first time. She clung to him, as much in relief as in ecstasy. Oh, yes, she thought, oh, God, how I love you. "I love you too," she said.

She started to say it again when he pushed her away. Close to snarling, he said, "Don't say that. You're lying." She didn't know what to think. "I don't believe it," he said, "you don't mean it," and then it hit her crystal clear. What the problem had been from the beginning. He didn't think he was good enough for her.

Compassion flooded through her. She had never felt more protective, more motherly. It left her breathless with excitement and desire. He truly did not believe she loved him. No, no, she said, he was wrong. He would find out.

A long time later she'd realize how right she had been about his feeling unworthy of her, never suspecting how this would burrow in and eat at them until nothing remained. But right then it seemed so simple. She was nineteen years old, and she was exultant.

It was soon afterward that Marie gave herself to him. She didn't think of it as sex. She saw it as an extension of profound love for the man she knew she would marry. It signified her total commitment to him. Still, she remained tense and anxious about it later, but not because she had done something wrong in the eyes of the Church. She was afraid it wasn't enough, that it didn't have the same meaning for him as it had for her. That was when she became possessed by the idea of marrying him right away.

She knew she'd have to drop out of college. But it didn't matter. She'd work, so that he could go to college instead. She'd find fulfillment through him. A woman's ultimate role, Marie thought then, was to be a wife. To be supportive and loving, stoic if need be, understanding, forgiving. She had only to look to her mother's example. It was, Marie told herself, how a truly good woman should be.

· 7 ·

Virginia was appalled. What about her education? Roque argued that she should at least finish out the year at Siena before making a decision. Their attitude incensed her. Virginia had left school to get married, hadn't she?

The next big problem was David's parents. He had been a late child, and they were both in their fifties. When she met them, they seemed to take to her. But as soon as his mother learned what was up, she told Marie she was making a mistake. Kind of fluttered around it. Said her son hadn't matured enough. He wasn't ready for marriage.

She and David could run off, of course. There was this place in Georgia that Marie had heard about where you could get married by a justice of the peace at fourteen even. But that was unacceptable. She would not marry outside the Church.

David's mother appeared a little afraid of him, and therefore not past spying on him. That was how Marie got the idea to write the letter. David was going to New Orleans with some friends for Mardi Gras. While he was away she would send him a note at home indicating that she was pregnant. She was sure his mother would open it to find out more of what was happening between them. He loved the idea, and it worked. His mother's opposition evaporated immediately. So did Virginia's.

They were married in Nashville at Christ the King Church on March 24, 1962.

There was one last crisis. The night before the wedding, after the rehearsal dinner, he turned to her and said, "Baby, please don't make me go through with this."

It was just cold feet, she thought. She didn't blame him. She was rather nervous herself. But this was the moment to be strong. It was going to be all right, she told him. He'd see.

"Please," he said, like a small boy. "I'm scared."

Well, she said, if that was the case, she'd have to start dating other guys. Marie always remembered saying that.

She wore a short white dress for the wedding. At the reception everybody said she had never looked lovelier. A black waiter hovered nearby, making sure she had everything she wanted. Did she wish cream for her coffee? "Yes, thank you," she said, smiling.

Eyes straight ahead, her new husband said out of the side of his mouth, "I caught that."

"What?" she said.

"Coming on to that goddamn waiter."

A friend of her parents was wishing her happiness. Marie could barely respond. She was having trouble breathing. She felt she might pass out. It was insane to think she'd be flirting with a waiter on her wedding day, black or white. She didn't know what to do, so she kept on smiling.

But she managed to push it out of her mind during their honeymoon. They spent three days in his motel, eating, talking, making love. She had known him about seven months. This was the longest stretch she'd ever spent with him.

· 8 ·

They lived in a three-room apartment in a Memphis development. His parents got it for them and also supplied the furnishings. Gradually she would learn how fearful they were of him. They didn't know how to handle him, so they indulged him. He had come and gone pretty much as he pleased.

He worked at the neighborhood market his father owned. All their food came from the market. They would just help themselves. Mostly they ate steak. Sometimes his father complained, but good-naturedly.

The first time she tried to broil a steak, she charred it beyond recognition. Well, she said, at least she knew how to boil an egg. He was not amused. She mistook a box of tea leaves for tea bags. She dropped the leaves in boiling water anyway, and after it overflowed, they quarreled. One day he wanted to know why she never baked a cake. He always had cake at home, he said. She didn't have a clue how to go about it. She asked his mother what the best cake mix was. To her consternation, Marie found that his mother made everything from scratch, including cakes. And not only was cake mix out, but only a certain kind of flour, Swans Down cake flour, would do. This was an aspect of domestic life she hadn't counted on.

Almost at once, he began complaining about her housekeeping. His mother kept a spotless house. She was the kind of woman who enjoyed starching curtains twice a month, even ironed her slips and bras. Marie was way out of her league. The biggest blowups she'd had at home in Daytona Beach were over the state of her room. At first she was resentful. But when she reflected on it, she decided maybe she was at fault. She wanted desperately to please him. She might not like it much, but it was part of the package. Wives cleaned houses.

She spent a whole day on the apartment, dusting, waxing, polishing, washing the kitchen floor, the sink, the bathroom, the garbage can, the windows. Next she did the laundry, put dinner on and waited expectantly. The place was glistening. When he walked in, she saw how surprised he was. He went around examining things. He disappeared into the bathroom. After a few seconds, he yelled, "Goddamnit, Marie, come look at this."

He was standing by the tub. In a rage. He reached behind the towel rack and held up a finger in front of her. There was some grime on it. "Look at that," he yelled again. "You call that cleaning, you fucking whore?"

Then he hit her. Open-handed, but really hard. She never saw it coming. She staggered back through the doorway. She gazed at him, stunned. Nobody had ever hit her before. She thought men hit women only in the movies.

Marie didn't start crying until she ran out of the apartment. She wandered around the streets for a couple of hours. Her face hurt. Oddly, though, his words hurt worse. She couldn't believe her ears. People didn't speak like that around her, much less to her. Around the house she had grown up in, "damn" was a heavy expression, which her brothers used once in a while.

She had no place to run to in Memphis, so she came back to the apartment. The living room was empty, the bedroom door closed. She sat there, still crying. When he walked out of the bedroom, she flinched. But he knelt beside her and said he was sorry. He didn't know what had gotten into him. Pressures he couldn't explain, he said. He swore it would never happen again, and she believed him.

They had dinner. Afterward, he took her hand. "Baby," he said, smiling, "everything looks real nice," and finally she returned the smile.

Later, friends of his came by, and they all went out to listen to some rock music and had a good time.

· 9 ·

All those vaguely formulated thoughts about working, so she could put David through college, so he could realize himself, went by the boards. About seven weeks after the marriage, Marie really was pregnant.

One thing, he sure was popular. All kinds of friends flocked around David. A lot of them were local kids, teenagers, high school seniors. You could tell which ones were headed nowhere. But there were others too, well-mannered, intelligent, clean-cut boys planning to go on to college. They all had one thing in common. They all looked up to him. At the heart of it, from what Marie could gather, was his fighting ability. By the time they were married he had stopped boxing. He hardly ever talked about it. But he had given her a pair of tiny fourteen-karat-gold boxing gloves he had won in a tournament. And she found a manila envelope full of newspaper clippings that showed what a star he had been.

Even so, his main reputation was based on fighting outside the ring. Marie had never seen anything like it in Daytona Beach or Nashville. In Memphis fighting was in. Boys fought at the drop of a hat at dances, at parties, in clubs. And he was the best. She constantly heard stories about this time or that, how he could whip anybody, beat him to a pulp, no matter how big, whether the other guy pulled a knife or had a bottle in his hand. Usually, she heard, it wasn't that he walked in somewhere throwing his weight around. Usually it was a buddy of his who had picked a fight first, or had gotten into trouble, and he'd jump right in and take over.

He also had another set of friends, mean, surly guys, mostly older than he, real rednecks. They seemed to admire him as much as everyone else. Marie despised them, especially the Tiller brothers. One of them, Charles, wound up in Brushy Mountain, Tennessee's toughest prison. Every so often on a Saturday afternoon the doorbell would ring and the Tiller brothers and their crowd would strut in, loaded down with six-packs of beer.

She'd be furious that David was glad to see them, furious at the way he let them make themselves at home, talking loud, passing around the latest copy of *Playboy* or watching a ball game on TV, dropping ashes, drinking beer, asking her to bring them more beer.

One Saturday she'd had enough. She went into the kitchen, closed the door, took all the beer from the refrigerator, turned on the tap to drown out what she was doing, popped the cans one by one and poured the beer down the drain. It occurred to Marie that it wasn't the smartest thing she'd ever done, but she was so mad she didn't care. By golly, it was her home too. She felt terrific each time she popped another beer can.

When she finished, she walked past them into the bedroom and lay down to read. She heard them carrying on. Someone said, "Hey, how 'bout more beer?" and another one said, "Okay, man, I'll get it," and then she heard a voice call her husband, "Where'd you put that beer?" and he said, "In the refrigerator," and the same voice said, "Hell, there's no beer in here." Marie heard them trooping into the kitchen, and one of them said, "Goddamn, look at them cans in that sack," and David hollered, "Marie!"

She went to the kitchen door. There were five or six of them jammed in there, kind of befuddled. "Yes?" she said. "Just who the hell do you think you are?" he shouted. "Goddamnit, Marie, what in hell do you think you're doing?"

She let it all out, shouting back full force. She was fed up. They all had no right coming in with that beer, she said. He knew she didn't like beer around, that his drinking was bad news for both of them, for their marriage, that she didn't appreciate it and she didn't give a hoot who thought what about it.

He shoved her aside, but nothing more. "Come on," he said to the Tillers, "let's get out of here." He returned very late. Pretending sleep, she listened to him stumble in, drunk, and that upset her. In the morning, after she got back from mass, he was up and quite cheerful. Didn't say a word about what had happened.

The other thing she couldn't abide was *Playboy* magazine. It seemed like every time the Tillers showed up, they'd have a copy and would leave it. At the time she considered *Playboy* plain pornography. The first chance she had, Marie would throw it out. David wasn't that ardent a reader and hadn't noticed. But one day he evidently had gotten into an article and when he couldn't find the magazine, she said it was in the garbage in the yard and if he wanted to dig through the garbage, that was fine with her, but look at it out there where it belonged. She would not allow it in the house. There was some toe-to-toe, high-decibel hollering about what right did she have to do that, but finally he just muttered something and stalked out.

Then she began to realize that his violence had little connection with anything she did. It appeared to come out of himself, without warning, often when she least suspected it. That was the spooky part.

It was the same with his morbid jealousy. When she was with him before they married, she'd flirt outrageously. But she cut it out afterward, and not only because she knew how he would react. She believed totally in the sanctity of marriage, that she had pledged herself for life, and to do anything to undermine it in the slightest was unthinkable.

She got to learn when he was on the verge of exploding. They'd be someplace, and his fingers would start to move, curling and uncurling, and all of a sudden the fingers stopped and it would happen. And after it had happened and some poor guy was on the floor, the veins that had been bulging in David's neck and temples would be gone, and you couldn't guess in a million years what had just occurred. He'd be completely at ease, relaxed, almost indifferent to his surroundings, as if he had some secret thought that mildly amused him. He was so incredibly quick. She once told him he reminded her of a cat, and he gave her a necklace with a black onyx panther.

One time at a party he was standing with his best friends, Mike Walsh and Phil Hicks. Marie liked Mike and Phil. They were the exact opposite of the Tillers, both college-bound, preppy types. A fourth boy was with them. She saw the boy pointing at her. The next thing she knew, the boy was unconscious. She found out from Mike and Phil that the boy wanted to know who the good-looking chick was, and when her husband asked which chick did he mean, that was it.

All the local fellows were so mortally afraid of him, afraid to look at her twice, she was sure the boy must have been from out of town. It turned out she was right. And on this occasion, in front of everybody, she screamed, "Are you crazy? How could you do that?" But he ignored her. Then she heard him say, after the boy had been revived, "Hey, man, I'm real sorry. I guess you didn't know that was my wife."

Another time she'd left a party early and walked home, annoyed at the persistent attention David was paying another girl. When she arrived at the apartment, he was there, waiting. God knows what would have happened if Phil and Mike hadn't been there too and dragged him off her. Even so, when she saw herself in a mirror, her eye was nearly shut, her lower lip puffed and cut.

· 10 ·

After each of these episodes he couldn't do enough for her. She would be touched by the way he walked places with her because of her constant car sickness brought on by the pregnancy. If there was a movie she wanted to see, even if it was five miles away, he'd walk with her. He'd hold her hand as though there wasn't anything he enjoyed doing more. She would be darned put out, she kept thinking, if she were the one who had to do it for someone else. And then, he made sure to go to Sunday mass with her, knowing how much it delighted her. Afterward they would go to Britling's cafeteria and gorge themselves on lunch. They would take so much on their trays that when they went for a table, the hostess would ask if they didn't want one for four, they must be waiting on two other people, and they would giggle over this. Their own private joke. They were together. She could hear strangers saying it. Just look over there. What a handsome young couple!

Of course, she felt the shame when the other things got out, like the time with Mike and Phil. But his friends didn't appear any more surprised than his parents. That was the way he was. Always had been. They remained the ideal, ever-popular husband and wife. The girls were thrilled she was having a baby. They'd tell her how they wished they were married and having one too. And at least she could be thankful that her own friends in Nashville and Daytona Beach, and her family, didn't know the bad parts of her marriage.

Then Marie's younger brother Bobby, just seventeen, came to visit. When Marie wasn't feeling up to it, the two men would take off together. At the Pig, Bobby was introduced to the Tiller bunch. Before he knew it, a fight broke out. A real melee with another gang. "Hey," David said, "you've been here a week and you haven't seen me fight yet."

Bobby looked on, bug-eyed. He saw somebody slam a car door on another boy's leg. Heard the scream. There were bottles, tire irons, even knives, everywhere. Nobody seemed to be without a weapon. Except David. He just stood there in the middle of the whole thing, taking away whatever the other guy had and then beating the hell out of him, very methodical, like a machine. Bobby couldn't get over it.

One night when Marie felt better, the three of them went to a party. No Tillers. Instead, there were some of her husband's old high school pals who had gone on to college. "Honey," Marie had said, "I sure wish you'd think about that."

It was late when they got home. Bobby began to make up the sofa in the living room. Marie was exhausted and wanted to get right to sleep. Besides, David had drunk too much beer. She was in the bedroom with him, pulling off her shoes, when he said, "Goddamnit, I'm sick and tired of you trying to control me." "Please," she said, turning toward him, "be quiet. Bobby'll hear you." "I don't give a fuck," he said. Every time he said something like that, it just chilled her. She got up from the bed. She had learned by now that it was time to leave. "Don't move," he said.

She saw his fingers curling and uncurling. "Don't move," he said again. She started for the door. But before she had gone a step, he was between her and the door. "I told you," he said. "Don't move." He was holding a nail file. "You move," he said, "and you get this." There was a knock at the door, and Bobby was calling, "Ree, what's wrong? What's going on?"

"Fuck off," her husband shouted.

It didn't make sense, she thought. He didn't use weapons. They were beneath him. Their eyes locked, though, and Marie knew he wasn't kidding. She remained absolutely still. He was right in front of her. She willed herself not to move. Do not move a muscle, she told herself. Suddenly he said, "You moved!" It all happened in a blur. She felt the stab, and then she saw the blood spurting from her hand. She cried out.

As soon as Bobby heard her, he jerked the door open. His brother-in-law's back was to him. Bobby threw himself at him and got an arm around his neck. Bobby was sawed off, not more than five foot five, but solidly built. He felt David struggling, unable to break the hammerlock against his windpipe. Bobby kept hanging on, squeezing, afraid to let go. Then he felt him seem to go limp. And now Bobby was afraid that he might be choking him. So he let go.

In a flash his brother-in-law was on him, fists raining in. Bobby remembered looking at him as he went down, how he had no expression. No outrage, nothing.

When Bobby came to, Marie was bending over him. She had a bloody towel wrapped around her hand. "Where is he?" Bobby said.

"I don't know. He just left."

Bobby helped her ice her hand, then bandage it. He washed the blood off his face. "How can you live with him?" he asked, and she said, well, he could be so caring, and he would always apologize, as if he hadn't been able to help himself. Maybe it was those guys he was hanging out with, Bobby thought. Next to them he looked real good.

It was all too bizarre. Bobby decided he'd better leave, and at daybreak he did. Marie begged him not to tell anyone in Nashville about it, and he promised not to. He wouldn't have, anyway. His style was to be closemouthed. And maybe his sister found it exciting on the edge of a volcano.

When David showed up, before he was hardly inside the front door, Marie tore into him. There was no excuse for what he'd done, she said. How *could* he? Actually stab her. And beat up her little brother. But he didn't respond. He walked right by her into the bedroom, and lay down. It was as though he hadn't heard anything she was saying. That was the first time she saw him practically catatonic. He stayed that way for hours, staring at the ceiling. Marie knew it was impossible, but she could have sworn his eyes never blinked.

Except for God, by way of prayer, she didn't have anyone to talk to. She couldn't bring herself to say, Listen, there's something wrong with my husband—he beats me up. She didn't know then that there were thousands of women, tens of thousands, who had fled into the dark in their nightgowns, as she had, battered and bloodied, terrified and ashamed. She thought she was alone, and that terrified her even more.

Immense guilt consumed her, mostly for having rammed through the marriage. She could never escape that. And she was also guilty for what was happening between them now. No one did what he was doing for no reason at all, she kept thinking, so she put herself on the rack. Somehow she was to blame too. And whether it was half, or more or less, it didn't matter, and she searched herself to see where she might have inadvertently upset or inflamed him.

· 11 ·

The baby was born a month late, on February 26, 1963, in St. Joseph's, a Catholic hospital in Memphis, and they named him Dante. Marie was twenty.

Her gynecologist was a woman. Her husband had insisted on that, and to tell the truth Marie was kind of relieved. Although she'd been a sex symbol as a beauty queen, she was sexually naive. When she was eleven, she had announced to Virginia that she had discovered how babies were made. A man kissed a woman, and the germs got all mixed up inside the woman. Virginia then explained the process of conception in very technical terms, which didn't exactly dovetail with Marie's romantic notions of love and marriage. Made it sound rather gruesome. That was about the extent of her sex education. The Pill hadn't come into use when she was at Seabreeze High, and the subject wasn't on the curriculum at Siena.

She was overjoyed at the change in her husband's attitude toward her for having given him such a magnificent son. He was there every day with flowers and gifts. From now on, things were going to be different between them. Marie had no doubt about it.

· 12 ·

Therese was born October 5, 1964.

They were living in Nashville then. David had gotten a job in the men's shop at Cain-Sloan, the city's leading department store. And not simply a sales job. He was in training as a buyer.

At first Marie had wanted another son. For all their rambunctiousness, boys were a delight. But she was completely taken by Therese. No bother at all. Never cried. Not even when she was soaked through. It disturbed Marie, however, that her husband wasn't relating to Therese. Fathers were supposed to be wild about daughters, especially after a son.

He started boozing more, staying out late. One night that winter he hobbled in on crutches, his foot in a cast, face all bruised up. Well, she thought, he'd finally lost one. Then she found out the other fellow was in the hospital. David had been so drunk he fell down a flight of stairs and broke his ankle after the fight was over.

The following week Marie realized her period wasn't ever going to come. She'd been waiting for it so anxiously. It just couldn't be, so soon after Therese. For all her love of babies, the thought of another child now, under the circumstances, left her practically suicidal. There had been all kinds of stories in the papers about the Pill, but it was still remote to her, and she'd been relying on the rhythm method. That required his cooperation, however, and she could almost recall the night. She'd been right on the line. All she could do was hope she was safe. She hadn't had a choice.

When she told him, he swung a crutch at her, as if it were her fault. Got her savagely in the back. Little Dante was watching. The next Saturday she was in the kitchen when she heard screaming in the living room. She rushed in and found her two-year-old son crying, "No, no," in front of the TV. A movie was playing. The scene showed a man slapping a woman around.

Marie was combing her hair when her husband came up to her and said to get out. If she didn't, he said, he was going to kill her. He said it very matter-of-factly. No emotion at all. That frightened her the most.

She called Roque. "Daddy, please come quick," she said. "I need you." She grabbed the kids and waited outside on the street. He can't do anything to me here, she thought.

Her father went back inside with them while she got some things for the children. Roque didn't say anything. Neither did her husband. It was the same old story. He never did what you expected.

She asked Roque to stop by Christ the King, where she prayed for guidance. After she came out, she tried to pull herself together. All she could think of was the new child she was carrying. How she'd manage. What her parents would say.

"Ree, it'll be all right," Roque said.

She said, "It's not what you think."

"Well, what is it, then?"

"I just can't tell you now."

"Honey, I'm your daddy. Who loves you more than I do? How can I help you if you don't trust me?"

The tears poured out of her, and that was when she told him she was pregnant again.

"Are you sure?" he said. "Have you seen a doctor?"

"I don't have to," she said. "I know it."

She remembered how her father looked at her. She'd had her ups and downs with Roque, and still would, but Marie would never forget how he was at that moment. With all the problems this news was going to cause him, how it would disrupt his own life, he held her and said, "Honey, why are you crying? That's marvelous. It's wonderful. You're bringing another baby into the world. That's no reason to cry," he said.

"You have two beautiful children. Now you'll have a third, like the others."

· 13 ·

Ricky was born September 27, 1965. After he was old enough to be left with a baby-sitter along with his brother and sister, Marie got a secretarial job with the Southwestern Company, a publishing house specializing in Bibles and Bible-related literature. She had moved out of her parents' home and was living in Vine Hill, a public housing project in Nashville.

David had returned to Memphis. She heard he was sharing a place with several guys, running crazy. Heard, too, he'd racked himself up in a motorcycle accident. Occasionally she'd hear from him directly. The calls would always come at night. "Why are you talking so quiet," he'd say, "who's with you?" and she would hang up, too tired to argue.

She was at Southwestern when the call came from his family. He'd been in a fight and had been stabbed in the stomach with a butcher knife. He was not expected to live.

She was allowed a couple of days off from her job. They knew she was separated, and she fibbed that her husband had been in a car wreck. She parked the children with Virginia and rode a bus to Memphis.

The way the knife had gone in, it barely missed his heart but went through just about every other vital organ. When Marie walked into the room, his mother was there, and she didn't know who else. It was like a deathwatch, she thought. Tubes were attached to him every-where. He was so pale. He couldn't speak. He waved feebly at the others to leave. As soon as they were alone, he mouthed, "I love you," and she sat holding his hand.

His condition stabilized. She had to get back to Nashville, to the children and her job. He began to recover. His doctors considered it miraculous. He stayed in the hospital for weeks. Then he phoned her. "I love you," he said, and she said she loved him.

One night at the Vine Hill project the bell rang, and when she opened the door, he was there, clutching a satchel, literally swaying. She had to catch him to keep him from falling. He was still pale. Released from the hospital, he had hitchhiked directly to Nashville, to her. Marie took him in. If this hadn't changed him at last, she thought, nothing would.

He got a job with the K Mart chain. He did so well that after four months he was promoted and transferred to the Atlanta area, where K Mart was opening new stores. She quit Southwestern and went with him.

For a while everything was fine. And then it went sour again. And then it didn't matter.

THREE

May 31, 1967. She'd never forget the date. Marie had come up to Nashville with the kids to celebrate her father's birthday. She was looking forward to it, and to seeing her brothers Chris, a year younger than she, and Bobby and her sisters Mary Therese, eleven years her junior, and Rosie.

Mary Therese went with her to the bakery to pick up the cake. Ricky was between them in the front seat. He was twenty months old. Marie had noticed some pistachio shells on the seat and brushed them off. On the way to the bakery she stopped for gas. After Mary Therese got out for a drink of water, Marie saw Ricky pick up a pistachio shell she had missed and pop it into his mouth. She reached in for the shell, got it out and tossed it through the open window on the passenger side of the car. Her sister had left the door ajar, and when Marie had finished paying the gas station attendant, she turned and saw Ricky outside the car. She immediately thought of the shell, that he had gone after it. She scrambled around the car and found him on his knees, a hand just coming away from his mouth. By the time she got to him, he had already started to cough, then really to choke. People came running from other cars. So did the station attendants. Marie pounded his back.

All of a sudden it was over. Ricky seemed okay. But it had been some scene. Everyone was shaken by it. Men and women stood around as Marie, holding Ricky to her, thanked them for their kindness.

She continued on to the bakery. Her sister apologized for not closing the door. Halfway there, Ricky began choking and gagging again. Marie slammed on the brakes and pounded on his back once more. She was desperate. He appeared to be strangling. Abruptly he returned to normal.

He toddled into the bakery with them, saying, "Cookie, cookie." Marie was at the counter waiting for her father's birthday cake when Ricky was seized again, this time worse than before. The other customers were transfixed. One of them cried, "Look at his lips! They're blue. Call an ambulance!"

With that he was perfectly all right, as if nothing had happened. "Well, sugar," the woman behind the counter said, "I guess it's gone. Kids always have something, don't they?" Maybe so, Marie said. But she stopped by the hospital at Vanderbilt University to be on the safe side. A doctor looked down Ricky's throat and put a stethoscope to him, and told her, "There's nothing wrong."

She had gone only five or six blocks when Ricky started wheezing. She wheeled around and raced back to the hospital. By the time she got there, he was breathing without trouble. This time, though, she insisted on an X-ray. "I'm telling you he's choking on a pistachio shell," she maintained. "*I know it.*" All the time she was saying this, Ricky was wandering around the room, peeking at various instruments, looking perfectly healthy. Nevertheless, the doctors took X-rays. The pictures were even brought out to her. Everything was fine. One of the doctors said there did appear to be a touch of bronchitis and gave her a penicillin prescription. It was as though the prescription was as much for her as for anything. She didn't care, as long as it was something.

That night Ricky slept without stirring once. Marie and the children stayed with her parents for three days. They had a lovely time.

· 2 ·

Back in Marietta, Georgia, where they had settled, she told her husband about the unnerving experience. He was only mildly interested, and Marie really couldn't blame him. When she looked at Ricky now, if she hadn't actually seen him nearly choking to death, she wouldn't have believed it herself.

About three weeks passed. On a Saturday afternoon she and David went grocery shopping while a teenage girl from across the street watched the kids.

When they returned, Marie knew instantly something was wrong. The front door of the house was wide open. A neighbor's car was out front. She ran inside. Three neighbors were there, scared, confused. The baby-sitter screamed hysterically when she saw her. "Marie, I promise I didn't do anything. I was in here and I just heard this sound."

Marie wasn't listening because she heard the sound too. She had never heard anything like it before, an enormous, incredible rattling. She flew into the room where Ricky was in his baby bed. It was a hot day, and all he had on was his diaper. He was lying face up. The anguish knifed through her. Ricky wasn't coughing or gagging this time. The rattling sound came from his fighting for every breath. Every time he took a breath, his little chest would literally collapse afterward. You could have poured half a cup of water in the hollow. It was the most grotesque sight she had ever seen. It was obscene, and it was happening to her baby.

She scooped him up and ran with him and her husband to the car, and they tore off to Kennestone Hospital. She rushed into the emergency room, clutching Ricky to her breast, crying "My baby, my baby! He can't breathe!"

She remembered someone snatching Ricky from her and telling her to follow, asking if he had choked on anything, and she was saying no, she didn't believe so, thinking they meant minutes ago, forgetting about the pistachio shell, which seemed so remote.

There was a swirl of doctors and nurses. Ricky was listened to, probed, X-rayed, and placed in an oxygen tent. They concluded that he must have ingested a foreign body. Marie called the baby-sitter, who said absolutely not, that Ricky had been sleeping when it started. Then Marie remembered the shell, and they said that was highly unlikely as the cause. It was so long ago. It had to be something more immediate.

Ricky did not get better. Her heart broke as she watched him inside the tiny plastic oxygen tent, gasping continually for breath, crying constantly, crying to get out of the tent to her. He couldn't eat and couldn't sleep. Even when he did nod off, the gasping never let up. He would be crouched on his hands and knees, and his head would droop from exhaustion, and then the sound of his own breathing, and the effort, would wake him. Sometimes he would finally keel over, but the awful heaving for air did not stop.

Marie never left the hospital. She stayed in his room. At night the nurses would find her sleeping for short stretches on a cot that had been set up alongside the tent. Her right foot would move in rhythm with his gasping. If there was a pause, the foot would halt and would not move again until his breathing resumed.

She kept talking about the pistachio shell, but it had been ruled out by now. The pediatrician attending Ricky decided that the trouble was probably laryngotracheal bronchitis, an inflammation of the larynx and trachea, and she prescribed a drug treatment.

Still there was no improvement. Once, Marie left him to go to the cafeteria for a cup of coffee, but being away for fifteen minutes was all she could stand. Then when she returned and opened the door to the children's wing, she heard it, this awful death rattle. Ricky's room was at the far end of the corridor, yet the sound of his breathing reverberated everywhere. The walls and ceiling of the corridor seemed to expand in and out around her, like giant lungs. She had been with him so ceaselessly that the sound had become part of her. Now, hearing it again after not having heard it, even for so brief a time, sent her reeling. "Dear God," she remembered pleading, "help me. Help my baby."

She saw the stricken faces of the nurses, their helplessness. Ricky's weight fell from thirty to twenty pounds in hardly two weeks. Nothing had worked. Dr. Robert Sessions, a surgeon, joined the case. One afternoon he took her aside. He was angry, and she wondered what she had done. "Where's your husband?" he demanded. "Why isn't he ever here?" She said that he was working, watching after the other two children, that a situation like this was very difficult for him. "I don't care," Sessions said. "I want him here. You need support. Where's your family? Why aren't they here?" She explained that her parents were in Nashville and that she had not called them, and he said, "You call now," and gave her a dime and stood by while she made the collect call.

"Momma," she said, weeping, "Mom, I'm at the hospital. It's Ricky, and you have to come down here. The doctor wants to talk to you." She couldn't go on, and handed Dr. Sessions the phone. "Yes," she heard him say, "the baby's condition is critical. It's possible he might not live through the night. Your daughter needs support. You must come at once."

Then he telephoned David himself and told him to get over to the hospital.

Sessions decided he would insert a bronchoscope down Ricky's wind-pipe in the morning in a last-ditch attempt to determine if he had indeed ingested a foreign body and, if so, to remove it. A tray of instruments was set up outside his room in case an emergency tracheotomy had to be performed during the night.

Marie was overcome with gratitude when Sessions ordered the nurses to take Ricky out of the tent, to rig up a system so an oxygen mask would come over her shoulder and she could hold him while he breathed through it. The risk was worth taking, he said. Ricky might relax a little in his mother's arms.

She could not stop the tears as she cradled him. The front of her dress was wet. Her husband, when he arrived, looked at them and knelt beside her and put his head on her lap. "Please stop crying, Ree," he begged. She had to pull herself together, he said, she was all he had. Marie was too occupied with Ricky then to dwell on the significance of what he had said, that it was his need he was thinking of. After a while he left, unable to bear it.

· 3 ·

It was her longest night. She sat in the dark alone, gently rocking Ricky. The gasping and the heaving continued, but every now and then his eyes would close, and she would think about putting him back in the tent because she realized that technically it was better for him, but whenever she tried to do this, he would stiffen at once and start to struggle feebly, so she kept holding him.

She began to curse herself for all the material things she had ever yearned for. There was this sofa she had seen in a store window that she wanted. She had dreamed of getting other things as well, but the sofa was easiest for her to focus on now, and she thought how could she have possibly been like that, how could any of it begin to compare with her baby's life, and she despised herself and swore that never again would she allow a material consideration to affect her. Then she thought of having to buy a coffin and picking the clothes for Ricky to wear in it. She implored God not to take him from her. Her prayers never stopped. She became one seething, feeling, living human prayer. She was vaguely aware of night nurses looking into the room, standing in the doorway for a moment and turning away because there was nothing they could do, and then she started praying for morning to come, eager for the bronchoscopy, thinking that at last something concrete and specific was going to be done to make her son better, and finally they took him off.

He was still gone when her mother came in and said, "Oh, Ree!" and embraced her, and they sat holding hands, waiting.

When Dr. Sessions walked into the room, his face was set, very solemn, but there was something in it that told her that Ricky was alive. "Your baby is resting comfortably," he said. He said that Ricky had suffered cardiac arrest on the table, but he had massaged his heart back to life and that it had a good strong beat. The bronchoscopy had found no evidence of foreign bodies, no pistachio shell, but there had been a great deal of mucus in both lungs, and he had done a tracheotomy. Later she remembered all this, but all that was registering now was that Ricky was alive.

When they brought him back, he was so ashen, unmoving. "He's dead, he's dead!" Marie cried, and a nurse said no, she was wrong, and it dawned on her that she thought he was dead because the gasping for breath had disappeared.

She cried out again when she saw the silver thing in his throat. "What's that?" And Sessions came back to explain it was the tube he was breathing through, that the tube was required to suction out the mucus, to clear his lungs, that it was only temporary.

The sight of it sent her nearer to collapse than she had ever been. Slowly Ricky awoke. When he saw her, he tried to say something. She saw his lips form "Momma," but there was no word, just a gurgling instead, and a vile, greenish slime bubbling out of his throat, out of the tube. There was more gurgling. She didn't know what it was until she saw the tears running down his face. He was crying, but the only sound he could make was the gurgling noise.

She watched horrified the first time they suctioned him, seeing them holding him down to keep him from thrashing free, his eyes beseeching her, the silent tears. But each time it became less horrible. She began to treasure the tube in his throat, even bless it. It was keeping him alive. He could sleep. There was some pinkness in his cheeks. His lips weren't blue anymore. Every so often she would pull down the sheet and stare at his chest. It looked like any baby's chest, except maybe a little bonier.

Nurses tended him around the clock, and after three days Marie's mother persuaded her to go home for the night, saying she would stay at the hospital. That night, as she was about to fall asleep, Marie sat bolt upright, wanting to run to the phone to see if Ricky was all right, but then a sense of peace settled over her. It was a mystical experience, her certainty that God had not let her go home only to take Ricky from her. Half asleep, in a reverie, she thought of Lazarus being raised from the dead, what it must have been like seeing blue skies and green fields and white and yellow daisies dancing in the breeze. She remembered how intense the colors were, and she came awake again, content that for now anyway everything was in God's good hands, and at last fell into a deep, confident sleep.

· 4 ·

Virginia took Dante and Therese back to Tennessee. In about a month the trach tube was removed, and Ricky went home. His brother and sister returned, and with endless wonderment and pleasure, Marie watched them playing. Even the marriage seemed to improve. David had just been named a regional sales supervisor. He was much less tense, and from time to time he could be utterly charming. His company's medical insurance policy had covered Ricky completely.

Everyone was having a good time at a cookout over Labor Day weekend. Suddenly, without warning, Ricky went rigid, convulsing, eyes rolling in his head. And Marie was back in the Kennestone emergency room. It was all so surreal. Staff people working on him, asking if he had choked on something, rushing him into X-ray. An X-ray technician said, "Hey, that's the same kid that was here before."

Dr. Sessions said that Kennestone just wasn't equipped to handle Ricky anymore, and it was decided that he should go by ambulance to Egleston Hospital in Atlanta, part of the Emory University medical complex specializing in seriously ill children.

Then she was standing next to a nurse who had been particularly kind to Ricky, and the nurse was on the phone to a funeral home requesting a hearse.

Marie finally lost control. She started screaming, "No, no, no! *Never!*" There was no way her baby was going in a hearse. The nurse pulled back, startled. She tried to explain that the hospital couldn't spare an ambulance for a trip like this, that it was common practice for hearses to double up, and Marie cried that she didn't care. She was still sobbing, thinking of Ricky in a hearse going not to a hospital but to a cemetery, when she felt the nurse's arm around her, the nurse telling her that it was all right, that she had located a regular ambulance.

Twenty minutes after his admission to Egleston, Ricky was undergoing his second tracheotomy, and then he went into an intensive care unit.

Marie was allowed in for five minutes every hour. She sensed a new professionalism in Ricky's care. She could actually go for a cup of coffee and not worry. Egleston was exclusively for children, but you didn't send a child there for a tonsillectomy. About fifteen babies were in the same unit. There were babies with deformed heads the size of watermelons, who never moved. There were babies with protruding spines. Right next to Ricky was another little boy with a trach tube in his throat. But the other little boy also had a malignant brain tumor. Sometimes she walked the corridors and saw the burn victims, infants in naked agony. On the one hand, she was relieved that Ricky was there. And on the other, she had to face the terrifying reality that he was there at all.

Infection was an immediate danger to him. First it was strep. He was placed in isolation, Marie with him. She wore a hospital gown, mask and rubber gloves. He was fed through a sliding window. All the utensils and plates were disposable. She was told that if she left the room, she would have to leave the hospital too. So of course she stayed.

And next, pneumonia. He began developing pneumonia the way other people got headaches, two or three times a month. You could tell that pneumonia was coming on when the mucus from his lungs got greener and was tinged with blood.

Marie learned to suction him herself. The suctioning had to be done frequently, as often as every fifteen minutes when he had pneumonia. The average was twenty or twenty-five times during the day, less at night when he was asleep. Every time the staff people approached Ricky to do it, he got frantic, afraid they would hurt him. Sometimes the bruises from the shots they gave him seemed to cover his whole body. But the doctors noticed that he calmed down when Marie touched him, held his hand. They suggested that she try learning the procedure, that it might be easier all around.

The suction machine was in a steel casing with rounded edges, about the size of a four-slice toaster, perforated so the heat could escape.

Several feet of thin plastic tubing ran to it and to a waste jar. There was another jar with a saline solution. She learned to keep her hand from trembling, to run some of the saline solution through the tubing to clean it out, to stick the tubing through the trach tube, to get it deep down into his trachea without causing him to gag too much, to turn the tubing so that it went first into one lung lobe and then the other, to make sure the tubing wasn't clogging, and if it was, to take it out and shoot more saline solution through it. The best part was how Ricky got to smiling when she began the suctioning process, as though he knew she was helping him.

· 5 ·

What passed for normalcy at Egleston, between crises, was Ricky in a private room, the doctors searching for the key to his condition. Marie was with him all the time, his brother and sister staying with her parents or her in-laws. A bed had been fixed up for her. She brought clothes, her hair dryer and just moved in. There was a TV, a radio, magazines. And mostly the waiting. Long periods in the chapel, praying.

Yet the Egleston doctors were flummoxed. They dismissed the laryngotracheal bronchitis theory as a joke. They listened to her story about the pistachio shell, and they bronchoscoped him endlessly. A miniaturized bronchoscope was flown down from New York to get a better look inside him. He was bronchoscoped a dozen times without success. No shell. Nothing. Specimens of his mucus were sent to medical research centers around the country, even to London. Nothing turned up. Whatever Ricky had was not recorded. They began to think that he might have some unknown birth defect. They told her that he might be able to live with his tracheotomy until he was five or six, and then be okay for the rest of his life. Or maybe he wouldn't ever see five or six. In fact they didn't know.

After three months Ricky had regained enough strength to be allowed to go home. Customarily, after a tracheotomy, the trach tube stayed put, for years if necessary. And while a birth defect remained suspect number one, there was a lingering suspicion that Ricky had some extraordinarily rare lung disease. So to prevent a possible buildup of infection, his trach tube would have to be changed daily.

The trach tube was sterling silver. It hooked into his throat. A flange held it in place. On each side of the flange there was a hole for a white string that went around his neck. Since Marie had done so well with the suctioning, the doctors tried to persuade her to learn how to switch the trach tubes. But she couldn't bring herself to do it. She had watched it being changed, had seen that split second when one was slipped out, the sudden gasp from Ricky unable to breathe until another was inserted. His life depended on the trach tube. The thought of something going wrong, of the opening in his throat closing, clogging up, before she could get the second tube in, was more than she could take. So, instead, she said she would make the eighty-mile round trip to Egleston every day.

One day, right after Christmas, she was on her way from Egleston, whizzing along the Interstate, with Ricky in the rear seat in a baby chair with some hanging toys that had been rigged up.

She heard a gasp. Well, maybe she didn't. She was never really sure. But *something* made her glance over her shoulder. She saw Ricky, his eyes huge, pointing down toward the floor of the car. And she saw his neck, the trach tube gone.

She veered off the Interstate onto the shoulder. She heard tires squealing behind her, horns honking. She bounced to a stop, climbed over the back of the front seat and on her hands and knees found it. Somehow the string had become untied. By then his face was bluish. Still kneeling, she reached up with one hand and parted the opening in his throat, and with the other pressed the tube into his windpipe. She did it without thinking. His face began to get color again.

She swerved across two lanes, jumped the center island and sped straight back to Egleston hoping for once that a cop would show up. Naturally, none did, even though she was hitting ninety miles an hour in traffic, propelled by the image of the germs swarming inside Ricky.

At the hospital, after the contaminated tube was replaced by a sterilized one, he was kept under observation. But nothing developed. Doctors clapped Marie on the back as if she had won first prize. Even she was pretty pleased with herself. See, she was told, we knew all along you could do it. So while Ricky was being monitored, she worked on how to change trach tubes. When she returned home, she had two more tubes. They went on the rolling three-tier medical table with the suction equipment and the cold-mist vaporizers that kept his congestion down at night. She would polish the spare tubes and boil and store them in baby-food jars. The baby-food jars were just the right size.

It cut her trips to Egleston to twice a week, for examinations and the antibiotic shots he still needed.

· 6 ·

She'd been so preoccupied with Ricky that she hadn't thought about her marriage. For a time it had remained on a reasonably even keel. Then all at once everything reverted to form. Unexpectedly, the way it always had.

In February '68, on the first Saturday of the month, Marie was doing some housework when she heard a commotion in the kitchen. Little Dante had apparently climbed up on the kitchen counter to get some cereal and had knocked it over. David was in a rage, not just spanking him but actually punching him.

Marie threw herself between them, screaming. Ricky and Therese came running in. Her husband was shouting it was all her fault, that this kid, all of four years old, had climbed up on the counter, what kind of a mother was she anyway? He whirled toward her, a kitchen knife in his hand.

Clutching the children, she cowered in a corner. Ricky was making bubbling sounds. My God, she thought, I have to suction him. Marie was sure she was going to be murdered on the spot.

She looked up, past the knife, at his eyes. They were glazed over, unseeing, and somehow she knew what she had to say, how to handle this. She spoke slowly, the kids hanging on to her. "Oh, baby," she said, "I'm so sorry for you. God bless you. God help you. Honey, I know you don't mean to be like this. I know you love me. I know how much you love our children. And I know how hurt you are inside."

She saw something snap in his eyes, like a camera shutter. He stared down at her, at the knife, as though he were seeing it for the first time. He dropped it and rushed from the kitchen.

She stayed crouched where she was, not daring to move. She heard him pacing, then stop. He had gone into their bedroom. She waited to be certain. She had to suction Ricky. She sent the other two outside to play, and then she picked up Ricky, the mucus oozing from his trach tube.

When she was finished, she saw her husband lying on the bed, face up, eyes unblinking. She had meant what she had said in the kitchen, and she felt a great wave of pity for him. She would never truly know what had brought him to that point at that time.

Afterward, it was the same as always. Remorseful. Contrite. Loving. Gifts for her and for the kids. Vows that it would never, never occur again, whatever it had been. But she knew now the marriage was finished. It was just that she was immobilized, unable to act.

A week or so later Marie was standing at the kitchen sink, doing the dishes, when she felt something grab her leg. She couldn't help shrieking.

But when she looked down, it was only Therese, who had come in and spontaneously thrown her arms around her mother's leg. It left her devastated. Her own daughter could not hug her without terrorizing her. And she knew then that she had to get away for good. She tottered to the living room sofa and sat down, hunched over, moaning. So unutterably sad.

· 7 ·

That day, in Nashville, Marie's brother Chris had a sudden urge to call his sister. He never could figure out why. They didn't talk that often, hadn't spoken since Christmas, as a matter of fact. It must have been ESP or something, he would think. But he never forgot the call.

He heard the receiver being picked up, then nothing. "Ree?" he said. "Hello, Ree, is that you? Are you there?" And then he heard this very small voice saying, "Yes." He could hardly hear her. "Ree," he said, "are you all right?" and there was no answer.

The first thing that came to his mind was that something had happened to Ricky, that perhaps he had died. "Ree," he said. "Is it Ricky? Is Ricky all right, Ree? Talk to me." Her voice came back on the line. It sounded very far away, as if she weren't speaking into the phone, as if she weren't really talking to anybody. "He's okay," she said.

It must be the marriage, he thought next. He knew the marriage was in bad shape, and about the violence. He pursued that. Was that what was wrong? "Answer me!" he shouted. But she didn't.

He knew his sister: decisive, headstrong, sassy. She had never been like this, practically in a trance. "Listen to me, Ree," he said. "I'm coming down to get you. I'm leaving right now. It'll just be a few hours. Hang in there, hear? Pack a few things for you and the kids. I'll be there. Ree, say something! Do you understand?"

There was a long pause, and through the sobs, she faintly said, "Yes," and Chris hung up and went to his boss at the storage company where he worked and told him he was taking the rest of the day off. His sister, he said, needed help real bad.

Chris brought his wife, Jeanenne, with him. He didn't know what he was getting into, and maybe another woman could help.

He arrived late in the afternoon. Marie looked as she had sounded on the phone. He had never seen her so passive, so out of it. There were dark, sad rings under her eyes. That was more shocking to him than anything. She was always so robust, full of vitality.

She hadn't packed, for herself or the children. Chris asked Jeanenne to do it. This seemed to make Marie come to a bit. Only she knew what to take, she protested. Okay, let's get moving, he told her. He hated being so sharp with her, but he didn't know how else to get through. And he was edgy enough himself, wondering when her husband might show up.

Then there was Ricky. Marie had not called Egleston. Chris made her make the call. She got one of Ricky's doctors, tried to explain why she was calling, then broke down completely, unable to speak. Chris took the phone. He said that his sister was in the middle of an intolerable domestic situation and had to leave for Nashville. Could Ricky make the trip by car? Chris got the impression that the doctor was aware of her problems at home. The doctor said he felt Ricky could ride it out safely but that Marie had to check in with the Vanderbilt hospital immediately. He gave the name of the specialist to contact, and he said he would phone ahead and forward the necessary data.

So they left. They had to stop several times for Marie to suction Ricky in service-station rest rooms. The last time, in the night, was somewhere around Murfreesboro, Tennessee, within hailing distance of Nashville. Walking up and down past the gas pumps, Chris kept thinking, I can't believe this is happening, it just isn't possible.

· 8 ·

Marie dreaded facing Virginia and Roque. But when the car turned into the driveway, both were on the porch to embrace her. Before

Marie could say anything, Virginia whispered, "It's good to have you home."

First thing, Marie brought Ricky to Vanderbilt. His Egleston records were reviewed. Once again she told the story about the pistachio shell. Once again Ricky was X-rayed and bronchoscoped. Once again the doctors found nothing. Their prognosis was the same as Egleston's: Ricky had some mysterious birth defect. It was touch and go. He'd either grow out of it, or he wouldn't.

She couldn't, of course, remain with her parents. The house could barely hold her and two children when she had been pregnant with Ricky. Now there was another child, critically sick with no end in sight. It was, besides, Roque's most precarious economic moment. He had left his job as a night copy editor with the *Tennessean* to launch a rehabilitation project, the Samaritan Center for Alcoholics. It had begun as a laymen's charitable exercise at Christ the King working with derelicts in Nashville. But Roque had found himself involved beyond anything he'd bargained for. Samaritan Center eventually became a substantial operation, but right then he was just starting out, getting backing, raising funds. He wasn't even drawing a regular salary.

He got an apartment for Marie and paid a month's rent—a hundred dollars. It was on the ground floor of a forbidding old stone house in a rundown section of south Nashville. It was a sunless place, with paint peeling from the walls, the kitchen filthy and awful. Roque tried to prepare her for it, saying he couldn't afford too much. But Marie couldn't believe she'd have to stay in a place like this, even knowing all the while he was doing his best. She didn't have any clothes for herself and the kids except what she had taken the night she left Georgia. About ten days later Chris borrowed a van from his boss and drove back down to move the rest of her belongings. When he arrived, everything was cleaned out and David gone.

Elizabeth Alexander, from Tennessee welfare, who was friendly with Roque and Virginia, helped out with beds and a sofa. Virginia contributed some tables and lamps and what food she could spare. Monsignor Leo Siener, pastor of Nashville's Cathedral of the Incarnation, had grown up with Marie's parents in Chattanooga. He was also diocesan director of Catholic Social Services, and chipped in with money for staples and clothes for the children.

It wasn't until after Marie moved in and was frantically attempting to clean up that she became aware of the roaches and water bugs. She couldn't recall when she had not been petrified by them. In a panic, she called Virginia, who had an exterminator come right away. But the roaches remained, darting out of kitchen cabinets, the stove, the crevices in the walls. Water bugs got into Ricky's suction machine.

She didn't know how she could keep his equipment sterile. At night in bed, praying for some end to it, she'd steel herself for the moment when she would have to turn on the lights to suction Ricky, and see the roaches. Lying there, she could also hear the rats scurrying in the walls. She thought rats were only in cities like New York and Chicago. She tried to think of them as mice. Mice were kind of cute, she'd tell herself. Like the pet hamster she had when she was small. But she'd listen to the sounds in the walls, and she knew mice weren't making them. One morning she went out on the back porch and nearly stepped on a dead rat. She phoned Bobby to come and throw it away, and huddled inside the apartment until he did.

· 9 ·

Ricky was then two and a half, and Marie remembered it all as though it had happened in slow motion. She was suctioning him. In the afternoon. Very routine. He'd been coloring with a crayon and a pad of paper. Afterward, she ran some saline solution through the suction tube to clear it. She was coming down with a cold, already had developed a slight cough, and she made a mental note to be sure to have enough surgical masks on tap.

For no particular reason she turned and saw Ricky on his back in the crib, holding the crayon, a blue crayon, over his head with both hands. All of a sudden he broke the crayon, and Marie saw a chip fall straight into the trach tube in Ricky's throat. She remembered fighting off her scream so as not to scare him. It was the worst thing imaginable. A foreign body inside him, going into his fragile lungs. She looked to see if the chip had dropped all the way through the tube. She couldn't find a trace of it.

She called Vanderbilt and was told to bring Ricky in immediately. Then she called Virginia to pick her up, and got a neighbor to take care of Dante and Therese. The chief resident was in the emergency room waiting for them. This time there was no question about it. Marie had actually seen the chip go into Ricky's windpipe, and minutes later he was undergoing his sixteenth bronchoscopy.

Marie and Virginia were led to a cheerless room. Institutional green. She remembered how haggard her mother looked. Virginia wasn't saying anything. There was nothing anyone could say. Marie wasn't sure how much time passed. Then the resident was coming toward her. A young guy, under thirty. And he was beaming. He had a cardboard cup in his hand, and he said, "I want to show you something," and she looked into the cup, expecting to see the crayon chip, and instead saw a grayish, oblong object about the size of her little fingernail. She knew instantly what it was.

"It's the pistachio shell," she said.

"Yes," the resident said, "it is. You were right."

The theory was that the shell had kept moving around in Ricky's lungs. Maybe there'd been a hint of something in an X-ray, but by the time he was bronchoscoped it had gone somewhere else, hidden in the pus and mucus. Left unsaid, naturally, was whether anyone had really thought there was a shell in his lungs to begin with. Not until the crayon chip had there been any certainty that anything was inside Ricky. The chip was never located. The crayon was analyzed and found to be vegetable-based, and the chip probably had dissolved spontaneously.

Later, when Marie would be told that what she knew was happening around her could not be, that she must be mistaken, and was then forced to fight for her reputation and professional life, if not her actual life, she would think a lot about all those doctors, all those experts, who had once told her she had to be wrong, and had tried to talk her out of believing what she had seen with her own eyes.

Ricky stayed in the hospital for observation. After two days, when she went into his room, the trach tube was gone. In its place was an innocuous Band-Aid. For the better part of eleven months he hadn't been able to speak. Marie remembered how, at his last birthday, he'd tried to blow out the candles and couldn't. Instead the air had come from the opening in his throat.

The first word he said to her was "Momma."

His transformation was astonishing. Back home, he raced everywhere with his brother and sister, yelling at the top of his lungs. It was as if those terrible hours in emergency rooms, sitting by his hospital beds, not knowing whether he would live or die, had never occurred. By then Marie's cough, along with all the tension, had brought on laryngitis. It was maddening. Now she was the one who couldn't talk.

Her own life changed as dramatically. Freed from ministering night and day to Ricky, she could get a job. But the first thing she had to do was escape her roach-infested place as fast as she could. Around the corner up on a hill, there was a development called Colonial Village. She'd seen a sign that an apartment was available. She called Monsignor Siener and asked if he could help with the first month's rent. He saw to it that she got the money right away.

FOUR

Monsignor Siener also helped her find a job. One of his parishioners was in the Nashville regional headquarters of the American Dairy Queen franchise chain. Marie went to work for him and four other men as office manager and girl Friday to them all. They were on the road most of the time, and she was more or less on her own, making five hundred a month.

But her life was going to be more than this, she promised herself. As soon as all the children were old enough to be in school, she would return to college. She didn't know quite how she'd manage it, but she never doubted that she would.

After a while she began attending parties. Went out on dates. It floored her that she was found attractive. She didn't believe she was even pretty, let alone beautiful, anymore. She remembered how once when she was punched around by David and was bent over, weeping and moaning, he had yanked her up by the hair in front of a mirror and said, "Look at yourself. You used to be so beautiful when I married you. Now look at you." And all she'd seen in the mirror was her tear-streaked, swollen face, with a red blob of a nose, and she sobbed more, which made it worse, and thought, yes, he's right, you know, she was really ugly now, and no one could ever want her.

She had recurrent nightmares about her husband chasing her across shadowy landscapes. She kept her phone unlisted.

· 2 ·

Virginia, and then Roque's mother, Rosario, whom everyone called Mamasita, first suggested it. The two most Catholic women Marie knew. "Ree, honey," Virginia said one day, "you haven't asked me what I think, but I really think you should get a divorce. It's just too dangerous for you and the babies," she said. "I'm worried to death about it." Next, Mamasita was in Nashville for a visit, saying how much she loved her and that she couldn't stand the thought of anything hurting Marie beyond what had already happened. "Please," she said, "please be divorced."

But the shocker was Monsignor Siener. Of course, he said, the Church didn't recognize divorce. Although she'd still be married in the eyes of the Church, she had every reason in the world to dissolve the marriage with a civil divorce. There were very probable grounds for a Church annulment too, he said, but that would take time.

During the early years of the marriage, she had gone to Monsignor Siener for counsel, and he had seen both her and David, sometimes together, but mostly separately. As he listened to Marie, it became clear that in her passion to marry she'd been looking for another kind of security because of what had happened to her parents, searching for someone to fall back on. And she'd picked a man who apparently filled the bill. Handsome, seemingly dominant. Only it turned out she was the dominant figure, providing all the support and encouragement, getting no appreciation and affection back. Only Marie's determination had kept the relationship going. Siener reluctantly concluded he was dealing with a classic instance of oil and water. The marriage was a real bummer.

She got the divorce on July 14, 1969. Recognized or not by the Church, it was heavy stuff, the crushing reality that so much of what she'd struggled for from the core of her being, suffered for, agonized over, was worthless.

It was handed down in Memphis, her husband's last known domicile. He seemed to have vanished. Her parents drove with her to

Memphis. On the way, they stopped for the night in the city of Jackson, where an old newspaper friend of Roque's, a man named Lois Laycook, had taken over his family's printing business. Inevitably, Roque and he got into politics, and Laycook started raving about his local congressman, who was in his second term. Young, a real populist go-getter, Laycook said. Just what the Democratic party needed. Listening to Laycook, you'd think this guy was right up there with the moon and the stars.

It was, she'd remember, the first time she ever heard the name Ray Blanton.

Marie hadn't even seen her divorce lawyer before. He'd been referred by another lawyer Roque knew in Nashville. Over the phone with him she had insisted on the minimal grounds. They met in the courtroom. Marie had never been in a courtroom, much less a divorce court. And she hadn't given any consideration to support, didn't anticipate getting a dime, so when the lawyer asked her how much she wanted—three hundred, four hundred a month?—she said it wasn't worth bringing up, and the lawyer looked at her as if she were out of her mind. She had to put in for something, he said, and she said okay, put down twenty dollars a week, and he said that was ridiculous. For God's sake, he said, she couldn't raise three children on that. She needed at least fifty, and they sat in the courtroom, haggling in whispers, and finally Marie agreed to thirty-five dollars a week.

Everything was going routinely, her lawyer talking to the judge, when she saw the irritation on the judge's face, and her lawyer was saying, "But Your Honor, that's all I could get her to do." Next thing, the judge said to her, "Young lady, please come up here." So she went up, alarmed, and the judge wanted to know what this was, asking for thirty-five dollars a week for three children. Was she independently wealthy? Did she really have three children? "Do you have money in the bank, young lady?" he said sarcastically, and she said, "No, sir, I don't, but we're getting by."

"Well," said the judge, "I want you to define for me why you're asking only thirty-five dollars a week. Is your husband sending support now?" And Marie said, "Your Honor, I don't know where my husband is. As far as I know, he's not working, and he's not sending anything. If he was working, he wouldn't be sending anything at this time anyway, and my theory is that if I ask for some astronomical figure, he'll never send a cent. But if I ask him for a small figure, maybe he'll send that. That's why I'm asking thirty-five dollars a week. Because I stand a better chance of getting a little than a lot."

While she was talking she saw the judge looking at her open-mouthed, and when she stopped, he threw up his hands and said, "All right, young lady, I resign. Let's get on with it."

And then it was finished. She was divorced. She didn't feel anything. Numb, maybe. And empty. After all the years of hurt, there wasn't even hurt. It was so anticlimactic.

Afterward, oddly enough, other women could be the most grating. My goodness, three children, they'd say. How do you do it without a husband? How can you manage? Marie thought about that a lot. She'd think of all the strain and fear when she'd been with her husband, the constant pressure of humoring him and worrying about him. She would think how now if she wanted to rearrange some furniture, she'd just do it without any bickering about it. And how she used to have to keep wherever they were living so spick-and-span, and now if sometimes she didn't feel like making her bed in the morning, she didn't, and if she didn't feel like doing the dishes, they stayed in the sink. She'd think about all the meals she'd fixed for her children, doing everything exactly right, her mother-in-law figuratively standing over her, and how now she might simply open a can of Chef Boyardee Beefaroni for them, which they not only seemed to prefer to her own cooking but appeared to thrive on.

Actually, she thought, the answer was that life was easier without a husband, at least her husband.

She started a night-school course in psychology at the University of Tennessee's Nashville branch. She wanted to know more about what made people tick, especially her ex-husband. And she began to think more about going back to college. She tried to limit her social life. I won't go out this Friday night, she'd say to herself. Fellows would call, and she'd say, "No, I'm on strike." And she'd get through Friday night and feel good about it.

Then, still in great anxiety about her marital situation despite the divorce, she took the final step to resolve it. She would seek an annulment.

Marie believed in God, and she believed the Catholic faith was the best path to God. She believed in the divine tenets of the Church, although, as her faith evolved, not necessarily in all of its human doctrine. She'd agree or disagree. Her fundamental relationship was with God, not the Church hierarchy.

Later, she would take a longer view of the Church's stand on civil divorce and remarriage. There could be extenuating circumstances, and the Church was too rigid, too unforgiving. She'd think about a murderer being able to repent and be returned to the Church. Or that a priest could abdicate his vows and then be married in the Church if he wished. Were a priest's vows any less binding than marital vows? Yet a Catholic who divorced and remarried was denied the sacraments. Excommunicated. And what about a marriage that was so unhealthy that it drew one or both of its partners away from God, and for some red-tape reason an annulment couldn't be obtained? Wasn't that throwing the baby out with the bath water? So many of the Church's rules and regulations had been designed for convenience' sake. Or discipline. It seemed to her that God was more forgiving than His Church.

Right then, however, an annulment was terribly important for her own peace, and she went to Monsignor Siener about it. She wanted to know if her marriage had been valid, true and sacramental.

In a sense, he said, an annulment was a misnomer. The Church didn't annul a marriage. All the Church could do was examine the original contract and the state of mind of the participants at that time, and the circumstances surrounding the marriage. Possibly there was no marriage to begin with, even though there had been a ceremony and children. The phrase the Church used was: *lack of maturity and due discretion.*

It appeared, he said, that her husband had lacked the capacity then to enter into a lifetime contract with one wife. Lacked the necessary emotional stability to do it. He had been under pressure to get married. He didn't want to be married. He felt he had been trapped into marriage. Failings applied to both of them, although perhaps more to him than her. But for Marie's part, Monsignor Siener said, she seemed not to have exhibited due discretion and had certainly displayed a singular lack of maturity and responsibility from the start.

He warned that it was not for him to decide. The process would be long and painful. It would have to involve both her and her husband. Questions had to be pursued and answered fully. Facts ascertained, witnesses brought forth. Under ecclesiastical law, a *Libellus,* a document introducing the case, had to be prepared. The diocesan marriage tribunal had to hear the case. The judge knew in advance that even if he ruled for an annulment, his decision would be challenged. The case would move on to the Court of Second Instance, an appeals court, in the Archdiocese of Louisville. Thence to the National Conference of Catholic Bishops in Washington.

And, indeed, nearly seven years would pass before her annulment was granted. It seared Marie to relive in black and white what had happened, to put down in writing, "Not sure," in response to how freely her husband had entered into the marriage. To acknowledge "he was afraid to be married" and that she had pushed him to where "he was more afraid of losing me." To admit: "I came up with the idea— to say I was pregnant, when in fact I wasn't."

But it was in the works at last. Her commitment to the marriage was over.

· 4 ·

In the fall of '71, when she was twenty-nine and all three children were in school, Marie returned to college full time. She thought about night school, but that would take forever. Besides, she wanted to go to the best, and the best was Vanderbilt, which didn't offer night-school courses.

Most of her friends were disbelieving. One said, "Marie, you're telling me you'll miss out on a good party just because you've got an exam the next day?"

"You wait," she said.

And how was she going to make it financially? She couldn't work at a regular job. Well, she and the kids would have to hunker down, was all. Otherwise, she'd always be on a treadmill. Maybe men didn't need a college degree to get ahead, but she figured women did for sure. Her mother, who had been the librarian at Christ the King Church on Sundays after mass, arranged to let Marie succeed her, and that brought in a hundred a month. She got a part-time job editing a business newsletter and another one handling correspondence for Nashville's congressman, William Anderson. There was a nice touch to that. She'd been Miss *Nautilus,* and Anderson had been skipper of the submarine when it made its historic voyage under the North Pole. Best of all, she could type the letters at home. And she'd seen the bulletin-board notices at Vanderbilt for typists to do theses, and she answered them. She also applied for student loans from every federally backed program she could think of, and she put down her pride and accepted welfare aid for dependent children.

The hitch was getting into Vanderbilt. For good reason, her junior college grades from Daytona Beach and the ones after her first semester at Siena were a mess as far as Vanderbilt was concerned. After considerable give-and-take, Vanderbilt recommended she first try a semester at Peabody College. While Peabody was a separate entity, physically it was practically indistinguishable from the Vanderbilt campus. Classes were even interchangeable, and the tuition was less.

Then something completely unexpected happened. When Ricky was so ill, a doctor in Marietta had complimented Marie on how well she was standing up under the strain, and she said her faith was her salvation, and he said he wished he had faith like that. They ended up fast friends, and the doctor, G. B. Espy, revealed that he had a retarded little girl living in Tennessee who was becoming too difficult for his ex-wife to look after. Marie said there must be special places that could provide the care and affection the child needed, and he said yes, there were and he'd been checking them out. But it became increasingly clear that Dr. Espy was having real trouble facing up to the situation. Marie got the feeling that among his circle she was one of very few who even knew about the problem.

After the pistachio shell was found in Ricky, she telephoned Espy with the good news and learned that his daughter's plight was not yet resolved. So Marie scouted around and found the perfect school for her, called King's Daughters, about an hour's drive from Nashville, and after the girl was admitted made it a point to visit her as often as possible.

Now, just as Marie was ready to begin at Peabody, Espy called to say hello and thank her again, and when she told him what she was about to do, he said he'd like to help out by sending her $500 every three months. Marie said she couldn't possibly accept it, and Espy said she didn't understand. When he was in medical school, he said, a man in his town had lent him money to make it through, and when he tried to repay him, his benefactor had said all he wanted was that Espy do the same for somebody else. By taking his offer, Dr. Espy said, Marie would enable him to honor that obligation. He was sure that in her turn she'd do the same, and she said she would.

She arranged her class and study periods between nine and four o'clock to be on hand for the kids. She had a gorgeous tan from the summer.

Her dark brown hair hung to her waist. She wore a shirt and jeans like the other students. Her first week on campus a freshman who couldn't have been more than eighteen made a pass. That really set her up.

· 5 ·

After one semester at Peabody she went right into Vanderbilt. She decided to aim for a double major in English and psychology. She also took on more part-time work doing market-research interviews. But all the jobs got to be too much. She'd try to study after putting the children to bed and wake up in the middle of the night, slumped over her books. She began dozing off in class. There had to be a better way, she thought. Something with shorter hours and at least the same money.

That was when she became a cocktail waitress at a Nashville club, the Villa. She dropped everything else she'd been doing except typing theses and handling the library program at Christ the King. Friday and Saturday nights, sometimes on Thursdays, she'd be at the Villa. She'd get home from the club, pay the baby-sitter, take off her boots and hot pants, flop into bed, and be at church for the eight o'clock mass, all prim and proper. She tried to imagine which would cause more consternation—one of the Christ the King mothers walking into the Villa, or one of the waitresses coming in for a book on the life of Saint Francis. It was just the sort of secret giggle Marie delighted in.

She never had more drive or enthusiasm than when she began the fall semester in 1972. By going to Vanderbilt straight through the summer, plus course completions that had been finally accepted from Daytona and Siena, she had enough credits to be in the junior class. Her grades were so good that she signed up for an honors program for her psychology major.

For some time Marie had realized that the marriage between her parents had become one in name only. That fall Roque finally divorced Virginia and remarried. Although Marie didn't go into a tailspin this time, she still reacted bitterly. She saw it more as desertion than divorce, and it would be a good while before she found it within herself to reconcile with Roque, to see that nobody was truly at fault, that the string had simply run out between her father and mother.

· 6 ·

The coughing began in earnest the following February.

Marie first noticed it around Christmas. Virginia remarked on it. "Ree, honey," she said, "it sounds like you've got a cold."

But the coughing fits went away. And then returned sporadically. By late February she started coughing nonstop and having chest pains. She went to her doctor, who had X-rays taken. Her pictures were fine, he said. When he weighed her, he asked if she'd been dieting. She was down ten pounds from her normal one-nineteen. No, she said, she hadn't been, and the doctor said perhaps it was indigestion and prescribed some over-the-counter pills.

It got worse, and she went back to the doctor. He examined her once more and said there wasn't anything wrong that he could see. He asked if she wasn't still in school. And if she didn't have three children to look after. And jobs besides. Yes, she said, and he said, "It's that simple. You're doing too much." The suggestion that her illness was psychosomatic bugged Marie plenty, but she thought, well, she better pull herself together. Not cough till she exploded. Pretend the hurt in her chest wasn't there.

She would drag herself into class and sit there unable to concentrate, so weak and dizzy she would have to leave, and go home to collapse. She went to another doctor, who found nothing, and a third, whose best remedy was a cough suppressant. But the coughing went on, the attacks so bad she'd sometimes cough until she threw up. Her weight continued to drop. The pain in her chest was excruciating. She'd be struggling through a lecture and think if she could only get home and remove her bra, the pain would lessen. But it didn't make any difference. Darvon was prescribed. No help. She was taking four or five Darvons at a time, hoping they would at least make her drowsy. The coughing and pain had turned her into an insomniac. She counted herself lucky if she could doze off for a couple of hours.

One evening she was so weak she couldn't even get up to prepare dinner for the children, and Therese, who was eight then, had to do it, running back and forth from the kitchen as she finished each step in making hamburgers.

"Momma, I put the skillet on the stove."

"All right, honey, now turn the light on real low."

Marie and the kids moved in with Virginia, who was living alone with her youngest daughter, Rosie. Both Marie's brothers were busy raising families of their own. Chris wasn't even in Nashville. And her other sister, Mary Therese, was a co-ed at the University of the South in Sewanee.

Marie went into St. Thomas Hospital for a battery of tests. TB was a prime suspect, but nothing showed on the X-rays. She was tested for histoplasmosis, and for a time was thought to have a severe case. It was, she was told, a lung disease prevalent in the South that came from bird droppings. Lots of people had mild occurrences without knowing it. Occasionally it could be bad, however, and possibly lead to blindness. But then that possibility was eliminated.

She left St. Thomas no better off. It remained a mystery, like Ricky's sickness, she thought. Except there was no pistachio shell. She'd stopped working at the Villa, of course, or typing theses, and was unable to attend classes anymore. Her only income was the salary Christ the King kept paying despite her absence and the five hundred dollars Dr. Espy sent every three months.

There was a new problem. Her boys were getting to be too much for Virginia, who had become increasingly infirm, and Rosie, at twelve, was hardly a match for them. Monsignor Siener had them stay at St. Mary's, a Catholic residence, during the week. Even though St. Mary's was only a few miles away, and they'd be home on weekends, Marie hated the idea. But there was nothing else to do.

In the middle of all this a full scholarship she'd applied for came through. It seemed so pointless. There were more doctors, more X-rays. She began gulping Percodan regularly for the pain. She was under a hundred pounds now. Near the end of June, shadows showed up in her left lung.

She was sent to a thoracic surgeon. He pointed to the shadows and said there was no doubt about it. She had cancer. A large portion of the lung had to come out. He stood her in front of a mirror and traced with his finger where the long, curving incision would be made to pry her ribs apart. The operation must be performed immediately, the surgeon said. He told Marie he was scheduling her into the hospital the very next day.

She left his office in a daze, certain her life was over.

It was, she would think, the hand of God.

As Marie's health worsened she phoned Dr. Espy to explain why she wasn't up to visiting his little girl at King's Daughters. He kept in touch and didn't hide his disgust at the kind of medical attention she was getting. She remembered how he was especially upset that she was on Percodan without supervision.

The afternoon she'd been at the surgeon's office and returned home robotlike, Espy happened to call. She told him about the surgery, and he said she must be mistaken, she had to be talking about a biopsy, and Marie replied there hadn't been any mention of that. He couldn't believe it, he said, and ordered her to get on the phone to the surgeon and ask if a biopsy wasn't to be done first, and to call him right back.

"Tell your friend he doesn't know everything that's been going on up here," the surgeon said, clearly irritated. "You've been X-rayed dozens of times. We've been keeping careful watch, and we don't have any more time to fool around. We know what we're doing."

Marie had barely finished relaying this to Espy when he was shouting at her not to do a thing until she heard from him. About an hour later he was on the line. He'd been in touch with a colleague and close friend at Columbia-Presbyterian Medical Center in New York City who was one of the best thoracic surgeons in the country—maybe the best— and had arranged for her to be admitted at once. Espy said he was taking care of everything, her flight included, and he didn't want to hear any arguments about it. Then he asked to speak to Virginia to make sure his message got through.

She went alone. Virginia wanted to come along, but her health wouldn't permit it. Marie had to be wheeled through the airport. When she was seated in the plane and looked out and saw the kids waving good-bye, the tears she'd been holding back came. She wondered if she'd ever see them again.

· 7 ·

Marie never questioned that she could address God. And in Columbia-Presbyterian the night before they were to open her up, not knowing what they would find, knowing only that a new set of scans had revealed something inside her, she took a spiral notebook and wrote a letter to Him.

Dear God,

I know that You have been good to me—always. Always You have seen fit to bestow great blessings on me, even when I in effect rebuked You by my immaturity, lack of gratitude, or acknowledgement that I owed <u>all</u> to You.

In spite of grave & repeated offenses, You gave me 3 beautiful children, & though I have at times suffered, always You have protected us, shown me how to survive, & kept us in Your bosom.

Now I tremble with fear of the unknown, & with discouragement. And yet I have been surrounded by love, flowers, gifts—and most importantly—prayers.

Always, in retrospect, I have attempted to learn from my mistakes, that I might at least profit from learning through experience (however regrettable). You have showered Your graces on me. You have exposed far more good to me than bad, & have truly given far more to me than <u>anyone</u>, <u>anywhere</u>, deserves.

Yet knowing, as I do, my complete undeservingness—I realize that now I fear You, my Father—that now You see fit to at last bestow justice, & perhaps take me from this world.

I do not fear hell. I know that Your arms are around me. But forgive me, Father, for my weakness now.

O ye of little faith! (me)

How I cling now to my faith. Have I ever abandoned it? Truly, no. Allow me, if it be Your will, to lead by example as I believe I can, others to You.

But if You want me now, help me, help me, help my precious little ones . . .

During the tests she could tell from the doctors' faces that they thought it was a malignancy. They decided where to go in for the biopsy based on the tomograms, an advanced form of X-rays. Even pointed out the exact spot on her chest. She tried to be brave. Couldn't it be a bit lower, she asked, so the scar wouldn't show in a bathing suit? They said not to worry her pretty head about that— that if it was nothing, there'd be a plastic surgeon to take care of the scar.

When she came to in the recovery room, a nurse was looking down at her. The nurse was smiling. Then Marie faded out, but she remembered the smiling face, and she knew everything was all right.

After she awoke again, there were more smiling faces hovering over her, and a voice was saying, "It wasn't cancer. Marie, can you hear me? You don't have cancer."

They never did find out exactly what it was. "If we can't come up with an answer," she was told, "maybe we'll name it after you."

But the heart of the infection apparently had been dug out. She started to feel better. She put on some weight. When she arrived at the hospital, she had hit ninety-three pounds. The coughing continued for a while, and with the cut in her chest it hurt. The worst thing, though, was the withdrawal from Percodan. The Columbia-Presbyterian doctors stopped it cold turkey. It wasn't as if she wanted a whole bunch of pills, she'd plead. Just something to get her through. They said no. She never should have been put on it the way she was, to begin with. She ought to sue those people who had been treating her, they said, and she thought no, she was just happy being in one piece.

Marie was kept at Columbia-Presbyterian throughout July to guard against a relapse. To occupy herself, she began doing handicrafts and made a doll for Dr. Espy's daughter. She tuned in on the Watergate hearings every day. She watched with particular interest a young Nashville attorney named Fred Thompson, who was constantly on camera as the Republican minority counsel.

She started thinking about the future, regaining her strength, putting her life together. The first priority was to finish her education. She couldn't wait.

The doctors had advised her to pass up the fall semester. But she discovered that her Vanderbilt scholarship had been granted solely for the 1973–74 academic year, and she wasn't about to let it go.

The last week in August her sister Mary Therese visited some friends in Florida and took Marie with her. Marie was fascinated by the ocean, finding its vastness and power a metaphor for the omnipotence of God, and one afternoon when her sister and the others had wandered off, she found herself alone on the beach gazing at it. All at once she had to be in it. She walked shakily to the water's edge, letting ripples of the tide wash over her feet, then waded farther out to where the currents swirled around her knees. She heard someone shout, "Hey, should Marie be in there by herself?" She was scared, but she felt so good at the same time, as though by just being in the sea she was connecting with life. She went in deeper. A wave knocked her down. She had the sensation of drowning. The thought flashed through her that she wouldn't ever be able to get up. But she did, thoroughly drenched. And she felt absolutely magnificent. Reborn almost. Like Lazarus rising from the dead in the dream she had after Ricky's tracheotomy. Hands were helping her back onto the beach. "It's okay," she was saying. "I'm fine."

· 8 ·

Her senior year at Vanderbilt was her happiest and busiest. She was accepted in poetry and creative writing seminars. And she also made the staff of the campus newspaper, the *Hustler*, covering politics. She had always remembered her earliest consciousness of politics. It was 1952, when she was ten, the Democratic National Convention was being held in Chicago, and Tennessee's native son, Estes Kefauver, was challenging Adlai Stevenson. Roque was covering it for a Nashville radio station, and she was allowed to stay up late to see it on television and listen to her daddy filing reports.

She interviewed the head of the Young Democrats on campus and subsequently joined up. Politically, at home, she'd been a spoon-fed Democrat. Once part of the Solid South, Tennessee had become a swing state. Right then the incumbent governor, the two U.S. senators and seven out of ten congressmen were Republicans, but after Watergate, Democrats could sense the kill. The talk was that a pack of candidates would be in the running for the 1974 gubernatorial primary.

Through the Young Democrats Marie was in on all the excitement, at party caucuses, voter registration, drives, rallies, fund-raisers. At these affairs she kept bumping into a politically active lawyer in his mid-thirties, about six two, with reddish-brown hair combed modishly forward so the bangs almost touched his eyebrows. No matter how many times they met, he'd come up to her with a big grin and say, "Hi, you probably don't remember me, but I'm Eddie Sisk."

In the primary election for governor, Marie, along with some of her closest friends in the Young Democrats, favored Franklin Haney, a millionaire developer from Chattanooga running for office for the first time, who seemed to embody the fresh start they wanted for the party. Marie was even offered a job to do advance work for Haney. It was tempting, but she couldn't take it. Because of the incompletes she'd gotten when she was sick, she had to continue at Vanderbilt through the summer to receive her degree. Once, when Sisk had reintroduced himself to her for the umpteenth time, he asked her whom she was for, and when she said Haney, he said he was with Ray Blanton. "Haney's got the money," he told her, "but we've got the people." Then he winked at her and said, well, anyway, she was a good Democrat and that's what counted.

Blanton won the primary in a field of twelve with about a quarter of the vote. Since Tennessee did not have a runoff, that made him the Democratic nominee against the Republican, Lamar Alexander. The general election in the fall of '74 attracted national attention. According to *Time* magazine, there'd be no better way to gauge the Watergate fallout. If Blanton was victorious, reported *Time*, "it would be an ominous sign for Republicans throughout the South—an area where they once entertained such high hopes."

Ray Blanton trounced Alexander. His margin was 120,000 votes— close to 60 percent of the turnout. Some comeback, everyone said, for a fellow who'd been wiped out in a senatorial campaign against Howard Baker Jr.—by 276,000 votes—only two years before.

But Marie had her mind on other things. After finishing up at Vanderbilt, she had gone job-hunting and was in for a downer. The country was in a recession, and it was as bad in Nashville as anywhere else, especially for women. And because of the children, she lacked mobility. She just missed out being managing editor of a monthly magazine published by the Nashville-based American Association for State and Local History. At the last minute someone with more experience got the job. Virginia suggested getting a certificate to teach English, but Marie was interested in teaching only on the college level, and that meant going back for a master's degree. Eventually she got work as the assistant to a top executive in a Nashville bank. But it was really a secretarial job, and she hadn't put herself through Vanderbilt for that. She was still living with her mother, and around Christmas, a time she had expected would be brimming with opportunity, Marie voiced her despair to Virginia. Why had she knocked herself out? For what?

In January she went to a round of inaugural parties for the Blanton administration and heard how there was going to be a clean sweep of Republican officeholders. A few days later she read a story in the *Tennessean* that Eddie Sisk had been picked as the legal counsel to the new governor.

She thought about it a little before calling him, certain the tables would be turned now. She even rehearsed saying, "You probably don't remember me . . ." But when she gave her name, he was on the phone immediately. "Marie, how are you?"

"Just fine, thank you, Mr. Sisk. Congratulations on your appointment. I know you're going to do a terrific job."

"Well, I appreciate that. What can I do for you?"

She said she'd like to come see him if he could spare the time, and he said sure thing. Why not tomorrow morning? Eleven o'clock.

PART II

FIVE

Assistant State Attorney General David Raybin was sore as hell. It had been more than two weeks since the Blanton administration took over, and an extradition officer still hadn't been hired in the legal counsel's office.

Raybin was supposed to review extradition papers to certify that they had been properly drawn up. It should have been routine, and usually was—until now. Now Raybin was getting angry calls, letters and telegrams from his counterparts all over the country. To make matters worse, the former extradition officer, a Republican who knew she wouldn't be kept on, had quit. Add the normal hiatus of the Christmas holidays and there was a backlog of cases amounting to almost two months.

Raybin had already complained to Eddie Sisk. Privately Raybin had concluded Sisk was a klutz, but he had been one of Blanton's key campaign aides, and from what Raybin gathered he was the Governor's personal choice as legal counsel. So Raybin had proceeded with some tact.

Then on the morning of February 4 Raybin found renewed demands for extradition action on his desk from three different states, and this time when he got Sisk on the phone, his tone was a good deal sharper. Somebody had to be lined up pronto, Raybin said. Things were getting out of hand. Extradition warrants were a two-way street. How did Sisk think other states were going to react when Tennessee wanted a fugitive returned?

Okay, okay, Sisk had said. He'd get to it.

Less than an hour later Marie was there.

The day before, when Sisk had told her to come on down, she said, "Do you mean come to the capitol?" and he said, "Yeah, the Governor's office," and the prospect of that was exciting enough.

She dressed as if she were going to church. In a way the capitol was also a sacred place. It was on top of a hill, the highest part of downtown Nashville, overlooking not only the city and the Cumberland River winding below but the rolling countryside for miles beyond, and she remembers the awe she felt going up the capitol steps and, after getting directions, walking under vaulted ceilings and along an expanse of marble corridor toward the Governor's suite.

The corridor was crowded, but nothing like the Governor's reception area, which was real pandemonium. Phones ringing, people darting in and out of doors, others whispering tensely on sofas and chairs, highway patrolmen standing by looking very official. She gave her name, and while she waited, she recognized some faces from their photographs. O. H. (Shorty) Freeland, who was from the Governor's hometown and his patronage chief, and Jack Strickland, Blanton's assistant for policy planning, and the new press secretary, Brooks Parker. All around her, Marie sensed the throb of power.

Then Eddie Sisk was grinning down at her, saying it was Eddie, not Mr. Sisk, and he waved a hand at the bedlam and explained it was because they were still in the transition period, and took her by the arm and led her through a door to where they could talk, he said. And they were in this large room with blue carpeting and blue brocade drapes, and it was hushed in there, and she saw the big, polished mahogany desk with the high-backed leather chair behind it, and the great seal of Tennessee up on the wall, and the state flag and the American flag, and suddenly she knew she was actually in the Governor's personal office. Yes, Eddie seemed to be saying, it was the Governor's, but the Governor was at his other office in the mansion. She wasn't really listening, though, her eyes riveted on the desk and the chair, thinking so this is where it all happened, where the decisions were made that affected every Tennessean, right in this room, behind that desk.

Eddie was talking to her, sitting on a velveteen sofa, and she was answering, she didn't know quite what, and tried to jerk herself back into the reality of the moment so he wouldn't think she was completely gaga, and Marie was aware of him saying, "Hmm, a double major in English and psychology," and studying her intently.

"Well, hell, I don't know, Marie," he said, "but I've got a job to fill right now that might interest you. Hold on here just a minute." He picked up a phone, and she heard him asking something about did it require having to be a lawyer, and then he turned back to her and said, "Marie, how would you like to be extradition officer for the State of Tennessee?"

Afterward he made sure to call Alex Shipley, Raybin's immediate superior, and said he could tell his boy to stop chewing on his nails, the job had been filled.

Sisk figured he'd swatted a lot of flies at once. Marie was a good-looking woman, which was nothing to sneeze at. She was a loyal Democrat, and her Vanderbilt degree was class. And she was a little naive. Hadn't even asked what her salary would be.

The way the day was shaping up, he might be able to get in a round of golf. If only it would stop raining. The two big passions in Eddie Sisk's life were golf and the fortunes of the University of Tennessee football team.

Virginia was the one who brought up the money. Marie had gone home and said, "Guess what, Mom? It looks like I'm going to be the extradition officer for the state," and Virginia had said, "That's grand, honey, what is it?" and Marie replied that she didn't rightly know what it entailed, and that Eddie Sisk hadn't been much help, except that she'd be working closely with him and they'd learn about it together. Then Marie described what it had been like being right in Governor Blanton's office.

"What does it pay?" Virginia asked, and Marie had to confess she didn't know that either. In her excitement she'd forgotten to find out.

Her salary, it turned out, was a letdown. $8,928.

Eddie must have seen it in her face the next day. He took her into the corridor and off to a corner away from everyone and told her that while he knew it wasn't the kind of money she should be getting with a Vanderbilt degree, he was positive she'd like working in the administration with him. "I want for you to know, between us," he said, "you'll be your own boss. You can pretty much come and go as you please, so long as you do your work. I'll trust you on that. And there's something else I want you to know. We'll be on the lookout to upgrade you so you can earn more. That's a promise," Eddie Sisk said.

Marie hesitated. She still hadn't committed herself. Yesterday afternoon, after she'd been to the capitol, another job possibility had come through with the Joe M. Rogers Construction Company, a worldwide contractor, with a starting salary of $10,000. The title had been administrative assistant to one of the executives, but it sounded suspiciously secretarial to her.

She thought about Eddie's assurance of better things to come. In the back of her mind she'd been toying about maybe becoming a lawyer someday, and being extradition officer, what little she knew about it, did have legal overtones. Besides, experience in government would be invaluable. And with Eddie, she'd be in the thick of it. She kept recalling her emotions in the Governor's office, the air of, well, majesty she'd felt in there.

So right in the corridor Marie told Sisk he could count on her to do her best—for him and the Governor.

About a week later she was having lunch with two old friends she had gone to school with at Christ the King, Polly Whitsitt and Cynthia Bruer. "Honestly, Marie," Polly was saying, "I don't see how you can work for Ray Blanton. He's just a darned redneck. Daddy says it's embarrassing."

Marie's anger was immediate. She looked at Polly and Cynthia, both comfortably off, and said if there was any more talk like that she was leaving, and of course nothing else was said, but the rest of the lunch was sort of strained.

To tell the truth, she didn't know all that much about Blanton. She'd voted for him in the general election because he was a Democrat, and that was enough for her. Especially following Watergate. Polly and Cynthia were acting like snobs, she decided, like a lot of Nashville.

· 2 ·

THE TENNESSEAN, *August 11, 1966*

Adamsville—Ray Blanton displayed a talent for getting votes few people thought he had when he narrowly defeated veteran Rep. Tom Murray of Jackson for the Democratic nomination for Seventh District congressman.

"I feel the rural people switched their support from Murray to myself," the 36-year-old Blanton said.

THE TENNESSEAN, *November 11, 1967*

Jackson—Rep. Ray Blanton, D-Tenn., described Vietnam war dissenters yesterday as "an unholy alliance of seldom scrubbed young upstarts, ivory tower utopians and misguided society dropouts."

NASHVILLE BANNER, *November 6, 1968*

... GOP nominee John T. Williams lost to Rep. Ray Blanton in the 7th District race—a special "target" district for the Republicans in their attempt to win a majority in the Tennessee delegation.

Blanton used his conservative image to poll a solid 67% in the sprawling district.

UNITED PRESS INTERNATIONAL, *November 24, 1969*

West Tennessee Rep. Ray Blanton, a Democrat, says Vice President Spiro Agnew "has struck a responsive chord in the minds of a vast majority of Americans" with his criticism of television reporting and commentary.

THE TENNESSEAN, *June 8, 1970*

Memphis—The children of wealthy families are more prone to campus violence rather than students of working class families, Rep. Ray Blanton said here yesterday.

THE TENNESSEAN, *November 4, 1970*

Rep. Ray Blanton, Democrat, of the 7th District, triumphed easily over Republican contender William Doss.

Blanton [had] indicated his support for the presidential candidacy of George Wallace in 1968, but has campaigned hard for the Democratic ticket this year.

THE TENNESSEAN, *March 14, 1971*

Rogersville—Rep. Ray Blanton said here last night President Nixon's handling of domestic issues is "inept" and called Nixon "the worst President since Millard Fillmore."

NASHVILLE BANNER, *February 11, 1972*

Franklin—Rep. Ray Blanton (D-Tenn.) has erased all doubts that he will attempt to oust Republican Howard Baker for one of the state's two Senate seats this year.

Speaking to the Williamson County Democrats here Thursday night, Blanton said, "The possibility of my candidacy for the Senate post ain't a rumor."

NASHVILLE BANNER, *November 8, 1972*

Democratic senatorial hopeful Ray Blanton said in Memphis the telegram he termed an "endorsement" from Alabama Gov. George C. Wallace will add to his margin of victory against incumbent Sen. Howard Baker.

THE TENNESSEAN, *May 8, 1974*

Noting that voters have lost confidence in the integrity of political leaders, former U.S. Rep. Ray Blanton opened his bid for governor yesterday.

"I will present voters with a clean, honest image and will carry on a clean, honest administration," Blanton said.

ASSOCIATED PRESS, *August 6, 1974*

Memphis—Ray Blanton, the Democratic nominee for governor, says a Watergate-conscious public will demand that Republican candidate Lamar Alexander explain his role as a pre-Watergate White House aide.

THE TENNESSEAN, *October 10, 1974*

"I'll match my record on civil rights against any Republican in the country," Blanton replied.

... during his administration, he said, discrimination will be banned "absolutely" in state government.

THE TENNESSEAN, *October 13, 1974*

"I'm proud to be able to go back to Washington to visit my friends," Blanton said.

"When my opposition wants to visit his friends, he has to go to the Allenwood, Pa., federal prison."

THE NEW YORK TIMES, *October 28, 1974*

Nashville—A former segregationist is trying to recapture the Tennessee Governor's office with a 19th-century populist appeal to the economically hard-hit of both races.

Ray Blanton, who is considered a "good old boy" in his native farming country of western Tennessee, says the Republicans and large economic interests are responsible for inflation.

NASHVILLE BANNER, *November 6, 1974*

An Adamsville farmer took a drive down on his river bottom land Tuesday, looked it over and pondered the rich, dark soil.

A brief plane flight later, the son of the soil was elected the next governor of his state.

· 3 ·

The big joke at the Belle Meade Country Club was that Betty Blanton, the Governor's wife, was set on redecorating the executive mansion. She'd been all over town looking at new linoleum.

The Belle Meade section was the redoubt of old Nashville money, of which there was a great deal. Belle Meade easily matched, arguably outdid, other enclaves of the nation's rich—Bel Air in Los Angeles, say, or Houston's River Oaks. It stretched for miles on the city's southwest corner, one opulent fifteen-to-twenty-room home after another, each with appropriate acreage. A sprawling, unnatural park, impeccable to the last blade of grass. Divided by Harding Road, Belle Meade, in a kind of ultimate stab at status, even managed right and wrong sides, indistinguishable to a visitor. The wrong, western side was where the Louisville & Nashville tracks ran along the road; the right side had a picture-book rock-strewn stream.

Belle Meade had been the site of America's first thoroughbred stud farm. The same limestone shelf underlying Kentucky bluegrass went right through Middle Tennessee, and it was the lament of many Belle Meade residents that they could have been preeminent in breeding and racing had not Baptist and Methodist fundamentalism raised hell early on. Now the political clout of old-time religion had been reduced to limiting liquor-store licenses to one per designated area, a modicum of government control that the Nashville establishment didn't consider worth getting exercised about.

There was nothing sweaty about Nashville's wealth. The city had a perfect physical frame as you came in from the airport. The big skyline building on your left was National Life and Accident Insurance. The one on the right was Life and Casualty. Founded in 1778, Nashville sat in the fertile Cumberland River Valley, and the first big game was land speculation. Then it became a major railhead, ideally positioned between the factories of the Midwest and the steel mills of Birmingham to the south. Lacking heavy industry of its own, it blossomed as a financial, commercial and educational center.

By the time Ray Blanton took office, Nashville had a population of around five hundred thousand with more millionaires per capita than any other city in the country. Until very recently its interests were almost all homegrown and home-owned. The Genesco mercantile conglomerate alone created at least fifty local millionaires. The first municipal bond underwriting in the entire South began there. The Kentucky Fried Chicken empire was conceived there. Hospital Corporation of America was headquartered there. So was Ingram Industries, with its vast holdings in oil, coal and shipping, and Associates Finance, America's second largest loan company. The list went on. Big insurance, big banking, big business. If anything was in short supply, it was an influential middle class. And unlike other Southern cities, such as Memphis and Atlanta, Nashville had a black population less than a quarter of the total. Still, reflecting the city's devotion to the dollar, the biggest black bank in the Southeast, Citizens Bank and Trust, was in Nashville.

There was also a rash of new millionaires, spawned by the country-music boom that came out of Nashville's Grand Ole Opry. But they lived mainly on the other side of town, to the northeast, and had little input into the power structure. Getting better traffic lights for Music Row was the kind of thing that concerned them.

The people who really ran Nashville, and thus shaped much of Tennessee's life, belonged to a group called the Watauga Association. The name came from the first organized settlement in the state, established in 1772, when Tennessee was still part of North Carolina. Amazingly, few Nashvillians were aware of its existence, but with the city as closed as it was at the top, the occasional reporter who caught wind of it got no place. Only members knew who the other members were. Most of them, however, lived in Belle Meade and could be found on the boards of Nashville's dominant institutions, including some of the media, and on the board of Vanderbilt University.

The membership, all white and all male, saw itself as the guardian of responsible, rational, conservative government. It desired, and obtained, right-to-work laws, no state income tax and a hands-off climate for corporate and financial dealing. It also greatly prized a sophisticated, urbane image for Nashville. The sign at the airport welcomed you to MUSIC CITY, USA. While the Watauga Association accepted this as a new economic reality, it infinitely preferred Nashville's old boast—Athens of the South. The advent of Ray Blanton was distressing. It was recalled how he had once likened himself to the average American who favored the TV show *Bonanza* over the Metropolitan Opera.

The irony was that Blanton, for all his populist talk, would have dearly loved to be invited into Belle Meade's establishment homes. As a congressman, he'd been on the District of Columbia Committee. That made him an important man in Washington, and he had developed a taste for power and its fringe amenities, reportedly even taking on a mistress in the best tradition of the nation's lawmakers. In his campaign for governor, he had made an issue of the use of the state Lear jet by the Republican incumbent, Winfield Dunn, who was unable to succeed himself under the Tennessee constitution. One of Blanton's first decisions after his election was, on second thought, to keep the Lear. He was going to be a mobile chief executive, he said, and needed fast transportation.

But right off, the gibes had come. The only thing he'd learned in Washington was that it was okay to wear colored shirts with ties. His wife had just finished posting the executive mansion lawn for her clothesline. His oratorical muffs—such as the "anals of history"—kept Belle Meade in stitches.

The insults went beyond jokes and stories. A Belle Meade family had donated a painting of Andrew Jackson to the Hermitage, the famous house Jackson had built for his wife in 1819 on the outskirts of Nashville, but agreed instead to have it hung in the executive mansion during Dunn's term. Now, with Ray Blanton in residence, the family wanted the portrait taken to its original destination. Blanton was enraged. The portrait, he decreed, was staying put.

It wasn't as if he hadn't tried.

Shortly after his inauguration, Blanton asked three prominent Nashville couples, committed Democrats, to dine at the mansion. The Governor, resplendent in a tailor-made blue serge, a white shirt and maroon silk tie, with gleaming gold cuff links bearing the state seal, greeted his guests in the mansion's elegant foyer. Then forty-four, he had extraordinarily broad shoulders that gave him an imposing physical presence. Betty Blanton, from his hometown of Adamsville, whom he had married when he was majoring in agriculture at the University of Tennessee, was at his side dressed in ruffled light blue taffeta, her hair a pale moon color. "You know my pretty wife," the Governor said, almost challengingly.

The atmosphere at first was stiff. To break the ice, Blanton's pet poodle was fetched. The poodle had a trick. When asked what he thought of Republicans, he rolled over and played dead.

After drinks were served, the Governor conducted a tour of the mansion. He was full of anecdotal lore. Kennedy slept here, Truman there. He mentioned that he wanted to have the mansion's official history revised. The most recent version, completed under Winfield Dunn, was too Republican-oriented. He paused by the portrait of Jackson. That was his kind of politician, he said. To the victor belonged the spoils. Blanton's face, as always, was devoid of expression. It was difficult to tell if he was kidding or being serious.

Over dinner he spoke in his flat, rural drawl about his determination to rebuild the state Democratic party, which had been splintered for so long into various liberal and conservative persuasions. Without Watergate, even his own election would have been in doubt. Lamar Alexander, saddled with his service as an aide in the Nixon White House, had been forced to disclose the names of all his financial contributors, and Blanton recalled with relish how he had turned that to his advantage. "We country people know it's the guilty dog that always barks first," he had said.

The wine, a guest remembered, was "some kind of crackling rosé." The servants, black, passed back and forth unnoticed. Suddenly, though, they became the focus of attention. After dinner the entire staff lined up behind Blanton's chair. They were all prisoners, he explained, mostly in for murder. Traditionally, if they performed their work satisfactorily, they could expect commutations when the Governor went out of office. At a nod from Blanton, each stepped forward to give his name, age, county of origin, his sentence and the circumstances of his crime.

Perhaps six convicts had finished their recitations before one of the women present, appalled, said, "I think I've heard just about enough of this."

No, no, Blanton said. It was all right. He'd talked to these fellows, gotten to know them.

But didn't he think that it was rather dehumanizing, she persisted.

Blanton gazed at her. There was an uncomfortable silence. Abruptly, he shifted the subject. Even though they were killers, he said, he wasn't bothered at all that they were in the house. It was a choice he had to make. Either keep them on or hire a whole other staff at taxpayer expense. He turned to his wife for confirmation, asking if she was uneasy being under the same roof with them. Mrs. Blanton, appearing a bit dazed herself, said no, it was fine with her.

His guests left, speechless. It had been like a scene from an old movie about the antebellum South, Massa Blanton, surrounded by family and friends, strolling out on the plantation porch at twilight to be serenaded by his faithful darkies.

When you came down to it, Ray Blanton didn't owe the existing power structure a thing. In the welter of Democratic gubernatorial primary candidates after Watergate, he had come up like a joker out of the deck. Conventional wisdom had him finished politically when he was trounced in his U.S. Senate try. But the national ticket in 1972 had been headed by George McGovern. If he'd known that in advance, he said privately, he never would have run. But he had trudged dutifully across the state and gained invaluable name recognition. And he had learned something else. In a desperate attempt to avoid disaster, he had embraced white supremacist George Wallace. All Blanton had gotten in return was the loss of a large chunk of the normally Democratic black vote, as well as wholesale desertions from the party's liberals.

So this time around, two years later, he was out promising the black leadership full participation in his administration, plumping for women's rights at every chance and telling labor he was the working-man's friend. It was truly a testament to the short memory of the American voter. Poll after poll showed Blanton as all things to all people. And he stayed a steadfast Democrat, hammering away at the handmaidens of Republican rule—big oil, big corporations, big grocery bills.

Once in, smarting under the snubs, he decided to stick it to the establishment and set about fashioning his own permanent coalition. From the contacts he had made as a member of the Foreign and Interstate Commerce Committee in Congress, he planned on bringing new industry to Tennessee, not only to create more jobs but to water down the hold of the entrenched oligarchy. His labor commissioner was the first in state history to come out of union ranks. He appointed two blacks to his cabinet. While most of his female appointments were on the second and third levels, he did make a woman his commissioner of revenue. As things stood, he would not be able to succeed himself. A constitutional convention would be held in a couple of years, how-ever, and he had every intention of seeing that provision changed.

On the surface it looked spiffy. The Governor announced the forma-tion of a "blue ribbon" panel to screen prospects for key positions in his administration. But in all the fanfare for excellence, he made sure to get certain people he wanted where he wanted them. He was a true believer in Jacksonian democracy and the spoils system. It took money to build and bind a political operation. The Belle Meade crowd, he'd say, was as big a bunch of thieves as anybody. They had just gotten there first.

It was his conviction that you couldn't really trust someone until you'd done something for him and he was in your debt, and that would be Blanton's great limitation—the outsider's paranoia. The trouble was that the people closest to him, the ones he felt comfortable with, who massaged his ego, were generally second-raters. Or plain greedy. And then there was family. He gave his brother Gene an unmarked office right in the capitol. His campaign manager, Jim Allen, whose Pontiac dealership made him the most visibly successful member of Blanton's inner circle, was named an unpaid consultant with unspecified duties and an unlimited expense account. He brought in young Clyde Edd Hood as a special assistant. Only twenty-two, Hood had been at the top of his class in political science at the University of Tennessee's Nashville branch. A fellow student remembered Hood telling him how he was going to hitch his wagon to a star and make a million dollars by the time he was thirty. The next thing the student knew, Hood was Blanton's campaign finance chairman. Now one of Hood's unannounced assignments would be to monitor the allocation of liquor-store licenses.

Among the tasks of the transportation commissioner was to oversee lucrative highway contracts. It was a cabinet-level position, and Gil Merritt, a former U.S. attorney for Middle Tennessee who was on Blanton's screening committee, conveyed three recommendations. Blanton looked at the list and asked how come Eddie Shaw wasn't on it. Shaw was an old Blanton crony. He owned a restaurant in Hardin County, adjoining the Governor's home county of McNairy. Didn't Merritt know Shaw wanted the job?

Yes, he knew, Merritt said, but there was no way he was qualified.

Well, hell, Blanton had said, Eddie Shaw was a friend. He couldn't insult him like that. It wasn't right. The least the committee could do was put him on the list.

Merritt agreed, and as soon as Shaw's name was included, Blanton appointed him. After all, the Governor explained, while the final decision on appointments was his, Shaw *had* been recommended.

Merritt had another go-around with Blanton over Eddie Sisk. Blanton said he had a right to pick his legal counsel. Merritt said he wasn't arguing that. The point was, while the attorney general would represent Blanton on matters involving the state, he was appointed by the Tennessee Supreme Court and by definition had a divided allegiance. The legal counsel would be Blanton's own lawyer, thinking only of his interests, protecting and advising him. Blanton, Merritt said, needed the best talent he could get, and Eddie Sisk didn't come close to filling the description.

Sisk had been Blanton's Senate campaign coordinator in '72. Subsequently there had been a charge of irregularities in campaign contributions, and a federal investigation was being called for. News of it cropped up in the press at the tail end of Blanton's gubernatorial run, although the timing made it seem like a Republican ploy. Since then Sisk had been questioned by the FBI.

Blanton told Merritt he didn't want any lawyers he didn't know around him. "I want Sisk," he said.

Maybe it was just a question of old-fashioned country loyalty and inbred distrust, Merritt confided to John Seigenthaler, publisher of the *Tennessean.* Traditionally Democratic, the paper had remained neutral in the primary before supporting Blanton in the general election, mostly because of his pledges to unify the party and to spur economic development throughout the state. "I think, though, he's going to have some chickens coming home to roost," Merritt said. "Ray doesn't want anyone telling him anything. He wants to do all the telling."

· 4 ·

Aside from the obvious fact that extraditions involved transferring those wanted by the law to and from other states, it became clear to Marie that Eddie Sisk not only didn't know what her precise duties were but was never going to find out.

Her first couple of weeks were maddening. Eddie had set up temporary shop in the Governor's conference room. In there with him, besides Marie, was his secretary, Janice Clinkenbeard, and a personable young man in his early twenties, Trent Hall, who had worked on the campaign. Eddie was running around in nine different directions. His preoccupation seemed to be filling jobs in the new administration. People seeking placements or favors streamed in and out. The phones rang incessantly. Occasionally the Governor himself would show up from the mansion, and there'd be a whole new flurry of activity. The only bit of sanity was supplied by young Hall. Every so often after hanging up the phone, he'd shout, "God, will somebody please get me a drink!"

Finally a pile of extradition warrants awaiting action was located. Marie went through them and, feeling slightly idiotic, started calling back to say, "We're all new here. The Governor's legal counsel would like for you to please give us a little while to get things in order." The rest of the time she spent drinking coffee and Cokes and wandering around the capitol corridors, meeting and chatting with legislators. The one thing she didn't do was bring Cokes or coffee to anybody else. She wasn't about to be taken for a flunky.

Sisk kept telling her not to worry. As soon as everything settled down he'd arrange for the two of them to go see Shipley and Raybin and learn what was what in extraditions. Then, since the legal counsel's regular suite on the capitol's lower level was being renovated, Sisk's operation was moved to the Andrew Jackson Building, a state office complex two blocks away. Now even the fun of being in the middle of the political hurly-burly was gone, although Eddie, of course, was still dashing over to the capitol every other minute.

At last Marie went to see Shipley and Raybin on her own, and found to her chagrin that they made the major decisions regarding the legality of an extradition. Her job was essentially clerical, tracking the papers, making sure the attorney general's office got them for review, and keeping district attorneys, sheriffs, police departments and appropriate officials in other states apprised about the status of the warrants. Sometimes, she was told, a hearing might be requested by a fugitive. This also was pretty cut-and-dried. The purpose of a hearing was not to determine guilt or innocence but simply to establish whether the fugitive was correctly named and if there was sufficient reason to believe he was in the area of the alleged offense at the time of its perpetration. What she had to be on the lookout for were hearing requests aimed solely at delaying the process.

During her session with Shipley and Raybin, Marie detected a certain coolness on Raybin's part, and she was right.

All Raybin knew about her was that she was a smashing-looking chick right out of college. Raybin was then twenty-six, and he assumed Marie was no more than twenty-one. He was engaged to be married, and wasn't interested himself, but he couldn't help remarking to Shipley after she left, "What's Sisk doing? Setting up a harem over there?"

As far as Raybin could see, Marie didn't have a discernible qualification for the job. While being extradition officer didn't require the greatest brain in the world, it demanded some legal knowledge and a fastidious attention to detail. For a long time it never occurred to Raybin that after the one briefing Marie had, extraditions moved like clockwork. Not a complaint.

· 5 ·

At the same time that Marie was trying to discover what an extradition officer did, George Haynes, an agent for the Tennessee Bureau of Criminal Identification stationed in Nashville, received an astonishing call from a lawyer named Rose Palermo.

She told him she had a client, Jerry Bates Long, who was appealing a fifteen-year sentence for armed robbery. Although he had been put into a work-release program, he was years away from parole eligibility. Long, she said, had previously been represented by another Nashville attorney, Arnold Peebles. According to Palermo, her client had told her Peebles was now saying he could arrange immediate executive clemency through the Governor's new legal counsel, Eddie Sisk. For $15,000.

In 1975, when Blanton was inaugurated, Haynes was beginning his seventh year as a TBCI agent. Before that he had been a trooper in the highway patrol. He was honored to belong to such an elite law-enforcement group. Short of the FBI maybe, the TBCI was as good as there was anywhere in the nation, unmarked by scandal, painstaking in its investigations. Agents were scattered across the state. Organized criminal activity was their chief target. They also helped out in rural sections where police resources fell short. Administratively the TBCI was under the Department of Public Safety. Blanton had just appointed a new public safety commissioner. A shake-up was going on as well in the TBCI high command, and some good men were being replaced, but Haynes couldn't conceive that the TBCI as an institution would be any different from what it had always been.

He found it even harder to believe what Palermo was telling him. It was crazy, he thought. The Blanton administration had been in office only two weeks or so. Still, Haynes had dealt with Rose Palermo in the past and knew her to be responsible. So he started checking around, and suddenly it wasn't that crazy. Before Sisk became the Governor's legal counsel, he and Peebles had been law partners.

Haynes called Palermo and asked her if Long would be willing to have his conversations with Peebles recorded. She said he would. Naturally, she expected consideration for her client, and Haynes said that if he cooperated and this panned out, he wouldn't have a thing to worry about.

Haynes instructed Long not to appear too eager. In all, there were three taped talks with Peebles, two on the phone and one with Long wearing a body recorder while on work release. Right off, loud and clear, the question wasn't whether executive clemency could be obtained through Sisk. Peebles described in detail how he'd already arranged that. The issue was money. When Long said he didn't know if he could put together that kind of cash, the price went to ten thousand. When Long expressed concern that Sisk might renege after being paid, it got to five down, the rest due when Long was on the street.

Haynes allowed himself the luxury of thinking he had cut off a major corruption conspiracy at the pass. He wrote up his report and forwarded it, together with the tapes, to TBCI headquarters. Considering who was involved, Haynes now needed authorization to proceed further. The next step was obviously to tie in Sisk—possibly by making a deal with Peebles, or using marked bills.

Haynes sat back expectantly. But nothing happened. Then he discovered that the TBCI had changed dramatically. As a senior field agent, Haynes had been called in to lead a series of gambling raids in Montgomery County, north of Nashville. A half-dozen joints were knocked off following an extensive undercover investigation. Haynes couldn't recall an operation of that size flourishing without a county sheriff knowing about it. The trouble was that Blanton's new public safety commissioner had been a Montgomery County trustee and former sheriff. Haynes remembered how the manager of one of the places he raided had screamed and cursed, "You sons of bitches was supposed to be kept out!" A couple of friends Haynes had at TBCI headquarters advised him to lie low for a while. The new commissioner, he was told, was enraged. Apparently he hadn't been told about the raids in advance and felt personally embarrassed. Then a verbal order went out to agents in the field that no more raids were to be conducted without first informing local sheriffs.

Haynes made inquiries at TBCI about Peebles. The feedback he got was to forget it. Peebles was a wacko. He'd been blowing smoke about getting Long out. That was a large assumption, Haynes thought, and in frustration he sent a copy of his report to the Nashville office of the FBI. But nothing came of that either.

Several weeks later his report of the conversations between Long and Arnold Peebles surfaced in a manner Haynes could never have imagined. Peebles was in the headlines in a totally unrelated case. It seemed he had lent a federal narcotics agent $10,000 toward buying a house. The sticky part was that the agent had been in charge of an investigation against a client Peebles was defending. Other murky financial deals between Peebles and his clients were also leaked.

But instead of an indictment, disbarment proceedings were filed against Peebles. Reporters were reminded of his excellent background, how his father was an admired lawyer and former DA, and that Peebles himself, after receiving his law degree, had clerked for the chief justice of the Tennessee Supreme Court. It was sad. Peebles was a sick person.

Instances of his erratic behavior were cited, his explosive temper, bouts of drinking.

It was at this point that his encounter with Jerry Bates Long was conveniently disposed of. The TBCI gave the tapes to the district attorney, who in turn passed them on to the Nashville Bar Association, not as evidence of Peebles' wrongdoing but as another example of his weirdness. Then Peebles temporarily surrendered his license to practice and entered a hospital for psychiatric treatment.

Under the circumstances, no one gave the slightest credence to Eddie Sisk's involvement. Nashville DA Thomas H. Shriver was quoted as saying he was "convinced Sisk did not participate in any way" in the alleged scheme, and that was the end of it.

Sisk released a brief statement denying he had ever spoken to Peebles about clemency for Long or anybody else and suggested that Arnold might benefit from medical care.

He and Marie talked about it afterward. It was, said Eddie, one of the prices you had to pay for serving the public, and she found herself commiserating with him.

SIX

While there were some who thought it was unconscionable for Peebles to have gotten off so lightly, that he had been propelled by the desire for a quick buck rather than by a sudden mental breakdown, no one entertained the notion that Sisk had played any part in the clemency bribe attempt. T. Edward Sisk, after all, had finally arrived, and he certainly wasn't going to risk everything in a fool caper like this.

No one considered that Eddie might be in a financial bind. But he was. The legal counsel's pay, $30,000, was less than he had hoped for, but the power and prestige the position promised, plus all those important contacts to be made, were irresistible, and Eddie liked to think big. Right off, though, he was in over his head. Starting with the fancy home he bought on Hillsboro Road to befit his new station. Not quite Belle Meade, but up there.

All his life Eddie had worked toward this sort of recognition. He was thirty-five, from Giles County on the Alabama line, in Blanton's old congressional district. After attending junior college in his hometown of Pulaski, he transferred to the University of Tennessee, where he met his wife, Claudette. She was one of the most popular coeds on campus, a champion baton-twirler and majorette with the UT marching band. Eddie was pretty popular himself. Men responded to his friendly grin and his enthusiasm for sports, and women found a lovable overgrown-teddy-bear quality in him. Eddie and Claudette looked to be your all-American couple. Once he had his law degree, he commenced doing all the right things. Got into the Heart Fund and Easter Seal drives. Became president of the Tennessee Young Lawyers Conference. And president of UT's Big Orange alumni chapter in Nashville. Went into politics too. In 1968, three years out of law school, he was on Ray Blanton's congressional reelection committee. In '72 he was statewide coordinator for Blanton's Senate try against Howard Baker. Two years later he couldn't afford to do more than handle Nashville and Davidson County in the Blanton gubernatorial campaign.

The trouble was, Eddie's private practice hadn't kept pace. He'd been associated with a couple of prominent law firms, but the partnerships he dreamed of hadn't materialized. And the truth was he never had cracked Blanton's inner circle—the redneck Mafia, it was called. Basically, Sisk had done what he was told. Now as legal counsel that would surely change. His reputation would be hugely enhanced. He'd be constantly at the Governor's side.

Sometimes, though, Sisk brooded over whether anyone, no matter how close, actually knew what was going on inside Blanton, except possibly his brother Gene. Blanton had this tight little group around him, but he had lines out to a lot of other people as well.

Bill Thompson was a perfect example. Thompson was a Democratic committeeman in Chattanooga. Eddie met him in the '72 campaign when Ward Crutchfield, the party chairman in Hamilton County, which included Chattanooga, introduced them and said Thompson was the man to work with on a day-to-day basis. They hit it off at once. Turned out Bill was as avid a golfer as Eddie, and he really knew his way around the city. Despite being white, he seemed to have access all through the black community. There would be a flap after the election about cash being spread in Chattanooga to cover the black vote, but nothing much came of it. From what Sisk could make out, Thompson was able to see Ray Blanton, or get him on the phone, most any time he had a mind to.

He was practically the first person to congratulate Eddie on his appointment. Before it was even announced. That was when Sisk confided in him about his money worries. Well, Thompson said, you know Ray would like his people to come out better than they went in.

· 2 ·

Ever since getting out of Columbia-Presbyterian, Marie had remained with her mother and Rosie, along with Therese and Ricky. Dante was in the sixth grade at the Morris School, run by the Franciscan brothers in Searcy, Arkansas. Dante's going away had been Virginia's idea.

Before Marie had gotten sick, the nearby public school that the kids were attending was as good as any in Nashville. Then busing began. Dante had the longest trip, to a poor black neighborhood on the other side of town, and was forced to give up team sports because Marie didn't have time to cart him back and forth. It was dispiriting for her. Philosophically she'd been for busing, one of the few parents she knew who favored it as a building block toward racial equality. But Dante's grades plummeted. He got into one fight after another. A disadvantaged child himself, coming from a single-parent home, he was surrounded by children even more disadvantaged, and she could see the relentlessly negative effect it was having.

After she moved in with Virginia, and the kids could walk to school, she was still concerned about Dante. Especially the fighting. Then one day Marie was coming down the stairs with Dante when he said, "Momma, wait a minute. I want to ask you something."

"Okay, honey," she said, and they sat on the steps.

He dug his elbows into his knees and said, "How much money does Daddy send you for us?"

His eyes were boring into her, and she said, "Well, honey, the truth is, really not anything."

"He doesn't send any money for us?"

"No, honey. Your daddy isn't able to. He's just now trying to get things together, and he's not able to. He will when he can."

"Why haven't you arrested him?"

The rage in his voice caught her off guard. She told him she didn't believe in that. "It would only hurt your daddy," she said. "And you know what? It'd hurt you more."

After a moment, he said, "Momma, if Daddy would send us money, we wouldn't have to live here at Grandmomma's, would we?"

So she started to have misgivings about that, but she said, "Remember, honey, it's because I was sick that we're here. We had our own place before, remember, and as soon as Momma finishes up at Vanderbilt and has a job, we'll have our own place again."

Virginia said Dante's biggest problem was that he had nothing but female authority figures around him—his grandmother, his mother, his teachers and baby-sitters. She told Marie she'd heard about this school in Arkansas staffed by Franciscan brothers. She said she had a friend,

Mrs. Luckett, a widow whose two boys, one Dante's age, were there and adored it. The Franciscans were good men, Virginia said, and Dante would benefit greatly being with them.

Marie was offended by the idea. Boarding schools were where parents sent their children to get rid of them. Besides, she argued, how could she possibly pay for it? Maybe something could be worked out, Virginia said. She believed one of the Luckett boys was on some kind of scholarship. And before Marie knew it, Virginia had Mary Luckett over for tea. Marie found her to be a charming, concerned woman, and she confirmed everything Virginia had said. The school had been a lifesaver—for her and her sons.

The instant Marie saw the Morris campus, she was struck by its beauty and tranquillity. After being prodded by Virginia at least to look it over, she had driven there in May '74 with Dante, who was sullen and resentful every mile of the way. She noticed he began to perk up a bit as they walked around the grounds and he took in the playing fields, the gym, a pond for swimming, the farmyard pets.

While he went off with the Luckett boys, she met with the headmaster, Brother Edwin. She couldn't keep the tears from her eyes as she explained some of her situation, how she would complete her courses at Vanderbilt during the summer, but, most of all, her apprehensions about Dante growing up without a father, how he needed to be exposed to good men and to good, positive discipline.

Brother Edwin asked her point-blank if she could manage the tuition. Frankly, she said, she had loathed the thought of sending Dante away, but these few hours she'd been at Morris had been a revelation. She'd come up with the money somehow, beg, borrow or steal it.

She was dumbfounded to hear him gently say it wouldn't be necessary. From what he'd observed, he said, Dante was exactly the sort of boy Morris wanted to help, and right on the spot he offered a full scholarship. The next hurdle was Dante. Another miracle. When he reappeared, wide-eyed, regaling her with his adventures, and she told him he might get to go there, he demanded to know why he couldn't start now. Why did he have to wait till the fall?

Yet it wasn't easy. She remembered the first Sunday mass at Christ the King after he went away, when one of his old teachers had asked if he was sick, and Marie explained he was at boarding school, and the teacher just said "Oh," and some parents who were standing around smiled knowingly as if a final verdict on her motherhood had been rendered. She wrote to him every other day, and it drove her crazy when she didn't hear back, even though she'd been told she would be hearing plenty if he was unhappy. She opened his first report card with trembling hands. All A's. Exemplary conduct. She called Brother Edwin to make sure a mistake hadn't been made. Then, after the Christmas holidays, when Dante had enchanted Ricky with tales of fishing expeditions, how he'd taken up archery, about a baby owl he was raising, Ricky was all over her to let him go to Morris too.

At home the girls were a marvel. Virginia, more and more confined to a wheelchair, had taught Rosie to cook, and Therese was learning fast. Although Rosie was Therese's aunt, they looked and acted like sisters. They posted work schedules on the refrigerator. One morning it would be Therese's turn to help Virginia bathe and dress while Rosie was in the kitchen fixing an elaborate breakfast—bacon, eggs, pancakes. By the time they were ready for school, they'd run the vacuum, loaded the dishwasher and taken out a roast to thaw for supper.

"Honestly," Marie once told Rosie and Therese, "I feel like I'm living in the grandest hotel," and Therese said, "Momma, it's fun."

Marie wished she could say the same about her job.

She had received a rather grandiose certificate declaring her to be state extradition officer, and Eddie had been nice enough to compliment her on how efficiently she was handling things, although the closest he got involved in what she was doing was when she told him that before an extradition warrant could be executed it had to be signed by Blanton. The Governor, he said, couldn't be bothered. She should sign his name herself.

"Are you sure it's all right?"

"Hell, yes, Marie," Sisk said. "You can do it. Just practice up."

She was the entire extradition staff. She hadn't wanted to be a secretary and now she was her own secretary. Once she'd been briefed by Raybin and Shipley, she was kept busy for about a month catching up on the backlog of warrants, but after that she had plenty of time on her hands. Her case load averaged perhaps fifteen a week, and it was so monotonously routine. She was still fascinated by the political process, and she killed hours watching the legislature in action until that too began to pall. Then she had an idea that would change everything.

Because of the renovations going on in the capitol, a number of other members of the Governor's staff also had been temporarily relocated in the Andrew Jackson Building, and Blanton's speech writer, a former reporter named Marion Peck, ended up in the adjoining office. Marion was always rushing from one appointment to the next, moaning about deadlines, typing madly behind closed doors. It seemed so exciting compared with Marie's dull days, and so she dug out the political pieces she'd done for the Vanderbilt paper and asked Marion if she could help with some of the speeches. Marion looked them over and seemed pleased, and gave her some research material for a trial run.

Marie wasn't planning on saying anything to Sisk until she got a final go-ahead from Marion, but while she was hunched over her typewriter, surrounded by research material, Sisk happened to stick his head into her office and said, "What in the world are you doing?" and she said she might be assisting Marion Peck with writing speeches. "How's that?" he said, and she said, a little abashed, "It was my idea. I have all this spare time, Eddie, and I want to be as productive as I can."

He didn't look so much angry as perplexed. He gave her a long, thoughtful look, and then he said, "Hold on just a minute." He disappeared and returned with a sheaf of papers, at least six inches thick, and dropped it on her desk. "If you feel like you don't have enough to do, your problem's solved."

"What's this?" she said.

"Clemency petitions," he said. "You know, when we let somebody out of prison early. I'm making you my liaison with the pardons and paroles board. You tell Marion Peck you'll be busier than you thought."

Eddie started saying that while he couldn't offer her more salary right then, it could lead to other things. Marie heard him but wasn't paying that much attention. She had glimpsed the top paper on the sheaf in front of her. It was a letter that began, *Dear Governor Blanton, I pray to God that you will find the compassion within you to hear a mother's plea,* and she was hooked. She was sure there wouldn't be anything cut-and-dried about *this.*

"What am I supposed to do?" she said, and he said, "Well, you go through all this stuff and get yourself acquainted, and we'll talk about it later. We get petitions most every day, and so does the board. Now some of these petitions," said Eddie, "are real deserving, and we are going to want to help out on them. Like this case here. I want you to get right on it. Look at this boy. Jimmy Carroll. Got mixed up with drugs, but he's a first offender. And he's straightened out, you can see right here. We want to flag this one and handle it personally. You call his daddy and tell him the Governor's office is on it, and call Stoker over at the board and tell him we're mighty interested in this case."

John Stoker was the administrative aide to the Board of Pardons and

Paroles. When Marie phoned him and gave the prisoner's name, Stoker asked what his number was, and she said she didn't know, and he said he had to know the number, and she said she'd try to find out but that she was calling for Eddie and the Governor. There was a pause, and Stoker said to give him that name again. And in an hour or so Stoker was telling her, "Yeah, well, there's a good chance for him, I'd say. Never been in trouble before. Only twenty. Let's see here, the original conviction was possession. Nothing more."

Marie told Sisk, "Eddie, I checked into that Carroll case, and John Stoker says this fellow does appear to be worthy of special treatment," and Sisk said, "Good, I thought so. You tell Stoker to schedule a hearing right quick. That boy's daddy was a big contributor."

"I thought it was because he's so deserving," she said.

"Goddamn," Sisk said, "of course he is. Just because his daddy contributed doesn't make him less deserving, does it?"

· 3 ·

In Tennessee a felon couldn't be considered for parole until he completed approximately half his sentence. As usual, with a statute that severe, a way was found around it. In this instance, executive clemency.

There were three types of clemency. One was an outright pardon by the governor, which wiped the record clean. It was not often used, however, because of the controversy it might stir up. The most popular form of clemency was a commutation to time served. In theory, once the governor signed it, this simply made an inmate eligible for parole. In real life, he always got out. Still a third clemency route, especially in cases that could cause a ruckus, was a partial reduction in time so that a petitioner could be quietly paroled at a predetermined date down the line. Generally, though, unless a convict was a headliner, clemencies and subsequent paroles drew practically no media coverage.

The pardons and paroles board as well as the governor were on the receiving end of clemency petitions, but it was solely the governor's prerogative to grant one. When Marie became Sisk's liaison with the board, all three of its members, each serving a fixed term, were appointees of Winfield Dunn, and Governor Dunn, it seemed, had taken clemency recommendations from the board quite seriously. Reviewed them himself, despite protests from his staff that he had better things to do. It was also Dunn's policy not to act on any petitions he got without the board's approval.

That was how he was going to do it too, Ray Blanton proclaimed upon taking office. No clemencies if the board didn't recommend them. As for the board itself, there wouldn't be an opening Blanton could fill for another year.

The board's chairman, Charles Traughber, was black. The Republican party hardly existed in the black community, and except for the fact that it was expedient to have a black on the board because of the prison-population mix, his appointment wasn't particularly political. He'd risen through the ranks of the Department of Correction, and had been suggested to Dunn by his corrections commissioner. Then Traughber got to be chairman with the backing of the black caucus in the state legislature, the heart of which came from overwhelmingly Democratic Memphis and Shelby County in the southwest corner of Tennessee. The black caucus wasn't that big in numbers, but it could make all the difference in a close vote.

Marie met Traughber a couple of weeks after she took up her liaison work. "Marie, come on in here," Sisk said. "This is Charles Traughber, and I want you to sit in on this conference Charlie and I are having. Charlie, this is Marie Ragghianti."

She noticed how Traughber flinched a bit when Sisk called him Charlie. "How do you do, Mrs. Ragghianti," he said, springing up, and she said, "Why, hello, Mr. Traughber, I've looked forward to meeting you." He was a medium-sized man, oddly built, as if two different bodies had been joined, slim on top and heavier from the waist down. He had a neatly trimmed modified Afro and was wearing what appeared to be an expensive vested suit. His shoes gleamed. He sat carefully erect.

Sisk was lolling back in his swivel chair, tie yanked down, feet on his desk. "Marie," he said, "Charlie and I were just sitting here talking about how we're going to handle this thing, this clemency business, and I told him you're going to be liaison for me and for the Governor. So, Charlie, if you can't find me, you just call Marie and she'll take care of whatever it is. And, Marie, I was just telling Charlie that the Governor isn't going to be interested in but a few of these cases. We know the board has got all the expertise and background, and we're going to let them use their discretion in ninety-nine out of a hundred cases." Now Sisk had his feet off the desk and was leaning toward Traughber. "Charlie, I can tell you this pretty much forthwith. I can tell you that the Governor—I mean, if that board recommends the

Governor release somebody, by God, you can count on it. You say this guy deserves to be let out, that's good enough for us."

He turned to Marie for confirmation. "Marie, you've been on the job only a short while, but have we sent anything back unsigned?"

"No, Eddie, I believe they've all been signed."

Sisk nodded solemnly, and his tone momentarily became quite official. "I don't mean to imply we're going to be careless. We're going to be reviewing things like we always have. But I want you to know we appreciate all the guidance and help you've given us, Mr. Traughber." Just the slightest emphasis on the "mister" part, Marie thought.

Then, as though every nicety had been observed, he was back in form, up from his chair, stalking about, rattling on. "And likewise," Sisk said, "I hope our cases will be viewed favorably by you all. Because the Governor's not going to do anything without your recommendation. We trust you, and we hope you trust us. Anyway, to get on with it, Charlie, as you and Marie know, this office is besieged with people asking for clemency consideration. Of course we can't possibly take care of them all, and there aren't going to be that many that have any merit to speak of. But those few that do, Charlie, we'll be checking with you, and me or Marie will be calling in on them. I know," said Sisk, like a coach exhorting his team at half time, "this is all going to work out real easy. Let's just see how well we can get everything done with a minimum of paper work."

As soon as he was certain Eddie had finished, Traughber, fingertips pressed together, replied, "Thank you, Mr. Sisk. We know how overloaded you are up here, and we are ready to aid you in any manner possible." Traughber spoke with stiff precision, as if he were creeping through a verbal minefield. "The board, of course, realizes there may be occasions when it is necessary to communicate by telephone. It would be, ah, helpful, however, if you or Mrs. Ragghianti could put your requests in writing."

Sisk was in his chair again, tilted back nonchalantly. "Well, you know, Charlie, we don't have time for a lot of— I mean, we don't want to get into a lot of formal memos," he said. "That takes time, and Marie here, she's already got more than she can handle. You know, she's extradition officer, and you can take one look at my desk and see I've got more than I can handle. So we'd really like to be informal about this whole thing. If Marie calls you, you know it's a call from me. And if it's a call from me," Sisk said, laying a look on Traughber, "you know it's a call from the Governor."

"We need it for our records," Traughber softly insisted.

Eddie waved a hand, as if in good-natured resignation. "Well, Marie —I know Marie isn't going to mind if she's got time, you know," he said without committing himself to anything. "We'll drop you a line, but I really—we don't want to get into all this. Time's time, you know. Hell, it takes a couple of days for a messenger to bring something over there, doesn't it?" The thought seemed to seize Sisk's imagination. "How long *does* it take?"

"It's not unusual if we discuss something in the morning for us to receive notification in the afternoon," Traughber said.

"Yeah, but you all run around a lot, Charlie. Never can find you. Well, we don't need to get into all that now. That's all right. Marie, you hear what he says. You do your best to get these things out. We want to help every way we can."

It had been vintage Eddie Sisk. Disorganized. Unfocused. Rambling on. Obviously he'd been trying to establish a relationship with Traughber, however ineptly, she thought. At the time, the message she heard was, You scratch our back, we'll scratch yours. We'll expect you to honor our requests unless it's impossible, and we're not going to ask the impossible. Let's keep things running smoothly. And there was nothing wrong with that. Eddie just didn't seem capable of making it that simple. It never entered her head there might be more to it. She had her job because of Eddie. She had complete confidence in him. She found him a fun-loving, likable, even considerate person, and the idea he could have a crooked bone in his body was inconceivable. Right then, for instance, the Arnold Peebles affair had cropped up in the papers, and everyone agreed how unfairly maligned Eddie had been.

Not even people who put Eddie down, like Jack Strickland, ever hinted that there was anything shady about him. Strickland worked primarily on economic development. He too had been relocated in the Jackson building. He was an attractive, dark-haired man, intense, disciplined and a touch arrogant, one of the few the Governor had around from Republican territory in East Tennessee. One day, bored with her extradition duties, Marie was in her office reading a volume of Dylan Thomas poems when Strickland wandered in. She'd been embarrassed, of course, at being caught reading poetry instead of processing a warrant, but all Strickland said was, "It's gratifying to see somebody around here with some sensitivity and intelligence. How can you stand working for a dunce like Sisk?" She was ready to concede privately that Eddie wasn't the sharpest legal mind in the world, but he was unswervingly loyal to the Governor and that counted plenty. She owed Eddie the same loyalty, and she defended him across the board. Loyalty, she thought, was an intangible you couldn't buy.

Toward the end of the meeting with Sisk and Traughber, Marie piped up. "Since we're all starting out on this, I sure would appreciate it if you two would remember to give me a buzz every time you get together, so I can keep track of what's happening."

"Good idea, Marie," Sisk said. "Fine, fine. I guess that about takes care of it."

After Traughber left, Eddie suddenly got more direct. He asked Marie what she thought about the board's chairman, and she said she'd been impressed by him.

Yeah, well, said Sisk, he could tell her one thing. If you were up for parole, it sure was a hell of a help if you were a black rapist from around Memphis or Shelby County.

"Eddie, you're terrible," she protested, and he said, "You know, Marie, that's what I like about you. You really look for the best in everybody."

Despite the sarcastic edge in his voice, she took it as a compliment. That was how a person ought to be, she felt.

Almost at once Sisk had her working on her first pardon. She was so new on the job she didn't realize what rarity a full pardon was. The recipient, Joe Allen Finley, was a young man in for burglary, and Eddie pointed out that the case was a fine example of how humane Ray Blanton could be regardless of politics. Finley's father, who owned a tavern over in Blount County, south of Knoxville, was a local Republican honcho, but that didn't matter. The father, Eddie went on, was awful sick and needed his son to run the family business. The trouble was that even though Finley was due for parole consideration any day, a parolee under state law couldn't deal in liquor. So a pardon was the solution. That was the kind of man Blanton was, said Eddie, and then he told Marie to move Traughber on Finley. There'd been enough delays.

There was more to the story, although she had no way of knowing it then. Finley's father did have a tavern and was a backwoods Republican boss, but this wasn't the only time he tried to get his son a pardon. During the last days of the Dunn administration, Dunn's press secretary received a call on Finley's behalf from an important Republican wanting to know how much it would take. The press secretary reported the inquiry to Dunn's executive assistant, and the answer was that pardons weren't for sale.

Within months, as it turned out, Finley had his pardon from Blanton. It went through so quietly there wasn't a peep in the papers. And for a long while not even Dunn's staff people who had been involved in the bribe attempt were aware that Joe Allen Finley was out and about with no prison record to his name.

In May, as the paper work for Finley's pardon was getting under way, it was time for the baccalaureate ceremonies at Vanderbilt that Marie had missed the year before because of her illness. Although she already had her degree, she wanted her children to witness the panoply of the occasion. She even brought Dante back from Morris. It was important, she believed, for them to witness a visible reward after the struggle to make it through college, a struggle they had shared.

When she told Eddie it was coming up and she needed the day off, he said to be sure to send an invitation to the Governor. "I can't do that," she said, and he said, "Hell, Marie, do it. He'll be impressed, you graduating from Vanderbilt and all." So she did, and before she knew it, to her astonishment and delight, a packet arrived containing a gold medallion, the state seal on one side and "Governor and Mrs. Ray Blanton" engraved on the other. Possibly it had been Eddie who had been more impressed. He had dropped out of Vanderbilt because of poor grades in his freshman year, although Marie didn't know that. It wasn't something he included in his résumé.

Then she was on her way to a conference of the National Association of Extradition Officials in Colorado Springs. She plunged into the workshop programs with such dedication that she was elected regional vice-president of the association for the Southeast. "How was your foray in Colorado?" Sisk asked after she returned, and when she told him what had happened, he said, "You're kidding." "I'm not, honestly," she said, and he said, "Damn, wait till I tell the Governor about that!"

It was this sort of spontaneous enthusiasm that made her truly care for Eddie, she thought. She felt so sisterly and protective toward him, especially when people like Jack Strickland knocked him. And she was fond of Eddie's wife, Claudette. Thought she was stunning. They had a daughter named Allison. Eddie was forever showing her the latest pictures of Allison, and that touched her perhaps more than anything. He was clearly a devoted father, and she reflected on her own, essentially fatherless children.

Claudette taught baton-twirling, which took her out of the city now and then, and sometimes when that occurred, Marie would have a drink after work with Eddie at the Capitol Hill Club, where the politicians hung out, or even dinner. And in a relaxed moment like that, she'd chide him about flirting with some of the glamorous secretaries on the hill. When he said it wasn't all his doing, she said she knew that, but he ought to remember none of those women could hold a candle to Claudette, and he'd laugh and say she was right. Of course, she was conscious of the sidelong glances when she and Eddie were together. It was an annoyance she resigned herself to. Sex and politics, it seemed, went hand in hand. Eddie would laugh at that too. "Come on, Marie," he'd say, "let's run away and put all these rumors to rest," and she couldn't help laughing back.

Eddie was absolutely incorrigible.

Like the time Virginia called her at work and told her she hated to say it, but she believed Ricky had helped himself to some change from her purse. Marie said she'd be right home and went in to let Eddie know why she was leaving. "Take it easy," he said. "I'll bet there isn't a boy in America who hasn't gone into a pocketbook at one time or another."

"Maybe so," she said, "but I guess the way I see it the prisons are full of inmates who were once little boys pulling stuff like this, with mothers who passed it off lightly."

"Okay," he said with a big smile. "Tell you what, though. If he goes to prison, at least we can get him executive clemency."

That made her laugh again. It seemed such a harmless joke at the time.

· 4 ·

Her new work absorbed her. She carefully read each of the clemency recommendations the board sent over and wrote up one-page synopses for Sisk. Some of the supporting material for the petitioners, of course, made you wonder why they weren't behind pulpits instead of bars. But there were others, as well, real cries for help, that wrenched her heart. She remembered one of the earliest that came across her desk, for a black man from rural West Tennessee, left motherless at five, his father remarried to a woman with nine children of her own, locked out by his stepmother and father at ten, according to the testimony of neighbors, and initially arrested and placed in juvenile detention for stealing food from local gardens. Arrested and incarcerated again for breaking into, incredibly, his own home, and finally, inevitably, for breaking into somebody else's home. In prison, however, he had an unblemished record, earned a high school equivalency diploma and had a job waiting if he got clemency. Marie had stared at the man's photograph, wondering how many other stories there were like his in the penal system. She reflected on her own life, her idyllic childhood, the fact that much of the anguish she suffered afterward was undeniably her doing, while this man had been a victim from the beginning, and it pleased her immensely to be a link in his return to society.

She started a card file to keep track of all the petitions the Governor received that Eddie was interested in. Each card had the pertinent data, the name of the inmate, his main sponsor, the nature of the crime, the sentence, parole eligibility and so forth, along with progress reports and comments.

Eddie's big question was always what was holding things up, even though she'd already gone through the whole litany about how before a hearing could take place there had to be a field investigation by a parole counselor, social and psychiatric histories compiled, prison write-ups, feedback from judges and DAs. The mention of a district attorney was sure to send him into a frenzy. "Those goddamn DAs!" he'd complain. "All they want is to lock a guy up and throw away the keys." And that wasn't hard to go along with.

The DA that got him worked up the most was Gary Gerbitz, down in Chattanooga. Gerbitz, according to Eddie, was a sneaky little Republican son of a bitch. Would send his own mother up if he thought it'd help his career. Marie got this assessment of Gerbitz in June, some seven weeks into her liaison work, when Sisk told her to check with Stoker at the board concerning an inmate named Billy Gene Cole.

Cole had served approximately a year and a half of a twenty-five-year sentence for armed robbery. Marie reported to Sisk that the board had already received a query on Cole and decided not to take any action for at least another three years. As she understood it, Marie told him, there had been an exceptionally strong letter of protest from the Chattanooga district attorney's office regarding possible executive clemency for Cole. Coming from Gerbitz, Sisk said, there was nothing exceptional about it. Gerbitz was a disgrace to the criminal justice system. Eddie said he happened to know about the Cole case. Before Cole was

tried, he said, the man had been offered a plea bargain calling for him
to do only eleven months. The case against him was that weak. But
Cole had elected to go to trial instead. It was, said Sisk, clear evidence
that Cole was innocent. Cole's mistake had been underestimating what
Gerbitz and his people were capable of doing in front of a jury. Probably had bad legal advice. All right, he said when he had calmed down,
he'd get on the horn to Traughber about this.

Around then a call from Kate Waller, a law student at the University
of Tennessee, was routed by chance to Marie. Kate explained that she
was writing a paper on capital punishment and wanted to view first-
hand the death house in Nashville. She'd been rebuffed by prison
officials and was now calling the Governor's office for help.

If there was one thing Marie admired about Ray Blanton, it was
his stand on capital punishment. During his campaign, along with his
commitment to women's rights and black advancement, he declared
his opposition to the death penalty, that killing someone did nothing
to solve the problem of crime, that, indeed, serving a life sentence
was far harsher, and that as long as he was the governor, no electrocu-
tions would be carried out. It was, Marie thought, the perfect answer
to the talk she heard about Blanton being an insensitive, unthinking
redneck.

Listening to Kate, Marie thought that here she was dealing with
prisoners and had never been inside a prison, so she said she'd not only
try to arrange a visit but would go along herself. As it turned out, all
she had to do was say she was from the Governor's office. She could
almost see the warden coming to attention on the other end of the line.

The front of the main state penitentiary, on a rolling plain west of
Nashville, was as unprisonlike as you could imagine. Painted yellow, it
looked as if it were a huge mysterious Victorian mansion, complete
with gabled windows and odd abutments, the kind you found in a
Charles Addams cartoon. But then there were the high yellow walls
extending from each side. And the steel gates sliding shut behind her
and Kate Waller that made Marie shudder at what a prisoner must feel
being brought through them, knowing there was no exit.

The warden was all smiles. Said he was afraid there wasn't much to
see, but Marie and her friend were surely welcome to look around.
What they wanted to see, said Marie, was some of the prison, of course,
and the death chamber. Also death row. That brought the warden up
short. Women weren't let in there. They'd be the first ever. Then he

brightened. Well, seeing as Marie was from the Governor's office, he said, he'd work out something.

The death house was a separate building in the yard, inside the walls. Crossing toward it, led by a guard assigned as their guide, Marie sensed the vast oppressive sullenness that hung in the air, the dejection, boredom, desolation. The eyes following her. It made her feel light-headed, as if she were walking a few feet off the ground. She wished she had something to hold on to.

The guard opened the door to the death chamber, and she saw the chair, straps hanging from it. Her stomach turned over. She saw the same horror in Kate's eyes that she was experiencing.

The guard offered an insider's tidbit. The TVA wouldn't furnish electrical power for the chair, so the prison had been forced to install a special generator.

That certainly was an unnecessary burden on the taxpayers, Marie remarked tonelessly, and the guard, as though dazzled by their unexpected affinity, said, "Yes, ma'am, that's just how I see it. Waste of tax money!"

The guard stepped to a corner of the chamber. "This here's the switch," he said. "I tell you, switch it a little more and we'd all be better off. I wish you'd speak to the Governor. He's a great man and I voted for him, but he's wrong about the chair. There's a need for this chair. I told the warden. I'll pull the damn switch myself."

"I believe you would," Marie said.

When they got into death row, the guard shouted, "Women here. Everyone dressed!" Another guard said, "Women? Women ain't supposed to be here," and their guard said, "Well, they are. Governor's office."

It was stifling hot. "Isn't there any air conditioning?" Kate said, and the guard answered, "We give 'em meals. Why the hell should we air-condition these bastards? Excuse my language, ma'am."

Marie was in eye contact with a young black pressing against his cage. "Hey, I hear the Governor's a good man. Don't like capital punishment," he said.

"That's right. How old are you?"

"Twenty-two tomorrow, ma'am. Been here since I was nineteen."

"What happened?"

"Shot two men in a liquor-store holdup. Didn't mean to kill 'em, but I did. Ma'am, please tell the Governor I'm not askin' for a motel or nothin', just to get rid of some of these roaches and flies, you know."

It seemed plain to Marie that what she'd witnessed just reinforced what she had been reading in the clemency files, that very few of these inmates had ever known the meaning of hope as she had, and somehow this had to be dealt with.

But mostly what she remembered was the sight of the electric chair, trying to imagine the inconceivable, trying to identify with somebody whose life could terminate in such a wretched symbol of man's inhumanity to man. And that afternoon, driving away from the penitentiary, she felt proud to be part of an administration which wasn't going to countenance the chair's use.

· 5 ·

More clemency petitions, as well as extraditions, were coming in all the time, and Marie had more or less forgotten about the Billy Gene Cole case.

Then on September 9, around three months after Sisk asked her to look into it, he announced Cole was taking a lie detector test. Sisk was on a real high. "You watch," he said, "he's going to pass that polygraph with flying colors."

It took her a moment to recall Cole, how upset Eddie was when she said the board had turned him down, and she assumed the test had to do with Cole's guilt or innocence in his armed robbery conviction. But even though Marie was supposedly Sisk's liaison in all clemency petitions, a great deal had been happening with Billy Gene Cole that she didn't know about.

Without her being aware of it, Eddie had informed Charles Traughber that he didn't care what some lousy DA was saying. He wanted another hearing on Cole, and damn quick.

The board thereupon convened and on August 7 voted unanimously to recommend cutting Cole's original sentence from twenty-five to ten years. But this wasn't good enough for Sisk. The message, he told Traughber, must not be getting through. He, *and* the Governor, wanted Cole out *now*.

Marie also didn't know that Cole's polygraph had nothing to do with his armed robbery conviction. While the pardons and paroles board was still squirming over Sisk's demand for an immediate clemency recommendation, Blanton's new director of the Tennessee Bureau of Criminal Identification passed on some unhappy news. A TBCI agent in the field had heard that one Billy Gene Cole was up for early release from prison. According to the agent, Cole was his prime suspect in a double homicide committed in East Tennessee several years before. The director said he thought Sisk might want to know this.

The next step on Cole's behalf had some novel reasoning. If Cole took a lie detector test that absolved him of complicity in the double homicide, his clemency petition could go forward as planned. One of the people involved in this approach was Cole's lawyer. The lawyer worked in a firm headed by Ward Crutchfield, the Chattanooga Democratic chairman.

Marie had no idea of any of this because most of the exchanges were directly between Sisk and Traughber, sometimes in person, usually over the phone. Traughber then relayed them to the rest of the board. And nobody on the board was running around talking about it. All Marie knew at the time was this guy Cole was going to take a polygraph, and the next thing Eddie was walking into her office and saying, "You won't believe it."

"What?"

"Cole flunked his damn lie detector."

"He did? You're joking."

"No, I'm not," said Sisk, although even he was laughing at what seemed to be the absurdity of it. Then he stopped laughing. "Anyway, tell Stoker we want the papers drawn up."

"What papers?"

"The clemency papers for Cole. That's what."

"But you just said he flunked the test."

For once Sisk leveled with her. There was a lot more to this than she knew, he said. Besides, Cole had been very nervous. He was going to have another test, but enough time had already been wasted. Those polygraphs weren't infallible. She'd be just as nervous if her whole life was riding on one g.d. test.

"Eddie," she said, "I can't call John Stoker and tell him in one breath that Cole failed the test and in the next to draw up the papers. What's he going to think?"

"Don't worry about it. I talked to Traughber."

"Well, let Traughber tell him."

"Traughber will tell him. But I want it coming from here too. I don't want any questions in anyone's mind about this."

Sisk didn't mention the double homicide business, although he did check with the TBCI to see if something more had developed in the investigation. Nothing had. And, for the record, he had a letter from Cole's lawyer about the bollixed-up polygraph that said, *We have no dissatisfaction with the way in which said examination was given, but*

*are merely speculative as to the total reliability of said examination.
. . . Please be advised that our client has agreed to a hypnotic examination.*

When Marie called Stoker and told him what Eddie wanted, there was a measurable silence before Stoker said, "Marie, are you serious?" and after she said yes, she guessed she was, he laughed weakly and said, "Well, I'm just here to take orders."

As the board's administrative assistant, Stoker, of course, could have filled Marie in quite a bit. But the pardons and paroles board was in another building, and except for one or two brief encounters, his only contact with her had been by phone or correspondence. As far as Stoker was concerned, Marie was an extension of Eddie Sisk, the Governor's legal counsel.

Despite the little she knew, the Cole case disturbed her a lot. It occurred to her that possibly Eddie's good nature was being taken advantage of. For one thing, although she was supposed to be in on all the meetings between Eddie and Traughber, she had noticed Traughber coming out of Sisk's office without ever having been told he was there. She'd even spoken to Traughber about it, pointing out that Eddie had a tendency to be disorganized and forgetful and to please remind him to buzz her whenever they were getting together. Traughber had said, "I'll try my best, Mrs. Ragghianti." It wasn't what he said so much as the tone. A touch sharp. Kind of a putdown. She started thinking maybe she didn't cotton to Traughber as she first thought she would.

She didn't know whom to talk to about Cole. Certainly no one in state government, or in Tennessee, for that matter. She couldn't take the chance. It could be completely misconstrued. Somebody might get the wrong idea about Eddie, and it would wind up in the papers. The Blanton administration didn't lack for political enemies as it was. It would be, Marie thought, the worst sort of disloyalty on her part.

Finally, though, she turned to someone she trusted completely, whose advice she respected. She had continued to visit Dr. Espy's little girl at King's Daughters as often as she could and would telephone him in Georgia afterward. So now, when she called him following her latest visit, the Cole case and her apprehensions about it came up, really by accident. It must have been in her voice because he asked if something was wrong, and she said yes and no, and then sketched out what was nagging at her.

First off, he said, she'd said it herself. Eddie was considerably more informed about the case than she was. And from what she'd told him, Sisk sounded like a decent man. It wasn't likely, moreover, that the Governor would have appointed him if he didn't know what he was doing. When she brought up the Chattanooga DA's protest, he asked if district attorneys raised Cain only about petitions coming from the Governor's office, and she said no, they also went after some of the board's clemency recommendations, and he said, well, Eddie was right. There was no getting around it. Some DAs were out for blood. Criminal justice was always controversial, one way or another, he said.

She hung up, relieved. She'd been seeing phantoms. It could have been Arnold Peebles all over again. And if she had any lingering doubts, they were dismantled in a hurry when the board sent over Cole's clemency papers. The board, after all, was an independent body. No question *it* knew what it was doing.

The papers on Cole appeared to be like those for any other clemency. The standard form had a distinctive green border headed COMMUTA- TION, was usually two pages long, and it summarized, complete with whereas this and whereas that, a petitioner's current situation, past criminal history, the nature of the felony, mitigating circumstances and rehabilitation prospects. A stock final paragraph said that in view of the foregoing, members of the board had voted to "recommend" whatever the clemency was, followed by their signatures. A separate NOW, THERE- FORE page was attached for the Governor to sign.

The Board of Pardons and Paroles in which Marie placed such faith had been legislated in 1972, and that was how Winfield Dunn got to pick its first three members. Before then it had been a part-time operation. The terms of the three members were staggered so succeeding governors could have a say in some, but not all, of the board's makeup. The theory was that this would maintain the board's integrity against political pressure. Apparently nobody figured the pressure would be there anyway, plenty of it self-inflicted.

At the time, board members were being paid about $23,000 each, with the chairman getting a thousand more. One member, Dorothy Greer, was up for reappointment in less than a year. She'd been superintendent of a state reformatory for girls. A second member, white-haired Joe Mitchell, also had come up through the corrections department. Looking to retirement and his pension, he had a term running two years longer than Greer's. Traughber's tenure was the longest, although he could be displaced as chairman. And while the statute said the Governor had to have good cause to remove a member, it was generally conceded that he had the right to decide how good his cause was. No one on the board doubted that he or she served at the Governor's pleasure.

The Cole clemency shattered every one of the board's guidelines. But after Traughber delivered Sisk's message about Cole to his fellow members, they did some fancy pretzel-bending and fell upon the lovely thought that if the Governor was bound to grant a clemency, there wasn't much they could do about it. They could have refused to draw up the papers, of course, or insisted on a written order. But that, evidently, didn't strike them as such a good idea. So, instead, they elected to solve everything by quietly substituting the word "submit" for "recommend" in the last paragraph of the commutation document. That way they wouldn't be responsible. If something unpleasant cropped up later on, it hadn't been the board's doing.

This exquisite point escaped everybody's attention. Certainly Marie, who knew less than anyone else about what was going on, didn't notice it. Sisk didn't either. Nor did Ken Lavender, the Governor's appointments secretary, who, it would turn out, actually signed Blanton's name to the clemencies, just as Marie had been instructed to do for extradition warrants. Even the state secretary, who also had to sign a commutation to make it official, didn't catch the distinction.

And no howl of protest arose from anybody who was aware of the shabby proceedings. No leaks to the media. Basically, it seemed, the issue no longer was the merits of the Billy Gene Cole clemency. In the end it was jobs that mattered. Going along to get along. In judging some people, at least, Eddie Sisk didn't look to be so dumb.

Blanton's TBCI director, whose name was Robert Goodwin, would explain that he was out of town when the Cole commutation went through. The Chattanooga district attorney, Gary Gerbitz, who would have been very much interested, was not informed about it.

SEVEN

Dalton, Georgia, was twenty-one miles south of Chattanooga on Interstate 75. They made carpeting there. Daltonians liked to bet that if you walked on a piece of tufted floor covering just about anywhere, it came from Dalton. So for a city with a population of only eighteen thousand there was considerable wealth around. Most of it was concentrated in a section on the west side of the city, known locally as Snob Hill.

The first Snob Hill robbery took place on the afternoon of September 2, 1975. Odell Edwards, a textile-mill owner, feeling ill, had returned home unexpectedly early. He found two white males inside wearing stocking masks and waving pistols. They tied him up, took his cash and demanded to know where his wife kept her jewelry. They seemed surprised at his arrival. Turned out they were really waiting for her. When Dorothy Edwards came in an hour later, the masked men also tied her up and stripped her of her rings, including one with a large diamond.

Three weeks afterward, on the morning of September 21, Coy Dennard, a woman in her sixties, the wife of a jute-and-yarn manufacturer, was getting ready to go out when the front bell rang. Through the peephole she saw what she described as a "clean-cut" young white man. Another man was standing behind him. The young man appeared to be lost. When she opened the door, she was immediately sprayed with

Mace, knocked to the floor and bound. Three diamond rings and a diamond pendant, worth $10,000 in all, were taken from her. Her pocketbook, containing $20, was also stolen.

At that point Bill Dodd, an agent for the Georgia Bureau of Investigation, entered the case. Though Marie never met Dodd, nobody would affect her life more in the next two years.

Dodd had been in the GBI for sixteen years, thirteen of them in Dalton and surrounding Whitfield County. He was forty-five, a little over six feet, about two hundred pounds. His brown hair was beginning to gray. He loved being an agent. When there had been corruption in the sheriff's office, Dodd was assigned to investigate and broke it up. Some of the men he worked with started calling him Serpico. Bill wasn't much for books and movies. All he knew about Frank Serpico was that he was a New York cop who was supposed to have ratted on other cops, and he was deeply hurt. His wife, Bette, however, had seen the movie and then read the book in paperback. She told him he ought to be proud, that it was the best compliment he'd ever gotten.

Again in about three weeks, early in the evening on October 15, George C. Stafford, the owner of several Whitfield County supermarkets, walked into his house and was blinded temporarily with Mace by two men who had crawled through a basement window. Stafford was known to carry large amounts of cash because of his supermarket business. As a matter of fact, before coming home, he had deposited $45,000 in a Dalton bank. He was relieved of his watch and $400 in his wallet and tied up in his bedroom. A few minutes later his wife, Doris, walked in and was also Maced. Approximately $11,000 in jewelry was taken. The Staffords were warned that if they called the police, there would be a return visit and their house would be blown "all to hell." Then the two men took off in Stafford's Cadillac, which was found abandoned on Interstate 75.

From the Stafford residence Bill Dodd could look down on I-75. Dalton, with its transient work force in the carpet mills, had a high incidence of theft and Saturday-night murders. There hadn't been anything like these robberies, though, and from the first, Dodd's suspicions wandered up the Interstate toward Chattanooga. But he figured there had to be a Dalton connection as well. Too much was known about which houses to hit and when the people in them would be alone.

One out of ten cases Bill worked on usually was what he called a whodunit, and these latest whodunits were especially heavy because of the clout the victims had in the community. To ease the tension of his job, Dodd rebuilt old cars from the frame up. He'd already done several Ford models, '32s and '34s, which he then sold to collectors. For the last six months he'd been putting together a 1965 Shelby Mustang that he intended to keep for himself. He had a special feeling for it. A car from his time. He envisioned it glistening white with blue racing stripes. But he knew now it would be a while before he could get back to the Mustang. Had Eddie Sisk known just how determined Dodd was to solve the Snob Hill robberies, it might have changed everything for him—and the Blanton administration.

Dodd picked up on the slenderest of leads. Some months before, there'd been a residential burglary in Catoosa County northwest of Dalton on the Tennessee line. A tip had been received by the under-manned local police that a Catoosa County drifter named Robert Earl Smith was involved, but no supporting evidence was developed.

The robberies appeared to have a three-week cycle, so early in No-vember Dodd advised the Dalton police to beef up patrols in the neighborhood and decided to take a chance and lean hard on Smith, who, he had learned, frequently visited Chattanooga. Dodd caught up with Smith the night of November 4 and told him he had enough on him to put him away for good. After listening to Dodd's description of his bleak future unless he cooperated, Smith caved in. Said one of the participants in the Catoosa County break-in was Wendell Allen (Butch) Barnes, who lived in East Ridge, a Chattanooga suburb. Also said he'd heard that the man who masterminded it was Tommy Prater, a Chattanooga fence.

Then the next day, November 5, Sims Lambert, the wife of Dalton's biggest construction supplier, drove her children home from grade school, opened her front door and was mugged by two waiting masked men who demanded her jewelry. With this fourth felony, the total in stolen property was approaching $100,000.

After a lengthy stakeout Chattanooga detectives, with Dodd pres-ent, arrested Wendell Barnes late in the evening of November 6 and booked him as wanted in Georgia for the Catoosa County burglary. The plan was to have Barnes spend the night in the cooler thinking things over and then Dodd would interrogate him in the morning about the Dalton robberies. But before Dodd could get to him, Barnes, ostensibly an odd-job carpenter with few resources, was sprung with extraordinary swiftness on $5,000 bond. The only way left for Bill Dodd to have another crack at him was to start extradition proceedings with Tennessee.

· 2 ·

In Nashville, early in October, Marie had added two more names to her growing clemency file. One was a white woman, Bobbie Jean King, convicted of fraudulent use of a credit card. The other was a young black man, Larkin H. Bibbs Jr., in for second-degree murder. Had anyone bothered to check, there would have been no apparent connection, other than the fact that they were both from around Chattanooga.

But Bobbie Jean King stuck in Marie's mind. At first, when Marie called Stoker, he couldn't locate any citation on her. Then it turned out she went by two other names as well, Bobbie Jean Carmichael and Bobbie Jean Hawkins. It also turned out she hadn't actually been in the prison system. Her credit-card conviction had resulted in a suspended sentence with probationary supervision, and even that had expired. When Marie queried Eddie about it, he said this was another instance of Blanton's compassion. The woman was in a custody fight with her ex-husband, and her record, what little there was of it, was being held against her. That's why the Governor wanted to give her a pardon, and Marie didn't need to hear anything more.

Ricky had joined his brother that fall at Morris, also on a scholarship, and was getting marks as splendid as Dante's, and for the first time Marie had some breathing room to think about herself.

She'd been dating a man, a stockbroker, whom she really liked, then half loved, maybe more. She couldn't tell. It was all so mixed up. But the idea of marriage disconcerted her. She didn't know why. The stockbroker had bright prospects, He was good-looking, and he was kind. Seemingly, a lot of problems would vanish instantly with him.

Together they went to a movie, *Alice Doesn't Live Here Anymore*, the story of a young wife and mother, suddenly widowed and forced to make her way alone, to take on the responsibility of a totally new and unexpected life for herself and her son, to find herself as a person before entering into another relationship. It had a stunning impact on Marie. She'd never seen a film that treated the female dilemma with such care and insight, and was dismayed years later to watch its sardonic, moving edge corrupted in a TV comedy series.

Marie, of course, completely identified with Alice. Even got a bit melodramatic about it. The discussion afterward had become quite heated. This man she thought she knew so well wasn't anywhere on the same wavelength. It wasn't that he hadn't liked the movie. Just that he couldn't fathom why she was getting so worked up. It was, after all, only a picture show.

The experience settled things for her. She hadn't come this far—from someone she could now hardly recognize, who had thought love and prayer were all you needed to change the world—to give up all that she had worked for. And she had a ways to go. After the boredom of extraditions, the clemency liaison work had helped, but not nearly enough. And so she decided she wanted to be a lawyer and started boning up for the Law School Admission Test, a prerequisite for entering an approved institution. If she had to, she'd get another job. With a new goal like this, it didn't matter so much what the job was.

Toward the end of September she wrote to Dante at school.

. . . I surely hope when you pray that you remember to ask God's guidance for me in regard to a career in law. Somehow, the more I think of it, the more determined I become to do it. It's almost as if I am propelled by an unknown force! But of course, that "unknown force" is my drive for independence—for all 4 of us. You may learn, I hope, from watching me, that most things are possible if you try long enough & hard enough! Of course, we've had a great deal of help along the way—but I have never stopped striving to better our lives. What this demonstrates is that we all need the help of others—but we have to work hard at all times in order to get it, or deserve it. I hope that eventually I will be able to give you & Ricky & Therese all the best things you need—like Morris School—without needing the assistance of other people's generosity (like the brothers at Morris!).

Darling, you know that I am thinking of you, & love you, & miss you. God bless you, & I thank Him for giving me you, my beautiful, gallant first-born son.

A big hug,
Mom

P.S. Here's that extra $5!

LSATs were given in Nashville twice a year. The next one was scheduled for Saturday, October 11. The evening of the tenth

Marie got to bed early to be ready for the test. She never made it.

The phone woke her around midnight. Dr. Espy was calling from California. His little girl, Anne, had suffered a grand mal seizure that brought on cardiac arrest, and she'd been rushed from King's Daughters to the intensive care unit in the children's wing at Vanderbilt hospital. He gave Marie his flight time in the morning. She went immediately to the hospital and learned there had been continuing convulsions and a second heart stoppage. The prognosis was very bad. Espy's former wife and her mother arrived. Marie felt like an intruder, but in their grief they seemed to welcome her being there. She accompanied them to the hospital chapel, weeping and praying with them.

Many times she had brought Espy's daughter to Nashville for a weekend and had been touched at how gentle the kids were with her. And at some point during the night she wrote to Dante and Ricky.

I am keeping a very sad vigil at Anne's bedside in Vanderbilt hospital. . . . I very much doubt that she will survive, but it's in God's hands. I know that what is best for her is what He will allow to happen. It is so very hard for us to understand why a child like her must endure all that she has, but we must remember to use it as an opportunity to be closer to God. God's present in a special way in her, & she has been the cause of a lot of love and good.

Please pray for her, & for her family, & for me, that I may help them in every way I can.

At daybreak Anne died. Marie met Espy at the airport. He took one look at her and said, "She's gone, isn't she?" and she held him as he broke down.

Marie had seen his daughter after her death, and a tremendous spiritual awareness swept over her as she looked down at the frail, serene face. Truly, she felt, Anne was better off than she'd ever been, and she felt the presence of God as never before. She felt it again as she drove Espy in from the airport. Marie had talked to Espy enough to know how totally hateful the relationship between him and his wife had become, and now, suddenly, he was asking with great tenderness and concern how she was. "We have to do exactly what she wants," he said.

And then *she* only wanted what he wanted. In the end Marie helped with the arrangements. The funeral was held in Espy's hometown in southern Alabama. Although it was a Baptist service, she arranged for

the minister to read from Saint Francis of Assisi. The prayer seemed
to fit right in.

> *Lord, make me an instrument of Your*
> *peace. Where there is hatred, let me sow*
> *love . . . And it is in dying that we are born*
> *to eternal life.*

She stayed with the Espy family for more than a week, making sure
the thank-you notes got out, drawing up an address list for a memorial
card that King's Daughters had printed, having a rose from Anne's
coffin preserved so Espy could have it.

She had called Sisk to say she didn't know how long she'd be away.
Eddie was quite amenable. "Use your own judgment," he said. "We'll
get by." She remembered how grateful she was for his understanding.

· 3 ·

With Wendell Barnes out on bond in Tennessee and, for the moment
at least, out of reach, Bill Dodd turned his attention to Tommy Prater,
now his chief suspect in planning the Dalton robberies.

If Dodd needed any more motivation, he got it when he did a
rundown on Prater and discovered his involvement in the shooting of
a Georgia state trooper several years before over in Walker County,
west of Dalton. The trooper had stopped a car that answered the
description in a sheriff's radio alert following a burglary and had been
seriously wounded by a 12-gauge shotgun blast. Although the man who
pulled the trigger received a ten-year sentence, Prater, in separate
proceedings, managed to sweet-talk his way out. While his fingerprints
had been lifted from the car, he wasn't in it when the shooting occurred. This time, Dodd told himself, it'd be different.

Besides being a fence, Tommy Prater ran a topless club called the
Classic Cat in a honky-tonk area on Market Street, one of Chattanooga's main drags. Prater was thirty-two, slightly built, with thin-
ning light brown hair and soulful eyes. Women, to Dodd's disgust, felt
motherly toward him. He lived, as a matter of fact, with his mother.

For all practical purposes, Dodd moved to Chattanooga. Sometimes
in the company of a city detective—in any event, always letting the
police know he was there—he kept tailing Prater. Saw him constantly

with Barnes, and another man, Bruce McBryar. Barnes and McBryar started doing carpentry and installation work at the Classic Cat. Now and then Dodd saw Prater driving around with a heavyset man. According to the detective Dodd was with, the man was well known in Chattanooga. William Aubrey (Bill) Thompson. Had a record. Gambling felonies that had been knocked down to misdemeanors. Some moonshining. His wife had committed suicide with a pistol. Kind of weird. Thompson apparently had been in bed with her at the time. Also moved pretty good in local Democratic politics. That part interested Dodd. Maybe that was how Barnes had gotten out of jail so fast.

Working Market Street the way he was, Dodd knew word might filter back to Prater. But he had to risk it. And he also knew he was on the right track. He found a man who had acquired a snub-nosed Smith & Wesson .38 pistol from Prater. The pistol was traced back to a residential break-in ten months before in Walker County. He turned up a woman who had purchased a diamond ring from Prater for $300. The ring, which appraised out at $7,000, was identified as one taken from a Fort Payne, Alabama, robbery in 1974. He found another woman who told him that Prater once gave her a briefcase to hold for him, warning her not to look inside. It was almost as though he had wanted her to, she said. So she did. The briefcase was full of expensive jewelry. When Prater came for the briefcase, she confessed to what she'd done. He giggled and gave her a diamond brooch, and said this was just a little of what he had.

But what Dodd wanted was the Dalton connection. On November 30 he paid a return visit to another woman who hung around Market Street. There was something about her that made Dodd think she knew more than she was telling. This time, with a Chattanooga detective along, Dodd was able to scare her with a soliciting charge. Then he hit pay dirt. The woman said she'd been present earlier in the fall when Prater, Barnes and McBryar were laughing and talking about some diamond heist with a big fat guy who had a mustache. She didn't know who the fat guy was, but he had driven off in a red Ford. And the Ford had Georgia plates. She was sure about the plates.

While Dodd was driving to Dalton that afternoon, it suddenly came to him. It came so hard that he pulled off the Interstate for a minute to absorb it. Maybe it was because he was so into cars himself, especially Fords, but Dodd had remembered reading that around the time of the last robbery a Dalton police patrol routinely reported stopping a red Ford near the house and questioning the driver.

Dodd called home and said he'd be late for supper. He went through the files and found the report. The driver of the red Ford was named Bernard Weinthal. A woman was in the Ford with him who Weinthal said was his wife. They'd been cruising so slowly, Weinthal had explained, because they were searching for the address of a baby-sitter.

Next Dodd looked up Weinthal. He had a small record. He was forty. Had been a middle-echelon executive in the carpet industry, earning $35,000 a year. Married a woman half his age and began having financial problems. Passed some bad checks and had been fired as a result. Was currently living in a trailer with his wife on property his mother-in-law owned. He was fat. And he had a mustache.

On December 2 Dodd got from the telephone company a list of Weinthal's toll calls for the past six months. There were many to a Chattanooga number, Prater's number, and Dodd got a court order to tap Weinthal's line. Right off, Dodd knew he was going to have problems. Weinthal was talking to Prater about "other jobs." Said he needed the cash. Couldn't sit still. But Prater kept putting him off. The time wasn't right, he said.

Dodd was hoping for another robbery so they all could be nabbed in the act. As he listened to the tapes, however, it was obvious Prater had been tipped to the investigation and wasn't about to set foot in Georgia. For a while anyway.

He wondered how much Prater knew.

· 4 ·

October 22, 1975

Dearest Dante:

Honey, it was so good to talk to you. Time seems to have "telescoped" for me, and I'm kind of losing track of things for that reason. Give me another week or so, and I'll be back to normal.

I was here in the office until 10:15 last night, trying to get caught up after missing so much work. But the good part is that I have an assistant (named Charlie) who just started and he is really a life-saver for me. He is real interested, and catches on to everything I say really fast. Also, he is a good worker. I spent the better part of the day trying to teach him about my commutation work. I know it is going to be an ENORMOUS help to me. Thank heaven for that!

*. . . I do hope you are continuing to remember Anne, even though she's
already a little angel, and her father in your prayers.*

She'd come back to work out of sorts, depressed. During her absence,
clemency cases and extraditions had piled up. They all seemed so
meaningless now. As she waded through the stack, her irritation grew.
She checked with the Nashville Bar Association and was told the next
LSATs wouldn't be until May. She was under the impression that the
tests were given nationally at the same time, and the woman at the
association didn't volunteer that there were different dates elsewhere.

Marie looked around the office, and she suddenly blew. Sisk's secretary was out shopping. Eddie himself was off playing golf. Another
secretary was buried in *People* magazine. The only thing a file clerk was
filing was her nails. Even Trent Hall, whom she liked, had been on the
phone for half an hour gabbing with his wife.

She waited till Sisk returned late in the day and stormed into his
office. "I've had it!" she said. "You come look at my desk. I've got
enough work to keep everyone in this place busy for a month, and they
all act like they're on permanent vacation. I resent it. I don't like it,
and by golly, I'm not putting up with it. I can't do all this stuff by
myself. It's getting completely out of hand."

Startled at first, Sisk now started grinning. "Hold on," he said. "You
won't believe this, but I was just going to tell you. I've got you an
assistant. Name's Charlie Benson." He'd been recommended, said
Eddie, by Fred Taylor, a highway trooper assigned to the Governor's
staff. Mostly though, Taylor drove for Blanton's brother Gene. Marie
got the impression Gene Blanton had been involved in this as well.
Benson was a law student. Originally the idea had been for Benson to
work directly for him, Sisk went on, but then he realized how overloaded Marie was with clemency cases. That's where he wanted Benson, he said. On clemencies exclusively.

That hurt her feelings, and she said so. Why not extraditions too?
Well, *she* was the state extradition officer, Sisk said. But he backed off.
Didn't mean she wasn't to do any clemencies. She and Benson could
divide them up. Marie didn't push it further. She hadn't told Eddie
about preparing for the LSAT or that she intended to try again and
might be leaving as a result.

Benson was taking night law courses at the Nashville YMCA. Was in
his fourth year. He was from Cocke County in East Tennessee, hard

by the Great Smoky Mountains. It was big moonshine territory. In Cocke County the law was considered an alien force. The per capita murder rate was said to be the highest of any county in America. It wasn't an ordinary Saturday night in Cocke County unless there were a couple of shoot-outs.

Charlie Benson certainly didn't look like your clannish, gun-toting moonshiner. He was about five eight, sort of pudgy, merry-faced, with twinkling eyes. As soon as you saw Charlie, you took to him.

When Sisk introduced them, he said, "Charlie, I think you're going to like working for Marie," and Benson had said, "Yes, sir! I already do." Marie let it pass. And Benson made up for it in his own fashion. He was away from his desk once when the phone rang, and she answered it. Then she overheard him saying, "Hell, no, that was my boss. You ought to come down and see her." Afterward they talked over coffee about how so many people saw everything in stereotypes.

She went through the office routine and explained how he'd be operating with the pardons and paroles board. She showed him her clemency card file, what the data on each card should be, and told him since there were two of them now, the file was more important than ever. It was imperative that the information be faithfully entered on the progress of every case, so if some question arose when one of them wasn't around, the other would have an instant reference.

From the beginning Eddie and Charlie appeared to be inseparable. Marie gave it no thought. She got along fine with Eddie and fine with Charlie at just the right distance. If they went off on golf dates or had drinks together, probably yakking about something really vital, like UT's last football game, it was equally fine with her. But she could see how hurt Trent Hall was. Eddie used to take Trent along to play golf. Now it was always Charlie. "They're like the damn Bobbsey twins," Trent had said.

One thing did irk her about Charlie, though. While he was eager-beaver bright and caught on quickly to what had to be done, she noticed after a couple of weeks that he wasn't holding up his end on the cards. She'd hear him on the phone discussing a clemency, the card file box in front of him, and when he had finished, he wouldn't make an entry. She put it down to innate carelessness. Some people were like that. It was tedious, she told him, keeping up the cards, but if they didn't do it, they'd have an unholy mess on their hands. Nobody would know what was going on. He agreed. He'd try to remember to do better.

Early in December she found a note from Sisk on her desk. *Marie, see me. TES.* She couldn't recall the exact date. It didn't seem so important at the time. Anyway, she went into his office, and Eddie said he wanted her to be on the lookout for some extradition warrants that might be coming in from Georgia. If they arrived, there'd most likely be four of them.

One would be for a guy named Tommy Prater, he said. He had forgotten the names of the other three, but it didn't matter. Prater was the main name to watch out for. As soon as they popped up, he wanted to know it. He had information, he said, that Georgia was trying to frame these guys.

"Sure, Eddie," she said.

If she thought anything, it was because this was only the second extradition Sisk had expressed the slightest interest in. The other had involved a Tennessee country-music star, Faron Young. Oklahoma had wanted him returned on a charge of indecently exposing himself to a teenage girl, and there'd been a flap about it in the press. The Nashville country-music industry was up in arms, and Sisk hashed over the problem with Marie. There was another version to the story, that the girl had barged into Faron's dressing room after his performance. But be that as it may, Eddie said, there was no way Blanton was going to honor the extradition. Didn't she know anyone from that convention in Colorado last spring she could talk to and cool the whole thing? The fact was Marie had met the legal counsel to Oklahoma's governor and had gotten along well with him. She called him, explained the situation, and the upshot was that Oklahoma dropped the warrant. A day or so later when she arrived for work, there was a glossy photo of Faron Young tacked to her door and on it, in Eddie's handwriting, *Dear Marie, Thanks for everything. Love, Faron.*

Now, when Sisk had finished with the Georgia business, she jotted down a note to herself, *Georgia / Prater / Let TES know,* and put it in a special flag file she maintained for extraditions that were going to have hearings. It wasn't unusual for a hearing to be requested even before a warrant got to her, and clearly there would be a hearing on this one. Sisk said Prater's attorney had already been in touch with him.

As Christmas, traditional clemency time, approached, a flurry of commutations and pardons went through, among them Larkin H. Bibbs Jr. and Bobbie Jean King.

The day of the office party young Trent Hall, who had remained with

Eddie working on legislative matters, came in and said, "Hey, Marie, help yourself to some liquor. There're a couple of cases out front, and Eddie said everybody can have some."

"Who from?"

"Bill Thompson."

She couldn't help making a face. Although they hadn't been introduced, Marie had disliked Thompson on sight, a beefy fellow she would see occasionally hanging around Eddie's office. Always with a big cigar in his mouth. Had black curly hair and wore flashy Hawaiian sport shirts and sunglasses. And it wasn't simply his dress. It was his whole manner. Sometimes, even when Eddie wasn't there, he'd be in Sisk's office, feet up, puffing on a cigar, using the phone, the WATS line, as if he owned it. One day she had asked Trent if he knew anything about the man, and Trent had said his name was Bill Thompson. Said he didn't know much more, except Thompson was involved in party politics in Chattanooga and he and Eddie played golf. "Why?" Trent asked, and Marie said, "Oh, I don't know. He's so obnoxious. Maybe it's the way he makes himself at home."

Now Trent was saying, "There's more than the liquor. Take a look."

She followed him to a heap of boxes. He opened one. Inside was a throw rug, or maybe a wall hanging, celebrating the forthcoming '76 bicentennial year. It was red, white and blue, with a gold eagle in the center. "What do you think?" Trent said. "There's one for each of us."

"I think it's awful."

"Oh, I don't know," said Trent, standing back, squinting. "It's not so bad. I'm going to try it out."

Finally Marie took one herself. Perhaps Dante or Ricky might want to have it.

Then at the party, Janice Clinkenbeard, Eddie's secretary, was showing off a bottle of Joy perfume. From that nice Mr. Thompson, Janice said. Wasn't it thoughtful of him?

· 5 ·

The tap on Bernard Weinthal's line in Dalton had been activated December 12.

Sometimes he'd be calling Prater four or five times a day. They had to get moving again. There were other jobs to do. He knew, Weinthal said, where the women lived who had diamonds on their fingers. He was out every day watching for them. But Prater wasn't having any of it. He knows something, Bill Dodd thought, frustrated. But the one thing Dodd counted on was that Prater didn't know they had pinpointed Weinthal. Or else Prater wouldn't be talking to him. Running the taped conversations, he kept rooting for Bernie. Come on, Tommy, he said to himself, come on down here.

Weinthal talked about how good the Dalton jobs had been. Well, maybe Dalton was too hot, Prater said. He was getting bad vibes from Dalton. They'd done too many jobs there. Weinthal said Dalton wasn't the only place. He knew plenty of places outside Dalton.

In the middle of all this Prater allowed he had a diamond, a big one, about three carats, that he was having trouble getting rid of. Weinthal went crazy. He was back on the phone saying he had somebody he could sell it to. Just get it to him, he pleaded. Prater at last said okay, and Dodd knew he was in business.

On the evening of December 28 he watched as a car with Tennessee tags drove up to Weinthal's trailer on the outskirts of town, and then left. Dodd let the messenger return to Chattanooga. The trailer remained under surveillance through the night, and in the morning Weinthal was followed into Dalton. He got out of his car and was on the sidewalk headed for a local jeweler when Dodd, armed with a search warrant, stopped him. "Mr. Weinthal, you're under arrest," he said, and reached into the watch pocket of Weinthal's vest, stretched tight over his protruding belly. Somehow Dodd knew the diamond was there. And it was. Out of its setting, in a glassine packet.

· 6 ·

ASSOCIATED PRESS, *December 26, 1975*

Preparing to begin his second year in office, Gov. Ray Blanton appears relaxed and in command, not only of the state administration but of the Democratic party in Tennessee.

He'd had only one problem of consequence.

Days before Blanton's gubernatorial election, the story had surfaced about illegal contributions in his 1972 senatorial campaign against Howard Baker. It had been largely discounted, however, because it had such a zany side to it. Besides the illegal contributions, there supposedly had been an attempt to sabotage Senator Baker's campaign train by greasing the tracks with Crisco. Whether this was to derail the train or to slow it on its appointed rounds was never quite clear. Blanton fielded the charge very well. Had audiences rolling in the aisles when he inquired how much Crisco it took to stop a train.

But the illegal-funding part wouldn't go away. An investigation had begun under a Nashville FBI agent, Henderson Hillin. Then it spilled over into possible funny money during Blanton's run for the governorship.

By the fall of '75 a federal grand jury was in session. As Blanton's 1972 campaign coordinator, Eddie Sisk had been subpoenaed, and denied knowing anything about anything. A number of others figured in the investigation, including Blanton's patronage man, Shorty Freeland, Chattanooga chairman Ward Crutchfield and Gene Blanton. All were equally insistent they knew nothing.

Still, the bad publicity dragged on, and Blanton met with John Seigenthaler, the publisher of the *Tennessean*. The paper had supported Blanton in the general election, and it was no secret Seigenthaler was a Democrat. A one-time Nieman fellow at Harvard, he had started out as a reporter for the *Tennessean*, made a name for himself looking into the Teamsters and ended up for a time as administrative assistant to Attorney General Robert F. Kennedy. He had a reputation for guts and was known to have what he called an objective attitude toward the FBI. Once, as Kennedy's on-the-spot emissary during the civil rights movement in the early 1960s, Seigenthaler was clubbed senseless in Montgomery, Alabama, while FBI agents stood by taking notes. It had become a famous story. Admittedly, the agents had no jurisdiction, but why hadn't they given him a hand? "I don't know," Seigenthaler would respond, "I was unconscious at the moment." Now he was being regularly listed as one of the ten most powerful men in Tennessee.

Personally, Seigenthaler thought the accusations against Blanton dating back to '72 had been a last-minute Republican dodge to save the governor's chair. He had been around long enough to know there was hardly a candidate who wasn't receiving money under the table one way or another. At worst, he figured, Blanton's people had been inept. Sophistication wasn't their strongest suit.

The governor's brother Gene, who was there when Blanton met with Seigenthaler, said he didn't understand what all this chickenshit fuss was, and the Governor said, "I'll tell you what it is. We got us a Republican President, two Republican senators and a Republican United States attorney. That good enough?"

Seigenthaler agreed the investigation was selective law enforcement, but he warned Blanton that in his opinion it wasn't going to go away, and his paper would have to continue reporting it. What Blanton needed, he said, was some first-class legal counsel. Sisk wasn't capable of handling something like this. Seigenthaler's advice was to retain Jim Neal, who had convicted Jimmy Hoffa and had been a key special prosecutor during Watergate. He was thought to be the best defense lawyer in the state.

The answer was quintessential Blanton. "No way," he said. "If I hire Jim Neal, everyone will think I'm guilty of something."

There had to be, the Governor said, a better solution.

In Nashville, agent Hillin thought he had a good case rocking along. He was uncovering dummy contributors, hidden donors, illegal corporate transfers, an apparently unreported $1,000 cash gift. But the indisputable, concrete heart of his investigation was the W-2 tax form of an employee of a Memphis trucking firm which showed he'd been drawing his regular salary while working full time in Blanton's campaign. This was tantamount to a corporate contribution, a specific violation of federal election laws. What's more, the employee had openly acknowledged it. Subsequently it was discovered that another employee had been used in the same manner.

Then Hillin's case collapsed. The owner of the firm, Frank Phillips, a longtime Blanton friend and supporter whom the Governor had put on the state Alcoholic Beverage Commission, swore it was all his fault. Hadn't understood the finer points of the election law. And Ray Blanton didn't know anything about it. The firm wound up being fined $3,000, and the Justice Department decided it would be too difficult to pursue the other allegations. Phillips continued to serve as an ABC commissioner. He had been guilty, said Blanton, of only a technical violation.

· 7 ·

That Christmas was the best Marie could recall since her adolescence. It was especially warm because her other sister, Mary Therese, was there. She was so fond of M.T. Yet it seemed she'd been the one sibling Marie had seen the least. First there'd been Marie's marriage and then M.T. had gone off to college at Sewanee. She was deeply religious. Trying to think her life through, M.T. had just returned from a trip through the Southwest, and the more she talked about how different and interesting everything was, the more Marie began to toy with the idea of studying law there. Maybe Arizona. Break away from Nashville. She asked the kids if they'd like that, and the boys said terrific—as long as they could keep going to the Morris School. Therese said she'd go, but only if Rosie came along. Then she and Rosie cooked the Christmas turkey.

EIGHT

Right after New Year's Janice Clinkenbeard was in asking Marie if she had heard anything on the Georgia extraditions. Said Eddie wanted to know, and when Marie said she hadn't, Janice said, well, here were the other three names to watch out for. Wendell Allen Barnes, Bruce McBryar and Reisto Bekovich. Every couple of days, it seemed, Janice was asking again. Got to be a real pest.

In Dalton, after his arrest, Bernard Weinthal had tried to bluster his way out. Dodd reminded him that in Georgia you could get the death penalty for this kind of armed robbery, and if Weinthal wanted to take the rap by himself in front of a jury, it was his decision. The robberies had been vicious. Homes invaded. People assaulted. A lot of squeals started coming out of Weinthal. He hadn't done anything like that. He fell apart. What would happen if he cooperated? He'd be doing himself a big favor, Dodd said.

Weinthal said he originally hooked up with Prater to unload carpeting stolen from Dalton mills. Besides Prater, Barnes and McBryar, there was a fourth guy named Bekovich, a professional fighter, who was involved as a lookout in the first robbery while Weinthal waited in the parking lot of a nearby Episcopal church. Weinthal was adamant about never having been inside any of the houses. Dodd believed him. None of the descriptions came close to matching him.

A Winfield County grand jury returned indictments in the middle of January '76, and extradition papers were immediately drawn up. In Georgia, with the approval of the district attorney, victims of a crime could retain a special prosecutor to press their case, and the four Dalton families had hired Erwin Mitchell, a former Winfield DA and two-term U.S. congressman. They wanted action fast.

At the time Eddie Sisk wasn't aware of this. Had no idea Georgia considered the case anything special. But even before the extradition papers arrived in Nashville, Marie got a call from her Georgia counter-part advising that they contained a technical error, and please return them so new ones could be issued. The Georgia extradition officer, Wanda Davis, didn't get into details for good reason. The technical error was nothing more than law-enforcement jealousy. Because of the prominence of the victims, the Dalton police, along with the sheriff's department, wanted to be identified as requesting the extraditions instead of the Georgia Bureau of Investigation. The whole thing was getting quite political.

Sisk was very smug when Marie passed on the news that the papers had a mistake in them. "I told you there was something fishy about this," he said. Also said he wanted to see the papers anyway after they came in. He'd had them for a week or so when Wanda was on the phone again, a little testy this time, asking why they hadn't been returned yet. "I'm getting all kinds of pressure," she complained.

"You don't know the half of it," Marie said.

· 2 ·

Of course, besides the Georgia extraditions, she had other extraditions and clemencies to contend with. But the only one that had an unusual aspect involved an inmate named Jimmy H. Pendleton, in for second-degree murder. Back in December Eddie had told her to get the board going on Pendleton. When the official commutation form was deliv-ered for the Governor's endorsement, Eddie walked in laughing and said, "Guess what? The board recommended the wrong Pendleton. They don't know their elbow from left field."

"Do you want me to start it over?"

No, he said, not right now. Maybe later. The case wasn't as meritori-ous as he first thought.

One Friday afternoon Charlie Benson picked up the metal box containing Marie's clemency card file. For a second she imagined he was going
to make some entries, but she remembered it was Friday, and Charlie's
habit was to leave early to drive across the state to spend the weekend
with his family in Cocke County. Often he left on Thursdays.

"What are you doing?" she said. "Don't tell me you're going to work
on the cards."

"Yeah, well, kind of. Eddie told me to take them home."

"I'm not sure that's such a good idea. Why?"

"He thinks maybe some of them are sloppy."

"I guess my abbreviations and all could be improved on, but that's
no reason to take them out of here," she said.

He said, "That isn't it. Eddie wants me to check out some things.
We all know the cards are okay, but there might be something in them
that could look bad if a nosy, off-base reporter got hold of them."

"Like what?"

"Marie, I don't know. It's just that Eddie thinks some of this stuff
in them could be misinterpreted."

It was getting sticky. She didn't want a confrontation with Charlie.
She liked Charlie. Once when she had brought Therese to the office,
Charlie had been especially patient with her, giving her a grand tour,
taking her down to the cafeteria for a Coke. He had confided in Marie
about his aspirations in law, and she had remarked that this job was
great for him because he was meeting all the right people, and he
replied, "Don't think I don't know it." So now she didn't want to spoil
their relationship. She said, however, to wait and went looking for Sisk.
He wasn't to be found, and Janice said she had no idea where he'd
gone.

Marie came back and said, "Are you sure Eddie told you to do this?"

"Yes, I'm sure, Marie. He said to do it last weekend, but I forgot."

It wasn't that she spent all Saturday and Sunday stewing about the
cards. She was annoyed, certainly, but it was more because it seemed
so ridiculous and paranoid of Eddie and Charlie. Sheer stupidity, real
two-digit-IQ thinking, to fret about what some reporter might conjure
up from the cards, even granting that one would get access to them.
The information, after all, was confidential, and the fact was that more
often than not any storm kicked up by the media centered on clemencies coming from the board, not from the legal counsel's office.

When Benson brought the file back on Monday, she flipped through the cards. As far as she could determine, they were all there. Then she saw the Larkin Bibbs card. She had filled it out herself, on two sides. Now the notations were sparse, and in Charlie's handwriting. She tried to recall what she had put down, but couldn't. That was the point of the cards to begin with. To refer to. Anyhow, the board had gone ahead and recommended Bibbs, so the case was closed.

She spoke to Eddie about it, though. It was, she said acidly, the sort of dumb, covered-wagon mentality that had led to Watergate.

Very funny, he said.

It would appear that there was some justification for Sisk's paranoia.

She'd been looking at the February 9 issue of the *Tennessee Journal,* a gossipy weekly political newsletter published by Lee Smith, a former aide to Governor Dunn. Despite the newsletter's Republican slant, it had some good inside dope, and Marie enjoyed reading it. All at once she was reading about her first pardon case, Joe Allen Finley.

> Several months ago Governor Ray Blanton exercised his constitutional authority to pardon Joe Allen Finley, son of a Blount County tavern operator and under sentence for grand larceny. Earlier Governor Winfield Dunn had declined to grant the pardon when the Board of Pardons and Paroles would not recommend that he do so. Since the board made no recommendation to Governor Blanton, Blount Countians and others remain mystified concerning the reason for the Governor's action.

Marie couldn't believe her eyes. She'd seen the Finley commutation herself. She got out a copy and went through it word by word. That's when she discovered the board had substituted "submit" for "recommend."

Considering where the item had been printed, her first reaction was that somebody connected with the board was trying to embarrass Blanton, and she went to Sisk about it. Eddie was slow catching on. "Aw, hell, Marie," he said, "what difference does it make?"

"How come they're always recommending their cases and just submitting one of ours? It *is* different."

Suddenly she had his full attention. "By God, you're right." Came right out of his chair and told her to go through every clemency that had originated in the Governor's office.

In all she found sixteen submits, among them Billy Gene Cole,

Larkin Bibbs and Bobbie Jean King. She gave the rundown to Sisk and a day or so afterward saw board member Dorothy Greer leaving Eddie's office. Dorothy didn't look too happy. Next it was Charles Traughber. He didn't look so happy either, and that hadn't upset her a bit. Marie half suspected he had leaked the Finley item. He was so sneaky, she thought. Even Charlie Benson agreed with that. Despite her reminders to Traughber to make sure she was brought in on clemency matters, he had continued to meet with Sisk on his own. Indeed, he'd become increasingly cool, although always correct. She had the distinct impression that Traughber didn't like women in general, and white women in particular, and she recalled Sisk's crack about Traughber and Shelby County rapists.

About a month later the board had hopped to once again. Eddie got a letter, dated March 22 and signed by all three members, confirming that the Board of Pardons and Paroles had in fact recommended "a commutation of sentence to Governor Ray Blanton on behalf of the following subjects." All sixteen names Marie had turned up were listed.

"They were getting too big for their britches over there," Sisk said. Told her he really appreciated her alertness.

Meanwhile the Georgia extraditions wouldn't go away.

She finally got Eddie to let go of the first set of papers and sent them back to Wanda Davis. When the revised papers arrived, she asked Sisk if she couldn't forward them now to Shipley or Raybin in the attorney general's office for review, and he said no, he wanted to review them himself. Normally it took two to three weeks just to process an extradition warrant, but Eddie still had the papers when Wanda was calling again in a couple of weeks to find out what was happening. And again. Then some attorney in Georgia named Erwin Mitchell was on the phone asking what the situation was.

"Eddie," she said, "what about those Georgia papers?"

"Well, I really haven't gotten to them yet. Give me a few more days."

He kept procrastinating, and the inquiries from Georgia mounted. She said, "Look, I have to tell these people something. Can't we get the papers over to Alex Shipley?" And at last he said okay. He'd talk to Shipley himself. There was no hurry on this, he said. One of the defense lawyers, who was with Ward Crutchfield's firm down in Chattanooga, had already advised him that all four men named in the warrants intended to request hearings, and that was going to take time. Georgia would have to wait.

The Tennessee hearing officer on extraditions was Charles Grigsby. Marie asked if she could notify Grigsby that these hearings were coming up and to start scheduling a date. At least that would get Georgia off her back. Yes, he said. But, by God, Tennessee was going to see to it that these men got due process. Sisk began working up a real head of steam. These guys were being railroaded. Georgia had some vendetta going against them. Had Marie ever seen a frenzy like this on any other extradition? No, she said, and he said that alone showed something was wrong, and she had to admit that perhaps he had a point.

· 3 ·

All of this had worn her down. There was now such an unpleasant aura surrounding her work. And she was really just a cog in Eddie's operation, basically doing what she was told. So Marie mailed in her application for the LSATs she had missed in the fall.

Then early in April Sisk took her aside. "Marie," he said, "do you know the parole board's the highest paid board in the state?" and she said, "No, I didn't," and he said, "Well, it is. I've been thinking. I think you should be on that board."

She'd recall later that he didn't speak at all about the opportunity to do something important. To contribute. Find fulfillment. Nothing like that. It was the money. But her thoughts were so jumbled she didn't realize it.

Dorothy Greer's appointment was up the end of June, Sisk said, and the Governor definitely wasn't going to keep her. Blanton wanted his own people in places like this. People he could trust. Who understood the meaning of loyalty. Marie, he said, knew better than anyone how the board had tried to undercut the Governor. Besides, he and she had worked well together. Everything would be more efficient, simplified. No more red tape. Cut down the time factor and so forth. And she got along well with Benson. Charlie would continue to handle the liaison work with the board. And Charlie could be the extradition officer. That way, said Eddie, smiling, she wouldn't have to worry about the Georgia business. He knew what a rough time she'd had in the past, with the kids and all. Now, with her new salary, she'd be home free.

She was absolutely overwhelmed. It was a leap beyond anything she had imagined. She would be in a position truly to make a difference in the criminal justice system. Independent. Using her own judgment, being her own person. It never crossed her mind it might be otherwise. The money, too, was a consideration that couldn't be ignored.

"Are you on the level?" she said.

"Yeah, sure I am. You know what the job's all about."

"But, Eddie, I mean, I don't know if I have the qualifications for it."

"Who's to say what the qualifications are?" he said. "You've got a degree from Vanderbilt in psychology, don't you? Think about it."

She had always believed she could do anything she wanted. But this was different. She could end up making an awful fool of herself in public. She went down the hall to talk to Jack Strickland. Jack hadn't changed his opinion about Sisk. He didn't rate Charlie any higher. After Benson had been hired, Jack started calling them Mutt and Jeff. He surprised her by saying he'd heard talk she might be going on the board, and when she expressed reservations about her background and experience, Jack said, "Are you kidding? Look at Mutt and Jeff. You've got more brains than both of them put together."

Charlie, of course, was excited. A raise for him and only the beginning for her in politics, he said. He was sure she would run for office one day, a big-time office, and she could count on him to be out beating the bushes for her.

Next, Sam Lipford phoned her for lunch. Sam was director of the state probation and parole officers, about three hundred of them. His country-bumpkin manner masked an acute political sensibility. "I hear rumors you're up for the board," he said, and she said maybe she had a shot at it. Marie couldn't have found a more sympathetic ear about her misgivings. Lipford was only two years out of college himself and had nothing on paper to warrant his directorship. But he was from Blanton's hometown. Had the right contacts, and by all accounts was doing a first-rate job. "Graduating from Vanderbilt is qualification enough," he said. He told her the Governor couldn't afford to take one woman off the board without replacing her with another. The corrections commissioner, C. Murray Henderson, was pushing for the warden at the women's prison, but Henderson was new on the job himself. Didn't know that many key people in the administration and, as Sam put it, would recognize the realities. With Sisk behind Marie, she didn't have a problem. Lipford liked to come on a little.

"I'll tell you one thing," he said. "You'll be the best-looking member on the board."

· 4 ·

On Easter Sunday, April 18, after the egg hunt at home, and mass, and brunch, she went to her office and read over again a ten-page hand-written memo from Dorothy Greer to Sisk. The memo was undated. Marie didn't know whether it had been written before or after Dorothy was told she wouldn't be reappointed, but Eddie had given it to her to summarize for him.

The memo ripped into Traughber. It said he was increasingly erratic, arrogant and incapable of rational management. His interpretation to the board of opinions from the attorney general's office had turned out to be completely at odds with what had been actually voiced. His directives required X-ray vision to comprehend. He retained official files in his personal possession for extensive periods and was spending most of his time "dogging" legislators about being named chairman again. Racism had become a factor. Traughber had chewed out John Stoker for reprimanding a black employee. Stoker had been out of line because he wasn't "a brother."

Marie thought about how much trouble the board was having with various DAs and judges. One DA had recently blown his top over an inmate's release by the board and had called Sisk. Marie discovered that the board had acted because there was a technical violation in the man's sentence which left the state liable to a lawsuit. All Traughber had to do was explain that the board didn't want the guy out any more than the DA did but it had no choice. Traughber, however, hadn't bothered. He was so incompetent, Marie thought. Causing all this grief for nothing.

She remembered cradling her head in her arms on the typewriter in the silent office, thinking that Dorothy Greer was on her way out, and that left Joe Mitchell, who was more or less a cipher, and Traughber, and it occurred to her that if she was going to be on the board, the one thing she was certain of was that she could do a better job than Charles Traughber, and if Traughber was the board's chairman, why shouldn't she be chairman instead?

It became so dazzlingly clear, and she spent the rest of the afternoon drafting a letter to Governor Ray Blanton telling him she should not only be on the board but be its chairman as well. Her interest, she wrote, was seeing to it that his administration was viewed in the best possible light, that when inevitably controversial clemency cases arose, they were explained properly to law-enforcement officials and the media. She had the expertise to do this, citing her work on the *Hustler* at Vanderbilt, her days as an active Young Democrat and her excellent, ongoing relationship with district attorneys and judges across the state both as extradition officer and nearly a year as liaison between the legal counsel's office and the board. She had worked closely, she noted, with his legal counsel, and her appointment would ensure a harmonious relationship with the board, which didn't exist now. She pointed out how under Traughber there had been a number of unnecessarily embarrassing incidents, such as the *Tennessee Journal* item on the Finley pardon. On the issue of clemency she stated that in her opinion it was logical and proper to help supporters of the administration whenever possible "as long as the ends of justice and truth prevail." As an afterthought, she underlined the last part, and at another time, when she looked back at the letter, with its gushy emphasis on loyalty and good public relations, Marie at least got some solace from that caveat. Probably nobody had picked it up. Or if anyone had, it was taken as Fourth of July rhetoric. Not something she really believed.

On Monday morning she told Sisk what she had decided. "Listen," she said, "why put me on the board if I have to be subservient to Traughber? Why shouldn't Traughber be subservient to us? He's had his shot and he's done a lousy job. Embarrassed you. Embarrassed me. Embarrassed the Governor. If I take over that job, by God, I want to do it right. How can I do anything if he's still chairman?"

She could see Eddie thinking it over. "Yeah, well, yeah. Maybe you're right," he said, and she showed him her letter. She saw his face fall. It was four pages, single-spaced. "Take your time," she said, "but read it." Later that same day he sent for her and said, "Okay, this is okay. You've sold me. But we've got to get down to brass tacks now. It isn't going to be all that easy. You've got to round up some more support."

Once she made up her mind to go, she went all out.

She contacted her father's old friend Lois Laycook and got him to write on her behalf. She also called another friend of Roque's, George Barrett, the Nashville party chairman and a prominent Catholic. She'd bumped into Barrett at a couple of functions when she was working as a Young Democrat at Vanderbilt. "You mean you're Roque's little girl Marie?" he had said. "If I can ever do anything for you, you just call." Well, now he could.

DA Richard Fisher wrote a perfect letter, although she barely knew him. Fisher was very active in the statewide association of district attorneys lobbying for tougher criminal justice legislation. Fisher had struck her as an especially fair, dedicated DA. She had speeded up an extradition for him and clarified some of the board's clemency recommendations. *Certainly, the duties of a District Attorney . . . and the decisions of the Board in the discharge of its duties cause serious disagreement on occasion. The personal involvement of Mrs. Ragghianti has effectively minimized such disagreement and misunderstanding,* Fisher wrote the Governor.

Marie's good friend Maribeth Freeman was secretary to Fate Thomas, the politically powerful Davidson County sheriff and a big Blanton booster. Thomas had been trying to date Marie, and when Maribeth sounded him out about sending an endorsement, he said, "You write it and I'll sign it." Marie even solicited a letter from James L. (Bud) Carroll, the Blanton contributor whose son had been one of her first clemency cases a year before. *Mrs. Ragghianti is a loyal supporter of the present administration,* Carroll advised the Governor. And, of course, there was her faithful benefactor, Monsignor Siener, who on the letterhead of the Cathedral of the Incarnation further identified himself as the former chaplain of the Tennessee State Penitentiary.

Within ten days Marie's blitz had produced better than twenty-five letters from key law-enforcement people, influential legislators and party figures and important Blanton financial backers, all calling for her appointment as chairman. Sisk seemed taken aback. As if amazed to discover a whole new side to Marie he hadn't suspected was there. "Hell," he told her, "you're doing better than I ever could." Then he said she needed to see corrections commissioner Henderson and also John Seigenthaler. He'd heard Traughber was putting up a fight.

"I don't know the commissioner," she said. "I can't walk up to a total stranger and ask him to recommend me."

"Just do it, Marie. I know he's going to like you."

So she asked for a meeting at the commissioner's convenience, and C. Murray Henderson replied, "A good-looking woman can see me anytime." When they talked, Henderson acted as though she already had the job, but if Marie felt it would help, why, he'd be glad to speak to the Governor. While there was a lot of "little lady" in Henderson's tone, it was more courtly than condescending.

Seigenthaler wasn't as easy. She tried several times to get through to him, and she was ready to give up. But Eddie insisted. Seigenthaler was the icing on the cake.

Paul Corbin, a former Kennedy operative who had worked with Seigenthaler in Washington, interceded. Corbin was frequently in Nashville and had once dated a woman Marie had grown up with. At first, when he talked to Seigenthaler about recommending Marie, the publisher said he didn't like the idea of becoming entangled in Blanton's appointments. Corbin kept at it, however, and Seigenthaler eventually agreed to see her.

It was her most difficult interview. Seigenthaler wasn't automatically impressed with her Vanderbilt degree. Wanted to know what made her think she was fit for the chairmanship. She said that for one thing she'd been acting as liaison between the Governor's office and the board on all matters having to do with executive clemency. She believed, she said, that she had a handle on some of the problems besetting the board.

"Like what?" he said, and she said, like PR. The board largely disregarded the media, and she thought that was a mistake. The media could play a crucial role in the interpretation of clemency cases. "I don't mean to sound egotistical," she said, "but I feel I could smooth over the rough edges that Charles Traughber hasn't been too adept at." And, she went on, she felt she also had a handle on the administration's goals regarding clemency and could be a real asset to the Governor.

"How's that?" he said, and she said that it was obvious the administration wanted to use clemencies as much as it could for political pluses, and that was all right, but someone was needed on the board who knew what was possible and what wasn't, so egg wouldn't end up on everybody's face.

Marie looked right at Seigenthaler and told him that for her the bottom line was the deep sense of commitment she had to what chairing the board entailed, that she saw it not just as a job but as a unique opportunity to have a positive impact on human lives.

Seigenthaler still hadn't said anything when he escorted her out of his office. In the city room, though, they ran into a young reporter who had worked on the *Hustler* with her. "You must know Marie," Seigenthaler said. "Our new pardons chairman."

When Marie reported this to Sisk, he said, "That does it. It's in the bag now."

As soon as Marie left, Seigenthaler called Blanton at the executive mansion and told him that for what it was worth, he thought Marie would make an excellent chairman. To his own astonishment, he found himself adding, "Ray, I just want you to know she's straight as an arrow."

It seemed such a gratuitous thing to say. Seigenthaler remarked on it later to Corbin, and Corbin shot back, "You were right. Sisk, and that whole crowd over there, are a bunch of crooks. I already told Marie, but she won't listen." All you had to do, said Corbin, was look at them in their polyester leisure suits.

One of Corbin's trademarks was his outrageous, gravel-voiced comments. Any number of people considered him a scalawag, a born troublemaker. Others, like Seigenthaler, thought him amusing. And as he had done so many times before with Corbin, Seigenthaler laughed off this latest sally.

· 5 ·

The first week in May, Marie dispatched the letter to Governor Blanton that she had drafted Easter Sunday. By messenger. The minute she did, she started fretting. Would the letter actually get to Blanton? Would Blanton remember who she was? Had all the other letters really reached him? She'd seen them, of course, since they'd been routed back to Sisk, but maybe Blanton's secretary had done that. Blanton was such a remote figure, even to the capitol hill staff. Very few people had access to him. She marveled at herself for even having the audacity to go after the chairmanship. She pictured Blanton opening her letter and saying to someone, "What the hell's this all about?"

In her pursuit of the job, she left the current clemency load to Benson. Extraditions were so routine they practically took care of themselves. Except the Georgia extraditions. The mere mention of Tommy Prater got her stomach churning. It had been one thing after another. Each of the wanted men had a lawyer, and getting them together for a hearing had become a nightmare. One attorney had gotten sick. The next one had a court conflict. It went on and on. And the phone calls had kept coming from Georgia. From Wanda Davis. Erwin Mitchell. Marie couldn't remember who else.

And then she received a call that laid her out. From a Mrs. Thomas

Lambert in Dalton, who said she was one of the victims of the robberies. Marie had no trouble picking up the venom in Mrs. Lambert's
voice. "I'm really sorry about the delay," she replied. "We've encountered all kinds of problems with these cases. First there was some kind
of error in the warrants sent by Georgia. Then, because of the number
of people involved, we've had considerable difficulty getting schedules
coordinated in order to hold a hearing."

Sims Lambert said, "You sit up there talking about hearings and
schedules, while I'm down here taking my children for counseling. My
children were with me when those masked men broke into our house,
tied us up, stole our property. My seven-year-old son has been terrified
to go into his own bedroom ever since. How would *you* like it if it
happened to you?"

Aghast, Marie immediately told Sisk about the call. "Eddie," she
said, "why don't we go ahead and send these turkeys back to Georgia?
You know we're not required to give them a hearing. I mean, the AG's
office says it's only a courtesy. We're not required to do it by law."

This time Sisk had a totally new slant. It just so happened, he said,
that he'd learned that Prater and a couple of the others had criminal
charges pending against them in Chattanooga, and that Tennessee was
damn well going to prosecute them before they were shipped off to
Georgia or anywhere else.

Marie said she guessed that settled it, then, and Sisk said he certainly
hoped so.

· 6 ·

By now the legal counsel's office had moved back to the capitol from
the Andrew Jackson Building, and Blanton's appointments secretary,
Ken Lavender, was on the phone telling her to come up. The Governor
wanted to see her right away.

She raced in to see Eddie and said you'd think they would have given
her some decent notice. "Look how I look," she said, and he said she
looked fine and to get going.

The Governor's chambers were on the floor directly above. She
started for the elevator but decided to use the stairs to gain time to
compose herself. Her heart was thumping so. On the landing she
paused and asked the Holy Spirit to guide her in her dialogue with
Blanton.

Earlier in the week she had gone to Christ the King Church to pray for help in her quest, and as if a veil had been lifted, she discerned a symmetry and form to her life she had not known before. All the pain and suffering from her marriage specifically, which had appeared so senseless, took on definition and significance. She would put all of it to use in understanding the pathology of the offenders who might come before her, and now on the landing that thought sustained her.

Ken Lavender was wavy-haired, kind of soft-looking. She saw Ken quite a bit. He was the one to whom she brought the commutation forms every week or so. This time, though, when he said, "Hi, Marie," there was a note of deference in his voice, and while she was still absorbing this Ken was opening a door and introducing her to Ray Blanton.

It was the same office that had filled her with such awe more than a year before when she'd been in there with Sisk—only now the Governor was there, and later she remembered her surprise at how Blanton rose to greet her, came forward to shake her hand and led her to a chair by the side of his desk and asked if she wouldn't like to have a Coke. "Yes, I would, thank you," she said, and she thought how extraordinary it was that the Governor of Tennessee had disappeared to pour her a Coke and was bringing it to her. Her apprehension fell away, and she was instantly in tune with the moment, poised, self-assured.

"Tell me," he said, "how you ever got interested in pardons and paroles," and it was obvious that he hadn't read her letter, so she went over what she had written, and it became equally clear he wasn't so much listening to her as studying her, mulling her over. He was as poker-faced as ever, but she thought she caught a glint of friendliness in his perpetually quizzical eyes—he liked her. She sensed a sexual tension in him, and of course she was right. There'd come a time when he would say of her, "She's the only woman who ever screwed me before I had a chance to screw her."

But right then he was gazing at her intently and saying, "Yes, Eddie's mentioned what a good job you've been doing." He had been hearing good things about her from many of his friends.

She'd been in there for perhaps a half hour when she realized this was the exact second to leave, and she stood up, and he stood up with her, and she reached across the desk and shook his hand and said, "Governor Blanton, I really want this job, and I deeply believe that I could be an asset to you and your administration," and he smiled and said he would be in touch. She felt his eyes on her as she walked out of the office, and going down the stairs she had just ascended so nervously she knew he was still thinking about her and she paused again and thanked God. She was sure she had it.

Two days passed without any further word, and the doubts began edging back. On Friday, May 7, she was at her desk when the phone rang and a voice said, "Marie, this is Bill Thompson."

"Oh, yes, Mr. Thompson," she said, wondering what this was all about. She'd seen him often, but couldn't recall ever having talked to him.

"You don't need to call me Mr. Thompson. Call me Bill."

"All right. Is there something I can do for you?"

"Well, I want to congratulate you. I just talked to the Governor, and he tells me you're going to be on the parole board. You're going to be the chairman."

She remembered being horrified at getting the news from this creep. Yet she had a sinking sensation that she was hearing it from the horse's mouth. "Oh, really," she said. "I wonder why he hasn't told me."

And Thompson chuckled and said, "Come on. I bet you knew all the time it was set." His tone became confidential. He knew the hard days she'd had, raising three kids, divorced, putting herself through school. "It's all over now," he said. "All that hard work's paid off, hasn't it?"

"That remains to be seen."

It was as though she hadn't said anything. "I'm a widower myself," he said. "Have a couple of kids. 'Course, they're grown now. But your troubles are over. You'll be on easy street from here on out."

Marie struggled to remain civil. He was, after all, a friend of the Governor's, and it was something she'd have to put up with. "I don't quite understand what you mean."

"Hey, I've been told you've got a brain in your head. You're not just another pretty face," he said. "Let's put it this way. You know, there'll be little side benefits and opportunities, and you'll be smart enough to see them and take advantage of them. Nobody has to know. It's like, you know, you're having an affair with somebody. At the end of the day, you go into the bedroom, close the door. Nobody knows what's going on. It's nobody's business."

That was all she could swallow. She didn't care how icy she sounded. "Thank you for your interest. I'm sorry, but I have to go see Eddie."

Nothing, however, seemed to faze Bill Thompson. He gave her his home phone number. "You hang on to that number now, honey. And tell Eddie to call me."

She hung up, nauseated. She went looking for Sisk, but he wasn't around. When he showed up later in the day, she told him what Thompson had said, and he said, "Don't worry about it, Marie. You've got to take Bill with a grain of salt. He was just trying to be nice."

"Yes, well, if you think that was nice, your perception and my perception of what's nice are poles apart. I don't want anything to do with him."

And then Sisk confirmed that she would be the board's chairman. "I was trying to tell you if you'd only give me a chance." The Governor was going to announce her appointment at his regular press conference the following Tuesday.

She was still upset. "Speaking of being nice, it'd be nice if he told me first."

"Well, hell, Marie, he's told me, and I'm telling you." Blanton's last reservation, he observed, was whether she was mature enough for the job. Then with a quick grin he said, "I can see the headline now. Blanton makes former beauty queen parole chairman."

"Oh God," she groaned, "that's all I need."

On Saturday she drove to the giant Hundred Oaks shopping mall, Nashville's niftiest, to look for something proper to wear. She had already determined it should be white. Symbolic for her, if no one else. It was slim pickings after Easter, however. She wanted a suit, but there were none to be had. Then she spotted a white dress with a jacket. She asked Therese what she thought, and Therese said it looked real good except the hemline was too long. The saleslady said it was impossible to have it shortened by Monday evening, and Therese chirped up and said, "You all have to do it. My momma's having a press conference with the Governor Tuesday morning," and the saleslady laughed and said, well, in that case, they'd make a special effort.

After that they looked for a dining table for their new apartment. Marie had located two apartments about a minute's walk apart in Valley Ridge, a residential complex in southwest Nashville, a two-bedroom one for Virginia and Rosie, and a three-bedroom one for herself, Therese and the boys. It had become harder and harder for Virginia to get around in the house where they had been living. Also there were the inevitable irritations of a grown daughter and mother together, compounded by the kids. Over the Easter vacation, when the boys were back from Morris, there'd been a disaster of sorts. Dante and Ricky spent a day cleaning up the yard. When they finished, they set a pile of trash and broken branches on fire and succeeded in burning down most of the garage as well. It had been quite a scene, complete with fire engines. Didn't do much for Virginia's nerves.

Virginia was delighted with the move. St. Henry's, one of Nashville's newer Catholic churches, wasn't more than a couple of hundred yards away, and she was acquainted with many of its parishioners. And for the children there were plenty of play facilities and a pool during the summer.

Marie's rent, $225 a month, was beyond anything she had ever dreamed of paying. But with her big salary hike coming up, she could manage it, and help out Virginia if she had to.

She tossed restlessly in bed all Monday night. Even started brooding over Eddie's wisecrack about the beauty-queen headline. That worried her more than Bill Thompson. Once she got to be chairman and he tried another call like that, he'd be in for some shock. Just thinking about it made her feel better.

Marie was habitually late. But on Tuesday morning, May 11, she took pains to be on time for the press conference. Packed Therese off to school as usual in her regulation blue-and-gray checkered jumper, white blouse and blue knee socks, and was halfway to the capitol before she realized she wanted at least one of her children on hand to witness the event. She turned the car around and headed back to get Therese out of class.

When they arrived, Eddie was pacing up and down in the corridor. "My God, you're late," he babbled, "I can't believe you're late," and she said she was sorry but she had something important to take care of.

And standing alongside Blanton as he announced her appointment, she saw Eddie in the back, behind all the reporters and cameras. Charlie Benson was next to him. They both seemed to have a faraway look in their eyes. She always remembered that. Later she would think that what they were seeing off in the distance were dollar signs. Lots of them.

After the conference was over, she returned Therese to school and drove again to the office. It was close to one o'clock now, and nobody was around. Talk about an anticlimax, she thought.

Then Jack Strickland was on the line. Was amazed that she didn't have any lunch plans. "I'm pleased and delighted," he said.

Strickland insisted on a bottle of champagne. It was her crowning day, he said. How did she feel about it?

She clinked her glass against his and said, "I'll tell you how it feels. It's only the beginning, Jack. The best is yet to come."

"Well, knowing you, I can believe it." Strickland looked at her and shook his head. "I've really enjoyed the last three weeks watching you in action," he said. "I've never seen anything like it. Those big politicos up on the hill. They all think they run the world. And you wrapped every one of them around your little finger. I don't know whether it was that smile of yours or that steely brain you have. Probably a deadly combination. But you did some job."

"Let's face it, Jack. I had all kinds of help, up to and including your support."

"Marie," he said, "you did it on your own. Don't forget that."

· 7 ·

She could never stop thinking about it. If Eddie Sisk's nephew hadn't committed suicide, which put Eddie out of reach, Jack Lowery never would have called her. And then what?

Jack's call came Friday evening, May 14, just three days after her appointment was announced. Marie had met Lowery about six weeks before. He was the Democratic mayor of Lebanon, a town some thirty miles east of Nashville. He was also a lawyer, and he had been in to see Sisk about clemency for a client, an inmate named Will E. Midgett, who was doing time for negligent vehicular homicide during a drunken spree. Midgett was in his sixties and in poor health. Turned out there was a question whether he was the actual driver of the car. Best of all, upon release, he would immediately go to Florida to live with relatives. That was always a big plus in a commutation. Let some other state worry. Marie reported to Sisk that there didn't seem to be any problems as far as the board was concerned, and Eddie told her to let Lowery know. Jack had supported the Governor, he said. Lowery returned with all sorts of documents buttressing his case, including material promising Midgett's move to Florida.

That same Friday, in the morning, Lowery had called to find out the status of the clemency. Marie put him on hold while she called John Stoker at the board. Stoker said he couldn't find the Midgett file. Maybe Traughber had it. Well, she wanted to speak to Traughber. This case had been dragging on too long. Next Traughber was hemming and hawing on the phone. He said he believed the file was with Joe Mitchell at home in Memphis and they'd have it on Monday, and Marie apologized to Lowery and said she'd be back to him on Monday for sure, and he said, "Okay, Marie, I understand how these things go."

She got home just after 7 P.M. Therese was off on a sleep-over, and Marie was looking forward to being alone, fixing herself a bowl of soup, soaking in a hot tub, reading some Yeats and getting to sleep. The week had left her wrung out.

She'd barely come through the front door when the phone rang, and it was Lowery. "Marie, I'm sorry to bother you like this. I tried to find Eddie, but I can't locate him."

"There's been a death in his family," she said, "down in Giles County."

"Yeah, gosh, that's too bad. But, Marie, I've got to talk to somebody. I even thought of calling the Governor. The most incredible thing happened. I mean, it just happened, less than two hours ago."

"*What*, Jack?"

Lowery said he hardly knew where to begin. Anyway, it was the end of the day. His secretary had already left, and he was phoning somebody when he heard a noise in his outer office and went out and found this man standing there, a guy with black hair and a beer gut, wearing a loud sport shirt, smoking a cigar.

Thinking the fellow was a potential client, he told him to wait until he got off the phone and then invited him into his office. The man identified himself as Bob Roundtree. Didn't beat around the bush at all, according to Lowery. Said he was there about something he thought would be of considerable interest to Lowery and a client of his, Will Midgett. Roundtree claimed he knew Midgett was petitioning Governor Blanton for clemency and he was in a position to guarantee clemency practically the next day—for $20,000.

"That's impossible, Jack," Marie interrupted. "That clemency's in the works. You know that as well as I do."

"Look, I'm only telling you what he told me. Who gets to see the stuff I gave Eddie?"

"Well, I saw it too, and Charlie Benson. And the board."

"Let me tell you," Lowery said. "This Roundtree knows everything from A to Z. He even knows about Midgett going to Florida, and even Midgett hasn't been told that yet. And Marie, this guy's a pro. It was like he'd done this a thousand times. He even wanted to retain me so we'd have confidentiality and started reaching for his pocket until I pointed out that obviously I was going to have to discuss it with Mr. Midgett."

Marie broke in and asked him to describe Roundtree again. The image of Bill Thompson jumped before her eyes. She thought she was hallucinating. It wasn't possible.

She hadn't heard the half of it, Lowery said. He asked Roundtree how he was going to pull this off, and Roundtree said he had connections right to the top. The Governor's office, the parole board. If it'd make Lowery happier, he wouldn't have to pay the twenty thousand until Midgett was free. "Your man will be out and on the beach in Florida—wherever you want him to be," Roundtree had said.

Lowery played along. Told Roundtree he'd need some time, and they finally agreed to meet in ten days. After Roundtree left, Lowery ran to the window and saw him getting into a black 1976 Cordoba. There was one other person in the car, perhaps more. He couldn't say. It was drizzling and misty.

He did copy the car's license number, though, and since he was the mayor, he called the cops to stop the Cordoba to find out whom it was registered to and who the driver was.

The information had been relayed to him this minute, he said. The car was in the name of "Bobby J. Hawkins." At least that was how Marie wrote it down, automatically assuming that it was a man. It would take her a while to connect it with Bobbie Jean Hawkins, the woman whose pardon she had processed last Christmas.

But she stopped thinking altogether when Lowery passed on the name of the driver. Just went completely numb. "It was, let's see here," Lowery said. "Oh yes, Tommy Ray Prater. From Chattanooga."

NINE

Jack was still talking, but Marie wasn't listening. Maybe she'd heard wrong. Would he please spell the name? And when he did, she thought, Could there be another Tommy Prater? Of course. That had to be the answer.

"Why?" Lowery said. "Do you know him?"

"No, no, I don't."

"Well, what's the deal? You sound funny."

She made a snap decision. She was speaking in confidence, she said, but she had an extradition case involving a Tommy Prater. Surely there could be more than one Tommy Prater. Didn't he think so?

"I don't know, Marie. Prater doesn't strike me as that common a name. You say he's in an extradition? I wonder what the connection is."

"My God, Jack, you know, there's got to be an explanation. Hey, I've got it. I'm going back and look at the papers. There may be a picture of him. Roundtree and Prater could be the same guy. At least we'll settle that."

She remembered walking past the capitol security guard and along the dimly lit, silent corridor, her heels echoing off the marble floor. Made it all the more spooky. And then she was letting herself into the legal counsel's office. When she turned on the lights, Eddie's door was open, his desk a familiar clutter. Poor Eddie. The tragedy in his family had hit him hard, and this was all he needed. With any luck, though, she'd have the whole thing resolved before he returned.

But when she combed through Prater's file, there were no photographs. She went through the files of the three other men. None there either. She called Lowery, and he said, "What should we do now? Should we call Eddie?"

"Jack, I don't see how we can disturb him at this moment. I mean, he was real shook up about his nephew. It was a bad scene. The funeral's tomorrow, so I expect he'll be home sometime Sunday. We'll just have to wait."

Lowery agreed, but the idea of doing nothing for two days hung heavy on the line. Marie said, "Listen, I'm the extradition officer. I'll request pictures from the sheriff's office or the Chattanooga DA first thing Monday." At least that was something positive. Still, there was a letdown. They were both so keyed up. Neither one of them wanted to get off the phone.

Lowery's description of Roundtree kept eating at her. "Jack," she said, "did you ever hear of a Bill Thompson?"

"Who's he?"

"Oh, he's some friend of Eddie's. A friend of the administration. In politics in Chattanooga. I'm surprised you haven't run across him."

"Why are you asking? Does he match up with Roundtree?"

"Well, yes. A little bit, I guess."

"But how would he know about Midgett?"

"That's it. I don't know. Look, Jack, forget I even said it. I mean, this is so far out. I don't know what I'm saying anymore. I better get on home. If you think of something else, call me there."

Better get a grip on herself too, she thought. It was cockeyed. What could a fugitive wanted by Georgia, a politician who was a friend of the Governor and an inmate up for clemency possibly have in common?

Around midnight Lowery cranked it up all over again. Said it was kind of embarrassing, but he had to have her opinion. Once, when he was discussing the Midgett clemency with Sisk, he'd said he was aware that sometimes things like this required special arranging, and if there was anything extra that had to be done, he was sure it could be worked out. According to Lowery, Sisk looked at him with a peculiar expression at first, but then told him not to worry. "Marie," Lowery asked, "you don't suppose Eddie got the wrong impression? Like I meant paying money?"

"Of course not, Jack," she said. "Eddie knows you better than that."

"Well, I would hope so, but all this stuff today has got me going every which way."

· 2 ·

This was getting out of hand. Marie wondered if she was botching things up. What if it got into the media? She could see the story now. Who knew about this? Why wasn't anything done? She began thinking that she should have called Sisk, after all. He could be inadvertently involved. The damage to him and the Governor might be incalculable.

She thought of Charlie Benson, home for the weekend in Cocke County. With the time differential, it was an hour later in East Tennessee, but Benson was still up. "Charlie, the most extraordinary, incredible thing has happened," she said, and she could sense Benson sitting straight up as she related the call from Lowery. "Yeah, yeah," he kept saying. "Then what?"

"Charlie," she said, "who does that guy remind you of?"

"Which guy?"

"Roundtree! I know this is crazy, but it's Bill Thompson to a T."

Benson's tone got sharp. "That doesn't make any sense. You're letting your imagination run away."

"Charlie, have you ever noticed how much time he spends in Eddie's office?"

"What are you driving at, Marie?"

"Well, suppose that Midgett file was on Eddie's desk and suppose Thompson came in and saw it. You know how I always worried about Eddie. He's so darn trusting. Trusts everybody. Suppose there's some reporter already picking this up. I'm worried sick."

"Listen, Marie, you didn't mention Thompson to Lowery, did you? Or Prater?"

All at once she felt guilty about Thompson, so she let that pass. Just answered the second part. Yes, she had said there was an extradition warrant out on a Tommy Prater. What was wrong with that?

"I don't think," said Benson, "you should be talking up these wild theories of yours until we know where we are."

"But shouldn't I call Eddie?"

"No! He's got enough on his mind. This can hold till Eddie gets back. Believe me, nothing's going to happen before then."

"I don't see how you can be so sure."

"Look, you told me the son of a bitch wasn't going to contact Lowery for another ten days. And besides, I'll bet he never does. Not in ten days, or ten years."

"What do you mean?"

"*Marie,* Lowery had the cops stop the car. You said it yourself. Whoever he was can put two and two together, for Christ's sake."

She had to admit she hadn't thought of that. Anyhow, she said, she was going to get right on the photographs of the four men wanted by Georgia.

"What in hell for?" said Benson.

"Maybe one of them is about five eleven, has black hair, a beer belly, smokes a cigar and wears Hawaiian print shirts."

"Cool it, Marie, will you? This could end up worse than you think. By running around on your own!" Benson's voice softened. "I wish I was there with you. You've had a long day and a big week. Don't worry. I'll tell Eddie how conscientious you've been. Wait for him. Let him make the decisions. And try to get some rest. I'm really tired. You must be too."

"Okay, Charlie, you're right," she said.

Close to 3 A.M. Lowery was calling once more. "Marie, I hope I didn't wake you."

"Are you kidding? What is it?"

"I've been racking my brains about something," the Lebanon mayor said. "Maybe I shouldn't be saying this, but I've heard rumors that the board can be bought. Now, isn't Charles Traughber from Chattanooga?"

"Yes."

"And Prater is from Chattanooga?"

"Right."

"And this Thompson character. Didn't you say he's from Chattanooga?"

She remembered Benson's warning. "Jack," she said, "I never should have brought his name into this. I mean, so what? *I'm* from Chattanooga, for that matter."

She was getting schizoid. With Benson, she'd been pushing Thompson. With Lowery, pooh-poohing the idea.

Despite the hour, she dialed Benson back. To her surprise, he appeared wide awake. Answered on the first ring.

"Charlie, I was just on with Jack Lowery," she said. "He was talking about rumors the board's on the take."

"Yeah, I've thought of that."

Marie told him how the Midgett clemency had been limping along. How, suddenly, this Friday morning, the Midgett file was missing. What about that? What about Traughber? It fitted.

For the first time Benson wasn't arguing. Perhaps she had something there, he said. What he was concerned about was not having the Governor, and Eddie, embarrassed.

"This all stinks," she said. "So help me, Charlie, if Eddie has somehow been taken in by Traughber or Thompson . . ."

"Goddamnit, Marie," Benson persisted, "why do you keep dragging Bill Thompson into this? Traughber's one thing, but Thompson's another. The guy isn't involved. I don't understand why you're always bringing his name up. What are you puffing on?"

"Charlie, I was only speculating."

She must have dozed off, although she had no sensation of sleeping. Didn't know whether it had been dreams or thoughts about Charles Traughber. But she was ready to believe anything about him. She'd been suspicious long before this. There'd been the Greer memo as well. And why had the Midgett case taken so much time? Once she started thinking about it, she recalled contacting the board two or three other times at Lowery's behest to see how it was coming. Now the file was gone. Supposedly in Joe Mitchell's possession. One more item kept haunting her. Eddie somehow was tangled up in this mess. However innocently.

She wore out the carpet waiting for 9 A.M. to call Mitchell in Memphis. She got his wife and then Joe was on, affably apologizing for not having called to congratulate her. They chatted briefly, and Marie said, "By the way, do you still have the Midgett file?"

"The what?" he said, and after she explained, Mitchell said he hadn't seen that one. Told her to hold on while he looked through some material he had brought home. No, he said, he didn't have it, but he remembered now that Traughber had talked about the case. Why didn't she give him a ring? He was pretty sure Charles must have it.

· 3 ·

Sisk finally answered his phone early Sunday afternoon. She had to see him. He was eating, he said. Couldn't this be put off till tomorrow? There was an edginess in his voice.

No, it couldn't, said Marie, it was urgent. She asked if she could come over later. He didn't want that. Said he'd meet her at the office in an hour if it was so important.

He was already there when she arrived. He was in a polo shirt, checkered trousers and sneakers. Marie had never seen him dressed like that, and she remembered thinking how youthful and athletic he looked. The annoyance he had exhibited before seemed to have disappeared.

When she finished telling him the story, he said, "Is that all?" It was as though he was being exceedingly tolerant of her for having dragged him to the office on a Sunday afternoon over nothing.

"What do you mean?" she said. "Did you hear what I just told you? A crime has been committed."

He stared right at her. "What crime?" he said. "No crime's been committed. No money has changed hands. Until it does, nothing's happened. Anybody could walk in on Lowery and offer to help get his client favorable clemency consideration. Unless something illegal was done, and unless money actually changed hands, where's the crime? No law's been broken. Jack's probably all worked up about this because he thinks it might affect Midgett's release. And it won't. I'll guarantee that."

What about Prater? she said. How would it look if it came out that a man whose extradition was being blocked had been driving a car in an extortion attempt? Prater had to be sent to Georgia first thing.

Prater, he said, *if* it was the same Prater, wasn't going anywhere. He'd promised a hearing on Prater, and he was living up to it. Even though Marie might not believe in due process, Sisk said, he did. And if she was to be the board chairman, she'd better learn what that meant.

She turned to Roundtree. It sure sounded like Bill Thompson, she said. Had Eddie ever seen Thompson without a flowered shirt, baggy pants and a cigar? "Hell, Marie," Sisk said, "there're maybe a thousand people within a mile radius that fit that description. Want me to look outside and see if I can locate one?" And then he said, a good deal more icily, "I didn't come down here to discuss Bill Thompson's wardrobe. Is there anything else?"

The pictures, she said. She was going to request them to settle exactly who was driving the car—and who might have been in Lowery's office.

She wasn't going to do anything of the sort, he ordered. She was the one who kept talking about it all ending up on the front pages, and it sure would if she went on rocking the boat. One way or another, everybody and his uncle would be sticking a nose into it, and it'd be her fault unless she got herself together and let him handle this.

Marie felt deflated. As though she'd arrived for a party and found out it had been last week.

Look, Sisk said, he'd get to the bottom of it. They had plenty of time. He'd call Lowery and set up something in case the guy came back. And he'd speak to Blanton about it. Did that make her feel better?

A thousand percent, she thought. Letting the Governor know was what she'd really been after, and as she and Eddie walked to their cars in the warm, bright sunlight, she felt relieved, even up. She remembered the strain Eddie had been under because of his nephew's suicide. That had to affect how he'd acted, and she reached out and touched his arm and offered her condolences again, chagrined that it hadn't occurred to her before.

When Marie returned to her apartment, she phoned Lowery and said Sisk would be contacting him. Also that he was going to tell the Governor. She reminded Lowery to be sure to write up a report of the incident, and he said, "Yeah, right," and thanked her for calling.

The next day she was barely at her desk when John Stoker was on the line saying that the board had scheduled a hearing on the Midgett clemency ten days hence. Stoker also said Mr. Traughber wanted to know if she was free for lunch. He'd meet her on the Legislative Plaza at noon by the cafeteria. She could hardly wait, she said.

To her surprise, Stoker was standing with Traughber. Oh boy, she thought, he's brought himself a buffer. She started off all sweetness and light. Appreciated Traughber's offer right after her appointment was announced to aid her any way he could. She really needed his expertise and support, she said, and he said his first advice was to take a nice long vacation. Get rested up.

Yes, she said, that wasn't a bad idea. Twenty minutes into the meal, she looked at him and said, "Charles, what about this Will Midgett case? Do you think there's anything unusual there?"

Marie thought he'd fall off his chair. He was just lifting a piece of meat to his mouth. The fork came down, clattering on the plate. His lips began moving, but no sound came out. She saw a muscle in his left cheek twitching violently.

"Of course," she said, smiling, "who knows what's going on with half these cases?"

"Well, uh, you know, we've got a hearing set up."

"Yes, I'm real pleased about that. There's been such a delay. Eddie'll be pleased too." Traughber, she said, appeared fatigued himself. Perhaps *he* ought to have a vacation.

She swept triumphantly into Sisk's office and told him how Traughber almost had a coronary when she mentioned the Midgett case. "You should've seen how his cheek was twitching," Marie said. "I mean, I'm telling you it was obvious this guy's in on the whole thing."

For once Sisk seemed intrigued. Agreed it was rather odd behavior. "I wonder what that means. But, hell, there's not much you can do with a twitching cheek," he said.

"I know that. It's a lead, though, and we have to follow up. Give me the go-ahead to get those pictures."

"Pictures? What's this have to do with pictures?"

"Eddie, something's going on," she said. "Now, I don't know if Traughber's got something going with Thompson, but—"

"Thompson!" Sisk yelled. His demeanor changed completely. His face flushed. "How did we get from Traughber's twitching cheek to Thompson?"

"Please, we've got to tell the Governor. Have you talked to him yet?"

"I've put in a call to him," Sisk said. "Do you want me to tell him about Traughber's cheek? Listen, Marie, quit playing Nancy Drew and get your mind on your job. I told you I'll handle this."

· 4 ·

In her calls to Lowery, she detected a new, subdued note in his voice. He said Sisk had called to assure him that in no way would any of this taint the board's review of the Midgett clemency. He hesitated, and said Sisk also told him he'd spoken to her and was going to see the Governor. "Marie, do you think he will?"

"Of course, Jack. Why wouldn't he?"

Another time Lowery said, "Well, I guess we've done all we can." It was as though he were wishing he'd never gotten in touch with her that Friday night. And she had the feeling he wasn't sharing everything he and Eddie talked about. She could just hear Sisk. Marie's, you know, a bit naive. Has to have time to grow into the job. Doesn't understand all the complexities yet.

"By the way, Jack," she said.

"Yes?"

"Don't forget that report."

"I won't."

She didn't doubt that he'd come up with something. If she'd learned one thing about political animals, it was the instinct to cover themselves. Whatever else happened, Lowery knew she knew, and who knew where it would wind up? Being an unguided missile, she thought, had its advantages.

It was all affecting her behavior more than she knew. In the middle of the week she had a date with the assistant corrections commissioner, Ramon Sanchez-Viñas. Sam Lipford had introduced Marie to Ramon at lunch one day. He was about the handsomest man she'd ever met, and in line with her old theory, she promptly put him down as undoubtedly shallow and full of himself. Dark, liquid eyes, startlingly lush lashes, a magnificent smile, a complexion she could only describe as luminous.

But she had discovered what a quick study he was—smart, sharp, perceptive. Along with the Hispanic heritage he shared with Marie, he had been raised a Catholic and was in the last stages of a divorce. If there was a drawback, it was that he was eight years younger than she. "That's all right," he needled her. "I prefer older women." Marie decided she liked him a lot. Now over dinner he was saying, "Where are you? You sure aren't with me." She wished she could speak to him about the Georgia extraditions and the visitation to Jack Lowery's office, but at that moment she didn't dare.

She told Charlie Benson, "You've got to help me on those pictures. I mean, what do we have to lose? You and Eddie are probably right, but let's look at the remote possibility this could hurt the Governor. Don't we need to head off that possibility?"

"Marie," he said, "I agree with Eddie all the way. You're making a mountain out of a molehill. If anybody's going to hurt the Governor, it's you."

She had another run-in with Sisk, the bitterest so far, on the Georgia extraditions. She'd learned that the hearing officer, Charles Grigsby, was out. The word was he'd been forced to resign. She said she supposed it meant Sisk would be handling the hearing, and Eddie replied that was correct, since a successor to Grigsby hadn't been appointed yet. And for her information, a hearing had been scheduled the last week in June. The earliest everyone could make it. Did she have any objections?

Marie felt chastened. Maybe she was pushing too hard. Who was she to question the Governor's legal counsel in the interpretation of his duties and responsibilities? For all she knew, the Governor might be taking steps she didn't know about. They didn't have to tell her what they were doing. Had every right not to, the way she'd been carrying on. Perhaps they believed she wasn't sufficiently discreet. Couldn't be trusted.

That was still her mood the next day, Saturday, when something closer to home was bothering her. The boys were away at Morris, happily ignorant of her tension, and poor Therese was bearing the brunt of it. The following week Marie would be off to the annual national convention of extradition officers. This time it would be nearer, in Annapolis, Maryland. She would have skipped it, except that she was a regional vice-president and had to be on hand to report the past year's activities. On top of everything, that had occupied her plenty.

True, Therese could stay with Virginia and Rosie, and hadn't complained a bit. But that didn't ease Marie's pangs of conscience. Therese was so entrancing. There were moments of role reversal that absolutely floored Marie. When they went shopping together in the supermarket, Therese would have a list all ready, something that never occurred to Marie, and as they went up and down the aisles it'd be Therese saying, "Oh, Momma, don't get that! That kind's no good." Or "Look at this, Momma, this is on special." Just the other night Marie had been reading when Therese started bustling around. "What are you doing, honey?" she said, and Therese said, "I think I'll do the laundry." Sometimes Marie couldn't believe Therese was her daughter. When she'd been Therese's age, she wouldn't have done the laundry without someone standing over her with a sledgehammer. Not in a million years.

So that Saturday morning Marie announced she was going to be Therese's slave for the day. She'd do the house. And she'd make breakfast. Then they'd spend the afternoon by the pool. She was serving up French toast and bacon when Eddie called. He was at the office, with Charlie, and he wanted her to come down.

· 5 ·

It started out pleasantly enough. "Marie," said Sisk, "Charlie and I've been sitting here discussing some things we're concerned about. Now,

I know you're concerned too, and I want for us to come to a definite agreement once and for all. You haven't done anything about those pictures?"

"No, of course not. You know that." She glanced at Benson. He was looking at the ceiling.

"Well, I want your solemn promise you won't try to get them," Sisk said.

"My solemn promise?"

"You heard me."

"Look, Eddie, let's forget about Traughber and Thompson. Let's concentrate on Tommy Prater. We all know a Tommy Prater was driving that car, and we all know there's a Tommy Prater Georgia wants. What's the matter with you?" She'd been floating on air, she thought, when her appointment had come through. She hadn't been kidding when she said she wanted to be an asset to the administration, and here Eddie was making it as difficult as possible. It was just like the business with her clemency card file. The same obtuse, covered-wagon mentality.

"Goddamnit," Sisk shouted. "You call the sheriff, or whoever you want to call over there, and somebody's going to say 'Why?' and the next thing that goddamn Gerbitz will find out, and before we know it, it'll be in the goddamn Chattanooga *Times.*" Sisk was pacing back and forth. "You're obsessed with those pictures. We don't need them. We have these guys. We know where they are. We're going to have a hearing. Georgia knows it. You know it. I know it. The Governor knows it. You want to know what they look like, come to the goddamn hearing! They're getting their day in court."

She was ready to give up when Benson jumped in. "Christ almighty, Marie, you've been ranting and raving about this every fucking second. You've been driving Eddie crazy. Why don't you wise up and lay off?"

She couldn't believe her ears. Right after she knew she was going to be the chairman, she had successfully lobbied for Benson to receive double her old salary as extradition officer and liaison with the board. "Who do you think you're talking to?" she said.

"The hardest-headed bitch I've ever met."

"I beg your pardon, Charlie. I don't appreciate that," Marie said, and turned toward the door.

"Aw, for Lord's sake, Charlie," Sisk said. "You're not helping." He told Benson to leave them alone. After a deep breath to calm himself, Eddie told her, "Marie, what do you suppose the Governor would say if he knew some of these wild allegations you've been running around making?"

It didn't take long for the message to sink in. Her appointment had been announced, all right, but at the rate she was going, Blanton could change his mind. And she could even be fired as extradition officer, just like that. While she was determined to get to the bottom of all this, she'd wait now until she was officially sworn in—in five weeks, July 1. It wouldn't be so easy to dispense with her then. "Okay, Eddie," she said.

The minute Marie stopped talking about photographs, about Georgia, Sisk actually became quite jolly. Told her he was going to attend the Annapolis convention of extradition officers with her. The Governor wanted to put together a task force to revamp the state criminal justice system, and Marie would be included. A federal judge had ruled that something had to be done about overcrowding in Tennessee prisons. The convention, Eddie said, might give him some insights.

As Marie suspected, what it provided him was some uninterrupted golf. She was sitting in the lobby of an Annapolis hotel, accepting congratulations on her new post, being told what a contribution to pardons and paroles she'd make, when she saw Sisk heading out for another eighteen holes, as if he didn't have a care in the world.

It was too much. She went to her room and dialed information for the Hamilton County sheriff's office in Chattanooga. By God, she was going to do it. She hadn't ever been pinned down on whether she would or wouldn't. The hell with Eddie. To hell with everyone.

She got a deputy, and identified herself as the state extradition officer. Said there was a hearing coming up on four men from the Chattanooga area. To make everything right and proper, she said, she needed their photographs. For some reason they hadn't been forwarded along with the warrants.

Pictures of them all might not be on file, the deputy said. He'd have to look. The Chattanooga police might have to be called. That was fine, she said. No rush. It was all routine. She said to make sure the envelope was addressed to her personally at the capitol and marked "Confidential."

"Yes, ma'am," the deputy said.

On Thursday, May 27, while Marie was traveling back from Annapolis, the board recommended clemency for Will E. Midgett. His sentence was reduced to time served with parole.

· 6 ·

In Nashville on Monday she met with Sisk about another conference —the annual meeting of the state's district attorneys, to be held in Memphis the following week. As part of the Governor's task force on criminal justice, Marie had suggested picking a couple of DAs for it, in effect co-opting them. Instead of having them snipe from the outside, why not have them on the team? Eddie liked the idea and asked for some names. She had put forward Richard Fisher, and also Gary Gerbitz. The mention of Gerbitz had him climbing the wall, and she said who better? Wasn't he the one causing the most trouble? Well, Sisk said, he'd have to think hard about that.

Then Marie excused herself. She had a doctor's appointment. Would be back in an hour or so. About six weeks before, she'd been unscrewing a recalcitrant light bulb. It shattered in her hand, and some fragments of glass had gotten embedded in her right index finger. She had picked out the pieces but apparently not all of them. Now the finger was swollen and throbbing painfully.

On the way out, she passed by her desk and saw the envelope from the Hamilton County sheriff's office, stamped "Confidential." She gave a quick, guilty look around, and took it with her.

That afternoon she was admitted to the Vanderbilt hospital for emergency surgery. "You have a felon in there," the doctor had said.

"A *what?*" she said with a burst of laughter.

"I don't see where it's so funny. You could lose the finger."

That sobered her up fast. "I'm sorry. It's just that— Oh, forget it," she said.

The next day she lay in bed, her hand wrapped in a bulky bandage and held above her head on some kind of pulley. Tubes were connected to her left arm feeding her intravenously with glucose and antibiotics. She shivered at the thought of having a missing finger. Her doctor told her it'd been a close call.

She had a parade of visitors. Sam Lipford, Murray Henderson carrying a basket of daisies, and, of course, Ramon. Both Charlie and Eddie came, and she watched horrified as Eddie stood there, a hand inches from the Hamilton County envelope on her bedside table, making jokes about the new pardons chairman walking around with a felon in her finger. But he never noticed it.

As soon as she could, Marie phoned Lowery, explained where she was and said she had the pictures. She had looked at them herself, but all she saw were the faces of four seedy characters, none of them resembling Lowery's description, and when Jack came to the hospital and examined them, he said, "Our friend Roundtree isn't in this bunch."

Well, she said, that left the cop who stopped the car, and Lowery said he'd show the mug shots to him, but he asked Marie if they really should be pursuing this any further. Wasn't it up to the Governor now? And she said they had no choice. It had gone too far.

Despite her doctor's admonition to take it easy, she was determined to go to the conference of district attorneys. It was too good a chance to pass up, being able to meet them all at once just as she was starting out, to express personally her desire to work with them on paroling problems. And she was also scheduled to speak to them as a group.

Eddie was busy politicking when she arrived at the welcoming reception in the Hyatt Regency Hotel. He immediately squired her around, introducing her to DA after DA, wisecracking about the felon when they inquired about her bandaged finger, noting that they were viewing not only beauty but brains, that she'd been a star student at Vanderbilt and that she'd bring commitment and dedication to her chairmanship. It was why Ray Blanton had selected her, Eddie said. With each DA she tried earnestly to get in a few words about how she knew district attorneys had been largely ignored in the past by the board, even to the point of not being informed when clemency was being considered on one of their cases. That would change under her stewardship, she said. She wouldn't invite their input, she'd insist upon it. All in all, she thought, she was making the right impression.

The district attorney she wanted to meet the most was the one Sisk didn't introduce her to, Gary Gerbitz. So on her own, she asked somebody if he wasn't there, and he was pointed out to her. He was about six foot one, slim, intense, square-jawed, Mr. DA himself.

She moved into a circle where he was holding forth. Marie was sure he knew who she was, but he didn't acknowledge her presence. It figured, she thought. He was Republican and anti-Blanton. Saw her as another instrument of the enemy.

She waited until the circle broke up. "I'm from Chattanooga myself, Mr. Gerbitz. Born there thirty-three years ago," she said, and gave him her best smile.

"Really?"

"Yes, and every time I go back, I'm struck that there's something about Chattanooga that sets it apart from other cities in the state. More cosmopolitan, I guess." She chose her words carefully. "Like politics. I mean, here you are a Republican district attorney in a Democratic city. How'd you do it?"

That got him going, and she listened patiently as he described the way he'd slaughtered the longtime Democratic incumbent. She asked if Ward Crutchfield was still running the show, and he said yes, as incompetently as ever. She mentioned a couple of other Chattanooga Democrats. Then she said, "Have you ever heard of Bill Thompson?"

Marie was stunned by his response. Bill Thompson was the scum of the earth. And slippery as an eel, he said. He'd been trying to nail Thompson for he didn't know how long. Thompson was in everything you could think of. Pulled strings all over Chattanooga. By the time Gerbitz was through, Thompson sounded like a Mafia kingpin instead of the party wheelhorse she'd been hearing about.

She wanted to get away from the subject of Thompson before it occurred to Gerbitz to ask why she was asking. She told him she was aware of how highly critical he'd been of the board and hoped they could meet to improve relations. Sometimes, though, the criminal justice system seemed to work at cross-purposes, she said. As Gerbitz probably knew, she was finishing up as extradition officer, and there was always a conflict of some kind, such as another state going after someone Tennessee wanted to prosecute first. She waited a beat. For instance, she murmured as innocently as she could, there was that Tommy Prater case. How was it coming along?

Gerbitz blew sky-high. Did she mean to tell him Prater hadn't been packed off to Georgia yet? Prater was a no-good punk, but the charges against him in Chattanooga were nothing compared with what he was up for in Georgia. Just receiving some stolen property. He'd already advised Sisk weeks ago, he said, that he wasn't going to stand in the way of sending Prater and those other jokers back.

Hastily she said she believed a hearing on the extraditions would be held the last week of June, and this appeared to mollify Gerbitz some, but he was still shaking his head when he said it was odd she'd mentioned Thompson and Prater almost in the same breath. In Chattanooga they were with each other all the time. Prater was at Thompson's beck and call.

Marie thought she would become violently ill on the spot. Felt the cold sweat pop out on her brow. Gerbitz was staring at her curiously. "Are you all right?" he said. "Is there something wrong?"

No, she said, she was okay. It was only that she'd had this operation on her finger and hadn't fully recovered. Would he forgive her for a moment?

She managed to nod her way past a couple of people and just made it to the rest room. Inside, she leaned against the door. The image of Thompson making himself at home in Eddie's office with a cigar in his mouth rushed at her. Her gorge rose. She braced herself on the wash basin, fighting waves of nausea. Tears were streaming down her cheeks. She gulped in air, bathed her face in cold water and finally began to pull herself together. With her good hand she did the best she could with her makeup. Combed her hair. She had locked the door, and there were repeated knocks on it. She couldn't stay in there forever. She would have to go out and mix and mingle as if everything were perfectly normal. She had to do it and she had to do it now, she told herself, and she did, walking past two irate women, saying she was sorry, she hadn't been feeling too well.

Gerbitz, thank God, had moved off. She didn't think she could cope with him again right then. She went off to dinner with a group. She didn't remember who was in it. Or what anyone talked about.

· 7 ·

In the morning she decided what she had to do. Part of it, she'd reflect, was because there remained less than two weeks before she would be sworn in, and it was really too late to reverse that. She'd been working over at the board almost as though she were already running it. She'd been introduced to all the DAs as the new chairman. Too many questions would be raised. The other part, the part Marie liked to believe truly motivated her, was that she wanted to be open with Eddie about the pictures. Show him he was going about the episode in Lebanon entirely the wrong way. That he was being badly, maybe fatally, used.

She waited till eight o'clock to call and say she wanted to see him. He groaned and said all right, come to his room. When she knocked on the door, he emerged in golf gear and said Claudette was dressing. What was it?

So in a hallway of the Memphis Hyatt Regency she told him she had ordered the photographs and had given them to Jack Lowery.

The color came out of his face. He looked up and down the hallway. She could see he could barely restrain from screaming at her. Actually he *was* screaming at her, in a whisper. His eyes bulged. His neck cords distended. It would have been sort of funny, if she hadn't been such a nervous wreck.

"You what?" he said in a strangled tone.

"I ordered those pictures."

"You promised me you wouldn't."

"I did not," she said. "Eddie, listen to me. I talked to Gary Gerbitz last night. He says that down in Chattanooga, Thompson and Prater are like ham and eggs."

Sisk's eyes rolled back. She thought they were going to disappear. "Gerbitz!" he said, his voice cracking now like an adolescent boy's. "You talked to him about this?"

"Eddie, give me some credit. Gerbitz doesn't suspect a thing. I just struck up a casual conversation with him. I know you don't want to believe it, and I'm sure Bill Thompson is a likable fellow, but Eddie, he's taking you for a ride, and you've got to see it. We've got to confront this. We've got to do something about it."

"My God, Marie. I'm going back to the original thing I told you. To this day, nothing has gone down, Marie. It's been a month, and no money has passed hands. Can't you get that through your head?"

"Eddie," she said, "I'm not trying to harm you. I'm trying to help you. You don't honestly believe I'd say anything to Gerbitz to embarrass us. Nothing's happened the way you put it, but something did happen. So nobody's going to know. But shouldn't *we* know? Isn't that better than living in ignorance?"

She reached out to him. He pulled away. "You better hope this doesn't get out," he said. "If it does, you're through, Marie. Finished!" He stalked back into his room, slamming the door.

Marie returned to her own room disheartened. She had to talk to somebody. And she thought of Murray Henderson, right there in the hotel. She'd come to admire him greatly since she first sought his support for the chairmanship. Highly intelligent. Thoroughly professional in his work. Dedicated, it seemed, to upgrading the state corrections system. Except that he sometimes hit the bottle—and both Sam and Ramon said it resulted from the unbelievable stress of supervising major penitentiaries—she couldn't recall a bad word about him.

The more she considered the idea, the better it came across. His appointment as corrections commissioner had been on merit. Henderson certainly wasn't any political crony of the Governor's. Marie remembered that once over cocktails the two of them started talking about religion. Murray was an Episcopalian. He had said it didn't matter what you were, even an atheist, if you'd thought it through. That was the important thing. She agreed absolutely. Murray, she thought, was a good man. Besides, Sisk liked him. Perhaps Henderson could help her with Eddie.

She dialed his room and said, "I hope I didn't wake you."

"Not at all. I was just getting ready to go to breakfast."

"Well, how would you like some company?"

"I can't think of a better way to start the day," he said.

At the table, Henderson told her she'd made a good impact on the DAs. Had heard them all talking about her.

Coming from him, she said, that was high praise, and he added, "You've got to watch out for them, though. They'll smile at you—and stab you in the back. All they're looking for is to make a name for themselves."

Henderson was digging into his fried eggs, over easy, when he said, "What did I do to deserve the honor of having breakfast with you?"

"Commissioner," she said, "I need your advice on something that I think is very important to all of us. When I say all of us, I mean you and me—and the Governor and Eddie."

"Eddie Sisk?"

"Yes, Eddie," and then she reminded him she was still officially the extradition officer, and there was an extradition that was being suspiciously obstructed, and along with this an extortion attempt in a clemency case. She'd looked into it, she said, and the two appeared to be linked and included at least one person who was a friend of both Eddie's and the Governor's. The thing was, she said, that she couldn't get Sisk to do anything.

All of a sudden Henderson wasn't so friendly. Forgot his eggs. Kind of jabbed at them on his plate.

"Maybe you could help Eddie see the light," she persisted. "He'd listen to you."

"You say you've spoken to Sisk?"

"Yes."

"Well, if I were you," said C. Murray Henderson, "I would concentrate not on what's happened in the past but the future. You've got a big enough job coming up as it is. When I was appointed myself, I didn't waste time worrying about past history. That's my advice. You've told Sisk. It's not your problem anymore."

She didn't argue. Henderson just wanted to get up and get off.

When she returned to her room, the only person she could think of talking to was Jack Lowery, and she'd already talked herself to death with him. But she phoned him to find out about the report. He'd been meaning to call her, he said. He was sending it on. He'd had to wait until the officer who stopped the car went over the pictures. It had taken a while because by the time the Cordoba was spotted, it was out of Lebanon and in another town, Murfreesboro. According to the cop there, the driver seemed to be the same Tommy Prater. He wasn't sure, but from the photographs, he also believed another passenger in front was Bruce McBryar. A third man was in the rear seat. The man had kept his head bowed, however, and the cop didn't have a good look at him.

So that was that. She felt none of the exhilaration she might have expected earlier. She told Lowery how dejected she was, about what had taken place in her conversations with Sisk and Henderson, her dread of what lay ahead. "What am I going to do?" she asked, and the next thing Lowery was saying was "Marie, Marie . . ."

She had started keeping a diary, and she wrote it down. What Jack said.

Forget all this, Marie. I know you have 3 children, & how hard you've worked to support them, putting yourself through school. Think about it, honey. After all these years, you at last have a GOOD job, one where you know you can care for yourself and your children. DON'T BLOW IT! I know it looks bad, but you can't change the system. You can fight & you can struggle—I know you have high ideals—but in the end, you'll lose, & your children will lose, too. DON'T TRY TO FIGHT IT! It was there before you got there, & it'll be there long after you're gone. I admire you, Marie. Not many could do what you've done. You have a chance now to enjoy life, & to enjoy the fruits of your labor. DON'T BE

DESTROYED! You deserve better. Honey, this system is huge and
YOU'RE JUST ONE LITTLE GIRL!

After she had hung up, she remained on the bed, eyes closed. Lowery
must have said "Don't let this destroy you!" five or six times. She felt
so alone.

· 8 ·

Lowery's six-page report, headed CONFIDENTIAL, was addressed to Sisk
and Marie. Stapled to it was a supplementary police report about
stopping the car.

While the report was somewhat antiseptic, considering Lowery's
initial reaction, all the main points were covered. Marie was irritated
a little that it implied Eddie was as anxious as she to get the facts, but
that was Jack touching every base. Most important, Lowery wrote that
Sisk had "indicated" he had discussed the incident with the Governor.

Lowery also advised it was unlikely he'd be receiving another visit
from the mysterious Roundtree. In halting the car for a driver's check,
the Murfreesboro cop unwittingly told the occupants he was doing so
at the request of the Lebanon Police Department. The report made no
direct connection between Roundtree and Bill Thompson. *The uniden-*
tified person in my opinion is from the Chattanooga area, wrote Lowery,
letting it go at that.

The ball, he concluded in so many words, was in the Governor's
court. Don't hesitate to call if he could be of further service.

The last week in June she attended a three-day conference of the
corrections department at the Henry Horton State Park in Columbia,
Tennessee. It would give her a chance to meet all the top prison
people, as well as regional parole directors, in a relaxed atmosphere.
But right off, one of the directors, a woman, delivered a passionate
plea, almost a speech, to Marie, imploring her to change the board's
attitude toward parole revocation hearings. A parole officer, she said,
didn't recommend revoking a parole lightly. Parole officers wanted an
offender integrated back into the community as much as anyone else,
but it didn't always work. The board, however, inevitably ignored
these recommendations, undermining the whole concept of parole.
Other parole officers agreed that parole regulations had no significant

impact on a former inmate's conduct. So it was worse than she had imagined. Not only were judges and DAs up in arms about the board's policies, but most of the parole officers to boot. Some even suggested it was hard to say where incompetence ended and payoffs began.

When she got back to Nashville, Marie learned that the long-delayed hearing on the Georgia warrants that Sisk was to preside over had been postponed again. Eddie had an unavoidable conflict in his schedule.

TEN

She'd bide her time. After Memphis, she stopped hounding Sisk about either the Georgia extraditions or Bill Thompson and the Will Midgett clemency. At that point Marie was stymied. Henderson had said to forget it. Lowery had told her to think of herself. Anesthetize thyself. Basically, all she had were suspicions. No real proof yet. She had to find someone she trusted. Someone who could help.

It was remarkable, though, how quickly Eddie reverted to his old friendly ways with her as soon as the whole subject was dropped. She could almost hear the wheels turning: Marie's finally got herself under control. A temporary aberration. She'd learn to get along. Had too much to lose. And, she supposed, there was always his concern about what she might do if her place on the board was snatched from her at the last minute.

Eddie called her on June 30 to get over to Justice Henry at the Supreme Court to be sworn in. She was taken by surprise. She'd thought it would be July 1, and that was why on her big day Sisk was the only one in attendance.

Reverentially, she read the oath of office prepared by one of the typists in the legal counsel's office and, to her horror, saw the ungrammatical insertion of a "that" in the sentence where she swore to "faithfully and impartially" discharge her duties. When she showed it to Eddie, he said, "Come on, it doesn't matter. There isn't time." "It does matter," she said, and right in Justice Henry's chambers, she borrowed some Liquid Paper and blotted it out, and then with her right hand raised, she declared, "I will administer justice without respect to persons and dispense equal rights to the poor and rich. . . . So help me God."

The early swearing-in gave Marie a jump on the Florida trip she had been planning. She was taking the Fourth of July week off to go to Daytona Beach. She'd been looking forward to it for a long time. The boys were back from Morris, and it would be the first vacation she'd ever had with all the kids. When Sisk heard about it, he told her that Bill Thompson had a condominium down that way. Maybe it was free, and she could save herself some cash money. He'd used it, he said, and it was real nice. His secretary, Janice, had too. Ask her. Marie had been thrown for a loop. Was Eddie somewhere in outer space?

An added attraction would be the drive itself. After years of beat-up, secondhand automobiles and a yellow Volkswagen bug she most recently owned, she had celebrated her chairmanship by buying a silver BMW 2002. She could have had a state car, but she would be on the road constantly, holding hearings and conferring with DAs and judges, trying to mend the breach that existed between them and the board, and she needed a car she could depend upon, especially traveling in the East Tennessee mountains, yet one in which she could comfortably load up her children when she had to. And she would receive a healthy usage allowance.

Ramon's mother lived in Fort Lauderdale, and he was thinking of visiting her the same week. It was decided they'd go together. He would stay over in Daytona for a day or two and rent a car to drive on. Marie had reserved adjoining motel rooms. He could bunk in with Dante and Ricky, while she and Therese shared the other room. Therese had taken to Ramon immediately. Started calling him Romeo, and the boys, of course, picked it up.

Marie warned him that riding with the kids might not be such a bargain. Sure enough, an hour out of Nashville she had to pull over, reach for a hairbrush and allocate a few licks. Ramon whispered, "Aren't you afraid you'll hurt somebody?" and she said, "Are you kidding?" By Chattanooga, he was brandishing the brush as well, but she was happy to note that a stern look from him sufficed after that. It was the old story, she thought. A man in the house.

She had been dating Ramon quite regularly. He had become involved in correctional work really by accident. Had a degree in urban planning and had been hired by the Dunn administration to program and evaluate prison population needs. He'd considered the project an interesting, temporary challenge but within three years had risen to be number three in the department. Marie had let him know bits and pieces of what was grinding at her. An extradition that was being politically fixed, or so it seemed. Funny business surrounding a clemency case. No details, however. No names. And Ramon hadn't pried. She found that gratifying. Besides his other attractive qualities, Ramon knew when to be discreet.

But now, having passed Chattanooga, actually speeding by Dalton, Georgia, on the Interstate, she began recounting the whole story. Just talking about it with someone who shared her values was therapeutic.

Ramon remembered at first thinking that this was cops-and-robbers stuff. Marie's imagination running wild. It wasn't possible. She was reading far more into it than was there. Her emotional intensity got to him, however. He could hear it in her voice when she described her breakfast with Henderson. How unresponsive Henderson had been.

Well, that was Murray. Murray was a team player. Honest, but didn't go looking for trouble, Ramon said. A disturbing thought seized him. He was glad he wasn't in her shoes.

"What do you think?" she said.

"From what you've told me," Ramon said, "Eddie's a crook."

There it was, out in the open. "Yes, maybe," she said. "Or maybe he's only being used. But it doesn't matter anymore."

He asked what she was going to do next, and Marie said she had to find someone she could turn to who knew the law. Sisk had said no laws had been broken. For all she knew, he was right. She was thinking of this lawyer, Bill Leech. After Maribeth Freeman had married State Senator Ed Blank, Marie had met Leech a couple of times at their house. Leech was considered a comer in Democratic politics. He was closemouthed, and everybody said integrity was his middle name.

Ramon said he didn't know Leech, and she said, "I could go to the FBI."

"You couldn't, not now, could you?"

She replied that she didn't know. "What should I do?" she said.

"Steer clear of Sisk and Benson, for sure."

But what then? One way or another, it always came out the same.

Nobody could tell her. In effect, everyone was saying this was bigger than she was. Whatever she did had to be her decision.

Ramon said it could get rough. Her new job and all. And the kids. That was too bad, she said. She wanted this job more than anything, but she had to chance it. At least she couldn't be gotten rid of that easily. Now she wasn't just another hired hand shuffling extradition papers. As for the children, she'd toughed it out with them before, and if need be, they'd do it again.

She meant it, Ramon thought. Every word.

The lady at the motel desk assumed they were a family. "Sign right here," she said to Ramon. "Ragghianti. Two rooms. We'll put in an extra bed for the children."

"No, I'll sign," Marie said.

"Hurray, we get our room, and Romeo and Momma get theirs," Ricky shouted.

"Wait a minute," Marie said, drawing them away from the desk. "You boys and Ramon are going to be in one room, and Therese and I'll be in the other."

"No, no, we want to stay together," they chorused.

"Listen," Marie said.

"Let them stay together," Ramon said.

"Momma, *please!*"

The desk lady was staring. "All right, okay, you all win," Marie said.

When Ramon met Marie, the word he heard around the corrections department was she was Eddie Sisk's girl friend. That was why she was on the board. He knew now that wasn't true, and he sensed he was getting to her. That night in Daytona Beach he made his move, but he got only so far before she said, "Hold up."

He didn't fight it. To tell the truth, he half expected it. Her Catholicism was the problem, he told himself. Marie was exactly like his mother. He wouldn't be able to bed down Marie unless they were married, or in a situation where marital vows were academic. And just coming out of a bad marriage, he wasn't ready to make that commitment. Wasn't even sure it would have made a difference anyway at that moment. He consoled himself with the knowledge that plenty of other women were homing in on him. He would, as he put it, split the sheets with them while he continued to see Marie.

Later, after things got bad for her and he would hear all the rumors that Marie was sleeping around, he would laugh. Let them have their fairy tales, he'd think.

· 2 ·

When she returned to Nashville, she phoned Bill Leech. In her heart, she wanted someone savvy to listen to her and say it wasn't what she thought. Marie chatted with Leech for a few minutes and said she would like to see him, and he said, "What about?" and she said she needed to do it in person, and he said, "Can you give me some idea?" and she said she didn't want to discuss it over the phone. He was tied up right then, he said, and would get back to her. Since Leech lived in Columbia, about forty miles south of Nashville, it wasn't as though she could walk across the street to meet with him.

After waiting a couple of days, she thought about trying him again, but didn't. She couldn't decide whether it was sheer annoyance at Leech—or a sudden ambivalence on her part.

Besides, she had plunged into being chairman.

Her office was on the Department of Correction's floor at the First American Center, a high rise four blocks down from capitol hill. She was in Traughber's old office. Now Traughber, like Joe Mitchell, essentially worked out of his residence, stopping by to pick up material for prospective clemency cases.

A man from personnel talked to her about salary. The range in her category was $24,000 to $28,000, he explained, unfolding some charts, and before she could say twenty-four was fine, he suggested $26,400, Marie being both a new member and the chairman. It was, he said, more than Traughber had been getting. There would be increases, of course, and she'd also have an expense allowance of around four hundred a month. Did that meet with her approval? he asked, and she thought, My God, yes! "Whatever you deem appropriate," she said.

Another fellow came by to see about redecorating her office. Most of Traughber's furnishings were in leather. She needed something feminine, yet executivelike, the decorator advised. Chairs along French Provincial lines, perhaps. A different sofa. A less massive desk. And curtains. He produced fabrics. Yellow with a floral design for the sofa.

A paler yellow for the chairs. "How about a silver tea service?" she said, laughing.

Actually, she would have liked a more feminine decor. She never got around to it. In the end her only personal imprint was a triptych on her desk with snapshots of Dante, Ricky and Therese.

She had more pressing priorities, it turned out. A manila envelope with confidential clemency material disappeared from her desk. She launched a frantic hunt. Finally John Stoker said, "Marie, I don't want to burst any bubbles, but this happens all the time. It'll show up. In a day, a week."

She called in Sherry Lomax, the board's executive secretary, and Sherry said, "Yeah, it happens. Stuff disappears, but before you know it, there it is again." Sherry was in her late twenties. She had silky bleached blond hair and could have been rather attractive if she hadn't been overweight. Ever since Marie's arrival, Sherry had been on an indispensability kick. She looked nervously at Marie. It was as if she, and everyone else connected with the board, had learned to live with the reality of missing files, and now all anybody wanted was for the new chairman to calm down. "I'll stay late if you want," Sherry said.

Three days later the envelope was miraculously back on Marie's desk. Then the log indicating which board member had a particular file was nowhere to be found. A week passed before it reappeared. So instead of selecting fabrics, Marie devoted herself to obtaining new locks for her office and the board files. Only she, Sherry and John were to have keys.

She learned that two females on the clerical staff were on work release. Also, a young black man named George Edwards was a parolee. Edwards rang a bell. He had been a prisoner assigned to the executive mansion whose sentence for armed robbery was commuted by Blanton the previous Christmas.

She decided to remove them. When Murray Henderson protested, citing budgetary and rehabilitation reasons, Marie said, "I want to help these people as much as you do, but you don't give an alcoholic a job as a bartender, and you don't give inmates and former inmates access to clemency files." Henderson appeared to be taken aback by her intransigence.

More material had mysteriously vanished. Normally a clemency file contained written comments by each board member concerning the petition under review. Marie looked up the Billy Gene Cole case. All the notes about him were gone. The same was true for Larkin H. Bibbs

Jr. Among other papers missing from the Bibbs folder was a Sisk memo to the board ordering clemency consideration. She was appalled to find that Bibbs had served only three months and two days in the penitentiary on his murder conviction before Blanton signed his release, and she recalled how Charlie Benson had rewritten the card for Bibbs in her liaison file. Charlie, it seemed, had tacked on an extra year to the prison time Bibbs actually served. Undoubtedly he would claim it was inadvertent. Indeed, everything was so conveniently sloppy that sloppiness itself could always bear the ultimate blame. Marie could hear it now: No crimes had been committed.

It also became clear that the board never included any derogatory data in a clemency inspired by Sisk. Then and there she resolved this was going to change. The board might be duty-bound to honor and investigate a request from the legal counsel's office, but if the case didn't stand up, it would be rejected.

She even found instances where hearings were conducted without available records. They'd been lost or mislaid. She began to go a little nutty trying to revise procedures from scratch.

That was why, she would think later, she made such a terrible mistake. First it had been Stoker, her administrative aide, complaining about Sherry Lomax. Next Sherry, as executive secretary, would be bad-mouthing John. It had gotten intolerable. One or the other had to leave. Marie associated Stoker with the old regime. Sherry was newer on the job and appeared so efficient and reliable. So Marie went to Sam Lipford and arranged to have Stoker become a parole officer and made Sherry the acting administrative aide. It was a decision she never ceased to regret.

Her first hearing, at the main prison in Nashville, was unnerving. The petitioner, a rather good-looking white man in his thirties serving a sentence for fraud, sat directly opposite her at the table. She immediately sensed an arrogance when he stared at her. He lolled back in his chair, almost leering. My God, she thought, this guy was coming on to her. As though that was all it would take. She remembered the sudden fury in his eyes when his petition was denied.

If she didn't have time to refurbish her office, at least she would redo herself. Her hair, which she usually let fall below her shoulders, she now pinned up or pulled back in a bun. She wore shirtwaist dresses. No more pantsuits. Nothing tight. She'd developed a slight nearsightedness, and glasses had been suggested for driving. She got a pair with a stern

tortoise-shell frame and made sure to have them perched on her nose
at every hearing from then on.

· 3 ·

There'd be many others, but no case better set the tone between Marie
and the Blanton administration than that of Rose Lee Cooper.

The Cooper clemency had started before Marie had been sworn in,
while she was still Sisk's liaison with the board. According to Eddie,
Rose Lee Cooper was in on some drug-related arrest, but there were
a lot of extenuating circumstances. Cooper had quite a few children,
currently in California, who needed their mother. And as soon as she
got clemency, she would quit the state and join them. Get the board
going, Sisk had said. Rose Lee Cooper was a black woman from Memphis, and the Fords were interested in this one. Marie didn't have to
be told who the Fords were. Memphis had come a long way since
old-time, segregationist Boss Ed Crump. The Fords, black and brothers, were in power now. Harold was a U.S. congressman, John a state
senator and Emmitt a state representative. John, said Sisk, was the most
interested.

Marie had barely settled in as chairman when Charlie Benson was
on the horn about scheduling Cooper for a hearing, and she took
another look. Rose Lee had a long history of drugs and prostitution. She
did have six children, four out of wedlock, but all were being cared for
by her mother. And from every indication, her present husband wasn't
exactly a candidate for the poorhouse. At the time of her arrest, she
had in her possession $25,000 worth of heroin and $3,500 of cocaine
concealed, as the report delicately put it, "between her legs." To top
everything, Marie told Benson, Rose Lee Cooper had hardly had time
to unpack her bags out at the women's prison. Forget it, she said. It
was a bad case all around.

"Schedule it," Benson said. "Eddie wants it."

She called Sisk and began to paint the same dismal picture. What
would he tell Senator Ford? Eddie said, and Marie said she'd call Ford
herself. The senator certainly wouldn't like the Governor embarrassed.
Maybe work release could be arranged for Rose Lee. Sisk grabbed on
to that. Agreed to have a hearing put off, for a while anyway.

But the pressure mounted. In mid-July Marie was at the Hyatt
Regency in Memphis on board business when Ben Haynes called.
Haynes nominally was deputy commissioner of personnel, but he was

right in there with the Governor. And even closer to the Governor's brother Gene. As a matter of fact, he said he was with Gene at that very second, in a hotel by the airport.

"We'd like for you to come out and have some drinks and dinner with us," Haynes said.

"Ben, I appreciate your thinking of me, but I just don't have the energy tonight." The thought of being with Gene Blanton repelled her. People could make jokes about Ray Blanton being a redneck, but Gene personified one. A friend of Marie's had seen him at a convention with a pack of cigarettes stuck in a rolled-up shirt sleeve. Can you imagine, the friend had said. The brother of the governor of the State of Tennessee. Marie hadn't doubted it for an instant.

"Hell," said Haynes, "we'll send a car for you. You don't have to drive."

"No, you don't understand. I'm awfully tired, and I have a lot of work, and I have to get up early." She sensed his displeasure. "Is there something I can do for you?"

Well, since she'd mentioned it, he said, there was this clemency on a woman he'd like to see helped. Really deserving.

"Oh. Who?"

"Let me see. Her name is, uh, Cooper, I think."

"A black woman from Memphis? Drug charges?"

"Right. That's her. Got a bunch of kids. She needs to be with her kids. Nobody's caring for them. It's mighty sad."

She'd had about enough of this, Marie thought. But she had to hand it to Rose Lee Cooper. For a downtrodden lady, she sure could turn out the troops. "Ben, I really appreciate how you feel. I've gotten quite a few calls on her. She's a fortunate woman. A lot of people are interested in her welfare. I'm sure you've talked to Charlie Benson, though. I'm afraid it isn't a good case."

"Oh," said Haynes, his voice getting hard, "you've already decided against this poor creature. Marie, I thought you were my friend, *our* friend."

"You know I'm your friend, Ben. I hope you're my friend. I'm trying to do what's best for the Governor."

"Is that it? Case closed, or what?"

"Ben," Marie said sweetly, "no case is ever closed. We're just now making a decision about a hearing. I'll let you know." She was about to broach the possibility of work release when Haynes hung up.

A week later, in Nashville, Benson called. "Goddamnit, Marie, schedule Rose Lee Cooper."

"Charlie, you know as well as I do I talked to Eddie and he said never mind."

"Well, I just talked to him and he said never mind what he said. Do it!"

When she phoned Sisk, he immediately went off on another tangent. "I don't understand," he said with some asperity, "why you and Charlie can't get along."

"Look, Eddie, Cooper is a bad case. Charlie has evidently promised somebody we're giving Cooper a clemency recommendation."

"Marie, do what Charlie says. Set up a hearing for Cooper now, today."

She took a deep breath and said, "I can't do that."

"Why?"

"Because we promised the DAs in Memphis we'd give them a month's notification on a hearing, and you backed me up. How's that going to look?"

"All right, goddamnit. Then send the damn notification letter today."

A new extradition hearing officer had been appointed to replace Charles Grigsby, and at the end of July he recommended that Prater and company be returned to Georgia. Sisk countermanded the ruling. The hearing officer, he said, had not followed procedures. The procedures called for "findings of fact and conclusions of law" only. The hearing officer was not supposed to recommend. That was the sole prerogative of the Governor.

In the state attorney general's office, David Raybin had moved up, and a young man named Bob Grunow was in extraditions. Marie bumped into Grunow, who told her, "Didn't you teach those guys before you left? I mean, what in hell are they doing over there?"

· 4 ·

It was the same as going to the dentist, she thought. The longer you waited, the worse it got, but you kept putting it off, hoping somehow the ache would get better. If Prater and the others had been sent back, just maybe she could have lived with everything else. She'd never know.

She clung to the idea that Sisk wasn't very bright. An unwitting dupe. Instead of crooked, she wanted to see dumb. But when you got down to it, nobody seemed to want to do anything. She needed legal advice badly. She tried Bill Leech again and wasn't able to reach him. She considered Gary Gerbitz. She was sure Gary would leap in with both feet. But he was a Republican, and that would immediately cloud the issue. The last thing Marie wanted was to turn this into a political football. She was, by God, still a Democrat.

She started thinking about Richard Fisher, who had written on her behalf to Blanton. In going through the board records, she discovered one of the reasons why. About that time Fisher had fired off a scathing letter to Traughber protesting clemency for an especially brutal murderer. *I don't care if he is the best prisoner in the entire system and the Wednesday night chaplain,* Fisher wrote. *Please reevaluate the methods you choose to lighten penitentiary burdens.*

Fisher was thirty-nine. On the surface he appeared to be more a ladies' man than a hard-nosed DA. But when Marie checked around, she heard nothing but good about him—foursquare and, best of all, a staunch Democrat, the first Democratic DA in his multicounty rural district northeast of Chattanooga. He had won by about six hundred votes in 1972, and his second time out he more than tripled that margin. He had even worked for Blanton's election.

She was going to be in Chattanooga in August, and she called to ask if she could see him. "You bet, Marie," he said.

Pangs of guilt about loyalty promptly descended upon her. Not the political kind. She was contemptuous of that, the sort of hack devotion that was held in greater esteem than competence or intelligence.

It was personal. She saw herself being called a ratfink, an informer. Despite everything, Eddie Sisk was her friend. Had hired her. That alone was a huge factor. There was also her obligation to the Governor.

Maybe she ought to resign. Take a walk. God knows, they could certainly get someone a lot more cooperative than she was. She thought about it. But she thought, as well, how people were always talking about contributing to society, yet how many of them ever got an opportunity to make a significant impact on the social scheme of things? In this job she was in a position to affect not only a few lives but many, many lives, in a way that mattered. She thought about being seventy, say, and looking back at this time and asking herself if she had done her best. Did she want to recall that she had turned her back on that challenge?

She searched her soul. Where did her loyalty lie? To Eddie? He could be maimed by this. To the people of Tennessee, however grandiose that sounded? Didn't she owe them? Or how about an inmate who knew the guy in the next cell was buying his way out?

Loyalty, Marie discovered, wasn't so simple. But she had to act. By not acting, she was being cowardly. So, of course, it was loyalty to her conscience that finally counted, and if it cut across a friendship, well then, the friendship was no longer viable.

She comforted herself with the thought that at least Fisher wouldn't jump at the chance to rip Sisk, or the Governor, to shreds.

Marie met him the afternoon of August 18 on the deck of the Ruby Tuesday restaurant in Chattanooga. It took her about an hour to go through the story. She noticed he didn't interrupt. When she had finished, she prepped herself for him to jolly her out of her foreboding. Tell her she was seeing things that weren't there.

Instead, he quietly said, "You've been under terrible stress, haven't you?"

"Yes," she said. "I think I've waited too long on this."

"We have to go to the FBI," Fisher said. Just like that.

"The FBI?"

"Yeah," he said, misunderstanding her response. The Tennessee Bureau of Criminal Identification was out of the question. Under the Blanton administration, it wasn't independent anymore, he said. Everybody knew it.

"Oh."

"You've really gotten yourself in the middle of something. Do you realize the magnitude of what you've told me?"

"Eddie says no crime's been committed," she said.

"Eddie knows better than that."

She remembered what Ramon had blurted. Sisk was a crook.

"I need your permission," Fisher said.

Marie was confused for a second.

"To go to the FBI."

She hesitated. The moment of truth. She hadn't expected this to move so fast. Dear Lord, the FBI. "You know how difficult this is for me," she said.

"Yes, I do."

"All right," she said. "Whatever you think."

The lunch crowd at Ruby Tuesday's was gone by the time she had arrived, the deck deserted. She had been so intent in her conversation with Fisher that she wasn't aware they had company. Marie caught him out of the corner of her eye. A man with a hat low over his face. And dark glasses. "That guy. Do you think he's watching us?"

"I don't know. Anyway, there's nothing we can do about it." She had brought along a copy of Jack Lowery's report. Fisher covered it with his arm and slid it off the table and into his jacket pocket. "I have to get going. Let's see what he does."

They were in the parking lot when the man with the dark glasses came hurrying down the stairs, looking all around. He stopped when he saw them.

"I'll be damned," Fisher said. "Well, he can't stand there forever. We'll wait him out."

At last the man got into a car and drove slowly away.

"Richard," she said, "I'm afraid."

She had every right to be, Fisher thought. But he said, "Don't worry. Maybe you won't have to be involved more than this."

Richard Fisher wasn't surprised at anything Marie had told him. He'd already picked up talk from ex-cons that money could spring you. And there was something else. Those Georgia extraditions were familiar. Last winter Fisher had been talking to a Georgia DA, and he remembered how the DA had been really pissed about some extraditions that were being held up in Nashville.

Still, Fisher wondered if he hadn't been a little hasty suggesting the FBI. Instant anger had consumed him while Marie was speaking. Here he was busting his ass to put people in prison, and there they were buying themselves out. But he had to be very careful. It was, after all, supposition, and it all could blow up in his face. He could kiss his career good-bye. It would be different if he were operating on his own turf. Now he'd be sticking his nose into somebody else's ball park. Namely, the Governor's. He admired Marie, saw how offended she was about the dishonesty of the whole thing, but she didn't appreciate how far this could go.

There wasn't any option besides the FBI that he could think of, though. It was some commentary on what had happened to state law enforcement under Ray Blanton. Fisher was going to live up to his commitment to Marie, but he would demand guarantees from the feds that nothing could be traced back to him. He needed protection. For that matter, so did she.

In Nashville, Jack Strickland made a passing remark to Marie about carrying on with certain DAs.

She took him right up on it. "What do you mean, Jack? Are you trying to imply you think I've got something going with a DA personally?"

"No," he said. "I know you better than that. But not everybody does."

Marie got this clammy feeling, remembering the man on the deck at Ruby Tuesday's.

· 5 ·

On August 22 she was getting ready to leave for a national conference of paroling and correctional authorities in Denver when Fisher called. He'd made contact with the FBI. Wanted her to give him those names again on the Georgia warrants. The FBI was very interested, he said.

Ramon drove her to the airport.

Ever since Daytona Beach, they had been drawing apart. When they dated, he wanted to relax. Have fun. Work into an easy relationship. But with Marie, it was always pardons and paroles, pardons and paroles. It didn't matter what they were doing. Dining. Swimming. Riding around.

On the way to the airport she was talking about Sisk again. Eddie was on vacation—at Bill Thompson's condominium, of all places. Or perhaps it belonged to Thompson's brother-in-law. She never could get it straight.

"Look," said Ramon, exasperated, "why don't you go to Blanton? If you think Sisk and Benson are doing him in, or Traughber, tell him. Maybe he doesn't know. Get it over with once and for all."

Marie found herself saying, "You're right. I'll be back on the twenty-sixth. Do me a favor. Call Sherry and tell her to make an appointment for me with the Governor."

In Denver, at dinner at the annual congress of the American Correctional Association, attended by officials from all fifty states, as well as the chairman and members of the U.S. parole commission, a woman from Indiana, seated at Marie's table, inquired as to the circumstances of her appointment.

Marie said, "I serve at the Governor's pleasure."

"Oh, honey, I bet you do."

That was the only sour note at the convention. She learned that Tennessee wasn't alone in the built-in conflict between corrections and pardons and paroles. Correctional officers were anxious to keep the prison population down. Overcrowding and riots were their chief concern, while parole people had to think about community life. She also discovered in Denver how exceptional Tennessee's executive clemency rate was. Very few other states used it as a release mechanism, usually as a measure of last resort in extraordinary situations.

There was talk of setting up new national release standards. Toward this end the groundwork was laid for a regional group, the Southern Paroling Authority. Marie was elected to the planning committee, along with Jack Scism from North Carolina. He'd been a reporter who uncovered corruption in the state parole system and wound up as chairman. If she only knew him well enough to discuss her own problems.

The first unsettling sign came from Nashville when Sherry Lomax called and said she'd spoken to Charlie Benson about the appointment with Blanton. Charlie said the Governor was going to be out of town.

Marie was infuriated. Why Benson? She wasn't aware he was the Governor's appointments secretary, she said, and Sherry replied sheepishly, "I guess I'm just used to talking to Charlie." Marie remembered seeing Charlie and Sherry huddled over drinks here and there. She decided, however, Sherry had acted out of ignorance.

Next Sisk was raging at her from Daytona Beach. It hadn't taken Benson long to pass the news. Traughber was a honeymoon compared with her, Sisk said. What did she mean trying to go around him to Blanton?

"Eddie, really," she said. "I don't need your permission to see the Governor. Calm down. Anyway, it seems he isn't available, so I won't be seeing him. Okay?"

"We'll talk about this when I get back," Sisk said.

Eddie, she thought, was having a lot of trouble adjusting to the idea that he couldn't order her around. Had even said on the phone not to get him wrong. He didn't expect her to be a rubber stamp. Which at least gave her a hollow laugh.

In Nashville, the morning of Friday, August 27, Marie spied a photo in the paper of Ray Blanton attending some local function the night before. So if he'd been away, he hadn't gone very far. She detoured by the capitol on her way to work and saw Blanton's limousine in its reserved parking space.

She found a spot for herself and marched into Ken Lavender's office and told him she needed to see the Governor. Ken told her, "He's got somebody with him. You'll have to wait awhile."

Marie called Sherry Lomax to explain where she was. Nobody else was to know.

Then she was standing in front of Blanton. He appeared cordial. She debated how to bring this all up. Incredibly, he made it easy. Almost as if he'd been expecting her. He riffled through some papers and handed her a letter. A clipping from the Chattanooga *Times* was attached. "Do you know anything about this?" he said. The clipping had a Dalton dateline and quoted law-enforcement officials regarding extraditions being mysteriously thwarted by Tennessee. The letter, from a constituent, was irate. The writer said he had contributed to Blanton's campaign and wasn't going to give another nickel if this was what he was getting for his money.

"Governor," Marie said, "now that you've mentioned it, these extraditions have been a subject of extreme concern to me. They've been a subject of great disagreement between me and Eddie."

"What's holding them up?"

That's where the disagreement was, she said. Marie tried to make it sound like a professional difference. She wanted the men sent back. Eddie wanted hearings on them, and the hearings had been delayed endlessly.

Blanton seemed more annoyed than upset. So she decided to let it all out. There had been other disagreements with Eddie, even violent arguments. There was more to these four extraditions. She told him about the extortion attempt in Lowery's office, and took a copy of Lowery's report from her briefcase and gave it to him.

Marie tried to read Blanton as he went over it. But there wasn't a flicker of expression. When he was through, she said, "You probably know that Bill Thompson and Eddie are pretty good friends."

"Yeah?"

"Well," she said, "Bill Thompson is also close to one of those men named in the extradition warrants. Tommy Prater. I have reason to believe the man identified as Roundtree in that report is Bill Thompson."

Stony-faced, he said, "If I was in a room and I saw Bill Thompson in one corner, I'd go to the other corner."

That was all. She felt compelled to keep talking. "Uh, Governor," she said, "one of the reasons I'm here is to get your philosophy on executive clemency."

"Philosophy?"

"Yes," she said, totally disconcerted. "I mean, it's amazing the number of people who contact me professing to represent *your* interest in specific cases. I get the feeling you don't know about half of them."

Blanton looked at her so directly, so openly. Without registering any emotion. Only now the tiny quizzical smile line on the corner of his mouth deepened. "You're right. I probably haven't been personally acquainted with more than two or three of them." No suggestion about how to rectify that.

Marie tried another tack. "An argument I've had with Eddie is the DAs," she said. "Frankly, I'm of the opinion that in clemency cases we should strongly consider the views of district attorneys. I believe they mirror their communities. I mean, they have to run for office too." She thought that was pretty clever, and nervy, connecting his political future with them.

Ray Blanton hardly blinked. "I've told Eddie," he said, "that he can't ignore those DAs."

Is this the way he always is? Marie thought. She'd heard the stories about him, of course. You never knew what Ray Blanton was thinking. When she'd been speaking, he *seemed* to be nodding. In agreement? She wasn't sure whether his head had moved at all. She wanted to cry out to him. Tell me what to do! She tried one last gambit. "Governor, how do you want me to handle the question of executive clemency? I have grave doubts about so many of the requests."

"Use your best judgment," he said. "That's why I put you there. That's what I expect."

She was exultant. That's what she wanted to hear. She waited for him to continue. He didn't. No further comment about the extraditions. About Bill Thompson. No exhortation that they had to get to the bottom of this. No hint that he'd be seeing Sisk about it. She didn't know what more to say. Their meeting was over. As Marie got up to leave, she said, "You can keep the report. I've got another copy."

"No, that's all right," he said, handing it back to her.

· 6 ·

Marie's mind whirled. Use her best judgment, he had said. Music to her ears. But what was the tune? She felt as if she'd been to Delphi.

And why hadn't he kept Lowery's report? Could he have been that uninterested? She had wanted desperately to tell him, Look, the FBI's involved in this now. The way he had been, though, she couldn't have done that.

She went directly to her office. She hadn't been there five minutes before the phone rang. She barely got out a hello when Eddie was screaming at her. At the top of his lungs. From Daytona Beach. "You goddamn bitch, you lied to me! Goddamn lying bitch!" His voice was almost unrecognizable.

She sparred for time. "Who is this, please?"

"You fucking well know who it is, you damn bitch. You lied to me. You went and saw the Governor. You told me you wouldn't!"

"Eddie, quiet down for a second."

Her interruption redoubled his fury. If anything, his decibel count went up a notch or two. She'd never heard him like this. "You knew what you were doing," he shrieked. "Couldn't wait for me to get out of town and run to the Governor. You talked to him about the Will Midgett case, didn't you? I'd like to slap your goddamn head off! Bitch!"

She wondered if he was foaming at the mouth. She attempted once more to speak, but his screaming reached a new peak. She held the phone away from her ear. His pitch was so high that she thought somebody outside her office might hear him. She put the phone down and went to close the door. Behind her she could pick up his distorted squawks. How did he know she'd seen Blanton? Had it been the Governor? Ken Lavender? The state police captain in charge of Blanton's security had seen her go in. Who else? Sherry?

She returned to the phone. Eddie continued to rant nonstop. "—ruin me," he was saying. "What more lies did you tell him? I never should've trusted you, you fucking bitch." She remembered how her husband used to scream at her. Only, he used to call her a whore, instead of a bitch. What was the psychological implication?

By now she knew better than to say anything. And gradually Sisk wound down. Got back to the Midgett case, and Lowery. She'd shot him down for good with Blanton. Who knew what she had said!

That cut two ways, she thought. Either the Governor had relied on him to run this whole operation and he'd fouled up, or the Governor didn't know anything about it. "If you'd shut up, I'll tell you," Marie said.

"You will?" He sounded surprised.

"Yes. If you want the truth, *he* brought up everything. Somebody wrote him a letter. Some voter. So I told him. And I would have told you. The Governor only listened. He wasn't mad at you at all."

"He wasn't?"

"No." That at least settled one thing. Blanton hadn't called Sisk. "I mean, there wasn't anything to hide. You told Jack Lowery and me you spoke to the Governor."

"Goddamnit, Marie, I never said that and you know it."

She let it pass. Oh Eddie, she thought. Then she said, "How did you know I saw the Governor?"

That got him going again. "I know every fucking move you make," he shouted. She pictured the man on the deck at Ruby Tuesday's. Sisk was still shouting when she put the receiver in its cradle.

Marie summoned Sherry. "The funniest thing just happened," she said. "I'm not here five minutes after I left the Governor, and Eddie Sisk's on the phone about it. And he's seven hundred miles away. How do you suppose he knew?"

Sherry looked at her, alarmed. "Marie, it wasn't me. Not after what you told me. Anybody at the capitol could have seen you."

That was true, Marie had to admit. And it was also true that she didn't want to believe it had been Sherry. Before Marie left for Denver, she had lobbied hard to make Sherry the board's permanent administrative assistant. The problem was she didn't have a college degree, and Marie was getting her a waiver. But Sherry had been in state government for a while, and Marie reflected on where her perception of power was. With the legal counsel, which was to say the Governor's office, or the pardons and paroles chairman? She decided to call the personnel department and tell the fellow there not to rush the Sherry Lomax promotion. In fact, to hold off on it until she got back to him.

She tried to focus on her work. The Cooper hearing was at last scheduled for September 2, and she knew that once a hearing on an executive clemency sponsored by the Governor's office had been set up, it never, ever, had been turned down. Marie looked over the letter from the Shelby County DA.

RE: Rose Cooper, No. 780555
  Indictment Nos. 37540, 37541, 37542
  . . . This office is advised that Ms. Cooper is a person with national connections in drug traffic and is not considered a casual user or offender. This office feels that under all the facts and circumstances

involved in this case, that it is entirely too early to consider any sort of
commutation for Ms. Rose Cooper.

· 7 ·

For sure, she and Sisk were on a collision course, and late in the
afternoon Marie telephoned David Raybin. She had mixed feelings
about Raybin. Chunky and round-faced, he wore wire-rimmed glasses
and vested suits, but he liked to come on tough. He had once told her
he looked on his job in the attorney general's office as a post–law school
graduate course. Really wanted to be a prosecutor. When Marie was
made extradition officer, he hadn't hidden his hostility. Kind of who's
this bimbo? And he was the only one who had turned her down when
she was seeking support to be chairman. He'd become counsel to the
pardons and paroles board. In effect, its lawyer, and he said to endorse
her would be a conflict of interest. She was put out, of course, but when
she dwelt on it some more, she decided, well, it showed he was a
stand-up guy. Acted on his beliefs. Besides, this time she only intended
to ask him a technical question as the board's counsel.

"David," she said, "I know it's Friday and quitting time, but I have
to see you. It's important."

"Okay, Marie. Come on over."

With Raybin, the reservations were mutual. When Marie had sounded
him out for an endorsement as chairman, he couldn't see anything that
qualified her. He figured she must be screwing Sisk or Blanton, or both.
But he had to confess that even before Marie had been sworn in, she'd
been to his office several times learning the legal intricacies of the
chairmanship, especially the suits in which Raybin constantly had to
defend the state against prisoners seeking habeas corpus writs, claiming
they should be paroled, their civil rights had been violated and so on.
Still, he had a low opinion of the Blanton administration in general and
Sisk in particular, and he saw Marie as owned lock, stock and barrel by
Sisk. Until very recently. A week before, Sisk had called and asked if
all three members of the board had to sign a commutation recommendation, and Raybin replied that there wasn't anything written down but
it had been the common practice. Raybin was intrigued by the query.
The only new element on the board was Marie. Perhaps there was
something he hadn't spotted.

He was absolutely bowled over when Marie strode in, refused a cup of coffee and said, "David, how can I be fired?"

"Fired? What are you talking about? Sit down, will you."

So she sat, and asked him again.

"Marie, according to the Tennessee Code, you can only be removed for good cause."

"I know that," she snapped. "But what's good cause? If the Governor doesn't like the color of my hair, is that it?"

"Don't be ridiculous, Marie. You're their baby. Their girl. They put you in there. You're in like Flynn."

"What about my perfume? If he doesn't like my perfume, am I gone?"

Raybin had never seen her so overwrought. She was up and down like a jackrabbit, pacing back and forth. "Just a minute," he said, and made a call. After he hung up, he told her, "It's what I thought. Good cause is pretty much what the Governor wants it to be."

"But it has to be in writing," she said. "It has to be explained, doesn't it?"

"Yeah, I suppose so. But so what? This is all hypothetical. Crazy." She saw him leaning back in his chair, eyes squinting. "Hold on," he said. "What's the trouble? Marie, you know if you're having problems with the board—that's what I'm here for. That's my job."

When she didn't reply, he said, "You sit there acting like you're having difficulty trusting me. Did it ever occur to you it could be a two-way street?"

"What's that mean?" This was going to be important, she thought. David, please say the right thing.

"Well, let's face it," Raybin said. "There's no love lost between the AG's office and Blanton. Maybe I shouldn't say it, but what I think of the administration is basically unprintable. They appointed you, so I could only assume you're their right-hand lady, and any reservations I may have shown toward you were for that reason, and that reason alone. And somehow I'm beginning to think I made a big mistake."

All at once she knew she was going to tell him. "David," she said, "if I confided in you about legal matters pertaining to the board, would you have to go to the AG?"

That depended. What were they? What was being done about them?

"What do you think of Richard Fisher?" she asked.

"I like Richard. He's a good DA and a good lawyer." Raybin looked at her. "And he doesn't shoot his mouth off."

So she told him about the Georgia extraditions and the Will Midgett clemency. And how she'd gone to Fisher, and Fisher had gone to the FBI.

Raybin said, "I believe every word. Look at this." He dug into his files and displayed a letter from a woman in East Tennessee written laboriously in pencil on lined paper. The woman said she'd given a Blanton patronage chief a down payment to get her brother out of prison. But nothing had happened, and more money was being demanded. The woman wrote that she'd worked hard for the money and wanted something done. Raybin had called the woman, and she said she had a canceled check. Raybin showed the check to Marie. He said Traughber was chairman at the time, and when he had called him about the case, Traughber said he couldn't find the file.

"Just like Midgett," Marie said.

Raybin said he hadn't known what to do. He didn't have any investigators for this sort of thing, or investigative powers when it came down to it. Seemed almost apologetic.

He asked if he could call Fisher, and she said yes, thinking that the FBI should also know about the payoff Raybin had described. Raybin spoke practically in code to Fisher, as if there were a tap on his line. And on the extension she could sense Richard wasn't leaping with joy that Raybin had been brought into this, but it was decided they'd all meet in Raybin's office the following Tuesday afternoon.

As she and Raybin left together, he said, "I'm not seeing the AG on this. You've done the right thing, and remember, you're not a little-bitty extradition officer anymore. You're in a powerful position, stronger than you think. If you have to, you can always go to the legislature."

Terrific, she thought.

· 8 ·

The Cooper hearing, at the women's prison in Nashville, was that same Tuesday, in the morning. Marie was on hand early to make sure the recording equipment was in working order. She'd been dismayed to discover the board had no transcripts of its hearings, and one of her first acts as chairman was to requisition dictating and recording machines. That's when it was driven home to her what a farce the board's independence was. The corrections department controlled the purse strings. Everything required the commissioner's approval, although in actuality Sam Lipford okayed the purchases. That in itself said plenty. Lipford, as director of parole and probation officers, should be reporting to her instead of to Murray Henderson.

This would be the first session of the board on tape. Traughber and Mitchell looked at her as if she had produced a live rattlesnake. David Raybin wanted the hearings recorded, she explained, smiling brightly.

With her fellow members on each side of her, Marie at last got a look at Rose Lee Cooper. Rose Lee was on the short side. Should be watching her weight, Marie remembered thinking. She was in street clothes. Smartly turned out. Her husband, quite a dandy himself, was with her. Clearly, they were both treating the hearing as a perfunctory affair. Marie thought Rose Lee might yawn at any moment. Upon being questioned, she did mention something about her children needing her presence.

After Cooper was led out, Mitchell leaned over to Marie and asked if this wasn't a case they were interested in up on the hill, and she said yes, but there was some controversy about it. She wondered what Mitchell would say if he knew what the controversy was. "Frankly," she said, "I don't see how we can possibly consider somebody who hasn't had time to hang up her things in the closet."

"I go along with that," Mitchell said.

Traughber didn't appear to know what to do, so Marie said, "This is a bad case, Charles. I talked to the Governor the other day, and he said he wants us to use our best judgment." She could see Traughber thinking that the Governor meant just the Cooper case. "I'm voting no," she said, and scrawled on her sheet in large letters, "Decline." Mitchell took a look and did the same. Then Traughber.

When Rose Lee Cooper was brought back in, as cocky as ever, and Marie announced the decision, her husband's jaw dropped to somewhere around his knees. "What is this?" he said. "What kind of setup is this?"

"You must realize that your wife has not served very much time of her sentence," Marie said. She didn't blame him for being incredulous. She wondered how much money had been involved.

Sherry Lomax looked up from the phone when Marie returned. "Charlie wants to know if the Cooper hearing was held."

"I'll talk to him myself," Marie said. "Charlie, I've got good news and bad news. I'll tell you the bad news first. The board declined to recommend Rose Cooper."

"Marie, this better be some kind of joke."

"It isn't a joking matter."

Benson started yelling, "I can't believe you're serious. You had the hearing and didn't recommend? I've already told people. Goddamn you, Marie, you've made a liar out of me."

"I haven't made a liar out of you at all."

"The hell you haven't. I told you. I already told people Rose Cooper was out."

"How could you? *Before* the hearing."

"Listen, stop fucking me around." Benson's voice was getting ugly.

"No, you listen to me," Marie said sharply. She wasn't about to submit to a replay of Sisk's Florida call. "My name goes on the dotted line. Not yours. The only lie around here would be if I said Rose Cooper deserved clemency. You got your hearing. That's all I promised."

There weren't any good-byes. She couldn't remember who slammed the phone down first. Marie never did get around to the good news. Although she had some reservations, the board was going to recommend in favor of another inmate named Gary Keene, whose commutation Eddie and Charlie were pushing.

Marie immediately dictated a letter to Governor Blanton, Attention Mr. Eddie Sisk, reviewing the Cooper case in detail. It concluded that due to Rose Lee's brief incarceration, her release shouldn't be considered until her normal parole date rolled around. Marie borrowed Ramon's secretary for the letter. The conversation with Benson had left a bad taste in her mouth, and she didn't want to have anything to do with Sherry right then. In fact, Marie began to think, Sherry's days were numbered.

That afternoon she met with Fisher and Raybin. Marie had talked to Fisher over the weekend, and he had been concerned about Raybin. She trusted David, she said, and she needed his help with the board. Also, she argued, he had come up with documentary evidence that added substance to her suspicions, and Richard had to concur.

There was a lot of tension in Raybin's office as they hashed over everything, but they all agreed that going to the FBI was the right step. Fisher assured Marie the FBI would be contacting her.

Well, where was the FBI? she said irritably.

Privately, Fisher was as much on edge. He'd already checked to find out what was happening, and had been told it was simply a matter of paper work. He said it was probably because of the security arrangements he'd demanded. Fisher had initially spoken to the resident agent in his hometown of Franklin. The report was to go to the FBI's field office for East Tennessee in Knoxville. Knoxville would send it on to the field office in Memphis before it got to Nashville. That way, Fisher explained, it would look as though Memphis, at the other end of the state, had originated the investigation.

What it amounted to was a major corruption conspiracy, Raybin said, and he wondered out loud whether Marie should approach Blanton. That was the one thing she had not told Raybin she'd done. Fisher remained silent. He hadn't been enthusiastic when she revealed to him that she'd seen Blanton. The more he had brooded about it, the more likely it appeared to him that Blanton might be in this. After hearing Marie's version of the meeting, Fisher kept remembering Senator Howard Baker's refrain during the Watergate hearings: What did Nixon know, and when did he know it?

Suddenly it was as if Raybin had been reading Fisher's mind. You know, he said, this could reach right up to the Governor. A sitting governor in the United States!

And for the first time, really, Marie felt the immensity of what she was doing.

· 9 ·

That night at home, when Therese was asleep, she wrote letters to her sons at Morris.

Afterward, before putting down some of the day's events in her journal, she leafed through it and saw the warning Jack Lowery had delivered to her in Memphis in June. You're just one little girl, he had said. Don't be destroyed! Think of your children!

Once, at Vanderbilt, she'd gotten into a heated discussion about ideals. Someone insisted every man had his price. "Well, I can't be bought," she protested, and was told, "That's because you haven't been in the right position yet."

And now, remembering her reaction then, she wrote:

I thought back to all the hard times that the kids & I had known, & all the meals of macaroni & cheese, & the cups of milk I'd borrowed, & the postdated checks that we lived on, & the juggling of bills & the jobs & the tears & the Ivory soap smells of my babies interspersed with the telephone calls of bill collectors—& I thought, too, of all the dates

I was asked for, & the marriage proposals, & the other proposals, & how easy it would have been, at any time, how <u>easy</u> it would have been to "sell out," to let some poor fool spend all his money on me & the kids, if I would lead him on, or sleep with him—but for me, in my simplistic fashion, it all boils down to a question of love and integrity; I couldn't let anyone spend money on me or my children unless I <u>loved</u> him, otherwise, it would have been a lie, a prostitution of myself and my little ones.

And so it is today. Even to "look the other way" when all this dirt is flying through the air would be to prostitute myself and my integrity.

PART III

ELEVEN

Henderson (Hank) Hillin Jr. was a walking FBI recruitment poster. He was forty-five, six foot two, in great shape from nearly daily tennis or handball. Had a taut-skinned, tanned face with a touch of gray in his sideburns and clear blue eyes that were warm and friendly—and, on demand, glacial. He was born in Nashville. In 1961 he had been stationed in Washington, D.C., in Soviet counterintelligence, when his mother fell gravely ill and J. Edgar Hoover personally had him transferred back to the city. Even now he always referred to the late FBI director as Mr. Hoover. He had since managed to remain in Nashville at some cost to his career advancement within the bureau. Still, there were compensations. As far as Nashville was concerned, he personified the FBI, and he had developed contacts throughout the capital that wouldn't hurt him one bit when he reached retirement at fifty. His last exploit had caused quite a stir. An armed fugitive had holed up in Murfreesboro, surrounded by FBI agents and state troopers, and Hillin went into the house and talked the man into surrendering.

Technically, Hillin was number two in the fifteen-man Nashville office. On September 15, however, the resident agent in charge was on vacation, and he was acting boss when the airtel—an FBI version of a mailgram sent over its own wire—arrived from Memphis with Richard Fisher's statement about Marie. Boy, Hillin thought, if this is right, it's going to blow the whole state Democratic administration out of the water.

Mrs. RAGGHIANTI desires to be contacted by the FBI on this matter, but wishes that it appear the FBI approached her at other than her request. According to FISHER, Mrs. RAGGHIANTI is anxious that she be contacted in the near future.

That was what Hank Hillin couldn't get over. In his twenty-two years with the bureau he wasn't able to recall when somebody at Marie's level had stepped forward voluntarily. The usual sources of information like this were lower-echelon employees in an organization with an ax to grind, or higher-ups out to save themselves.

Hillin had never forgotten how his investigation into Blanton's illegal campaign contributions had been cut off, and he was sure there was plenty more rotten in Blanton's regime, but the truth was he hadn't expected anything with this potential. If the information in the airtel panned out, it was obviously only the tip of the iceberg. Yet if he took the case himself, it would look as though he was grabbing all the goodies. So, regretfully, he assigned it to a young organized crime agent named Phil Thune. Phil had been burned on another investigation recently, and this would boost his morale. Hillin immediately tagged the case as a "183," a RICO, which was an acronym for the Racketeer Influenced and Corrupt Organizations Act, a fairly new statute Congress had passed to deal with the infiltration of legitimate enterprises "through a pattern of racketeering activity." From then on, the Tennessee pardons and paroles matter carried the FBI file classification "Memphis 183-40." The "40" was the local number.

Eddie Sisk had calmed down after his return from Florida. Even told Marie that she was right. He had talked to Blanton, and the Governor wasn't upset. Meanwhile his newest twist on the Georgia extraditions was to give the wanted men polygraph tests à la Billy Gene Cole. It was becoming more ludicrous every day, she thought. Eddie was attempting to have Tennessee try Prater and his pals when by every accepted extradition standard their guilt or innocence had to be decided in Georgia. Well, it was out of her hands. She did mention what was going on to Fisher, however, and Richard decided to lay one on

Sisk. His letter, addressed to Charlie Benson, was innocuous enough on the surface. No explanation of why it had been dispatched.

Would you please advise the status of the extradition of Beikouvitch, Barnes, McBrayer and Prater, (I'm not sure of the spelling of the names) and the reason for the delay in a determination.

> *Very truly yours,*
> *Richard A. Fisher*
> *District Attorney*

The letter had an electrifying effect on Sisk when Benson showed it to him. All he needed was someone like Fisher to be poking around. At once he phoned Special Prosecutor Erwin Mitchell in Dalton to assure Mitchell that the extraditions were going through. It was simply a question of paper work, Eddie said. Governor Blanton would be signing the warrants the moment they were processed. Three or four weeks at the outside. The next thing a bemused Mitchell knew, Sisk was calling again. He happened to be in Chattanooga on business. Wanted to know if he could drive down to see Mitchell, and Mitchell said of course.

Eddie showed up with Benson in tow. He stayed perhaps twenty minutes. Mitchell remembered how agitated Sisk was. How he kept saying he didn't want Mitchell to get the wrong impression. The delay in the extraditions had not been political in any way. It was just that there had been so many defendants and lawyers. Mitchell dryly replied that he was glad to hear it. He noticed that Benson had trouble maintaining a straight face while Sisk carried on. Mitchell resisted the temptation to inquire what had triggered Sisk's abrupt turnabout. The main thing was to have Prater back for trial, and he put in a call to Bill Dodd to relay the good news.

About then, Ramon Sanchez-Viñas tried to help Marie out. He knew she'd seen the Governor, but Marie had been evasive about the details. Ramon could tell, though, that the meeting had not gone well. He figured it was probably because Blanton hadn't taken her seriously.

Next Ramon got a taste of what Marie had been experiencing. Benson began pressuring him about putting an inmate on work release. Ramon said he'd have the corrections department's screening committee look into the case, and Benson, invoking Sisk, said that he didn't give a damn about any screening committee. Put the guy on work release now. Ramon asked a friend of his, Steve Cobb, a young Democratic legislator from Nashville, to set up an appointment with the Governor.

Sanchez-Viñas and Cobb saw Blanton early in the evening in his study at the mansion. Blanton was having a Scotch and cordially offered them drinks. After Cobb and Blanton finished discussing some pending bills, the Governor asked what had occasioned their visit, and Ramon told him he had reason to believe there were people in the administration cutting deals on prisoners. Blanton wanted to know his source, and Ramon said that Marie was getting a lot of heat on clemencies from Benson—and Sisk. Blanton, working on another Scotch, said Marie had been taken over by the district attorneys. She was not sensitive to overcrowding in the prison population. Ramon, of all people, should know better.

When Ramon started to argue, Blanton suddenly dropped his famous mask. Marie was headed for big trouble. He knew for a fact, he declared, that she was boozing it up and screwing every man in sight. In particular, she'd been sleeping with that goddamn turncoat Richard Fisher.

Blanton's outburst left Sanchez-Viñas and Cobb nonplussed. It was inconceivable to them that the Governor had any role in this. Ramon couldn't think of what else to say. He knew perfectly well that Marie didn't drink excessively. It seemed, though, that Blanton was having a problem in that regard.

· 2 ·

On September 20, the same day Fisher wrote to Benson about the Georgia extraditions, Marie fired Sherry Lomax. The last straw had been an act so brazen as to defy belief.

Sisk was still plumping for a clemency recommendation for Gary Keene, a University of Tennessee student serving time on a drug charge. Marie had examined his file and couldn't find anything suspect, and reminded herself not to be prejudiced just because Eddie was involved. It was probably because he was such a big UT booster. And while the Knoxville DA, Ron Webster, had protested the clemency, Marie decided to recommend anyway. Keene was a first offender, had a good institutional sheet and basically was deserving of consideration.

For the record, however, she included the DA's comments in the commutation write-up.

Marie rarely saw a commutation after it had been signed by her and forwarded to the legal counsel's office for the Governor's approval. But this time she did, when she went over to talk to Sisk about another matter. The first thing she noticed on the familiar green-bordered form sitting on Eddie's desk was that her signature was now in Sherry's hand. And the objection from Webster was missing.

Back in her own office, she said to Sherry, "Did you change the Keene write-up and write my name on the change?" Sherry looked right at her and said, "Yes, I did. Eddie told me to."

"Get out," Marie said. "You're supposed to be working for me, not Eddie." Marie stormed in to see Sam Lipford to make it official. "You get that girl out of my office or I am personally going to throw her out the window." Sam said, "Who, Sherry Lomax?" and she said, "You've got it."

Marie waited in Sam's office. He returned and said, "Well, she's leaving, and she's crying," and Marie replied, "That's the saddest story I've ever heard."

Sherry was still packing her things when Marie went back, already feeling a little remorseful. There were tears in Sherry's eyes, but aside from that she didn't seem so shaken. Her parting shot was that Marie would be sorry for this. She'd only tried to do her best, she said. For everyone. Clearly, Sherry had placed her bet, and it wasn't on Marie. "I don't believe there's any more to discuss," said Marie. Before she knew it, Murray Henderson was lining up another job for Sherry.

That afternoon the receptionist told Marie a Mr. Thune wanted to see her, and her heart leaped to her throat when Phil Thune came in and displayed his FBI badge.

She got up quickly and closed the door, and tried not to act nervous. But it gave her such a start having him there. The Memphis airtel had advised that Marie wished to be interviewed in the office. She'd forgotten she had said that to Fisher. At the time it seemed the forthright thing to do. Now she wasn't sure how smart it was. Then she recalled that an FBI agent had contacted her last summer about the status of an inmate, so if Thune was recognized, his presence could be easily explained away. Thune struck her as clean-cut and earnest.

Thune had already run a computer check on Marie and discovered no citations. Additional inquiries, though, turned up the talk that she and Sisk had had an affair and had fallen out after a lovers' quarrel. Privately Thune found the information in the airtel hard to believe. It was such an outlandish scheme. Nevertheless, Marie's direct, almost dispassionate account of what she knew didn't escape his notice. There was no tone of the angry girl friend. If anything, there was a tinge of sadness in her voice. And nothing judgmental, even when she described Sisk's curse-filled phone call from Florida. She didn't go after the Governor either. In her meeting with Blanton, she said, he seemed to be unaware of the situation. The only antipathy Thune could detect in Marie was when she spoke about Traughber, especially his role in the strange disappearance of the Midgett clemency papers. Thune spent better than two hours with Marie. His nine-page, single-spaced report on the FBI's standard "302" interview form was added to "Memphis 183-40."

At Sam Lipford's suggestion, Marie replaced Sherry with Jim Grisham, a quiet thirty-two-year-old corrections department administrator who'd been working at the main prison. Sam said Grisham was just what she was looking for—competent and absolutely trustworthy. Jim was eager for the promotion, and Marie felt a little silly trying to explain that the job might be more than he had bargained for without being able to elaborate on what she meant.

She showed Grisham around. As she had done when she was pardons and paroles liaison for Sisk, she had started a clemency card file on requests from the Governor's office. "Now, Jim," she said, "the most important thing you're going to have to deal with is this card file over here." She walked over to the box and lifted the lid. And gasped. The box was empty.

She excused herself and went into her office to call Sherry. Where were the cards? Sherry said she didn't know what Marie was talking about. Marie said, "You were the only one who had a key besides me. Where is it? The file isn't even locked."

"I left the key in my desk drawer," Sherry said.

Marie cornered Lipford. "I've heard Murray is getting Sherry another job. Fine. But I want the record to show that I, Marie Ragghianti, fired her because she was a liar and a thief. I want it in her personnel file."

"Hey, Marie," Lipford said, "take it easy."

At home that evening she thought of her old liaison file, the one that included Larkin Bibbs and Billy Gene Cole, and early in the morning she drove to the capitol and headed for the legal counsel's office. She knew that practically nobody, except the receptionist, arrived before nine-thirty, so Marie walked in on the dot of nine, returned a "Hi" to the girl on duty and went to Benson's desk. If they wanted to get into a swiping game, she could play it too. The file box was still in place, gathering dust. She took the cards and walked past the receptionist again. "See you," Marie said.

There was a clerk on the pardons and paroles staff named Cynthia Trainor, who hadn't hidden her admiration for Marie, and now Marie called her in and said, "Cynthia, I'm going to ask you to do something very, very important and highly confidential. Nobody is to know about it. I want you to take these cards over to the copier in the basement of the Andrew Jackson Building and make two copies of these cards front and back and bring them back to me. If anybody wants to know what you're doing, you tell them you're doing something for me."

Cynthia was back within an hour. It was the first of many copying assignments she would undertake in the Andrew Jackson basement. Not once, even when Marie had become a pariah to just about everyone in the administration, did Cynthia break faith.

Late in the day, when everybody had left work, Marie replaced the original cards in the liaison file.

The next morning she confronted Sisk and Benson about the missing cards from the board file, and finally Sisk admitted that Benson had them. He had every right to see them, Eddie said. Who could tell how his name was being used? She and Charlie would have to work it out. Benson tried to switch the subject to Sherry. How could Marie have fired a sweet girl like her?

"I want those cards," Marie said. "They're not Sherry's. They're not mine. They belong to the board." If she had to, she said in a fury, she'd go to the Nashville district attorney, Tom Shriver, and swear out a complaint.

She was reaching for the phone when Sisk said, "Charlie, give her the goddamn cards." They both looked frightened, she remembered thinking. Like two cowering bunnies.

In the afternoon she reported the episode to Phil Thune. Then she drove to the Vizcaya restaurant in southwest Nashville. Marie knew the owner and could count on getting a secluded table. She was getting together at last with Bill Leech. She had told David Raybin about Thune's visit, and David said he thought she should have an attorney advising her, and this time in her call to Leech she said she had to see him immediately. It was imperative.

Leech caught the urgency in her voice. He was a lanky man, with a boyish face and light brown hair that had a hint of a cowlick. People easily talked about his being governor or a U.S. senator someday. In 1971 he had presided over the Tennessee Constitutional Convention, and he planned to be similarly active in one scheduled for '77. It was fashionable in Nashville for some very sophisticated operators to play the down-home country boy. But at heart Bill really was one. He had a farm in the little town of Santa Fe, an hour's drive from the capital, where he raised beef cattle. Leech liked to get up at 5 A.M., don a straw cowboy hat and work the farm for three hours or so before going to his law office in nearby Columbia or to the other one he maintained in Nashville.

At the Vizcaya, when she'd finished the story, Marie saw that Leech, like Fisher and Raybin, didn't show the least surprise. She couldn't help thinking, Where has everybody been all this time?

All Leech said was he wished she'd gotten to him sooner. He wasn't sure the local FBI was the right way to go. Didn't know Thune. And didn't think much of Charles Anderson, the local U.S. attorney. In his opinion, Anderson was weak, a Nixon appointee and very defensive about it. Going straight to the Department of Justice in Washington might have been better.

"Well, it's too late now," Marie said. She also wanted to say she'd tried twice to see Leech during the summer, but she bit her tongue. It had been her fault too, not pushing as hard as she could.

Leech asked when she was going to see Thune again. Marie replied she didn't know exactly. Thune had just said he'd be in contact. Leech told her he wanted to be present at their next meeting, and she said, "Wouldn't that look funny, having a lawyer with me?" Wouldn't that make it seem she was guilty of something?

Did she want a lawyer or not? Leech said sharply. Abashed, Marie said she would call him the moment she heard from the FBI.

After Marie left, Bill Leech sat in his car, thinking. It was difficult to believe that Sisk would be doing this on his own. He was the kind of guy who followed orders.

The irony was that Leech was responsible in large measure for where

Sisk was. When Blanton was ready to make his senatorial run against Howard Baker, he'd asked Leech to manage the campaign. Leech wasn't a Blanton fan and ducked out, using his representation of the Tennessee Farm Bureau Federation as an excuse. It could lead to conflicts of interest, he said. Unfazed, Blanton had asked if Leech had any recommendations for the job, and Bill suggested Eddie Sisk, that politically active assistant DA in Giles County.

Now, driving down Harding Road, Leech stopped to phone David Raybin. Despite the hour, could he come by Raybin's home for a minute? Ostensibly, Leech went there to ascertain what Raybin thought about Marie. What he really wanted was to check out Raybin. Leech knew Richard Fisher and was confident he'd keep quiet. Raybin, however, was an unknown quantity. Leech's first concern was Marie's physical safety. If word got around in the prison population that she was blocking deals to get convicts out, she could be in terrible danger.

After a lengthy conversation with Raybin over a bottle of Chivas Regal, Leech was convinced he didn't have to worry. David had said, "I've told Marie that the main thing was for her to survive. I told her to pretend to be going along with everything."

· 3 ·

Phil Thune had completed three 302s on Marie. His interview with her, her telephoned report about firing Sherry and another telephone report about the missing card file.

Date of transcription: 9/28/76

... Following a heated argument with BENSON and SISK, the files were returned to Mrs. RAGGHIANTI, however, she stated she was not sure whether the files were complete or not.

The first week in October, Joe Trimbach, the special agent in charge of the Memphis field office, told Hank Hillin he had read the original Knoxville memo with Fisher's statement and the subsequent reports by Thune. The case looked as if it could go somewhere, Trimbach said, and he wanted Hillin to take over. Hillin was concerned about what this might do to morale in the Nashville office, especially Thune's, but

Trimbach said he was assigning the pardons and paroles investigation to him anyway. From now on Hillin would be the case agent.

Hillin was too well known around state offices, so he and Thune met Marie and Leech the afternoon of October 8 in the parking lot of the Sunflower supermarket past Belle Meade. From there they drove into Percy Warner Park, twenty-seven hundred acres given over to woodland, playing fields, picnic grounds and bridle paths. At that time of the year during a weekday the park was all but deserted. Even so, Hillin pulled in behind a log cabin built as a visitors' refuge from rain.

Marie was immediately taken with Hillin. He appeared to be so sure of himself, but not in a wise-guy way. He engendered instant confidence. He was, she thought, the kind of person you were glad to have on your side. She remembered how a uniformed park attendant had come up to the car rather officiously, wanting to know what they were doing there, and how Hank hadn't said anything, just showed him his badge, and the attendant had said, "Oh," and hurried away.

She handed Hillin the Xeroxes of her liaison card index, as well as her new board file. Marie also gave him a list of the sixteen executive clemency cases that the board had submitted instead of recommended before she became chairman. She explained that she'd ordered a log to be kept from now on on all phone calls regarding clemencies, who was calling and why. Then Marie gave a blow-by-blow account of the Rose Lee Cooper case.

Bill Leech had warned her simply to state the facts. Let the agents make the conclusions. She did her best, but during a pause, when Hillin was scribbling down something, she said almost abstractedly, "You know, I can't believe I'm really involved in all this because Eddie was my friend." She turned toward Leech. "Wasn't he, Bill?"

Before Leech could answer, Hillin said, "You've got to forget all that."

"But you don't know what he's like. He could really be nice. He's got this little girl he adores. He can't— I mean, he's not all bad."

"How can you say you care about what happens to him when he doesn't care what happens to you?" Hillin said. "You have to forget all that because what you're doing is so important. You have no idea how important what you're saying and doing is. One of these days you're going to be the golden girl in the State of Tennessee."

"Golden girl?"

"Yes. People are going to admire you and read about you."

It had never occurred to Marie to ask for anonymity in any of this, to say "Don't use my name." Nor would she. That wasn't her style. But she wasn't so certain people would react the way Hillin described. "To tell you the truth, I'd just as soon nobody knew," she said.

The meeting in Percy Warner Park lasted about an hour and a half. Right at the end, for no reason at all, the Jimmy Pendleton clemency back in January popped up in her head, the one where Sisk had said to skip it, they'd gotten the wrong Pendleton, and she told Hillin about it now. Only because it had been so odd, and that alone made it suspicious.

Leech said afterward he'd been very impressed with Hillin. They didn't have to worry about going to the Justice Department.

The one thing she hadn't mentioned was the hearing coming up on George Edwards. The parolee she had wanted off the board's staff. She knew Hillin and Leech would tell her to forget that too. Lie low. Don't make waves. But by God, she thought, despite this investigation, she was still the board chairman and she was determined to preserve the integrity of the pardons and paroles system, to live up to her oath of office, no matter what.

And she was drawing the line on Edwards. The pressure Sisk was bringing to bear on a pardon for George Edwards made the Cooper business look like kid stuff. At another time Marie might have gone along with it. Not anymore. Since she'd become chairman, she had learned how extraordinary a pardon was supposed to be. The board's own regulations held that an ex-con could petition for a pardon only when he had demonstrated a worthy record *after a minimum of five years from the termination of sentence.*

Edwards didn't come close to qualifying. A personable young black serving a fifteen-year sentence for armed robbery, he'd been the maître d' at the Governor's mansion when Blanton commuted him to time served so he could be paroled. But a parole legally remained sentence time, and Edwards had two years to go on that, plus the five years required for pardon consideration. Edwards might be a prince among men. All Marie could think about, however, were the form letters going out from the board every day to former inmates throughout the state instructing them to try again in five years—and then maybe a decision would be made on whether or not to recommend a pardon.

The reason for the pardon was even smellier. Jim Allen, Blanton's campaign manager, had been awarded a juicy franchise for a Nashville liquor store—on the edge of Belle Meade, the only one for miles around. And Edwards had gone to work for Allen. The hitch was that

Tennessee law prohibited anyone convicted of a "moral turpitude" crime to engage in the sale of retail liquor. A pardon would fix that. Just like the Joe Finley pardon when she had started as Sisk's liaison with the board.

It didn't make sense that all this muscle was being applied on behalf of Edwards, and Marie wondered what kind of leverage he'd acquired in the months he had been a clerical worker for the board before her arrival. On October 12 she voted to reject the Edwards pardon petition on the grounds that it did not meet the board's rules. Joe Mitchell seemed surprised, but as usual he went along. Traughber appeared even more confused, although he also voted to decline.

Two days later other clemency hearings were being held at the Shelby County Penal Farm in Memphis when Marie was told she had an urgent call from the Governor's office. A phone was brought to her. Mitchell was on her left, Traughber on her right. Eddie Sisk was on the line, berserk about Edwards. Goddamn this and that. "Oh, yes," she replied, as sweetly as she could, "I meant to tell you. I haven't had a chance."

"Goddamnit, Marie," Eddie hollered, "Edwards has got to have a pardon. With or without you. Where's Joe and Charlie?"

"They're right here."

"Let me speak to Joe. Goddamnit, put him on."

"Hello, Eddie," she heard Mitchell say. Marie watched the expression on his face. He began to go ashen. He glanced nervously at her as he listened to Sisk. In a way it was very funny, she thought, and she had to keep herself from laughing. "Why, uh, no, we, ah—there's been some misunderstanding," Mitchell was saying, and then, "Yes, sir, oh yes, no problem, no problem."

Traughber was next. Marie could make out Sisk's voice from where she sat. Mitchell's and Traughber's eyes locked. They turned to her. After the hearing they didn't say a word. Just looked kind of dazed, and Marie knew the days of traditional unanimity in the board's votes were over.

Sure that her chairmanship was at an end as well, she decided to go down fighting. She called the Nashville *Banner* and asked for Larry Brinton, the paper's star investigative reporter. Brinton had been trying to talk to her for weeks. In September Marie had agreed to see him, and they'd met in the Sheraton Inn coffee shop. No sooner had she seated herself than she spied Paul Corbin walking in. Corbin was close not only to John Seigenthaler but to the Davidson County sheriff, Fate Thomas, and Marie had fled.

Brinton kept trying to see her, and she'd been putting him off. Now it was different. Marie had a gut feeling that Brinton was the one reporter she could confide in, at least a little. Brinton had been writing an exposé of a bid-rigging scandal involving the sale of surplus state property in the Blanton administration, and she figured that the George Edwards case would be right up his alley.

Marie arranged to meet Brinton by the same cabin in Percy Warner Park where she had been with Hank Hillin. When she had told him about Edwards, Brinton asked, "What's behind this?" and Marie said, "I don't know. It's just typical of what I've been going through."

"What would you say if I told you I've heard the reason you've got this job is because you slept with Eddie Sisk—and Ray Blanton?"

"Larry, that's nonsense. I can't prove it, I guess, but it just isn't so."

"Okay, I believe you. But something's going on. I hear you're working with the FBI."

That sent her reeling. "I don't know what you're talking about," she said. And as quickly as she could, Marie phoned Hillin. "It was a shot in the dark," he assured her. "Believe me, nobody knows."

Hillin was partly right. But some of Blanton's chickens were already coming home to roost. George Haynes, smarting over the Arnold Peebles fiasco, and Charles Lee, another crack agent of the Tennessee Bureau of Criminal Identification, just as unhappy with the politicization of the TBCI, had been supplying Brinton with inside details about the surplus-property racket. Lee had broken the case. His reward was an assignment in southwest Tennessee to track down some cows that had been allegedly rustled from a farm owned by a friend of the Governor's father. Lee was about ready to quit. In the meantime he, along with Haynes, were no longer reporting anything to the TBCI. Instead, they went to the FBI, and both Haynes and Lee told Brinton that they had a feeling the feds were sniffing around Tennessee pardons and paroles.

Brinton spent several days digging for backup on Marie's story about George Edwards. Anyone working in a liquor store had to fill out a state-authorized employee's permit. Brinton stopped by the Alcoholic Beverage Commission to see if Edwards was on file and hit pay dirt.

One of the questions was whether the applicant had ever been convicted of a crime, and the answer, clearly not in George's handwriting, was: *Yes (Personal pardon from Governor).* What made it rather awkward was that the application was dated August 12, exactly two months before Edwards had even had his hearing.

Brinton's piece, under a four-column headline, was front-page news in the *Banner.*

> Everything appeared set for ex-convict George Arthur Edwards to receive a pardon from Gov. Ray Blanton.
>
> The 25-year-old Knox County armed robber seemed to have all the right things going for him—including an apparently illegal job at a liquor store owned by Jim Allen, confidant and former legislative liaison officer for Blanton.
>
> Most of all, Edwards believed his pardon was imminent. When he filed an application last August with the State Alcoholic Beverage Commission for a permit to work at Allen's Belle Meade Liquors, someone wrote on it that Edwards had already received a pardon from the Governor.

At Marie's suggestion, Brinton asked Traughber how Edwards could have thought on August 12 that he was going to get a pardon, and Traughber said he didn't know. Lee Hyden, the ABC director, didn't know either. As far as Brinton was concerned, Hyden was lying through his teeth. He had been handpicked by Blanton. Hyden did what he was told.

After Brinton's story, nobody, not even Sisk, mentioned George Edwards to Marie for quite a while.

· 4 ·

Jack Strickland asked her to come by.

October 16

At the outset, he told me he wanted to quote Scripture. "You must serve to lead," he said. Immediately, I was taut with apprehension. So I listened, without comment. Jack went on to say how essential that it was, & that there are those who don't like my "style," & those who say

I have no "compassion" in dealing with my staff (Sherry?). There are those who say I'm ambitious, & those who say I'm "trying to do too much too soon."

And, he warned me, I need to be careful—very careful about whom I trust, my "peers" especially. What had I said, & to whom, that could be used against me? I thought of Sam. Also Ramon, & the Commissioner.

There are people, important people, against me, he said—but "it's not too late." Not yet. We know the problem, he said, now we find the solution. Again & again, he returned to the theme that I must "serve" in order to "lead."

She had spoken to Fisher, and Raybin, and Hillin, and Leech, and to some extent Ramon, and in each instance she felt constrained to be strong and matter-of-fact, the chairman. Yet all this emotion was building up inside her. She was truly terrified. She felt so alone. She wondered what it would be like if she had a husband or a lover to confide in, cling to. But she realized she didn't know any man who would have put up with what she was doing, not for a minute, she thought.

She had to let something out, however. She was so keyed up. So scared. After the Edwards hearing she'd been certain she would be thrown out by the administration, publicly humiliated. Even after she had met with Brinton, she had no guarantee that his story would ever be published, or that it would do any good if it was.

Marie thought of her father. When Roque had finally left Virginia and remarried, Marie didn't speak to him for a long time, but then she had come to recognize over the years that he had a right to his own life. Now, though, she needed him desperately and drove out to his office at Samaritan House, his alcoholic rehabilitation center, and she poured it all out, and he gazed at her in utter amazement and incredulity and said, "Why, these people are nothing but a bunch of crooks."

"Well, Daddy, that's probably the case," she said, "but more important, these guys have got to be ready to fire me. I'm surprised they haven't done it by this time, after this George Edwards thing. There's sure to be a lot of publicity," she said, "and it's going to be embarrassing to everybody, and, you know, I felt like I should come and tell you. Because it's something that's going to affect you too, and Mom, and my kids."

She saw her father raise his eyebrows. It was such a characteristic reflex. And his face suddenly lit up, and he said, "Baby, I'm so proud of you. Who cares if you get fired for doing the right thing? I've never been prouder of you in my whole life than I am right now."

He was, she remembered, just the way he had been when in the misery of her marriage she blurted out that she was pregnant with Ricky, and Roque had held her and said it was the most wonderful news to know that she was bringing a beautiful new baby into the world.

She clutched him and sobbed in relief.

On October 18 Marie had an astounding session with Eddie Sisk. She contacted Hillin about it at once.

Date of transcription: 10/29/76

. . . SISK asked RAGGHIANTI if she had said anything to Chattanooga, Tennessee District Attorney GARY GERBITZ "about the Will Midgett case" or if she had talked to RICHARD FISHER, Cleveland, Tennessee District Attorney.

SISK said "I'm very disturbed—my source at the Federal Courthouse told me that RICHARD FISHER has gone to the FBI about a matter relating to commutations and your name (RAGGHIANTI) was tied to it." RAGGHIANTI denied the allegation to SISK, whereupon SISK said "You're sure you haven't said anything," and pressed her for an answer. RAGGHIANTI told SISK that several weeks ago she did talk to FISHER about some Georgia extraditions, but denied the above. SISK seemed pacified but later repeated the allegation and she told him again it was the Georgia extraditions.

Late in the afternoon of October 18, 1976, SISK came to her office and told her he had been thinking about their conversation and it was probably "those extraditions." SISK did not pursue the matter further.

Hillin still thought Sisk was operating basically on guesswork. Hillin had contacted Gary Gerbitz for a rundown on Bill Thompson, and conceivably word had filtered back. Marie also had told Hillin about the man with the dark glasses when she met with Fisher, and Fisher, of course, had written the letter asking about the Georgia extraditions. In the Nashville FBI office not that many people were aware of the case at this point, and only one secretary was typing the 302s. Like Leech, Hillin didn't think too highly of Anderson, the U.S. attorney, and if there was any kind of leak, it probably was coming from him. For a

while, anyway, Hillin was determined to keep Anderson in the dark as
much as possible.

On October 19 extradition orders were signed in Nashville directing
that Prater, Barnes, McBryar and Bekovich be taken into custody and
delivered to Georgia authorities. Attorneys for the defendants immediately said they would appeal on habeas corpus writs. Prater's lawyer,
from Ward Crutchfield's firm, argued that the original warrants from
Georgia were defective because one of the alleged victims hadn't signed
them. McBryar's lawyer claimed his man wasn't the right one. The
warrants had the wrong spelling—"er" instead of "ar." Bekovich,
meanwhile, had disappeared.

The Chattanooga *Times* quoted Sisk as saying by way of explanation
for the long delay, "This is the most complicated extradition proceeding we have ever had. Normally only one person is sought in an extradition. In this one we had four, who were represented by three lawyers."

On the twentieth Marie was in Knoxville for the annual conference of
the Tennessee Department of Correction at the Hyatt Regency. The
conference was a social occasion more than anything else. Which was
okay. A lot of these people, the parole officers and counselors and so
on, put in long hours, and it was only fitting that they have a chance
to get together for a good time. When she got there, she saw Commissioner Henderson falling-down-drunk during the hospitality hour and
being led away by Ramon. Then there was an amateur hour, people
singing and otherwise doing their thing—and drinking. Plans for the
rest of the evening were being made by various groups, and she was
being included in them all.

She had to get away. She left the group she was with as though she
were off to powder her nose. She went to her room and lay on the bed
in the dark. There were repeated knocks on her door. She listened to
voices calling her name. She didn't answer. The phone rang incessantly.
She took it off the hook. But the knocks and calls and rings kept
ricocheting in her head. It was as if dozens and hundreds and thousands
of people—maybe the whole world—were trying to get her to join their
festivities. Yet she couldn't. She was alone. Not part of their life.

Marie began to weep. Everything seemed so alarming and threatening and frightening. She thought about having to lie to Eddie. Was
there an okay lie? She detested the idea of lying. "Don't think about

it," Hank had said. "That's not the issue. Think about those prisoners who can't buy their way out, Marie," he'd said. He knew that would get to her. Exactly the right line. A new morality.

Hank had said Eddie was only bluffing about what he knew. It was easy for him to say. But FBI or no FBI, she knew that in the end she was on her own. Even Bill Leech was echoing Hillin—that she had to hang in there, that everyone was depending on her.

She felt like a patient whose doctor had just pronounced terminal cancer. You knew the doctor wasn't kidding. Still, every fiber in your body rebelled against the news.

· 5 ·

On October 21 she drove back to Nashville. She stopped on the way and telephoned Bill Leech. Leech's usual easygoing tone had disappeared. He'd been trying to reach her at the Hyatt Regency, he said. Where *was* she?

On the road, she said. Well, he had to see her. Couldn't talk over the phone, he said, and gave her directions to his farm in Santa Fe.

When she arrived, he told her that in the morning the FBI was going to raid the legal counsel's office as well as the board's. To make it look right, she was going to be handed a subpoena along with the other board members, as well as Murray Henderson, Sisk and Benson, and he didn't know who else.

But why? she said. The investigation had barely gotten off the ground. He didn't know that either, Leech said. Only that the FBI had learned clemency papers were being pulled out wholesale up at the capitol.

TWELVE

Just act like it was any other day, Leech had said. So she tried. The
morning of October 22 Marie kept her appointment with Mike Kettenring, the news director of WSM-TV, NBC's Nashville affiliate. Part of
her continuing effort to improve the board's media relations.

The talk with Kettenring was going well. It had developed that he
also was Catholic. Marie was so into her hopes for the board that she'd
almost forgotten what else was happening that day. The phone on
Kettenring's desk rang, and he said, "It's for you," and when she took
the receiver, Jim Grisham, who never cursed around her, was saying,
"Goddamn, Marie," and she said, "Yes?" and Grisham, practically
incoherent, said, "The FBI. The FBI is up here taking everything.
Hundreds of files. Over at the capitol too. You better get here quick.
They're asking for you. Hurry!"

"Thanks for your call, Jim. I'll be there," she said as routinely as she
could and told Kettenring, "I'm needed at the office." She left fast.
Kettenring would be finding out about the raid any second, and Marie
didn't want to be on hand when he did.

Barreling toward downtown, she thought about Sisk and Benson.
What should she do? To carry this off, she decided she would have to
call them. She pulled into a gas station and phoned Benson. "Charlie,
what's going on?" He said, "You ought to know."

"What do you mean?" she said. "Where's Eddie?"

"Eddie can't come to the phone because his office is full of FBI agents," Benson said.

"What are they doing?"

"Taking our files out."

"Oh, my God, Jim says they're carrying out our files too. I've got to get up there. I'll talk to you later."

"*Sure,*" Benson said. There was a lot of ugliness in his voice, and she swallowed hard.

Why hadn't Hillin given her some notice about the raids?

In fact, the decision had been made on the spur of the moment. TBCI agent Charles Lee was dating a woman in the Governor's office, and she had told Lee a whole bunch of commutation papers were being moved. Lee passed this on to George Haynes, who called Hillin on October 21, and the FBI, sensitive enough to what had happened to Marie's clemency cards, decided to go in at once.

When Marie got to the board's offices, it was filled with photographers, reporters and TV camera crews. And FBI agents. Grisham was beside himself. "I don't know what to do," he said. She felt bad that he was unaware of what was going on. "We have to cooperate," she said. "Give them whatever they want. If there's a problem, refer them to me." Reporters were shouting questions. "I can't talk to you now," she said. "I have to find out what's happening myself." Hillin appeared, playing it straight. "I'm sorry for the inconvenience, Mrs. Ragghianti," he said.

She and Hank went into her office. She told him to be sure to get the notes that board members wrote to each other during clemency investigations. They could be very revealing in cases like Billy Gene Cole and Larkin Bibbs. When a clemency petition was decided one way or another, the inmate's file was returned to the central-office records, but these notes were retained by the board and kept in alphabetical folders.

Hillin asked if Leech had gotten in touch with her. He apologized for not alerting her himself, but there hadn't been time. He explained that he had received a tip about commutation documents being taken from the legal counsel's office, and as he spoke, Marie started to get uneasy.

There was a statute requiring that each commutation, after it had been signed by the Governor and the state secretary, be formally summarized on one page and inserted in chronological order in a large leather ledger maintained in the Governor's office. The point was to enable any citizen to look up a particular commutation, although that hardly ever happened. Of course, each summary could have been prepared and inserted on the spot, but of course it wasn't. Instead, the custom was to take the commutations out of the files and summarize them in bunches, and that, Marie realized, was what had triggered the raids. Sisk and Benson may have been intent on doctoring everything in sight, but this was one time they weren't guilty. The raids hadn't been necessary—at least not now.

In all the pandemonium, Marie was trying to tell this to Hillin when Cynthia Trainor appeared at the door. She had a telephone message from Judy Hill, one of the secretaries in Sisk's office. *Need to get typewriter back. Charlie needs it. So nothing else can be tied into anything.*

"What typewriter?" Hillin said, and Marie had to think for a minute. Then she remembered. So much had been going on that she'd had trouble keeping up her journal by hand, and in September she'd borrowed the IBM Selectric she used when she had Benson's job. Still, the message didn't make sense.

Hillin asked her to call Sisk to find out more. Eddie sounded in worse shape than Jim Grisham had when he phoned her about the raids. Babbled on about five FBI agents in his office handing out subpoenas, seizing records. Even confiscating typewriter ribbons. So that was it, Marie thought.

"They're taking our records too," she said.

He wanted to know which ones. Said he was certain they'd gotten Will Midgett's. They were after everything he had on Midgett. Who else? Who else?

"Well, I don't really know," she said. "It seems like maybe Bill Cole and some of those other cases."

"My God," Sisk said.

"I don't understand about the typewriter," she said.

"You've got it, don't you?"

"Yes."

He said he had to have the typewriter, but mainly the ribbon, and it was at that moment, she would think, that she knew for sure about Eddie. If he could get worked up about a typewriter ribbon, worrying what was on it, there was nothing really left to debate.

The typewriter was home, she said, and if he wanted it that much, she'd send someone for it. But there wasn't any ribbon. You used a film cartridge on a Selectric and threw it away after using it once. The concept eluded him, and at last she said, "Eddie, take my word for it. You don't have to worry about a ribbon, I swear."

"Okay. But Marie, don't tell them anything."

She hung up. By now calls were coming in from TV and radio stations and newspapers throughout the state, and Hillin said, "Don't tell them anything."

It was, she remembered, the only time Hank Hillin and Eddie Sisk were ever in agreement.

· 2 ·

THE TENNESSEAN, *October 23, 1976*

FEDS SEIZE STATE FILES
ON CLEMENCY, PARDONS

NASHVILLE BANNER, *October 23, 1976*

FBI PROBING PAROLE PAYOFFS

She gave some inside stuff to Brinton, and reminded him to look into the Larkin Bibbs clemency. Bibbs had been rearrested on a heroin charge. But Brinton's lead came from another source—U.S. Attorney Anderson.

> The FBI today is probing the possibility that payoffs were involved in political pressure allegedly exerted by a "top" state official to obtain clemency, commutations or paroles for prison inmates.
>
> Three persons, including Mrs. Marie Ragghianti, chairman of the State Board of Pardons and Paroles, have been subpoenaed for testimony before a federal grand jury here. . . .
>
> Sources close to the Governor's office have told the *Banner* Mrs. Ragghianti and Sisk have had "heated" arguments concerning the disposition of commutation cases and that Gov. Blanton had been informed "weeks ago" of the problems between his legal counsel and the board chairman.
>
> Rumors have circulated for several months about Gov. Blanton granting executive clemency to a convicted slayer who served only four months of a 15-year term.
>
> Larkin Herman Bibbs, 26 . . . was committed to

the state prison in August 1975, and Blanton gave
him executive clemency in December.

THE TENNESSEAN, *October 24, 1976*

Gov. Ray Blanton's legal counsel denied yesterday that payoffs ever have been involved, to his
knowledge, in the granting of pardons, executive
clemency or sentence commutations for state prison
inmates.
"I deny that has ever happened," said Nashville
attorney Eddie Sisk. "The FBI didn't mention
payoffs to me."
. . . Sisk works with the [pardons and paroles]
board, referring to it requests from relatives, friends,
or from inmates. He said his office sometimes realizes that a particular person is more likely to be
eligible for consideration by the board because of his
or her record.
"I don't know if you could say we recommend.
We might say, 'this looks like a good case,' " he
said.

· 3 ·

Blanton himself was unavailable for comment. He was in Washington.
After having entertained a hundred United Nations ambassadors in
Tennessee as part of his economic development program, he had been
named chairman of the gubernatorial committee for the sixteenth
annual UN concert and dinner at the Kennedy Center. Henry Kis-
singer was to pay Blanton a special tribute for his "UN Visits Tennessee" forum.

Brooks Parker, Blanton's press secretary, said that the Governor was
cognizant of the subpoenas and that "his office is cooperating fully."
The Governor, Brooks added, would have more to say on the subject
when he returned to Nashville.

Sam Lipford could see the party line coming. Murray Henderson had
already told him that the raids were just a fishing expedition. The FBI
was out to get Blanton any way it could. Next, Lipford thought, it'd
be a Republican plot.

As he read the news reports, Sam had to shake his head at himself.
He'd gotten a tip about the FBI only a few days ago and had ignored
it. Sam had been on the varsity basketball team at Adamsville High and

liked to go down to the Y for a pickup game now and then. He was in the locker room dressing when this lawyer mentioned that he'd heard the FBI was getting very interested in the corrections department. Lipford tried to pump him, but the lawyer said he didn't know any more than that. Sam figured it might have to do with some staff improprieties at the main prison. He thought the conversation so inconsequential that he hadn't bothered to tell Henderson, and before he knew it, the FBI showed up. Lipford had been in his office when Murrell Pitts, the director of inmate records, rushed in and said he'd been handed a subpoena for a number of files. From then on, Lipford would be constantly reminded of the FBI visit. He'd go to the files to look up some inmate and would find a note instead that said *Checked out to the FBI* with the date it had been taken.

Sam began thinking about Marie. Last June, Henderson had told him she was saying that there was gross malfeasance in executive clemencies. Even that money was being passed. Henderson had said she was overreacting to rumors and gossip. Lipford remembered that during the summer Marie had said something to him about Charlie Benson pressuring her, but nothing about money changing hands.

Basically, Lipford agreed with Henderson. Marie was probably getting this dope from inmates, and with inmates you couldn't afford to overreact. Inmates bombarded you all the time with charges of wrongdoing, and you had to be very careful about them. After all, that was the business of the corrections department—inmates.

Lipford also had gotten feedback about problems between Marie and Traughber. But so what? Sam didn't like Traughber, but Marie's predecessor on the board, Dorothy Greer, had problems with Traughber too. That was the difference between Dorothy and Marie. Dorothy knew how to handle Traughber. Knew how to compromise. She was an experienced administrator, while Marie was a novice in management. She didn't know how to handle people on an administrative level. Was always acting impulsively. What counted was whether she liked someone or not. All you had to do was look at Marie's personnel troubles, Lipford thought. There had been the business with John Stoker and Sherry Lomax. And then with Sherry alone. And finally he'd had to bail Marie out by finding Jim Grisham. That wasn't the way to operate.

But Lipford had to admit he didn't know Marie all that well. He'd had minimal contact with her by phone during her extradition days. The first time he paid any real attention to her was when Sisk suggested that she might be going on the board because of her academic credentials. The surprise had been the chairmanship. Whispers of Marie's bed-hopping made sense. Sam had an eye for the ladies. But he soon recognized that with Marie he had run into a stone wall.

Now Lipford allowed himself a private laugh. Surprise, surprise. Maybe Sisk and the others hadn't known Marie all that well either. The unfunny part was where this FBI thing might go. If it got out of hand, a lot of jobs could go down the chute, Sam Lipford decided. Including his.

The bar at the Belle Meade Country Club hadn't buzzed like this in years—and not about the FBI and pardons and paroles.

One of the few persons in the Nashville power structure who had any truck with Ray Blanton was Ed Nelson, the president of Commerce Union Bank. Nelson was short, balding, fastidious. For some reason that his fellow club members couldn't fathom, Nelson liked Blanton, or at least was amused by him, and when Blanton had said he wanted to bring a delegation of United Nations officials to Nashville to help Tennessee's trade, Nelson had backed the project.

So, of course, Blanton took Nelson along with him to the big UN affair in Washington. The White House chief of protocol, Shirley Temple Black, was there. Blanton, flushed and on a high, had downed several Scotches when he asked Nelson if he wanted to meet *the* Shirley Temple, and Ed said he sure would, and Blanton hustled him over, and Nelson was extending his hand as he heard the Governor say, "Shirley, I want you to meet Ed Nelson, one of the most distinguished citizens of our state. Ever since he was a little boy, he's wanted to fuck you."

In retrospect Nelson thought it was kind of funny. The way he told it at the Belle Meade Country Club he still had his hand out, looking at the stunned expression on Shirley Temple's face, and suddenly she wasn't there anymore.

After that, whenever there was a reception requiring the presence of Nashville's elite and the Governor walked in, husbands hurried to their wives and escorted them to the nearest window, mumbling how pretty the city's new skyline looked at night.

· 4 ·

Late Friday afternoon, the day of the raids, Sisk had called Marie back and said he wanted to see her, and they arranged to meet at the Capitol Hill Club. Eddie was in a complete sweat. How could this have happened? he was saying. Did Marie think the acting DA over in Lebanon, Tommy Thompson, had done something? He seemed to recall Jack Lowery telling him he'd reported the Will Midgett business to Thompson. But those goddamn FBI agents had also been asking about Bibbs and Cole, so what the hell was going on? Eddie got a nervous tic in his voice when he was upset, somewhere between a hiccough and a mild belch, and Marie had never seen it so bad. It was coming every ten or twenty seconds. All at once he said he had to call Bill Willis. Sisk had been associated with the law firm of Willis and Knight, one of the most influential in Nashville. Willis himself was counsel to the *Tennessean.*

She listened to Sisk say, "Hold on a minute," and next he was asking her if she had a pen, and she fumbled through her purse and found one and handed it to him. As she did, she noticed emblazoned on the pen *District Attorneys General Conference.* It was too late to retrieve it, and Marie watched Eddie, on the phone, glancing at the pen, scrutinizing it and then squinting his eyes toward her. It was an unpleasant instant. As though they both knew what was on each other's minds. After Sisk had hung up, he wasn't the same. More guarded. But he didn't come out with anything.

Except for Larry Brinton, Marie didn't want to talk to any reporters, and to escape the media she asked her father if she and Therese could spend the weekend at his condominium in the country north of the city. She had thought of Virginia, but too many press people knew how often she was there.

October 24

. . . for the first time, the media & the general public learned of the federal probe. All eyes are on me. Those "in the know" suspect I am behind the probe. Those "not in the know" probably believe I'm one of the targets of the probe. A very devastating period for me. I can only pray to God & ask His blessing.

On Monday Marie couldn't hide anymore. She didn't know quite what to do. Then she decided she had to act normally. And the most normal thing would be to go to the capitol and see Sisk.

The prospect rattled her. In a way, it was the hardest thing yet for her to do. Up till now, it seemed, she'd been so caught up in events, so emotionally charged, that her actions had almost come out of themselves. This time she was making a calculated decision.

It was about as awful as she'd imagined, going down the capitol's central corridor. She might as well have worn a leper's bell, she thought —along with a sign that said *Judas*. People seemed thunderstruck at actually seeing her there. Secretaries peered at her as though she were some exotic object, the last of a species. Edd Hood and Al Wise, another Blanton special assistant, were walking toward her, did a double take, and went right by without saying a word. That's what she recalled more than anything. Nobody saying hello.

The string was broken by Larry Brinton. As she neared the legal counsel's office, she bumped into him. "Hi, Marie," he said, grinning, "what's new?" She could have killed Larry. *"Please,"* she said. "Go away."

FBI agents were still taking material from the legal counsel's office. When Marie entered, Benson glared at her with undisguised hatred, but with the agents there he didn't say anything. Trent Hall was openmouthed. Janice Clinkenbeard looked petrified when Marie asked where Eddie was. "Upstairs, I think. Want me to ring him?"

"No, I'll find him." She went up the same stairs she had mounted six months ago for her job interview with Ray Blanton. My God, she thought, had it been just six months? She found Sisk with Brooks Parker, the press secretary. As soon as he saw her, he sprang up and took her into an empty office. Oddly, he was about the only one she'd encountered that morning who reacted to the sight of her with anything approaching equanimity. He even seemed glad to see her. That was Eddie. Either hot or cold. She wanted to tell him that he had to do something about all of this before it was too late. But she'd tried and failed so many times, and now, she guessed, it *was* too late.

All he wanted to know was what else she had heard. And she replied truthfully, "Nothing." She'd sequestered herself the entire weekend. Sisk had left the office door open, and Marie saw people passing by in the hall, glancing in, startled to find her and Sisk huddled together. Larry Brinton peeked in at them at least twice. Larry appeared perplexed.

· 5 ·

Fresh from hobnobbing with national and international figures in Washington, as well as having been partied by old congressional colleagues hailing his elevated status, Ray Blanton returned to Nashville and launched a tirade against partisan political hatchet men.

It was a giant conspiracy, he declared, aimed at affecting statewide and national elections ten days hence. Jimmy Carter was running against Gerald Ford. And, more to the point, Jim Sasser was challenging Republican incumbent Senator Bill Brock. Blanton had backed Sasser, a studious, low-keyed lawyer and former state party chairman, for the Democratic nomination over the flamboyant John Jay Hooker Jr., a maverick member of a Belle Meade family. An early poll had shown Hooker with the greater name recognition, but Blanton nonetheless went the other way, and Sasser had won the primary easily.

The conspiracy part had been supplied by Sisk. He had learned that the day before the FBI raids, U.S. Attorney Anderson and the editor of the Republican-oriented Nashville *Banner* had lunched together. That was all Blanton needed, and he went right on the offensive. First his press office spread word of the lunch, and then released the text of a telegram the Governor had dispatched to U.S. Attorney General Edward Levi.

I HEREBY REQUEST AN IMMEDIATE INVESTIGATION OF THE U.S. ATTOR-NEY'S OFFICE FOR THE MIDDLE DISTRICT OF TENNESSEE. THE EVENTS THAT HAVE TRANSPIRED SINCE FRIDAY, OCTOBER 22, 1976, LEAD ME TO BELIEVE THAT THE U.S. ATTORNEY'S OFFICE IS BEING USED BY U.S. SENA-TOR WILLIAM E. BROCK III, AND HIS POLITICAL SUPPORTERS AT THE NASHVILLE BANNER FOR THE PURPOSES OF TRYING TO ENHANCE HIS CAMPAIGN FOR REELECTION TO THE U.S. SENATE. FURTHER, THESE EVENTS LEAD ME TO CONCLUDE THAT, ONCE AGAIN, THE FBI IS BEING USED TO FURTHER PARTISAN POLITICAL INTERESTS. . . .

Then Blanton put out an even tougher declaration.

Friday, the U.S. Attorney for the Middle District of Tennessee, appointed by President Nixon at the recommendation of William E. Brock III's campaign manager, ordered FBI agents to conduct a so-called "raid" on the office of my counsel at the State Capitol.

They had a subpoena issued at the request of the same U.S. Attorney. The agents told members of my staff they did not know the purpose of the investigation or what specific cases were in question.

I know why they were sent. Because an election is only days away, and Senator Brock is "in trouble." Let me tell you why I don't think Brock deserves to represent the people of Tennessee. . . . He supported the corrupt administration of Richard Nixon. He praised a corrupt Vice President, Spiro Agnew. At the Republican national convention four years ago, William E. Brock III led the young people of his party to support a dishonest President and Vice President.

Privately, Blanton wanted to know who the hell was behind the raids. The names always came down to Gerbitz, Fisher or Marie. The best Sisk had been able to pick up was that it was a DA. Sisk personally thought it was Gerbitz. A Republican with fancy political aspirations. From Chattanooga and after Bill Thompson's hide. You couldn't dismiss Fisher, though. So active in the DAs' legislative conference. Charlie Benson, of course, was convinced it was Marie. But Sisk couldn't see Marie going to the feds. She'd never had it so good, and she had those three kids to support. It wasn't possible she would risk throwing everything away. At worst, she'd done some complaining to Gerbitz or Fisher. Well, said Blanton, Murray Henderson had better straighten her out. Sisk was thankful about that. He wasn't being blamed for Marie. And the truth was why should he be? A whole phalanx of Blanton people had backed her for the chairmanship.

It was so difficult to figure where Blanton was at, Sisk thought. Sisk took his cues from Bill Thompson. After all, the Governor himself had called Sisk about the Billy Gene Cole clemency. *On Thompson's behalf.*

The reaction to the Governor's wire to Washington and his statement about the raids was beyond the administration's wildest dreams. A Blanton axiom was that when you were attacked, you came back swinging. Never explain. The more you explained, the more defensive you sounded. And guilty.

But first thing, the *Banner*'s editor, Ken Morrell, issued his own statement admitting he'd lunched with the U.S. attorney the day before the raid but claiming it had been a chance encounter. When he entered the cafeteria, a mutual acquaintance suggested he join Anderson's table. Only pleasantries had been exchanged, he said.

Anderson, instead of ignoring Blanton, also sent off a telegram to Washington and released the text. He said that the investigation into pardons and paroles had not originated in his office and he had nothing to do with the timing of the raids. Furthermore, he was out of town when the whole thing started. I DO HAVE SENATOR BROCK'S CAMPAIGN BUMPER STICKER ON MY PERSONAL AUTOMOBILE, the U.S. attorney's wire read. MY WIFE HAS BEEN WORKING AS A VOLUNTEER AND HAS CONTRIBUTED TO THE CAMPAIGN. SHE ALSO HAS A BROCK BUMPER STRIP ON HER CAR.

That sparked considerable chortling in the Governor's office. The U.S. attorney was coming off as a henpecked bumbler who either wasn't in command of his office or was lying. But something else in Anderson's telegram did arouse interest. Anderson said that the investigation had been initiated by several responsible Tennessee state officials. Pressed by reporters, he went further. Three officials were involved, all Democrats, elected or appointed. Marie remembered thinking, Why doesn't he just name me, Fisher and Raybin?

David Raybin had barely finished reading Marsha Vande Berg's story in the *Tennessean* about Anderson's three unidentified Democrats when Vande Berg was in his office. She wanted to talk about pardons and paroles. Raybin was trying to decide whether she was there because Anderson had leaked his name or merely because he was the board's legal adviser. Then Vande Berg asked him if he had gone to the FBI, and he said no. Technically, it was the truth, but Raybin felt uncomfortable about the evasion. Yet he couldn't think of any other way to protect Marie. He was bracing himself for the same question about her. All Vande Berg asked him about Marie, however, was if he had ever gone out with her, and that was an easy no. The same old stories were making the rounds, Raybin thought, chagrined to recall that he had once fallen for them himself.

When Vande Berg called her, Marie sensed a hostile attitude. Seemed as if this was turning into a media fight, the *Banner* anti administration and the *Tennessean* pro. Marie told Vande Berg what Bill Leech had said to say. Since she was under a grand jury subpoena, she couldn't comment.

On Blanton's orders, Murray Henderson arranged a press conference for the board members five days after the raids. Joe Mitchell never made it. His car had broken down, he said. Marie arrived at the tail end and again said she had been advised that it would be improper to answer any questions because of the grand jury.

But Traughber came through for the administration. The *Tennessean* quoted him as declaring he knew of no pressure from Blanton and no payoffs for inmates seeking early prison release. Asked if the board had ever been informed of the Governor's wishes in a specific case, he replied, "Not that I know of."

At the Capitol Hill Club Richard Fisher was going in as Sisk was coming out. Sisk was weaving noticeably and blocking his way. Fisher was responsible for the federal investigation, Sisk said suddenly, his arm cocked back, fist doubled. Well, this is it, Fisher thought. "I'm just a DA," he said. "I do my job whenever and whatever it is." There was a DAs' meeting in Nashville, and another district attorney, Buck Ramsey, happened by at that moment and grabbed Sisk's arm. The steam went out of Sisk. "It's either you or Gerbitz," he muttered, walking off, and Fisher realized Eddie really didn't know anything.

All in all, though, Sisk himself was feeling pretty chesty. He had gone screaming to the *Banner*'s publisher after Larry Brinton's initial story about the FBI raid, and the paper had backed down, offering him prominent space to reply. Eddie's statement, printed in full, said the Brinton report was nothing but innuendo and reckless disregard for the truth. He denied, among other things, exerting any undue pressure involving pardons, commutations and extraditions. He also flatly denied having "heated" arguments with Marie over commutation cases or that Blanton had been informed "weeks ago" of problems between him and the board chairman.

Eddie's windup was reminiscent of his performance in the Arnold Peebles affair.

I am a relatively young lawyer who left a rewarding private law practice to go into public service. I did so at a financial sacrifice to make a contribution to government.

I have worked hard to conduct myself in a manner to bring credit upon myself in all that I did . . . In order to be able to engage again in the honorable private practice of law, it is vital that my reputation for integrity be above reproach.

· 6 ·

It was the limbo she was in that Marie couldn't abide. She had gone into the Capitol Hill Club and somebody had started chirping—like a canary. And she'd heard the snickers.

A woman parole officer called her from Memphis. She said, "Mrs. Ragghianti, I just want you to know that it's the first time in all my years in corrections that I felt like someone was trying to do something about this mess." That had been nice to hear, but the point was Marie really wasn't able to say much in return.

A week after the raids she dropped in at a cocktail party that marked the end of the meeting of the district attorneys, the same sort of conference she had attended last June in Memphis. And right away Bill Pope, a DA from the southeast part of the state, around where Fisher and Gerbitz had their districts, said loudly in front of everyone, "Hey, Marie, you blew the whistle on them, didn't you? Good going!" She didn't know how to react. She felt her cheeks go hot, and she couldn't wait to get out.

That did it. On Saturday she dropped Therese off at Virginia's and drove again to Roque's place. It was a lovely autumn afternoon, the sun slanting through the colorful foliage. So incredibly peaceful.

She sat alone on the lawn under the trees, and after a while she took a pad she'd brought with her and began writing an announcement. She wanted all the speculation over and done with. She was the one who had brought about the investigation, and she wrote how and why she had done it. She would call a press conference on Monday.

She went inside and showed the statement to her father. "Daddy, I can't stand it anymore," she said. "Here, read this."

Roque said she should of course do whatever she thought was best, but he urged her to speak first to Bill Leech. And Hillin as well. What she intended to do could drastically affect the investigation.

She phoned Leech. "I've had it. I've written a statement. I'm having a press conference, and say I'm behind this thing. Everybody knows it anyway. You should see what it's like walking down the capitol halls. Everybody on the hill knows it. Everybody in corrections. I'll bet every reporter in the state knows it. You should have heard what they said at the DAs' conference. You should have heard Bill Pope yesterday. I feel like a fool carrying on this charade," she said. "What's to be gained? I'm going to get fired anyway. I'd rather go ahead and lay my cards on the table. Tell people 'Yes, by God, I did it. I'm the one.' "

Leech was worried not only about Marie's physical safety but also about her financial situation. He wanted her to keep her salary as long as possible. He knew, though, this wouldn't cut any ice with her. Instead, he tried arguing that to go public at this stage would blow the investigation. Mess up the show.

"It won't mess up anything," she insisted. "I've given Hank everything I can."

"You can't do it, Marie."

"Bill, this whole thing is crazy. Do you realize what a stupid mistake the FBI made? After all I've gone through, they went up there and raided the darn capitol when they didn't have to. All they had to do was make one lousy call to me, and all this could have been avoided. It's insane!"

"Marie, promise me you won't do anything until we've talked to Hank," Leech said. "Call up Hank."

So the phone calls began. Between her and Hillin. Between Leech and Hillin. Between her and Leech again. Hillin importuned her to reconsider. Finally it was decided that they would all meet Sunday evening at Leech's farmhouse in Santa Fe. The road past his house wasn't well traveled. Anyone nosing around would be quickly spotted.

The living room walls were faced with hand-hewn hundred-year-old hickory logs. Limestone for the huge fireplace had been quarried on the property. During her one previous visit, Marie had fallen in love with the house. It seemed to represent a simpler, purer time. Leech lived there alone. He was recently divorced, and on the verge of remarrying. Before everything was over, naturally, there'd be all kinds of rumors about Marie and Leech.

Marie brought Roque with her. Leech was putting on coffee when Hillin arrived with Toy Fuson, the Nashville resident agent. "Toy, I want you to meet a woman of great courage," Hillin said, and Fuson shook her hand and said how indebted they were to her.

Leech started off by saying that Marie was feeling tremendous pressure and that everyone was there to discuss the ramifications of her declaring her role in the investigation. Personally, he said, he could understand what she was enduring, but he was concerned that such a disclosure might be premature, that it might be better if she waited and declared herself at a time when it counted more.

Hillin picked up the theme. The investigation was barely under way. What Marie was contemplating not only would jeopardize it but would also terminate her usefulness. She might think people knew what she'd done. Really, though, they didn't. She felt that way because *she* knew. The FBI needed her where she was, he said. Besides, it was no moment to throw her job away. If she would only hang in. He too was aware of what she was going through, said Hillin, but he was convinced she was equal to it.

Hillin turned to Roque and said, "Mr. Fajardo, it's hard for me to be talking like this in front of you because Marie's your daughter, and if she were my daughter, I'd be wanting to protect her, and I guess I can't ask you to feel anything except that."

And Marie listened as her father responded that while he was outraged by the idea of her losing her livelihood for doing the right thing, instead of those in the wrong losing theirs, he wasn't about to tell her to do this or that. It was her decision, and only she could make it.

"Okay," she said. "I'll go along with you all. For now."

· 7 ·

With Blanton railing away at the Republicans, Jim Sasser's candidacy all but disappeared in the media. But on Election Day, November 2, Blanton clearly won the first go-around. It was a Democratic sweep. Sasser beat Brock almost three to two in the U.S. Senate race. And Tennessee gave Jimmy Carter 56 percent of the presidential vote, his largest margin in the country outside of Georgia. By any standard, Ray Blanton had a big I.O.U. coming to him in Washington, D.C.

Election evening TBCI agent George Haynes stopped in at Ray Judge's gun shop in Franklin County near the Alabama border. Haynes was thinking of getting a Smith & Wesson Airweight Bodyguard .38 revolver. It was a lot lighter than his standard issue. After about an hour, when Ray was closing up, he invited Haynes to accompany him to Democratic headquarters.

As the returns came in that night and everyone was celebrating the Democratic margin, Haynes heard this fellow talking about a liquor store he was going to open and announcing that he was calling Edd Hood right then and there to find out what was what with the license. Mention of Hood, one of Blanton's special assistants, got Haynes's attention. Haynes couldn't tell if Hood actually was on the line, but he caught the conversation at his end. Fifty-five hundred had been paid already. When was the damn license coming through?

Good Lord, Haynes thought, they're selling liquor franchises too, and the next day he reported what he'd heard to the FBI's Nashville office.

THIRTEEN

So liquor franchises went on Hank Hillin's agenda, but pardons and paroles remained the priority case.

The timing of the raids had been a big blunder, but there was no use worrying about it now. Hillin comforted himself with the thought that many papers might otherwise have been destroyed. For instance, one gem had been unearthed that certainly wouldn't have remained in existence much longer. A handwritten note from Bill Thompson to Eddie Sisk, dated June 20, 1975.

Would you please discuss the matter of a time cut for William Cole, 73060, with the Governor. I would appreciate it very much if you would contact me by phone (615-825-0548) and let me know Monday how this matter stands. Thanks, Bill Thompson.

Right away that tied in a lot of interested parties on the Cole clemency. And showed beyond a shadow of a doubt that Marie wasn't smoking something funny.

Hillin had already obtained a mug shot of Bill Thompson from Gary Gerbitz and shown it to Jack Lowery in Lebanon, and Lowery had identified Thompson and Roundtree as one and the same person.

Hillin hadn't stopped there. He checked the radio log of the Lebanon police department to make sure a call had gone out on the black

Cordoba that Prater was driving. He also talked to the Murfreesboro officer, John Lasater, who had intercepted the car. Lasater confirmed that Prater was behind the wheel, and when he saw Thompson's picture, he said it sure looked like one of the other men.

Barring some big break, Hillin knew that was how this case would be put together. Bits and pieces, each substantiating the other, to make a picture for the jury. And maybe there would be a break. Marie had pointed him in the right direction. There'd be incidents she didn't know about, but it was a hell of a start. And she was indispensable in another regard. By the nature of the case, most of the witnesses would have records. Their credibility would be savaged. Defense lawyers would have a field day with them. But Marie was a white-glove witness, unstained. The trouble was she hadn't actually seen money pass hands, deals being made.

In the beginning Hillin had planned on asking her to wear a wire. Entice Sisk into damaging discussions. Hillin would have coached her on that. But once he met her, he knew this wasn't feasible, not now anyway. She was still too ambivalent about Sisk. Felt too sorry for him. Hillin had tried to get her to realize what a dog Sisk was, and he would try again. Maybe she'd change. He had this feeling, though, that she wouldn't do it under any circumstances. Marie was one strong-minded woman.

Conventional wisdom put Sisk down as dumb, but when you looked at the whole thing, he wasn't really all that dumb. You could see that Sisk was as guilty as sin, but only if you wanted to. Making a case stick against him was another matter.

You had to nail down that there was a scheme to extort money from people seeking to avoid extradition or to get out of prison early. You had to show that a conspiracy was in the works here, that money or its equivalent had been exchanged, that there'd been influence-peddling of a criminal nature. Suppose you got Thompson. What then? Was he simply acting on his own, letting people think he had Sisk in his hip pocket? As it stood, Sisk could argue he was just doing Thompson a favor, however imprudent. The kind of thing you did for a friend. How did you rope in Sisk? Or Blanton? Blantons, the guys at the top, played it cute. Kept layers between them and the actual deed, like Mafia bosses. There was also certain to be a sense among those being investigated that they were all-powerful, untouchable. The Governor's office was no small shield. Getting anyone to crack wouldn't be easy.

You didn't have to go further than Arnold Peebles. Marie had reminded Hillin about Peebles. So had George Haynes, for that matter. Hillin could kick himself for having ignored the bribe attempt at the time, thereby joining a vast army. But there wasn't much to be done now. The inmate, Jerry Bates Long, had said his piece. His conversations with Peebles had been recorded. But Sisk had claimed he didn't know anything about it. Peebles had gone off for psychiatric help, and Hillin heard he was making a miraculous recovery. Word was that he'd be reapplying for his license. It wasn't likely Peebles would risk his prospects to practice law again by changing his tune, whatever the truth was.

With a Larkin Bibbs, it was the same dead end. Gerbitz had gotten reams of press copy with Bibbs. "I'm tired of this happening," he'd thundered. "What kind of explanation can they give for letting the man out this quick?" And now that Bibbs was headed back to the pokey after his heroin bust, you would think he'd be anxious to make a deal. Spill everything. But Hillin had discovered that Bibbs was a hotshot pusher for a violent black gang in Chattanooga running drugs throughout the Southeast. Undoubtedly, that was why his clemency had been greased in the first place. He'd be expecting a repeat performance. And even if he didn't get it, he'd be afraid of having his throat slit for talking. Hillin gave it a try anyway. But when he spoke to Bibbs, all he got in return was an insolent, silent stare.

From the cartons of documents the FBI seized, though, there had to be tracks. Some sort of pattern. As Hillin sifted through them, he saw a couple of avenues worth exploring. One was Jimmy H. Pendleton. All set to get clemency and suddenly didn't. Obviously, something had gone wrong. Hillin decided to send Dick Knudson out to chat with Pendleton's wife. Knudson, a young agent in the Nashville office, had quite a knack with people.

There was another, even better possibility. As Thompson's driver and gofer, Tommy Prater must have been around a lot of things. But best of all, Prater turned out to be Billy Gene Cole's cousin. Now, wasn't that an odd coincidence? And from the rundown Hillin had on him, Tommy didn't come off being so tough. Slick was the bottom line on Prater. Several arrests, but practically no time served. Squeeze him a little, and he might want to negotiate. Prater had been picked up after the extradition warrant was signed, and a motion was routinely made to get him out on bond. Hillin asked Gerbitz to contest his release. Let Prater stew in the Hamilton County jail.

Irvin Wells, an FBI agent in Chattanooga, went to pay Prater a visit.

· 2 ·

The grand jury subpoenas handed out during the raids were answerable November 8, and that was awkward. Momentum was important in a case like this. After all the hoopla, indictments would be anticipated, and there weren't going to be any. This particular grand jury was winding up its term. Marie and Jack Lowery would do their thing and lay the foundation for the next grand jury to be convened. Of course, you always hoped for some perjury, especially from Sisk. Besides Sisk, Murray Henderson would be making an appearance, along with Traughber, Mitchell and Dorothy Greer.

In his turn, Henderson explained that the pardons and paroles board was financially controlled by the Department of Correction. Beyond that, he said, he had little contact with the board. When asked about the Bibbs and Cole clemencies, he testified that he was unfamiliar with either one. Later he told reporters, "If I had known of any irregularities, I'd have been the first to report them."

Traughber insisted that he was unaware of any undue pressure from the Governor's office regarding clemencies. Mitchell said he just went along with the rest of the board. Dorothy Greer, however, testified how the board had decided to "submit" rather than "recommend" certain clemency petitions that the Governor was interested in.

Sisk admitted knowing Bill Thompson from politics, but he said his only business dealing with Thompson involved possible investments in coal land. Thompson had approached Sisk, as both a friend and a potential investor, for his opinion about the coal deals. He acknowledged that Thompson made inquiries about the status of Prater's extradition to Georgia. There was nothing unusual about this, he said. People were constantly asking about pardons, paroles and extraditions, and the policy of his office was to be as cooperative as possible. As for any delay in the extraditions, Georgia hadn't helped by fouling up the papers to begin with. In the Will Midgett business, Sisk said he couldn't see where a crime had been committed, and anyway the Governor's office wasn't supposed to initiate criminal investigations. That was the job of the TBCI and the local DA, and Sisk said he'd been told by Lowery that the acting DA had been informed. He had no hard information on Bob Roundtree, Sisk maintained. Lowery hadn't told *him* Roundtree could have been Thompson.

"Stay with the questions," Bill Leech had told her, and she said, "Suppose they don't ask the right ones?" and he replied, smiling despite himself, "Marie, *listen* to me."

She began to worry about the impact of her testimony—hoped that it'd be, well, fair. It was going to be an extraordinary time for her, she thought, but however devastating she might find the experience, it had to be even more unbearable for Eddie. At least she was on the right side.

The morning of her grand jury appearance Marie went to mass and communion at the cathedral. She had gone there so she could look for Monsignor Siener and ask his blessing. But when she went to the residence, she was told he wasn't in. The bishop, James Niedergeses, was on his way out, however, and Marie introduced herself as Virginia and Roque Fajardo's daughter, and Bishop Niedergeses said oh yes, he'd been reading about her. She explained why she had come, that she was concerned about the effect her testimony would have on the lives of people who had been her friends, people who had families and children, and Niedergeses placed his hand on her head and prayed aloud that her words would be an expression of God's will.

Bill Leech was waiting for her at the courthouse. Lights, cameras, reporters. Are you nervous, Mrs. Ragghianti? Do you have anything to hide? Are you going to tell what you know? She couldn't believe it. That somebody would actually ask her that.

And next she was in the grand jury room being sworn in, and to her amazement, the foreman was Stephie Freudenthal, an old friend of Virginia's, who worked at the Mills bookstore in Belle Meade. It made Marie feel at ease. She recalled all the times Stephie had sat in Virginia's living room. The U.S. attorney, Anderson, was asking the questions, but Marie concentrated on Stephie as she talked. She remembered how Stephie smiled and nodded back, almost clapping her hands once or twice.

"Are you familiar with the case involving Will E. Midgett?" Anderson said, and Marie answered, "I am." That was the way it began. She was on the stand for nearly three hours, far longer than any other witness. When she emerged, Leech looked at his watch and rolled his eyes. The length of her testimony wouldn't be lost on the administration. But Marie felt good about the grand jurors. There'd been twenty-three of them, black and white, men and women, white- and blue-collar —alert, interested, supportive. Right at the end there had been a colloquy between two jurors. One said the Governor couldn't be expected to run everything himself, it would take nine hundred hours a day, and the other said, "He is the one where the buck stops for the State of Tennessee."

After two days of bringing witnesses before the grand jury, Charles Anderson announced there hadn't been enough evidence for any indictments.

Don't worry, Hillin said to her. She'd been terrific. This was just the start.

On November 11, in Chattanooga, Judge Russell Hinson refused to grant habeas corpus writs to Tommy Prater, Bruce McBryar, Wendell Allen Barnes and Reisto Bekovich. Hinson ordered that the four men remain in custody while he considered their pleas for bond. Gary Gerbitz, who fought the bonds, told reporters that the FBI had requested and received material from his office on Prater and the others.

Defense attorneys from Ward Crutchfield's firm had argued that the delay in the extradition proceedings was not that uncommon. Witnesses testified that all four had been in Tennessee when the Dalton robberies took place. In response, Bernard Weinthal was produced, and he swore he had met with the defendants in Dalton on the dates in question. Judge Hinson ruled that it had not been shown beyond a reasonable doubt that the defendants weren't in Georgia when Georgia said they were. Defense attorneys declared they'd carry the case to the Tennessee Court of Criminal Appeals.

Agent Wells reported to Hillin that Prater claimed to know nothing about payoffs for pardons and paroles. On the other hand, said Wells, Tommy didn't seem too happy about being in jail.

· 3 ·

After her grand jury appearance, it wasn't as though people stopped talking to her, but if Marie happened to be in the cafeteria having a cup of coffee or a sandwich, all they did was say hello. Hardly anybody sat down with her. Even a cool customer like Sam Lipford. Or Ramon.

She had thought a great deal about Ramon. How guarded he'd

become. Before the FBI raids, Ramon had invited her for dinner out at his place in Goodlettsville, not so far from where her father lived. Ramon Sanchez-Viñas was a first-rate cook, and he had promised a chicken cordon bleu with a great white wine. It was exactly the sort of thing she adored.

Goodlettsville was country, and that night as she drove through the dark, winding roads off the Interstate, she caught sight of a van behind her. The van had an aerial.

Once she reached Ramon's he started in on her to quit her obsessive behavior as chairman. It was one thing to be concerned about her work, but she had to have some perspective. There was only so much she could do. Ramon didn't spell out the meeting he'd had with Blanton, and, of course, did not realize she had already gone to the FBI. He warned the route she was taking could lead to disaster. "Honey, you've got to watch out. If they can't get you professionally, they'll do it another way," he said.

The evening left her disquieted, defensive and strangely discombobulated. She and Ramon weren't speaking the same language any longer. She left about ten-thirty. At a crossroads gas station she glimpsed the van with its aerial. She jerked the BMW around and raced back to Ramon's. She told him she believed she was being followed and asked if she could spend the night on his sofa. He looked at her as though she was flipping out, but she didn't care. Luckily, Therese was staying at Virginia's. In the morning there wasn't any sign of the van.

Marie told Hank Hillin what Ramon had said. She didn't mention the van. In the clear light of day it was rather melodramatic. Perhaps she'd been seeing things.

If she had said anything to anyone about the van then, it would have been to Kevin McCormack. Kevin would have eaten it up. He worked for Sam Lipford, and of all the corrections department personnel, he was the only one who appeared unfazed by her travails with the administration. Indeed, Kevin, twenty-seven, curly-haired, bespectacled, was avid for inside details. "Come on, Marie," he'd say, "what's happening? You know plenty more than you're letting on." And he'd always do it with such an outrageously malicious glint in his eye that she would end up laughing. Kevin was a delight, and despite his gossipy nature, she noticed how industrious he was. On Saturday mornings, when she'd go to the office to catch up, he would be there more often than not, typing away on reports.

Of course, Sisk wanted to know everything that had gone on with the grand jury. Marie was as vague as she could be. She pointedly did not inquire what he had been asked.

She remembered how Eddie kept tapping his pen on the desk top. Frankly, he said, he, *they*, were at their wits' end about her. The pen-tapping got to her. She recognized that whatever affection she had for him was based on memory. A lot of water had run under the bridge.

"Like what?" she said. "You all are wearing me out with your accusations. I wanted to be helpful, and you wouldn't let me. You want to order me around, period. You have no regard for anything I say, much less my professional opinion. Do you think I want to make you look bad? I wanted you to look good. You and I know what's wrong. It's this investigation. That's all."

He said she was the most ungrateful person he had ever met. She'd been given one of the best jobs in state government, and she'd stabbed them in the back. He didn't know whether she had started this thing, but he was convinced she had something to do with it, running around, befriending every goddamn DA in Tennessee. He'd told her none of them could be trusted. All they cared about was being reelected. They'd try for mileage on anything they could. Raising hell about a clemency was just another way for them to get votes. Grab a mike and embarrass Ray Blanton was the name of the game. He couldn't understand how she'd let herself be taken in. She was so naive. The big mistake was thinking she was mature enough for the job. If she kept it up, he couldn't say if she could go on being the board's chairman. Look at the mess she'd made, he said.

That infuriated her. "How can you say such a thing?" she said. "What kind of job could I do if all I thought about was being the chairman? Of course I want to be chairman. But if every move I made was calculated on that, how good would I be? Good grief, Eddie, I thought you knew me better. *You,* of all people!"

· 4 ·

It was one of her nights to get to bed early. Thanksgiving was two days off, and Dante and Ricky would be home from Morris. She wanted to get rested up for them.

Therese had come in to read on the other twin bed in Marie's room and had fallen asleep. Marie got the phone on its first ring and came wide awake. A man's voice said, "Hold on for the Governor," and the next thing, Blanton was saying, "Marie?"

"Yes, Governor," she said, and he said he wanted to know what the hell she was doing. "Governor, I'm in bed." He said he didn't mean that, she knew what he meant. What was she trying to do to him anyway? Was this how she expressed her gratitude and loyalty?

Therese stirred. Marie tried to keep her voice down. She thought Blanton's words sounded a little slurred, but it was hard to tell whether he'd been drinking or if it was that rural drawl of his. "Governor, can you be more specific?" she said.

What was the story on her and her boozing and her carrying-on? he said. "What's the matter, can't you hold your booze?" She remembered that distinctly.

"Governor, I hardly know what to say."

He repeated, "Can't you hold your booze?"

"All I can say is that I hardly drink."

Yeah, well, he said, and then he said he had reports she had some pretty cozy relationships with the DAs. He understood she even had something going with an FBI agent.

"Governor, what are you talking about?"

"Hell, you know more about it than I do. That's for sure." For a moment his voice trailed off, as if he didn't know what to say next. Be in his office at noon tomorrow, he said abruptly. He didn't want to continue this on the phone. "All right," she said, "I'll be there," and he said, by God, she'd better be.

Marie called Bill Leech and related what had happened, and said there was no way she would keep the appointment. She wasn't going in to accept the humiliation of being fired like this, and Leech said, "You've got to see what he says. We can do it." What do you mean, *we?* she thought.

With Hank Hillin it was the same. She had to find out what Blanton was up to, he said. The only thing that riled Hank was Blanton's remark about her and an FBI agent. Blanton could have said she was sleeping with Hugh Hefner, whom she considered about the lowest form of human life on earth, or even Al Capone, and it wouldn't have bothered Hank for a second. But an FBI agent? Perish the thought!

November 24, 1976
The Day before Thanksgiving

What hell—a visit with the Governor himself, & practically a <u>promise</u> of severance. "Two months." He said he thought maybe he had made a mistake in appointing me, that I "talk too much." "To whom, Governor?" "What's the matter, can't you hold your booze?" "Governor, I hardly even drink. That's all I can say." (It reminded me of the telephone conversation last night, when he made a similar comment, & I said, "Governor Blanton, I am not an alcoholic," & he backed down somewhat.) But today he was full of wildly ludicrous accusations about how I had "talked too much," & he even went so far as to say I had <u>broken the law</u> by discussing confidential records with the wrong people (which is patently absurd). I said, more than once, "Governor, I would welcome the opportunity to confront these people in your presence," but he always seemed to ignore that, never giving any names, always being evasive.

When I asked for names, he said his sources were "impeachable (sic)" and that he didn't believe rumors and that too many "impeachable sources" had told him about me & that I was the cause of this whole investigation & did I know what it was like to have all your closest friends being interrogated & hounded by the FBI with a bunch of fairy tales? I said, well, the entire thing has been unpleasant for me, as well. And he said, "Well, your own mouth got this whole thing started, and if you don't put a stop to it, I'm going to." I asked what he meant and he said if things continued he would be forced to ask for my resignation, & I said whatever for and he said didn't I realize I had broken the law?

I said, "Governor Blanton, I can't think of anything further from the truth. I have done nothing but uphold that Board & defend the Administration to the best of my ability—to my friends, to the public, to the Grand Jury & to the FBI . . ." He turned quickly & interrupted. "Are they still investigating?" he asked. "I don't know—not to my knowledge," I replied.

And I wondered at what point, at what moment, at what hour I had allowed myself to become so enmeshed in such corruption—and where was the admiration I had felt for this man who sat before me now— behind the most important and prestigious desk in Tennessee—and my heart ached, & I hurt, & my idealism was shattered, but I couldn't back away. I knew I would never resign. As if reading my thoughts, he said,

"I assume you would have the stature to resign if it came to it."

"But why, Governor, when I've done nothing but uphold my job to the absolute best of my ability." (I thought of Eddie Sisk & Gene Blanton & Charlie Benson & Traughber & Ben Haynes, etc. etc. ad infinitum—all of whom enjoy his public support.) And I said, "Governor, I wish all of your aides and assistants were as loyal & as dedicated to defending this State & you as I have been."

And then I recalled the telephone call from Eddie—in Fla.—to me —in Denver . . . and today I knew, at last & irrevocably that the Governor is my enemy. And so I can only speculate as to how horribly off-base I've been about him—trusting & trying to ignore the wisps of smoke, much as I did when it was over with Eddie & Charlie, trying to ignore all the signs, trying to believe, trying to love, to be optimistic— always afraid of being an alarmist.

Hillin and Leech were both elated. See, she'd ridden it out. Hadn't been fired at all. Bill wanted to know if Blanton really had said "impeachable" sources. Psychologically, he found it interesting. Marie said she didn't give it much significance. She remembered the time she had wanted to write speeches for Blanton. That was when she'd learned about some of his gaffes. "Impeachable sources" was in the same league with "anals of history."

When she was in Blanton's office, she'd had this fantasy of saying to him, "Governor, if we can just get together, level with each other, perhaps everything could be worked out. Let's do it! A lot of these problems will evaporate in the light of understanding," and he'd say, "What's going on, Marie? Is it possible there's something I don't know about? Have you seen things I'm not aware of?"

Marie could picture Hank Hillin going through the roof over that. And, of course, the inescapable fact was that Blanton hadn't wanted to know anything. On that count, he was completely guilty.

Thanksgiving Day 1976

I am determined to enjoy my children and family today, but it is so hard for me to abandon the encroaching feelings of despair. Yesterday was a nightmare to me—although it was reassuring to discover that Bill has evidently been thinking through the procedural framework for a hearing if I am fired.

I don't know what I'll do if it comes to it. I cannot imagine a greater spectacle nor humiliation, and yet I will NEVER resign.

I can still hear the Governor. He seemed mildly incredulous—enough that he momentarily lost his poker-countenance—"Did I understand you to say that you won't resign?" "But Governor, in all respect, I have done nothing for which to resign."

"Marie, you have broken the law, don't you understand that? A part of your job has been to maintain the confidentiality of those records, & you haven't done it. . . ."

Again (for I had said it before) I said, "Governor, if anyone besides yourself were saying that, I would probably laugh; that's how absurd it is. I have worked long hours—I no longer have a social life—and even my children have been deprived of me (which is wrong) because of the long hours I've worked. I have been dedicated—to the Board, to the people of Tennessee, to you. No one can say otherwise."

"Well, they're saying it, Marie." (Even he didn't sound convinced of his own words.)

"But who, Governor, & what? I wish to confront these people, and in your presence." And then, "Governor, do you know what I came into when I arrived at that Board? Disappearing files, disappearing logs, disappearing mail, that's what. Telegrams, addressed to me, which never reached me . . . I changed locks, even. But Governor, do you know what they told me about those things when I got there? They said not to worry about it, that things had always been like that, & that the files, sooner or later, would turn up, & not to worry about it! But I did worry about it . . .

"Governor, are you planning to fire me?"

"Marie, that's up to you. If things don't improve, if I get the same reports—I'm giving you 2 months to show what you can do."

Of course, it was impossible to continue. Since I hadn't done the things he implied I had done, I couldn't possibly stop doing that which I had never done. I wondered what he would try to say I had done. And I realized we would have a new U.S. Attorney in just a little over 2 months. So that's it, I thought to myself.

· 5 ·

After the holidays she saw Sisk. "You know, Eddie, there seems to be an awful lot of stories going around about my so-called promiscuity," she said, and he gave a sort of half-embarrassed grin and told her he didn't know who could be saying it. He didn't know anything about it.

That was funny, she said. She didn't know about it either, but evidently more than one person did. "You should talk to the Governor and hear what he has to say. He called me on the phone the other night—"

Sisk interrupted. Yeah, he said. The Governor had been drinking that night. They had tried to keep him from calling her, but they weren't able to.

So they were having meetings about her, sitting around the executive mansion, discussing her. She shouldn't have been surprised. Nevertheless, it was chilling to have it confirmed. She wondered who *they* were, besides Blanton and Eddie. Gene Blanton, Ben Haynes, Jim Allen, probably. Who else? Her friend Jack Strickland? Jack had gotten cooler. She remembered his warnings to her—about serving before leading.

"Well," she said to Sisk, "I don't think he was drunk when I talked to him in his office. He says I'm having affairs with every DA in the state, half the judges and half of the FBI."

She'd messed herself up, Sisk said. Being with the wrong people. Being immature, obstinate. Take George Edwards, for instance. Edwards was one of the nicest guys he'd ever met, Sisk said. Marie knew very well that the Governor *himself* wanted George Edwards pardoned. Why wouldn't she go along?

How could he bring up George Edwards now, she thought—in the middle of all this, in the middle of a pardons and paroles scandal? Had the meeting at the mansion also been about Edwards? Then it dawned on Marie that the Edwards pardon was going to be resurrected. It was vintage Blanton. Suppose the Edwards case didn't have a connection with what the FBI was investigating. Edwards was personable and intelligent—had been a college student when he was arrested. It was entirely possible that Ray Blanton had taken a real liking to him, working as a convict maître d', hovering over the Governor's table.

Suppose Blanton rammed through the Edwards pardon, despite the headlines about payoffs. The public could easily start thinking there wasn't anything crooked about it, or why would the Governor take the risk? And if there wasn't anything crooked about Edwards, maybe all this other stuff in the media was so much garbage.

The trouble was the other stuff was real. "Eddie, I don't have a thing personally against George Edwards," she said. "But how can you expect me to recommend for somebody like him when every day I sit across the table from guys, young and old, who deserve as much consideration —and some maybe more. How can I tell them they don't meet the guidelines for clemency if they and I both know the evening news reported George Edwards got pardoned?"

She was mad enough to say that the petitioners she had to face also knew that other inmates were buying themselves out, but she didn't. She just said the Governor could do whatever he wanted to. The board had its guidelines, though.

They didn't need her goddamn vote, Sisk shot back. They already had Traughber's and Mitchell's.

"I'm sorry you feel like that," she said. Eddie actually looked baffled.

Leech and Hillin might think she was home free, but Marie sure didn't. You couldn't get away from it. As things stood, the Governor could fire her, chairman or not, practically on whim. That was the essential weakness of her position. Blanton had given her two months. He really must be looking forward to the change of administration in Washington and a new U.S. attorney in Nashville.

She began considering legislative allies against a dark future. Marie remembered how David Raybin had buoyed her with the thought that she wasn't a nobody in government anymore—that there was a reservoir of clout available to her in the legislature.

Her aim would be to make the board, and therefore herself, more autonomous. The quickest way was budgetary independence voted by the legislature, and a new legislative session would be convening after the first of the year. That was why Marie settled on State Senator Douglas Henry as her departure point.

Henry was from Nashville. Chairman of the Finance Ways and Means Committee. A man of medium height, slightly heavy, mild-mannered, he came off as so very well intentioned that other legislators tended to mock him a bit behind his back. But the fact was that no one in state government got any money for anything without a little cooperation from Douglas Henry.

Although Marie had met him only in passing, Henry promptly said he'd welcome an appointment with her. The hitch was that he was a gentleman of the old school, and they went through this song and dance about where they'd meet. He'd come to her, he insisted. Blanton was calling her everything but a whore, and here was Henry saying it was inappropriate for a lady like her to do the visiting. Wouldn't hear of it. All Marie needed was for Murray Henderson to spy Henry knocking on her door. Finally she persuaded the senator that it would save them both time if she passed by his office. She had other business to take care of on the hill after she saw him.

Marie arrived armed with all the board regulations, a copy of the standards of the American Correctional Association and pertinent sections of the *Tennessee Code Annotated.* She was going to get into this gingerly with Henry, but she was determined to let the chips fall where they may. Even if she looked to be the biggest chip with the farthest to fall.

"What can I do for such a charming young woman, meaning no disrespect," said Henry as he ordered coffee. "I realize what high office you hold." She told him she appreciated his valuable time, occupied as he must be with the forthcoming legislative session. Eyes twinkling, he said yes, things did have a way of perking up when the legislators were around. Well, now, what could he do for her?

There was plenty of shrewdness behind those merry eyes, Marie thought. Henry hadn't alluded in the slightest to the headlines that everyone on the hill was talking about.

She was there for his help, Marie began. And the legislature's help. She wasn't sure how much he kept up with the board's activities, but he probably knew the board didn't have its own budget. That appeared to surprise him. "I thought we allowed money for you people," he said, and she said yes, there was money allocated, but it was part of the corrections department budget.

"Of course, the law says the parole board is independent of the Department of Correction," she said. "But, Senator Henry, you know how these things go. That statute can say it all day. The bottom line, though, is it isn't so. Nobody can be independent without control of his own budget."

Henry sat back and lit his pipe. Marie could see she had his interest. Whatever he had expected from her, it clearly hadn't been this. He asked if there were any immediate problems.

She knew Douglas Henry was dedicated to law and order. One of her biggest problems was parole revocation hearings, she said. Parolees charged with violating their paroles were being released again because key witnesses weren't brought in to testify. The legislature had voted money to finance the board's subpoena power, but when she went to the corrections department, she had been informed there wasn't any money left.

"You mean they just let them go?" said Henry, leaning forward now, puffing furiously, and Marie said, "Yes, sir. So, obviously, this is of grave concern to us and to the welfare of the people of Tennessee." She was

careful not to attack Murray Henderson. "I don't blame the commissioner. I appreciate the dilemma he's in, what with prison overpopulation. But there's a fair way to mitigate all this by giving the board its
own budget."

"That seems very basic. Fundamental," Henry said. "What else?"

Well, Marie thought, here it is. The board should be completely
autonomous, she said. Especially in regard to the appointment and
removal of board members. She pulled out the national standards she
had brought along, and built on them. There should be nominating and
confirmation committees on appointments, and review committees on
removals. In Tennessee, if a board member was concerned about his
job, he might feel tempted to recommend whatever action he thought
his appointing authority wanted. That was better than saying "the
governor," she figured. Made it less personal.

"You having problems in this area, Mrs. Ragghianti?"

"Well, Senator Henry, before I go any further, I really need to ask
you to keep my remarks confidential, for the time being at least.
Frankly, without beating around the bush, I have to mention this
investigation that's going on. This *federal* investigation."

"Ah, yes," Henry said, "do you think there's anything there?"

"I wish I could say I didn't. The reality is—from my perspective—
that there is. And I'm in an almost untenable position right now. Eddie
Sisk and the Governor are very unhappy with me. They feel perhaps
I'm the cause of it, if only because so much of what's being examined
are matters that I've complained about."

Rest assured, said Henry, that their conversation would remain private. He said he was appreciative of her trust in him. If she would only
give him a little time, he would study the material she had provided
and reflect on what she had told him. He was, he added, deeply
impressed with her grasp of the situation after having been board
chairman for such a short while. They'd be getting together again, he
said.

Marie departed jubilant. She'd sensed a certain distaste for Blanton
in Henry's demeanor. Maybe she had pulled something off for herself
—and the board.

· 6 ·

On December 4 Marie was elected president of the Southern Paroling
Authority at its organizational meeting in Atlanta. Jack Scism, the

North Carolina parole chairman she had met in Denver when they first discussed the idea, noted that she seemed terribly distracted. Suddenly she was telling Scism what had been happening to her. Having unearthed corruption in his own state system, Jack would understand. He said he had to hand it to her, and Marie replied she didn't have to have compliments from him, of all people. After all, he'd done the same thing. Yes, Scism said, but he'd been an investigative reporter at the time. It was his job. Being chairman was something else. Scism said that if she ever needed his help or advice, he was available.

After she returned to Nashville, Hank Hillin told her that agents had combed through the papers they'd taken and couldn't find any file on Bobbie Jean Hawkins, a.k.a. King, a.k.a. Carmichael, whose car Prater had been driving. Marie and her new secretary, Ernestine Hicks, launched another search without success.

But Hillin said they'd lucked out on the copies she had made of her old liaison file. Among the original cards missing following the raids was the one for Larkin Bibbs, even though it already had been sanitized by Benson.

Marie didn't ask how the investigation was going. Early on, she had decided not to. She was afraid she might inadvertently let something slip out.

Meanwhile, the drum roll had started for George Edwards. During Marie's absence, Traughber had scheduled another hearing.

Blanton's Alcoholic Beverage Commission director, Lee Hyden, announced that the permit granted Edwards to work in a liquor store was legal and proper. Only a person convicted of a moral turpitude crime was prohibited from having a permit, Hyden declared, and armed robbery wasn't on the list.

Jim Allen, identified by the *Tennessean* as a friend of Blanton's, was quoted as saying, "I think this is the most despicable thing I've ever seen done in politics. They're making a sacrificial lamb out of this young man . . . a sharp young black boy that got into trouble when a bunch of college kids went out one night."

Edwards himself gave out several interviews. In one he blamed a "personal vendetta" against him by Marie. "I don't know why," the quote went. "I only met the lady about four times." In another, "This is a political thing where they are shooting at the Governor and Mr. Allen."

Personally, Edwards said, he didn't drink.

The hearing was held on December 10 at the Shelby County Penal Farm. Probably to cut down the media presence, Marie thought. Still, a dozen or so reporters showed up. There was a commotion when Traughber and Mitchell, citing an obscure board rule, voted to exclude them from the actual deliberations.

Marie listened as Mitchell said that in his opinion George had really tried. Had stayed out of trouble. Had a college education or close to it. Deserved another chance. And Traughber said he agreed with Mr. Mitchell. Mr. Edwards had proved himself. Had earned a new start in life.

They both wrote "recommend" on their sheets, not even bothering to notice Marie was putting down "decline," never expecting it. The majority had spoken, and every board vote so far had been unanimous. "Wait a minute," she said. "Not one fact in this case has changed since the last vote. You know it and I know it." Mitchell's face rarely displayed emotion, but now it was mottled with indignation. She was just going out of her way to embarrass everyone. Marie could see that Traughber, however, was almost smiling. As if enjoying the thought that she was driving a few more nails into her own coffin.

The reporters were let in, and Traughber announced the decision. One reporter asked if it had been unanimous, and when Traughber said it didn't matter, the shouts erupted. Who voted against, and why? Traughber was still trying to say it didn't matter, the majority was what counted, when Marie said, "I did, because there are no new facts. Mr. Edwards, unfortunately, doesn't fit the board's published guidelines for pardon consideration. In fact, he's violating his parole right now by working in a liquor store. It's unfair and inequitable to other prisoners."

Sam Lipford remembered how enraged Murray Henderson was when he learned of Marie's vote. "Goddamnit, why's she doing it? Can't somebody handle her?" Henderson hollered. "Can't you talk to her? I've never seen anyone so goddamn bullheaded. Doesn't she ever compromise?"

Lipford figured Henderson must be getting plenty of heat from the Governor about Marie. Sam was sure that in Blanton's view of the administrative setup Marie worked under the corrections commissioner.

· 7 ·

Date of transcription 11/23/76

. . . PRATER stated that he had never paid money to any State Official or to any other person in order to prevent his being extradited from the State of Tennessee to the State of Georgia. He stated he had no knowledge of any other person who had done so. He stated he has never been approached by any person or persons who offered to prevent his extradition in return for being paid cash.

That report was sent in by Chattanooga FBI agents Irvin D. Wells III and Sidney A. Perry. They also interviewed Barnes, McBryar and Bekovich with the same results.

Prater, though, was getting edgy. He'd been in the Hamilton County jail for a month now with no end in sight. Worse yet, his fencing operation was going to hell. Only he could run it, and he wasn't there.

Tommy, with his boyish good looks and sad eyes, could charm himself in or out of most anything. A cat used to landing on his feet. But, suddenly, nothing was working right. He had this feeling in his bones that he was headed for Georgia no matter what. When the extradition papers first came in, damn near a year ago, a detective in Chattanooga called him on a Friday. Told him he didn't have to come in until Monday. Which he did, and immediately went out on bond. And everything had been fine until now. It was *now*, the present moment, not the future, that got to Tommy Prater the most. He hated being cooped up. What he missed was his block on Market Street in Chattanooga, where the topless joints and honky-tonk bars blazed at night, where the smart guys hung out—where the action was. Market Street was Prater's whole life.

Around the end of November, he called Bill Thompson. He liked Thompson, and had liked doing things for him. Liked driving him around, being close to him. Bill was big-time, and not just in Chattanooga. Even pulled a lot of weight with the Governor. You never knew, Prater thought, when it could come in handy, and it had. Except something had gone wrong, and he called Thompson and said he wanted his money back so at least he could pay his attorney to get out on bond, be back on Market Street, and Thompson had said, "I don't know nothing about no money."

"Bill, I need help," he said. "You know the whole program on this, I need help." But Thompson didn't want to hear about it anymore. Thompson had done all he could. "Okay, Bill," Tommy Prater said, and then he called his mother and told her to get in touch with that police detective they knew. When the detective came to see him, Prater said, "Tell the FBI I will talk to them. Do you know any of them? You know, somebody you can really trust, because these people are powerful, and I'm scared."

"Yeah, I know one man," the detective said, and on December 6, the same day Hank Hillin was meeting with Marie in Nashville about the missing Bobbie Jean Hawkins file, agent John Benton went to visit Tommy. The next day Benton, along with Irvin Wells, telephoned Hillin and told him Prater was ready to spill his guts on the pardons and paroles case, but they were unfamiliar with many aspects of what he was saying. Hillin better hightail it over to Chattanooga himself.

PRATER stated he wished to make two requests of the interviewing agent: one, that he be given an opportunity to make bond, since he is currently confined at the Hamilton County Jail under no bond; second, that any assistance he renders to the FBI be made known to local authorities in the State of Georgia.

Prater was shrewd, Hillin thought. Prater knew the FBI could deliver on the bond but couldn't make promises on the Dalton robberies. There wasn't any question, though, that Prater expected something to be done about Georgia, and Hillin would give it his best shot—depending on how good a talker Prater was. Tommy insisted he hadn't participated in the robberies. Received the stolen property, yes, but hadn't actually gone into the premises waving a gun and spraying Mace, or anything like that. "We'll see what we can do," Hillin told him.

Hillin arrived in Chattanooga on December 8, and from the start Prater was very good indeed. According to Prater, when he first faced extradition, he had said to Thompson, "I'll just have to get an attorney in Georgia and go ahead and sign and go back down," and Bill said, "You don't have to." Thompson mentioned an extradition involving some country-music star that the Governor didn't okay. Bill made it sound as if there had been a lot more to it than he was saying. If Tommy and the others wanted to stop their extraditions, it could be done. For $5,000. Each.

Prater had already seen how Thompson could operate. When Tommy's cousin Billy Gene Cole was denied clemency consideration, a guy on Market Street had said why didn't Prater see Bill Thompson about it, and Thompson said the clemency would cost ten thousand. After that, Prater stayed close to Bill. He told Hillin how he and Bill went right into the penitentiary and sat with Billy Gene while Prater explained to his cousin what the deal was. First Cole would go before the board and get a sentence cut, at which time half the money had to be paid. The rest was payable when Cole was all set to get out. And that was precisely how it had happened, even when Billy Gene flunked his lie detector test. Prater even had to shell out $35 for the test, he told Hillin.

Prater filled in the missing pieces on Jimmy H. Pendleton. In Nashville, agent Dick Knudson had reported that Pendleton's wife said her husband was supposed to be released but wasn't able to raise the cash. She didn't know the details. Prater said Cole was the one who spoke to him and Thompson about Pendleton. The price had finally been fixed at five thousand when Jimmy claimed that was all he could manage. But after his papers were sent to the Governor's office, he couldn't even make that, so the clemency was canceled. Thompson was pretty upset about this, Prater said, and a new rule was instituted. Nothing would be done for an inmate unless there was money up front.

Prater also knew about the Larkin Bibbs clemency. This black dude in Chattanooga, Sam Pettyjohn, had said, "I need to see Bill. Tell your man to get in touch with me. I have to see about getting somebody out." Prater wasn't surprised. By now, he said, everybody along Market Street knew Thompson was the man to see for that. So he and Thompson went out to Pettyjohn's place, and Pettyjohn said there were these people who wanted a boy named Bibbs out of the pen. He'd been locked up for murder. Fifteen years. Thompson said he would have to make a call, and he did on the spot. It was a long-distance call, Prater said. The kind where you dialed "1" first. Thompson left his number, and pretty soon the phone rang, and after Bill had been on for a time, he told Pettyjohn he'd be in touch within two days. Then, when he was, he said it would run fifteen thousand. Once Bibbs was freed, according to Prater, there was a problem collecting the final five thousand due. But these people that Pettyjohn had mentioned, who were pushing dope all around, in Nashville, Memphis, down in Atlanta and Birmingham, anted up at last. Pettyjohn came by with a man carrying a brown paper bag and counted out the hundred-dollar bills. Prater was there with Thompson, watching.

Yes, said Prater, he was driving the black Chrysler Cordoba the afternoon Thompson saw Jack Lowery. They were headed for Nashville when Bill told him to get off the Interstate for Lebanon, and they parked in the main square. Thompson hadn't said anything about what he was doing. He went into a building, and after he came out, he told Prater to step on the gas. It had started raining heavily, and Prater was worried about the slick roads and being stopped for speeding. He asked Thompson what was going on, and Bill laughed and said he'd tell him later. When Prater saw the Murfreesboro squad car flashing its lights, he was sure it was for speeding. But the cop only asked for the registration and his license. The cop said the Lebanon police had requested a check. That was all. Afterward, Thompson told Prater just that "Sisk said the man was trying to get some help for the man."

More than anything, however, Prater linked up Thompson and Eddie Sisk in a payoff conspiracy. One morning the previous February, he said, he met Bill at Blaylock's restaurant in Chattanooga and gave him a $2,000 down payment to keep from being extradited. The two thousand, in hundreds, was in a regular white envelope. Thompson put the envelope into his coat pocket. Butch Barnes joined them and gave Thompson another thousand in cash. Thompson took the envelope out of his pocket and stuffed in the new bills, also hundreds.

They all drove to Nashville. Thompson told Prater they were meeting Sisk in front of the Capitol Park Inn, but when they arrived, Sisk wasn't in sight. Thompson made a phone call, and they drove around the city for a while. Then Bill said, "Let's go back to the Capitol Park." Prater remembered how Thompson was uptight and said to Barnes, "Butch, don't pay any attention to this man when you get out of the car." "Okay," Barnes had said.

This time Sisk was standing there. Thompson ordered Barnes out of the rear seat and told him to wait inside the hotel. Sisk got in, and Bill instructed Prater to drive to the basement garage. While he was doing this, Sisk gave Thompson a large manila envelope. Bill opened it and looked briefly at some papers. Prater never knew what the papers were. He parked by the garage elevator, and Thompson said to leave him and Mr. Sisk alone. Prater got out, and Sisk took his place. As Prater was starting away he glanced back and saw Thompson hand the white envelope to Sisk. It was the first time he'd seen it since Chattanooga. He remembered how the envelope had been bulging so with bills that the flap stuck out. Prater noticed the flap was still sticking out. A couple of hours later, Thompson said to him and Barnes, "You ain't got no worries."

Ask Butch, Prater told Hillin. Barnes would back him up. And Bekovich had been with him and Thompson at Lebanon. He'd talk too. Hillin wanted to know about McBryar, and Prater said Bruce didn't like Thompson, but he didn't like anybody now, it seemed. McBryar looked to be doing his own thing.

When Hillin and Benton interviewed Barnes, he corroborated Prater's version of the events beginning at Blaylock's restaurant. The only thing he couldn't verify was the white envelope passing from Thompson to Sisk. Barnes had been in the lobby at the time.

Bekovich tried to be helpful. Yeah, he'd been in Lebanon with Tommy and Bill, but the trouble was he had been so many places with them, it was hard to remember sometimes. If Tommy said he'd been in Lebanon, though, it must be so. He would go along with Tommy on that. Hillin decided Reisto perhaps had been in one too many prizefights. Wasn't quite the grand jury witness he had in mind. McBryar, as Prater predicted, refused to say a word. Just that he was going back to Georgia.

Through the U.S. attorney's office in Nashville, Hillin obtained a court order placing Tommy Ray Prater and Wendell Allen Barnes in federal custody. Next Hillin went to see Gary Gerbitz about personal-recognizance bonds for Prater and Barnes. When Gerbitz heard that Prater was fingering Thompson, he was only too happy to oblige.

U.S. marshals brought Prater and Barnes to a jail in Gallatin, northeast of Nashville, on December 11, the day after George Edwards was being recommended for a pardon in Memphis. A new federal grand jury was in session in Nashville, and on December 14 both men told their stories before it. Their appearance was secret.

Hank Hillin felt as though he'd hit a gusher. He tried to argue Prater out of returning to Chattanooga. There was a good chance of getting Prater into the federal witness protection program, he said. There'd be some restriction of movement, but it'd be a lot safer than Market Street. Prater wouldn't listen. He could take care of himself. Besides, he pointed out, there wasn't that much to worry about. If Thompson thought Prater could hurt him, he would have gotten him out of jail to begin with. Even so, Hillin remained concerned about Prater. Hardly a day passed that he didn't call Irvin Wells or Prater's mother to find out if Tommy was all right.

In Dalton, it wasn't until the end of December that Bill Dodd discovered that his prize catch had apparently vanished. Dodd couldn't learn a thing, except that the feds were involved somehow. Special Prosecutor Erwin Mitchell didn't anger easily, but when Dodd reported what had happened, Mitchell immediately put in a call to Governor George Busbee of Georgia.

And right off, Dodd began to get a queasy feeling about the continued well-being of his own key witness, Bernard Weinthal.

FOURTEEN

Amazingly enough, Marie's role in the investigation had remained a guessing game, and through Christmas of 1976 Hank Hillin hoped it would stay like that. He still had ideas of persuading her to record conversations with Sisk. There was always the danger of grand jury leaks, but so far, so good. There hadn't been a peep, for instance, about Prater's appearance, and after a couple of go-arounds Hillin had at the U.S. attorney's office, Anderson had quit spouting off.

Within the Blanton administration Charlie Benson had insisted that Marie was behind the federal probe. But most everyone else thought as Sisk did. Why in the world would she do it? What was the point? Marie had it made. A high-paying, prestigious job that half the people in Tennessee politics would give their eyeteeth for, and no financial resources to fall back on to support herself and her children. Besides, *she* wasn't being investigated. Had absolutely nothing to gain by going to the FBI. And what did she really know anyhow?

In Sisk's opinion, Hillin was responsible. Hillin had been trying to get something on the administration ever since his big inquiry into illegal campaign contributions blew up. Sisk remembered how Hillin had grilled him. Had him dragged before a grand jury. Mr. FBI had ended up looking silly and didn't like it. Now he wanted to get even.

Nevertheless the pardons and paroles thing wasn't withering away. There already was talk about another grand jury hearing in February.

Bill Thompson had told Sisk he'd heard that Prater might be in federal hands. FBI agents had been visiting him in the Hamilton County jail, and all at once Prater had disappeared. But who'd believe a punk like Prater, trying to deal himself out of facing heavy criminal charges in Georgia? It was obvious, though, even to Sisk, that Marie in her lunacy was at least talking to the FBI. The Governor was fed up. That was what counted.

Getting rid of Marie quietly was the problem, and Eddie Sisk came up with a diabolical solution. Before he was appointed legal counsel, Eddie had been handling the appeal for John Sneed, a young black convicted of murdering a drug dealer and his wife. They had stayed in contact, and Sneed was looking for executive clemency. Sisk explained that right then he was having a lot of problems with the board chairman, and Sneed said, hey, he could tell Sisk a thing or two about Marie. According to Sneed, he had this white girl friend named Sheryl who knew Marie when she was working her way through Vanderbilt as a cocktail waitress at the Villa. The two women had gotten acquainted, said Sneed, because they both hung out in black nightclubs in Nashville. Sisk was all ears when Sneed said Sheryl told him that Marie used to pick through the purses of the Villa's female patrons for cash and credit cards. Afterward, the two of them would take off to Memphis or Chattanooga on spending sprees. Not even a photograph on an identification card stopped Marie, Sneed said. She was so slick at makeup that she could change her appearance to fit the I.D.

Sisk didn't doubt the information for a second. Everyone had a skeleton in the closet, and goody-goody Marie wasn't an exception. He instructed Sneed to get onto Sheryl for more details. If this worked out, Sneed was as good as out of the pen. Sisk assigned Benson to follow up with Sneed. They'd confront Marie with what they had and force her resignation. Benson loved the plan. But what pleased Sisk was how much the Governor liked it. Especially how Marie would have to resign. Ray Blanton, Sisk remembered thinking, hated to fire people.

Until the advent of Tommy Prater, Hillin's investigation had been the kind of trench warfare he detested—slogging through the seized records of suspect inmates. Trying to find tracks, seeking some pattern. Who had sponsored particular clemencies? Who had written letters? Who had made prison visits? Were there any connections?

Now, with Prater, there was more immediate direction. Prater's credibility was vital. Prater had spoken about going to the penitentiary in Nashville on the Cole, Bibbs and Pendleton clemencies. And there it all was in visitation permission memos written by the warden's secretary, the dates exactly right, preceding each clemency recommendation.

Subject: William Cole
Date: 9/10/75
Mr. Thompson, Mr. Prater and Mr. Beckovich have permission to visit with the above named resident when they come to the institution.

Subject: William Cole
Date: 10/8/75
Mr. Bill Thompson, Mr. Prater and Mrs. William Cole will visit with the above named resident this afternoon.

Subject: Larkin H. Bibbs Jr.
Date: 12/4/75
Mr. Samuel Pettyjohn has permission to visit the above named resident on Friday, December 5, 1975.

Subject: Jim Pendleton
Date: 2/6/76
Mr. Bill Cole, an ex-resident, has permission to visit the above named resident today.

There was more. A sign-in log for W. A. Thompson and Tommy Prater to see William Cole, #73060, on May 21, 1975, another for W. Thompson to see Larkin H. Bibbs Jr., #76623, on November 25, 1975. Hillin asked the secretary if anyone special had arranged for the visits, and she said yes, there had been calls from the Governor's office, from somebody who worked for Mr. Eddie Sisk, although she couldn't recall the name. Was this a usual thing? Well, she said, now that Hillin had mentioned it, she wasn't able to remember it ever happening before.

Prater had told Hillin that to raise the ten thousand required to spring Billy Gene Cole, he had taken out a $5,000 note from the United Bank in Chattanooga, and so had Cole's wife, Beulah. A United loan officer confirmed the transactions. Five thousand to Prater on August 12, '75, and five thousand to Mrs. Cole two weeks later. Prater had explained that he needed the money to help get his cousin out of prison. The loan officer claimed he thought that Prater was talking about a legal fee. Once Cole was out, the bank's records showed that the original loan to Prater was consolidated with the one Cole's wife had received.

Hillin kept digging away. He located the polygraph expert Prater had said he hired to give Cole a lie detector test. Yes, the man agreed, it had been Prater. Prater had told Hillin that he had seen Bill Thompson pass the white envelope to Sisk at the Capitol Park Inn in early February. Hotel records showed that Thompson had registered there on February 4, 1976. Room 161. And in Huntsville, Alabama, the brother of Wendell Allen Barnes admitted borrowing $1,000 on his brother's behalf, also at United. He said Wendell had told him he had to have the money to stay out of jail. Then it turned out that Thompson's brother-in-law was a vice-president of the United Bank of Chattanooga. Piece after piece was falling into place.

Hillin's hot streak ended when he went to question Billy Gene Cole and his wife, then living on the outskirts of Nashville. Hillin sensed that Cole disliked him. The chemistry just wasn't there. Hillin was too threatening a figure. Clearly, Cole was afraid that if he talked to Hillin, he could wind up back in prison, his parole revoked. He refused to say anything, bank records, prison visits or not. So once again, Hillin called upon Dick Knudson's engaging manner. Agent Knudson started dropping by to see the Coles. How were they getting on? Was there something he could do for them? Knudson could chitchat for hours, and pretty soon the Coles were warming up to him. Hillin would have to wait it out.

Meanwhile Hillin continued going over various commutations pushed by Sisk or Benson that Marie had blocked. One was Rose Lee Cooper's. Another was for a convict named Charles Winters. Not only had Winters escaped once, a fact mysteriously missing from the board's files, but a DA's telegram to Marie protesting clemency was never seen by her. At the time Sherry Lomax had been Marie's acting administrative assistant. Still another commutation plea involved Marvin Grantham, in for armed robbery. When Grantham appeared before the board, there hadn't been a single letter of community support for his release, not even the customary offer of a job.

A fourth case was especially disturbing. Sisk had wanted Marie to look into a recommendation for a Ronald Sotka. She discovered that he was serving one hundred ninety-eight years for a vicious multiple murder. Consideration of Sotka was beyond belief, an evaluation officer had raged at her. She tried to explain that when the Governor's office asked for an investigation, she had to follow through, and the officer yelled there was nothing to investigate. Ronald Sotka was a psychopathic killer. He was one guy who really deserved having the key thrown away. Just write up a report, Marie said. She would take it from there.

The Sotka incident intrigued Hillin. Prater had said he phoned a man with a funny name staying at the Holiday Inn off the Vanderbilt campus to set up a meeting on a clemency. From what Hillin got from Marie, the time frame fit. Sotka's brother was eventually located in Ohio. He conceded that he had gone to the Holiday Inn to find out about freeing Ronald. A man called Bill Cole told him the price would be twenty thousand. Cole had pointed to himself as living proof that it was worth every penny.

· 2 ·

The February grand jury, concentrating on the Bibbs and Cole clemencies, heard a dozen witnesses from Chattanooga. Nothing spectacular, but Bill Thompson's tracks were all over. More pieces for the puzzle. Jack Blaylock, the owner of Blaylock's restaurant, said he'd written to the board offering Bibbs a job after Thompson asked him to. Bobbie Jean Hawkins testified that she had lent her Cordoba to Thompson during May '76. But diamond-ringed Sam Pettyjohn denied knowing anything about how Bibbs got out. He and his wife wrote letters on Bibbs's behalf simply as good neighbors. Pettyjohn was a wheeler-dealer in Chattanooga's black community, with a big foot in the underworld. Hillin figured Sam wasn't talking because he was terrified of the drug ring Bibbs had been working for, and in a way Hillin didn't blame him. He'd have to have a little sit-down with Pettyjohn.

In the *Tennessean* Sisk was quoted as saying there had been nothing improper about either the Cole or Bibbs case. According to Eddie, both had been granted executive clemency at the request of the pardons and paroles board. U.S. Attorney Anderson announced that while there would be no indictments at this time, the FBI was going to keep on hunting the facts.

About then, the Blanton administration's expectations of a quick fix from a new, Democratic U.S. attorney began to fade. Senator Jim Sasser wanted someone of stature, and had more or less settled on Howell (Hal) Hardin, the presiding judge of the second circuit court in Nashville. But Hardin was vacillating. A lot of his friends warned him that he didn't need to stumble into quicksand like this. He also heard that Anderson was running around telling everyone Hal Hardin was being handpicked to whitewash the pardons scandal.

Sisk brought Blanton's inner circle more bad news. It was all true about Marie's thieving, every word, John Sneed kept insisting at the main prison, but his girl friend just didn't want to get involved. And without her corroboration, they might as well forget it. So the next final solution for Marie was dreamed up. For better than six months a task force had been in the works to restructure state criminal justice procedures. Sisk hadn't paid it much heed. For Eddie, it was mostly show time. There had been some discussion, though, about expanding the board to perhaps five members. Now Sisk got very interested in that idea. Go ahead and pack the board, and have it elect a new chairman. Instead of forcing Marie to resign, neutralize her. Moreover, Sisk was willing to bet his life that an egomaniac like Marie wouldn't be able to stand playing second fiddle. She'd quit on her own.

· 3 ·

In the middle of all this, Jim Grisham wanted out as Marie's administrative assistant. He couldn't take the pressure anymore, he said. Half the time he didn't know what was going on. Couldn't sleep at night thinking about it. Couldn't stand the hostility all around Marie, which was spilling over on him. At lunch he told her how she was always after him to keep up the clemency card file, and how Benson was telling him not to do it, making a point of the fact that he was speaking for the Governor's office. All he wanted, said Grisham, was to be left alone to do his job, but nobody would let him. He told Marie how fond of her he was, and how much better off everybody would have been if she'd been the board chairman a lot earlier. He was going to request a transfer, he said. He was letting her know first, so she would have time to find a replacement. Marie felt such a sense of loss. But there wasn't anything she could do. She understood. She told him she deeply regretted his leaving. How important he had been to her. Until he came along, there hadn't been anyone with the board she could trust.

It was Sam Lipford who suggested Kevin McCormack. Ever since she had gotten to know Kevin when they both worked weekends at the office, she had become increasingly taken by his exuberant, sometimes brassy, mischievous manner—and his thoughtfulness. The first Saturday they were at the office, he had asked if he could get her coffee and a hamburger. Later, they got into the habit of having a beer at a place called the Judge's Chambers. He was a Notre Dame graduate, he said, and Marie liked that. His twin brother was a priest, although he himself had trouble making it to church. He had been in corrections work almost from the moment he was out of college, on the rehabilitation side, beginning as a parole counselor. He said he had wanted to make a social contribution. Trying to bring ex-inmates back into the mainstream of life was enormously fulfilling. This, of course, caused her to like him even more.

And Kevin made her smile. She remembered, after the FBI raids, how people around her, even Ramon and Sam, would stare at her but would never dare say anything. Kevin came right out with it. They were at the Judge's Chambers when he said, "Marie, how do you suppose this thing got started?"

"I wish I knew."

"Yeah, I bet," he replied, eyes narrowing theatrically.

"I'll tell you what, though," she said. "If you ever find out, I wish you'd let me know."

"Waitress," he said, "would you bring this lady another beer? I think she needs one."

McCormack was Lipford's assistant director in the probations and paroles division. Oversaw all the staff work throughout the state, as far as Marie could make out. Had the right to sign Sam's name to various directives. But the same qualities in Kevin that she found so attractive apparently rubbed Murray Henderson the wrong way. And after Kevin got into a feud with some field counselors—more a personality conflict than anything else—Henderson wanted him fired. Lipford attempted to dissuade Henderson, but the commissioner was adamant.

That was when she learned of Kevin's availability. Henderson even thanked her for getting him out of his hair. At first Kevin was reluctant. She had never seen him with such a hangdog look. Hurt and humiliated. And the truth was that being her administrative aide was something of a comedown for him. So Marie embarked on a selling job. She told him about the Southern Paroling Authority and how she would need him with her for its convention. Also the American Correctional Association's next national meeting in Virginia Beach. His help and advice would be essential. Then she played her trump. Before Kevin knew it, she said, his old probations and paroles division might be reporting directly to her. She had really big things in mind now that the legislature was in session. Kevin would be very much involved. It was highly confidential. Marie knew there was a lot of political animal in Kevin, and she could see the interest shining in his eyes. Jim Grisham and Kevin McCormack were light years apart in that respect.

After a couple of days he said, "Count me in. Marie, goddamnit, I admire you. You've got more balls than anyone I know."

"Kevin," she said, "I wish you'd restrain your risqué language."

In all that had happened to Marie, and was yet to come, nothing would be more painful to her, would haunt her so, than the memory of those conversations with Kevin. If she hadn't been so persuasive, Kevin McCormack would still be alive. Nobody would ever be able to tell her different.

· 4 ·

The legislative maneuverings Marie spoke to Kevin about had begun when she found herself being shunted aside by Sisk on the new criminal justice statutes the administration was supposedly preparing. For as long as she had been chairman, she'd been part of the Governor's task force. Her area of responsibility was in sentencing and paroling. The task force findings would then be the basis for the administration's bill. But by the end of January nothing was being done about it. She would call Sisk, and Sisk would put her off. She thought at first that all her work had been in vain. Blanton didn't·want any substantive changes. It never occurred to her that she was to be the target of a packed board.

She had continued to see Senator Henry, and Henry probably was going to drop something into the hopper. But Henry wasn't a fighter. She started thinking about State Representative Roger Murray. Marie had met Murray when she debated him on the merits of capital punishment. Murray had been nice about it. Told her she'd won the debate, even though she hadn't convinced him.

Now there was a good deal of chatter that Murray had eyes on the governorship. As it stood, Blanton couldn't succeed himself. A state constitutional convention scheduled for later in '77 might change that. Then again, it might not—or might not cover Blanton.

Marie went to Murray's office. The talk got around to the federal investigation. Murray wanted to know how serious it could be. Pretty serious, she ventured. Gradually she introduced the idea that it might be wise if Murray disassociated himself from the administration on pardons and paroles. Have his own package. She had plenty of material, she said. Murray liked that. Could Marie write him a memo? Be happy to, she replied.

Bill Leech was upset about the memo. Didn't understand why she had to put it in writing. Didn't want pieces of paper floating around. This was no time to rock the boat. Marie didn't tell Leech that to do otherwise would be awkward, seeing as how she had promoted the whole thing. She just said that Murray had asked for it, and she had to oblige. It was her duty as a public servant. To be on the safe side, she decided to add a disclaimer that the memo represented only her personal opinion and comments as requested by Murray.

By now Kevin was in on the plan, and they wrote the memo together. Murray was hooked. Wanted more specifics. And in a fourteen-page draft Marie incorporated all her dreams to give the board real power and political independence. Instead of a board, there'd be an autonomous commission with its own budget. Commission members would be nominated by a committee consisting of, among others, the state attorney general, the president of the DAs' conference and the speaker of the House of Representatives. The governor would select one of three nominees for each spot on the commission. Only the committee could remove a member. Probation and parole officers would be directly supervised by the commission, not the corrections department. DAs or counselors had to be on hand at parole revocation hearings. Current blurred lines of authority were clearly delineated.

Monday, March 28, the administration went public on Marie. That was when, driving in for an early breakfast meeting, she glanced down at her copy of the *Tennessean* and saw a front-page headline that a Blanton criminal justice bill would likely lead to her ouster, and then read that she'd been a constant irritant to the administration. Couldn't get along with anybody. That the Governor desired to remove her as chairman, although he was willing to keep her on as a member of the board. Kevin helped her prepare her response to the press: all she was trying to do was uphold her oath of office. That same afternoon Murray's proposed legislation was announced. It was almost a mirror image of what Marie had written for him.

Sisk went berserk the next day. Screamed at Marie to get over to him at once. Kevin stayed home "sick," so she brought her secretary along for protection. But Eddie told Ernestine to wait outside, slamming the door in her face.

3/30/77

"The Governor and I couldn't BELIEVE the statement you gave out!" He pitched his voice into a high soprano tone, evidently mimicking me: "I have only tried to uphold the oath of my office . . . and I hope the Governor supports me!"

. . . he proceeded to lambast me, accusing me of being "behind" all the bills but the Administration's. He also said, "What about that memo you wrote Roger Murray?" (I almost fainted.) I waited on him to pull out a copy of the memo, but with each passing second, I realized he was bluffing. He didn't have the memo, and hadn't seen it.

He then abruptly changed the subject. "Marie, you have been so goddamned defiant—the Governor—nobody—can believe it. Here we gave you one of the best jobs in State government, and you have defied us at every step of the way!"

It was her last chance, Sisk had said. If she supported their bill, she could stay as chairman. They'd fix that. She told him it would be difficult for her to support a bill she had only read about in the papers.

He wanted to know if there was something the matter with her hearing. She was going to support the bill or she'd be fired. If he were the Governor, he said, she'd have been long gone. And there was another thing she should know. They were building a file on her. She better keep that in mind. "And when we need it, we'll use it," he said.

Marie remembered how Hank Hillin had hinted around about her recording Eddie. For once, she wished she had a device so people could listen to these threats. About firing her. The file they were building on her!

The administration pulled out every stop to keep the Murray proposals from coming out of committee. Also others by Senator Henry.

Kevin returned from having lunch with Benson. Visibly shaken. She had encouraged Kevin to see Sisk and Benson as much as possible. "I'm zero with Eddie and Charlie," she had said, "but you can find out things. Pretend to be their friend. Knock me if you have to."

And now Kevin was telling her, "Marie, you're finished unless you go along with them. You've got to give up."

"You're joking. After everything we've done?"

"Marie, they're holding all the cards. Forget it, Marie. They'll hurt you. They said so."

When the Murray bill was defeated, she tried to buck Kevin up. Attention had been focused on the problem. There'd be amendments to the Blanton bill. Murray had a subcommittee that would be holding hearings. At least some of what she hoped for would be salvaged.

"You don't understand," Kevin said. "It's over."

She could see he was scared. It had been a mistake sending him into the enemy camp. But she didn't realize how deeply they had gotten into him. Missed it completely. Later, she would think how obvious the signs were. And she would know then how much the pressure had affected her. Trying to run the board. Trying to fight the administration. She was getting fuzzy around the edges. Not being alert. She'd already had a fright.

One morning she awoke, unable to rise. My God, she thought, I'm paralyzed. Instantly the specter of the tumor at the base of her mother's spine came to her. Had she inherited some congenital disease? Marie waited until Therese was off to school before she called for help. At Vanderbilt hospital X-rays and other tests showed nothing. A doctor asked if she had been under any tension recently. Well, she said, she was the pardons and paroles board chairman, and he said that made the diagnosis rather easy. Tranquilizers and three days of bed rest should do it.

Representative Murray said he hoped Marie didn't mind the way he had used her. With a straight face, she replied that she was glad to have been of help. Then Murray told her about the round of hearings on pardons and paroles that he intended to preside over. Trusted she'd be a witness. They were standing in the garage under the Legislative Plaza. All at once Marie disclosed Sisk's threat to fire her.

"You wouldn't say that under oath, would you?"

"Sure," she said.

· 5 ·

April 26, 1977— Tuesday— 7:45 P.M.

Kevin just called with some incredible news. "Are you sitting down, Marie?"

"What is it?"

"Get this: Charlie Benson has been suspended."

"What are you talking about?"

"I'm telling you, I've seen the letter. It said, Effective today, Mr. Charlie Benson is suspended from the payroll (or something like that). He's suspended, that's all! I don't know whether he's placed on another payroll or what . . ."

Hank Hillin thought he had his big break.

According to Edward F. Bell, extradition hearing officer in the state secretary's office, Benson had come to him with a bribe offer to stop a car-theft extradition warrant on one of Charlie's Cocke County in-laws.

Bell reported the offer to his immediate superior. The two men went to the state secretary, Gentry Crowell. Crowell took them to the attorney general, who advised them to go to the Nashville DA, Tom Shriver. Shriver knew the normal investigating body, the Tennessee Bureau of Criminal Identification, was under Blanton's thumb, and suggested the FBI.

After Hillin found out about it, he started having problems with U.S. Attorney Anderson. Hell, it was a state case, Anderson said. But Hillin argued that it was part of the whole pardons and paroles conspiracy, and Anderson finally said okay. When Bell agreed to wear a wire at his next meeting with Benson, Hillin warned Crowell not to say anything to the Governor.

Hillin got a pretty good first tape as Benson discussed preventing the extradition with Bell. Then Bell told Hillin he had heard Crowell was going to speak to the Governor after all. Hillin asked Crowell to come to the federal courthouse. He reiterated to the state secretary that telling Blanton was the same as telling Benson. There'd be a cover-up, and Bell's life could be on the line. Cocke County people were nothing to fool around with. Hillin played the tape Bell had recorded. He remembered how Crowell sat there, his head bowed, and promised not to talk to Blanton.

On Friday, April 15, Hillin got a second recording that was even better. Benson would be in Cocke County over the weekend and on Monday would be back to Bell with the money. Three big ones, Benson said. It was a tough wait for Hillin. Once he nabbed Benson in an actual payoff, the whole case could crack wide open. Except the payoff never took place.

When Hillin discovered what had gone wrong, he was speechless with rage and disgust. State Secretary Gentry Crowell had kept his word about not speaking to Blanton. Instead, he told Carl Wallace, the adjutant general of the Tennessee National Guard, whose reputation was far more as politician than warrior. Wallace lost no time putting in a long-distance call to the Governor, then in New Orleans. Wallace was instructed to contact Sisk at once. Eddie was in Knoxville attending a convention of state trial lawyers. Right afterward, Sisk headed for Newport, Benson's hometown, and that was the end of any more meetings with Bell.

Crowell's explanation sickened Hillin. Wallace was an old friend, Crowell said, and he felt he had to seek his advice and counsel. As far as Hillin was concerned, Crowell knew perfectly well Wallace would tip Blanton. Crowell was going with the power. It was as despicable and as craven an act as Hillin had encountered in all his years as an agent. And so disheartening. From what would have been a dramatic turning point in the investigation, he was back to slogging again.

The Governor made a great show of having Benson suspended while the TBCI looked into the matter. Then Benson was quietly reinstated. The TBCI, said Blanton, had found no malfeasance. In Tennessee, it seemed, Blanton could do whatever he wanted—and get away with it.

Toward the end of April, Hillin got another jolt. Charles Anderson told him the public integrity section of the Justice Department was going to take over the case. He showed Hillin the memo he had sent to Attorney General Griffin Bell requesting it. The case was strong and should be vigorously prosecuted.

If it was so strong, Hillin replied, why didn't Anderson continue it himself? This was his way of saving it, Anderson said. Otherwise everything would be lost. He'd learned that Hal Hardin had decided to accept the U.S. attorney appointment. Hillin didn't buy Anderson's paranoia. He knew Hardin and considered him capable and honest, and the thought of case control in Washington left him vaguely uneasy. But there was nothing he could do about it, so he went back to work.

The only solace he got out of the Benson fiasco was Benson's arrogance at trying to pull off a bribe attempt while the investigation was still in gear. Maybe that same arrogance would crop up again.

· 6 ·

Joe Hannah was number three in the TBCI. He liked to think of himself as a dedicated career man despite what had happened to the TBCI since Blanton assumed office. Some of the premier agents, like Charles Lee and George Haynes, were quitting or about to quit. Hannah, however, had family responsibilities to think about. It was a choice you had to make, he decided. Hannah was over the field agents, and he knew he was being constantly circumvented. At least one agent was reporting directly to the Governor's brother Gene. As long as he wasn't personally involved, Hannah figured he'd try to hang in. Do his job the best he could.

Sometimes, though, something just rose up to smack him in the face. A complaint had come in about a car with plates that turned out to be TBCI cover tags. Hannah went to the car pool at the communications center to check it out and learned the tags were being used by Fred Taylor, the highway patrol lieutenant who was Gene Blanton's driver.

Then there was the surveillance van for the organized crime division. Where was it? Oh, yeah, he was told. It was out on that woman up on the hill, the one who was giving the Governor so much trouble.

FIFTEEN

The Murray subcommittee hearings were being billed as an examination of the "mechanics" of the pardons and paroles system. Marie testified on May 9.

Bill Leech knew it was useless to try to talk her out of it. But he cautioned her to be careful about what she said. It wasn't worth losing her paycheck if she didn't have to. "Go slow," Leech said. "Walk easy with them. Don't stir up the animals." Besides her financial situation, for herself and the children, Leech continued to worry about her plain physical safety, although he hadn't brought that up for fear of upsetting her. It was no secret he was Marie's lawyer, but most everyone assumed it was to counsel her about the grand jury. No point in getting anyone thinking beyond that. Which was why he didn't go with her.

When Marie walked into the hearing room, the press was on hand in battle strength. Even the TV news anchors. Murray had made sure his people got out the word that this was a session not to be missed. He knew a big story when he saw it.

MURRAY . . . Mrs. Ragghianti, have you ever been threatened while trying to perform your official job?
MARIE Once.
MURRAY When was that?

MARIE   A few weeks ago. I don't remember the exact date. I possibly can figure it out. The Governor's legal counsel did threaten me.

MURRAY   Where did this threat take place?

MARIE   In his office.

MURRAY   All right. Now, this is Mr. Eddie Sisk that you're talking about?

MARIE   Yes.

MURRAY   Is he the Governor's legal counsel?

MARIE   Yes.

MURRAY   What was the nature of the threat?

MARIE   Well . . . to make a long story short, he did inform me that if I didn't support the bill, probably I would be fired.

MURRAY   In other words, he threatened you with the firing on the pretense of authority if you did not support the particular bill that the administration wanted, regardless of your personal feelings about it?

MARIE   Yes.

She heard some papers being rustled and a couple of tentative coughs. Then a general buzzing. A half-dozen reporters were already dashing out the hearing-room doors. The buzzing got louder, and Murray, looking very somber for the TV cameras, gaveled for silence. Marie saw Carol Marin, the Channel 4 co-anchor, studying her intently. She couldn't decide what was in Carol's mind—whether it was admiration or if Carol thought she had gone bananas.

Word spread through the capitol corridors about what was happening before Murray's subcommittee, and it was SRO for Sisk's testimony after the lunch recess. When Marie returned to the hearing room, all the murmurs stopped for a second. People were staring at her, pretending not to. Every time she looked around, eyes darted away. She saw Eddie fidgeting in a chair off to one side.

Just before the afternoon session started, Ed Parker, a radio reporter, went up and grabbed Murray's microphone. "And now, ladies and gentlemen," Parker boomed out, "on our left side here sits Miz Marie Ragghianti, the sacrificial lamb, and over there on the right is the Governor's hatchet man, Mr. Eddie Sisk." That broke the tension. Everybody laughed. Sisk even managed a grin.

For Marie, the comic relief was momentary. She was really uptight. She expected Sisk to deny everything, and it would come down to her word against his. Again, she wished she had a recording of what he'd said. Here it is, gentlemen. Clear proof. But she had forgotten that the Blanton style was never to be defensive. And Eddie, standing at the witness podium, half ringed by the subcommittee, hands flailing the air, his body twisting this way and that, jumpy as hell, his voice by turns sarcastic and righteous, did his best to follow the game plan. He told the subcommittee he didn't have the right to fire anybody, and that was that. In long, rambling statements he said Marie had been on the task force the Governor had appointed to draw up the bill, that the task force had met for months, that he himself had been at some of the meetings when Marie was present and that she had never once voiced any opposition to the legislation, and that as far as individual cases before the board were concerned, since that also had been raised, there was nothing wrong sitting down with the board and asking it to consider such cases favorably, that if the Governor felt strongly about a particular case, he was certainly within his rights to advance his arguments and the board was obligated at least to give the Governor, or for that matter Sisk himself, or anybody the Governor chose, an audience to hear these arguments, solely on the merits, of course.

When it got down to the nitty gritty, though, Sisk floundered into confirming the essence of what Marie had said.

MURRAY   Mrs. Ragghianti, when she was testifying, indicated . . . that because of differences over proposed legislation that you threatened her to be fired. Is that correct or incorrect? Some several weeks ago, a few weeks ago?

SISK   Well, let me say this . . . I can't remember the entire conversation, but I—I don't know whether the word "fire" was used or not directly, but I do know I—that she was told that the Governor would certainly not look favorably on her supporting some—some bill other than his, because as far as the administration was concerned, there wasn't but one bill, and that was the one that had been recommended by the task force.

MURRAY   All right. That fairly represents what Mrs. Ragghianti testified to over the legislation, and you certainly don't refute that you may have said "fire"?

SISK   I don't—I don't recall the exact—the exact language that was used, but I certainly did—did say that I looked with disfavor on this and I felt that the Governor would, if in fact she was supporting a bill other than the one the task force had recommended.

That was it. The whole thing had gotten too tender for the Democratic house majority leader, Tommy Burnett, one of the sponsors of the Blanton legislation. Another sponsor, Steve Cobb, the young Nashville legislator who had gone with Ramon to see Blanton about Marie's allegations, not only told Burnett to count him out but said that he would speak against the bill if it got to the floor. And before the day was over, Burnett announced that the administration bill was being withdrawn. Burnett told reporters, "I felt like it had become a politically explosive issue that is not meaningful at this time." He said that he had not consulted with Blanton.

When reporters tried to reach the Governor, his press secretary said that he would have no comment.

· 2 ·

ASSOCIATED PRESS, *May 10, 1977*

Nashville—Chairman Marie Ragghianti of the state parole board said Monday she once was threatened by an aide to Gov. Ray Blanton with loss of her job if she failed to support a bill to enlarge the board.

Marie had never seen Bill Leech so mad. She was so used to Leech's affable ways that it took her a second to recover. Then she argued back. The administration bill was only window-dressing. And she could have said a zillion more things. She could have told, for example, how Eddie had warned her she better watch her step, that a file was being kept on her. What would the media have done with that?

It didn't matter, Leech insisted. What she had done was unnecessary. It was injudicious. Inflammatory. There was too much at stake. She flared up at that. She didn't need him or anyone else to tell *her* what was at stake. "By God," she said, "the people of Tennessee have a right to know at least some of the things that are going on."

Finally they both cooled off.

This exchange took place the day after she testified, and things were never quite the same between them. In the evening one of the biggest legislative social events of the year was on tap, the annual reception of the powerful West Tennessee Democratic caucus. He sure *hoped* she wasn't going, Leech said as calmly as he could. It was exactly what she should be avoiding.

The truth was Marie was dying to go. After Sisk's inept performance and the withdrawal of the bill, her phone had been ringing all day with compliments about how stand-up she had been. She loved it, and she wanted more, and she told Leech that as a matter of fact she had thought about dropping by just to say hello. And he began getting exercised again, telling her she didn't need it, that the whole administration would be there, up to and including probably the Governor, that she had antagonized them all enough and this would only be rubbing their noses in it, and what she needed to do was stay home. Suddenly tired of squabbling, she said okay, she wouldn't go.

After work she stopped in at the Capitol Hill Club. As soon as she got there, her adrenaline began pumping again. A group of men at a table waved to her to come join them. Jim White, a state senator from Memphis, said, "Marie, what we want to know is how you manage to stay out of Eddie's clutches" and everyone started laughing. She didn't understand why until White showed her. That morning the *Tennessean* had run front-page pictures of her and Sisk at the hearing, separated by a column of type, as if they had been debating each other. Sisk had his arms extended, fingers clawing out, and White had folded the page so Eddie seemed on the verge of strangling Marie. "Well," she said, "it isn't as easy as it looks."

They all applauded. The folded front page was passed from table to table. You could follow its progress from the bursts of laughter. She sipped a Lite beer. A lobbyist said with great earnestness, "I admire your courage." She knew that if it had gone the other way, the lobbyist wouldn't have come near her. But she didn't care. More politicians streamed into the club for a quick pop before going on to the reception. She wished she were going herself.

She started talking to a short, stocky legislator from Knoxville named Ted Ray Miller. It turned out that Miller could use a ride to the reception, and she said she would ride him out, that it wasn't but a little bit out of her way. Actually it was, the reception being at the Rodeway Inn, which was dead east of the city near the airport, while she lived southwest, off West End Avenue.

When they got to the Rodeway Inn, Ted Ray said he couldn't

believe she was passing up the party, and she said maybe she would go in for a couple of minutes. The second she walked in, she was glad she had. The place was packed, and almost the first person she saw was Tom Wiseman, who had run for governor himself and who everybody said was going to be appointed a federal judge any time. Wiseman had a wide, friendly smile for her. He put out his hand and said he'd been hearing people talk about her all day, about how impressed they were at her fortitude. "You keep it up now," Wiseman told her.

Even people she didn't know were coming up, shaking her hand and congratulating her, wishing her well. All she heard were words like courage and integrity. It was glorious! She didn't see Blanton anywhere. But she saw Sisk momentarily on the other side of the room. There were so many people milling around, and the room was so large, that it was easy enough for both of them to avoid bumping into each other.

Somebody brought her a vodka and tonic. A lot of DAs were there, and that made her feel extra good. If there was one group that she felt was on her side, it was the district attorneys. Al Schmutzer, the Cocke County DA, gave her a big V-for-victory sign. The moonshiners in Cocke County were said to have put a $50,000 price tag on his head. Marie could never get over how blasé Al seemed about it. Richard Fisher was also there. After the intensity of their meetings before going to the FBI, she and Richard hadn't spoken that much. Kind of wait and see for both of them. He raised a glass to her from several feet away.

Gary Gerbitz grabbed her arm. "Hey," Gerbitz said, "you were terrific at the hearing. Did Eddie really threaten you?" Before she could answer, Gerbitz laughed and introduced her to one of his assistants. Gerbitz said why didn't they have a bite after the reception, and Marie said that it was a great idea.

She was just starting another vodka and tonic when she saw Sheriff Fate Thomas taking her in. She couldn't tell whether he was staring or leering at her. He was right out of Central Casting, jowly and paunchy, with a bulbous nose, string bow tie and ruffled shirt. Probably had checked his cream-colored cowboy hat. He'd written an endorsement letter for her when she was campaigning for chairman. Now he was being mentioned as Blanton's top candidate to replace her.

Seeing the sheriff made her remember Bill Leech's warning, and she felt a wave of guilt. Then, as if on cue, she turned and found Leech himself confronting her. "Marie, you told me you weren't coming here," he said, and she said, "I'm on my way out, Bill. I promise. I just gave Ted Ray Miller a ride, is all."

· 3 ·

She didn't want to leave, but she did, and went to the parking area and got into her BMW.

The Rodeway Inn was on Briley Parkway, a four-lane thoroughfare that was part of the belt system circling Nashville. There was a stop sign as you came out of the Inn's driveway onto Briley. To the left, if you turned right as Marie did, the parkway had a long, sweeping curve that let you see any oncoming traffic for three or four hundred yards.

Going along Briley, she thought about the reception and what an exhilarating experience it was. Tom Wiseman's words had been particularly thrilling. It went to show, she decided, that people did care if you gave them a chance. And she swore to herself that she would call Bill Leech in the morning, to apologize and to explain.

Then she saw the flashing blue lights of the Nashville Metro police in her rearview mirror. She had a tendency to speed, and the first thing she did was look at her speedometer. But she was doing less than forty, so she was sure the lights weren't for her. She glanced around to see if there was a wreck anywhere, or a fire. There wasn't.

The blue lights continued to flash. All of a sudden a siren sounded, and she realized that not only were there no wrecks around, but no other cars were in sight.

Marie pulled off Briley by a gas station at the Vultee Boulevard intersection, precisely a mile and three-tenths from the Rodeway Inn, still not alarmed, thinking maybe they wanted to ask her something, or maybe her taillight was out.

A motorcycle cop eased past her and parked in front of the BMW. He asked her for her license. She gave it to him and watched him go back to his motorcycle and use the radio. She wondered why, but mostly she began wishing he would turn off the flashing lights. Her silver BMW was familar to many of the people at the reception, and she was afraid one of them might come this way and recognize it.

The cop, Don Heath, returned and asked her if she had had anything to drink, and she said that she had just left a reception of the West Tennessee Democratic caucus and that she had drunk perhaps one and a half vodka and tonics—she couldn't be certain how much was left in the second one—and that was it, except for, oh yes, a Lite beer much earlier in the evening.

Heath went back to his motorcycle and made another radio call. By now five minutes more or less had passed, and she leaned out her window and said, "Officer, couldn't you turn off the lights?" and he replied, "No, I'm sorry, I can't."

The first alert bells began going off in her. When Heath returned this time, she said, "What's the trouble, Officer? Is something wrong?" And he said, "Well, we'll find out," and she said, "How's that?" and he replied, "We're waiting on the Batmobile," and she said, "You can't be serious," and he said, "Yes, I am." He wasn't smiling when he said it.

The Batmobile was a Breath Alcohol Testing vehicle of the Nashville police. She remembered reading somewhere that the department had acquired three of them to take the guesswork out of drunk-driving arrests. She relaxed once more. Let them give her the test. This was one of those things she'd have to get through. She didn't have anything to worry about.

It seemed like forever for the Batmobile to show up, and those darn blue lights started fraying her nerves all over again. Finally it arrived, a white van with blue lettering on the sides.

Annoyance got to her as she walked to the van, the indignity of it all. There were two officers inside. One of them explained that she had to blow into a kind of balloon, which measured the alcoholic content in the blood. The numbers came up on a computer. "Then what?" she asked, and he said that if she registered a tenth of one percent, it was a DUI—Driving Under the Influence.

Marie blew into the bag and watched the reddish digital numbers blink rapidly and stop at .04. She smiled and said, "That's it, I guess," but the officer administering the test said, "You didn't do it right," and she said, "What didn't I do right?" and he repeated, "Well, you just didn't do it right. You need to do it again."

She started to object, and then she thought, What difference does it make? She blew into the bag a second time, and the numbers registered .07, and she said, "That's really it now, huh? You said it had to be point one-oh for DUI, didn't you?"

She remembered how the two officers did not respond, how they looked at each other sort of confused. She started out of the van on her own and said to Heath, "I guess it's okay for me to go," and he told her that her BMW had been towed away. "But how will I get home?" she asked, and suddenly she knew she wasn't going home. She tried joking. "I thought it was point one-oh," she said. "I had point oh-four and point oh-seven. You don't add them up, do you?"

She became frightened. What was going on? *Why* was her car towed before she'd even finished the test? She looked at Heath. He was standing there saying nothing, almost, it seemed, daring her to make a scene.

She recalled what Bill Leech had said, how he had tried to warn her and she had not listened, and all at once she knew why this cop was not answering her, even looking at her, why she had to take the test twice, why her car had been towed away, why she wasn't going home.

Getting into the patrol car was the worst part. When it finally arrived, *its* lights were flashing too. She was put into the backseat, all five foot three of her with her little pocketbook, separated from the two cops in front by a heavy metal screen.

For the first time panic squeezed her. She was caged. It was as though she were already in jail, and she thought of all the inmates who had been before her trying to get uncaged, and she told herself not to forget this, that the experience might enable her to gain new insights for her work. Still, despite the ignominy, her resignation remained, the realization that there was nothing she could do.

She felt so small, silently holding her pocketbook on her lap, gazing at the metal screen. The cop riding with the driver swiveled his head around to look at her. He turned away, and then turned right back again. "Say," he said, "didn't I see you on TV last night?"

"I don't know," Marie said. "I didn't see the news last night." It was funny, but true, and the truth seemed terribly important.

"Well, wasn't your picture in the paper this morning?"

"Yes," she said. "You must have a good memory for faces."

"Hey," the cop said to his partner, "you know who that is? That's the chairman of the damn paroles board!"

The cop driving peeked back, startled. The car swerved. "Goddamn," the first cop said, "watch where you're going."

After that neither cop said anything.

She flinched when she got out of the car at police headquarters. She was sure flashbulbs would be popping off. But there weren't any.

She was taken to night court. She went past two drunks. One was slumped glassy-eyed against the wall. The other was sprawled out on the floor. She saw spittle running out of the corner of his mouth. She stepped around him, and as she did he reached out for her ankle. She avoided his grasp, but his fingers brushed against her leg, and she remembered the shiver that ran through her.

She stood before a judge. Heath was also there. The judge apparently recognized her. He said to Heath, "Do you know who she is? Why is she here?" And she heard Heath say that she had almost hit him, that she had gone through a stop sign coming out of a drive and had almost run him down.

Marie couldn't believe her ears. She wasn't able to swear she had braked to a full stop leaving the Rodeway Inn. But she sure hadn't barreled out onto Briley either. She distinctly recalled looking to see if there was any oncoming traffic. Later she would think how could it be said that she had nearly plowed into a cop on a motorcycle and he then followed her for more than a mile before arresting her? But now she just closed her eyes and shook her head and said nothing.

The judge told Heath he wanted to speak to him privately, and they disappeared. Thank God, she thought, it's all going to be taken care of. She was vaguely conscious of people sticking their heads into the courtroom, nosing around, curiouslike. When the judge returned, he directed her to go with Heath. They went into another room where there was a clerk behind a window. The clerk started writing up a report. She saw him put "DUI" right near the top. She waited for Heath to say something, and when he didn't, she meekly said, "I only registered point oh-seven, so it can't be DUI, can it?" and the clerk looked at Heath and said, "Did she register point oh-seven?" and she heard Heath saying, "Yeah, yeah."

She swayed slightly, seized by vertigo. Images were swimming in and out of focus. She tried to concentrate. The clerk—at least she thought it was the clerk—said that she was allowed a phone call, and maybe she should call her attorney. That snapped her back. If there was one thing she was certain of, it was that she could not face the humiliation of calling Bill Leech.

Finally the report was written up as a "reckless driving" charge. "Subject pulled from private drive," the narrative read, "and did not stop and was also cutting the center lane." There was no mention of almost hitting anybody.

Something was said about posting a $200 bond, and Marie said she didn't have that kind of money with her. Perhaps she wanted to call a member of her family? No, she replied, she couldn't possibly do that. Because of the time Marie needed to prepare for her legislative testimony, Therese had been staying at Virginia's. There was no way Marie would phone her mother at this hour.

She sensed a growing discomfort around her, a lot of agitation in the air. She saw it especially in Heath. "You mean," he said, "no one's coming to get you?"

"I told you there's nobody I can call."

"But that means I have to take you up to the fourth floor."

It was as though this hadn't been counted on at all. A black cop said, "Ma'am, a lady like you don't belong on the fourth floor."

She shrugged helplessly. She had no idea what the fourth floor was, except it sounded awful. Eventually she learned that it was the holding area for female prisoners.

She was standing by an elevator with Heath when another police officer, tall, young, came out of nowhere. He whispered to Heath, and the two of them walked off. That was the last time she saw Heath.

The new cop returned by himself. "Listen," he said, "I know you don't know who I am. But I know who you are—we have a mutual friend—and I'm going to help you."

She didn't know what was going on, but someone wanted to help her. She'd been rescued. "It's all right," the cop said. "I'm going to take you home."

The new cop said his name was Ronnie Woodard. In his car, driving her, he told her he couldn't say who their mutual friend was, that he had been sworn to secrecy. She listened, not really listening, dazed. By now it was nearly 3 A.M. She heard him say that he could talk to the judge if she wanted, and get this business straightened out. And then he mentioned something about sure being able to use a cup of coffee.

All her warning bells went to full alert again. She knew it was probably nutty, but she did not have anything left this night, no moorings, no reference points. Nothing. For all she knew, he meant every word he said. The only thing she could think of, however, was saying yes, fix it up with the judge, and then being charged with attempted bribery, or inviting him in for coffee and having someone burst in afterward, accusing her of impairing the morals of a Nashville police officer.

She had this compulsion to get out of the car as fast as she could. And when Woodard slowed in front of her apartment, before he had even stopped, she had the door open and was on her way out, saying, "Officer, I can't thank you enough, you were so kind," and running up the steps, already fishing out her keys, and getting inside and slamming her own door behind her, locking it.

Only then, alone, did Marie begin to sob. Huge, convulsive sobs. If they could just see her now, she thought. On the pardons and paroles board she was known as Hardhearted Hannah.

· 4 ·

She awoke at five-thirty in the morning, wide-eyed, nerve endings twitching. She went to the door for the *Tennessean.* She couldn't find anything about her arrest. She made herself some coffee and turned on the radio for the six-o'clock news. No mention there either.

She tuned in the *Today Show* to catch the first local news segment. Still no word. She began to think she was overdramatizing the incident, however nightmarish it had been, that running a stop sign was not such a big deal, and she better get a grip on her imagination. To work out the knot in the back of her neck, she went through her morning exercises twice.

At the office nobody said a word, not even Kevin, who always seemed to know everything that was going on.

Then, around 11 A.M., Becca Cottrill called. Becca was the press relations woman for the Department of Correction. Marie and Becca weren't that chummy. For one thing, Becca resented the fact that when Marie wanted to get an announcement out to the media, she did it herself.

Becca was very officious. "Marie, what's this?" she said. "I've been getting some inquiries. Were you arrested last night for drunk driving?"

Her heart sank. She wondered how they knew anything, and then she realized, of course, that they were all going to know. She was astonished at how evenly she managed to respond. "No, Becca, that's not true."

"Oh?"

"Look, I was arrested for reckless driving, but that makes it sound worse than it was. They say I went through a stop sign, and there's a grave question in my mind whether I actually did."

Becca's tone got a little defensive. "It's just that I have to have an answer."

"Well, now you do," Marie said, and hung up.

She wondered how much it had gotten around, where it had started. She decided to call Sisk to get a reading, using an upcoming clemency case as a pretext. A call like this would catch him off guard. But she didn't have to go that far. Young Trent Hall answered. He was one of the few in Eddie's office whom she had remained friendly with.

"Marie," he said, excited, "what's this I hear about you being arrested?" "Really?" she said, and he went on, "Yeah, I heard you were arrested last night. Everybody up here is talking about it. I hear you gave 'em hell," and she said, "*What?*" "That's right," he said, "I heard you put up a hell of a fight, cussed them out, hit them with your pocketbook. Right on!"

That rattled her, and she said too quickly, "Trent, *where* did you hear that?" and she could sense him shifting gears at the other end of the line, suddenly having second thoughts about saying too much. "Oh, I don't know," he said. "Everybody is talking about it, that, you know, you put up a real good fight." She didn't press him. He was probably repeating verbatim what Eddie or Charlie must have said ten minutes ago.

"Trent," she said very calmly, "you know me better than that. I don't go around cursing people and hitting them," and he cleared his throat and said, "Sure, Marie. I only wanted to make sure you're all right. You all right?"

She had to talk to somebody, and she called Kevin in. She told him what had happened during the night, and what she had just heard about it. She remembered how he clenched his fist and said, "Those goddamn bastards!" and that somehow made her feel better.

She had a BLT in her office, and skimmed through the early edition of the *Banner*. There was no mention of her, so maybe it would remain all talk. She had to leave for Memphis for a conference of paroling officers in the western part of the state. On the way she was to stay overnight in Jackson at Lois Laycook's. Her father's old friend had wanted her to meet a heavyweight Blanton financial contributor from Jackson. It never hurt, he had said, to know people like that. Even though the date had been set for several weeks, she would have canceled had it not been for the Memphis conference.

But Marie got through the dinner okay. Both men, of course, knew about her testimony before the Murray subcommittee. Most of their questions, however, centered on Sisk, what kind of a guy was he, and had the Governor really made the right choice? The evening wasn't easy. She couldn't get it out of her head what their reaction would have been if they had known about her arrest.

Late the next afternoon Dwight Lewis, a reporter for the *Tennessean*, reached Marie by phone in Memphis. Lewis covered the corrections department and the board. Lewis said he had been told about a DUI arrest, and did she have any comment? Marie knew Lewis was particularly close to Traughber, but he refused to say who his source was. It hadn't been a DUI, she said. The charge was reckless driving, going through a stop sign. She went through the whole thing again, hoping it would end there. Lewis, however, claimed that his editors considered it news. She asked when the story would appear. Tomorrow, Lewis said. Friday, the thirteenth.

She immediately thought about the kids. The boys were closest. The Morris School in Searcy, Arkansas, was a couple of hours from Memphis. She'd go to them first, then get back to Nashville to talk to Therese. It was important that they hear about it from her, in person, before they picked it up from someone else.

Marie was racing to get to the school before 9 P.M. Nine was the cut-off hour for visits. She was about ten miles from Searcy when she heard the siren. She looked at the speedometer. She'd been doing ninety.

"Young lady, do you know how fast you were speeding?" the trooper said, and she burst into tears, already seeing more headlines. Startled, he said, "What is it? What's the matter?" and she said she was trying to get to the Morris School to see her sons, and if she didn't arrive by nine she wouldn't be able to.

The trooper took her license. She saw him use his radio. He was gone perhaps ten minutes. Oh God, Marie thought. He's checking with Tennessee to see what they had on her. She watched him return. Would he take her in?

He gave her back the license. "All right," he said, "I'm not giving you a ticket. You go on now, and don't be in such a hurry. I had the dispatcher call the Morris School, and they said you can see your sons after nine. You know how to get there?"

"Oh, yes," she said. "Oh, thank you. Thank you."

"Boys," she said, struggling to keep from crying. "I want to tell you something just between us. Except it may get in the papers, and I hope you all won't be upset. But the night before last—you know how I've been writing to you that a lot of people who used to be my friends have really turned against me—well, the night before last, Momma was at this political reception and when I was leaving, guess what? I got arrested."

She saw Ricky's eyes widen. He's too young to understand all this, she thought. She concentrated on Dante. "Some of these people are really mad at me, and maybe that had something to do with it. I hope you know me well enough to know I wasn't out carousing, or anything like that. But the truth is, this officer arrested me. Sometimes politics isn't much fun."

"Momma," Ricky broke in, "you're going to sue them, aren't you?" and she said that by golly, she sure would like to, and she thanked them for standing by her. There wasn't a prouder momma in the whole world, she said.

She drove back to Nashville to tell Therese before she went off to school. Marie dreaded facing Virginia. The night before the arrest, she'd had dinner with Al Schmutzer and another DA. Therese was with Rosie at Virginia's but had wanted Marie to stop by for her. It was past eleven before Marie arrived, and Virginia had said rather sharply, "Ree, where have you been?"

"Good heavens, Mother, it's not even midnight."

Virginia said, "Don't you ever do this to me again. I've been frantic. I was about ready to call the police."

"For God's sake, for what? Mother, I am thirty-four years old. I have three children, and you're beside yourself worrying about me? Don't you think you're being a little ridiculous?"

And now, driving through the darkness on I-40, Marie bit her lip in chagrin, regretting the anger she'd displayed, thinking how valid her mother's concern had been. She found herself dozing at the wheel, the BMW half off the concrete, bouncing on the shoulder. She pulled off the Interstate and tried to sleep for a while. The huge trucks hurtling past kept waking her.

Marie just did catch Therese, and afterward, over coffee, Virginia was wonderful. "Well, it's so obvious. Blatant," she said. "You give testimony one day, and you're arrested the next." Therese came home from school and said, "Everybody says you were set up, Momma. What's that exactly?"

THE TENNESSEAN, *May 13, 1977*

PAROLE HEAD GIVEN TRAFFIC CITATION

. . . Asked if she thought her being stopped was politically motivated in any way, she said, "That's more than possible, but I hope it's not true." The officer could not be reached for comment.

Marie dragged herself into the office. An elderly corrections department clerk named Rudy worked in a cubbyhole she had to pass. "Ma'am, I read about you in the paper this morning," he said, "and I just want to say something. I want you to know that I'm praying for you."

She was immensely touched. "Why, thank you, Rudy."

"Yes, ma'am," he said, "if you've got a problem, you just need to do something about it."

"What's that?"

"If you've got a problem with alcohol, you need to face up to the fact. If you don't, you'll never be able to do anything about it."

There was a telephone memo that Ronnie had called. Ronnie? Then she remembered it was the cop who had taken her home. She didn't return the call.

· 5 ·

May 21, 1977
Saturday

Dearest Dante,

Therese and I are in Jackson, where we spent last night. I was absolutely exhausted. After arriving here, I visited the Adult Probation Parole Office, then Lois Laycook. Lois is a friend of Grandaddy's, & now mine. He is politically savvy, & a long-time supporter of the Governor. He did, in fact, recommend my appointment to the Governor. Since that time, as you know, a lot has happened. In talking to Lois yesterday, I sensed a pervasive sadness in his demeanor—regret, perhaps, for what he sees, and wishes he didn't see. He let me know that the Governor is out to get rid of me now, although he asked that I not quote him. I believe he is deeply disturbed by what's happening.

You must pray for me . . . Most of all, you must maintain your faith in God, in justice, & in the ultimate & inevitable triumph of good over evil.

Sometimes I recall the words of Winston Churchill, that "the malice of the wicked is reinforced by the weakness of the virtuous." Please pray that the good people of this state do not shy away from their responsibilities to actively uphold the law, not just simply to fail to break laws. Too many people think that as long as they don't break the law & "mind their own business," that is enough. That is not enough, nor will it ever be.

Laycook had asked to see her.

"Lois," she said, "I have to apologize for not telling you about the arrest. I just couldn't."

"Ree, you don't have to apologize to me. I think it's despicable. I thought you were very impressive in what you had to say the other evening. I phoned the Governor on your behalf, and I wish I could tell you it did some good. But I'm afraid it made things worse. Soon as I mentioned your name, he started cursing. Blew up. I've never heard him like that."

At groundbreaking ceremonies for major new construction at Vanderbilt University, State Senator Ed Blank was passing the time with Mayor Richard Fulton of Nashville when Governor Blanton walked up, that mysterious little half-smile working the corner of his mouth. "Say, Dick," Blank heard Blanton remark to the mayor, "I want to thank you for arresting Marie."

SIXTEEN

In a way, Sam Lipford had to laugh. All through the flap about the various criminal justice bills up on the hill, C. Murray Henderson kept ranting about what Marie was doing to undermine the Blanton administration. Henderson was the kind of man who believed you supported your boss to the bitter end, no matter what. He also didn't understand how you could kill the goose that was laying the golden eggs. When Henderson failed to get anywhere with Marie, he asked Sam and Ramon to try. It was the same old story. "Can't you do something about her?" he said to Lipford. "Can't you handle her? I can't handle her, can't you?"

"Hell, Murray, I can't handle her either."

"Well, go down there again and find out why she's doing it." Lipford would come back and tell Henderson it seemed to be a matter of ethics, and Henderson would yell, "*What?*" Henderson appeared to be having a hard time grasping that concept as opposed to the reality of political loyalty, so Lipford got more specific. "Murray, she's convinced something's going on, and she's determined to blow it up."

Lipford believed Marie about the ethics stuff. He'd noticed when he was sent off to reason with her, she never became personal, except about Charles Traughber, and that was all right with Sam. He found Traughber pretty slippery himself. Lipford had a sneaking admiration for Marie and tried to persuade her she was on a self-destruct kick.

Then she went too far even for Lipford. Quite aside from the legislation she was backing, Marie had gotten an opinion from David Raybin in the attorney general's office that under existing law the probations and paroles division—Lipford's division—should be reporting to her instead of to the corrections commissioner.

Technically, Lipford thought, she might be right, but he wouldn't have lasted two minutes with the administration if he had gone along with that. They had a knockdown fight over it.

"It's the law," she said.

"You're talking like it's gospel or something, and it isn't. Anyway, it isn't gospel that anybody has paid any attention to traditionally. It's just Raybin's opinion."

"Look it up."

"I don't have to look it up," Lipford told her. "I know where my paycheck is coming from. I know where the power is, Marie. That's *my* gospel."

She could sympathize with Sam and his anger about Raybin's opinion. The wording in the *Tennessee Code Annotated* was a little tricky, but when you studied the clause, Lipford and his field officers were under her. The whole thing had made Kevin more skittish than ever.

She felt so alone again. Didn't anybody care? The same sort of desolation and helplessness swept over her that she'd experienced after she had run from her husband for the last time, living in that roach-infested horror, existing on handouts, trying to maintain Dante and Therese, trying to keep little Ricky alive.

There had been that exhilarating feeling after her subcommittee testimony, but it all dissipated with the news of her arrest. It didn't matter if people thought she'd been set up. That was precisely the point. The administration had asserted itself. Showed it could do as it wished. She was damaged goods. Vulnerable. A loser. Sam Lipford had put it very simply. Being right didn't count. Jobs were on the line. The legislature, meanwhile, had adjourned. Supposedly there was to be another grand jury session in July, but people were saying it was a wild-goose chase. Hank Hillin told her not to believe everything she heard.

Her head whirled. There was so little time, and so much to do. A kinetic madness seized her. It was as if by staying in perpetual motion, she would make everything right. She sped across the state night and day, holding hearings, meeting with district attorneys, judges, community groups. Sleeping in her car by the side of an Interstate, being jolted awake by the roar of trucks became commonplace. She would open her eyes at daybreak wondering where she was, how she got there. Once she attended an evening meeting in Gatlinburg on the eastern edge of Tennessee and drove all night to be at 8 A.M. clemency hearings at the penitentiary in Nashville. She remembered being less than thirty miles from Nashville, that close to home, unable to drive another mile, and stopping at some motel and collapsing for an hour before pushing on. Fear stalked her. What they might manage to do to her on one of those dark roads. She'd leave word at the office that she was headed for Memphis, and drive to Chattanooga instead. She prayed constantly for the strength to persevere.

She was beset in mean ways. She had wanted to attend a workshop at Vanderbilt in human services management that would lead to a master's degree. The tuition was $1,000. As it happened, that was the amount set aside annually in each division of the corrections department for those employees who desired to further their education in a manner that would benefit the department. Marie applied for the money through the probations and paroles division. Henderson turned her down on the grounds that if he gave it all to her, nobody else could participate in the program. Then she discovered that she had been the only person to apply for a grant.

She learned of a departmental plan to have Traughber represent the board at the next American Correctional Association conference. How could they contemplate such a thing? Well, said Henderson, she'd been bitching a lot about how Tennessee didn't meet national standards. Maybe another view was needed.

· 2 ·

In June of '77 agent Dick Knudson, having visited Billy Gene Cole and his wife week after week, month after month, told Hillin, "I think I've got them."

The timing couldn't have been better. After the Benson blowup, the investigation had come to a virtual standstill. Joe Trimbach, the agent in charge of the Memphis office, was putting on heat. What was happening? Where are we going? Washington was starting to ask questions.

With Cole, Hillin played the heavy to Knudson's good guy. If Cole didn't cooperate, he could count on a federal indictment. On the other hand, if he did, he could expect immunity. The words tumbled out of Billy Gene, substantiating everything Prater had said. He'd paid ten thousand for his clemency. Bill Thompson had arranged it. Cole admitted being the go-between with Ronald Sotka's brother. He would testify before the grand jury.

Knudson had done an incredible job. Hillin noticed how the Coles treated Knudson almost as if he were a member of the family, anxiously glancing at him for his approval. Instead of the intransigence Cole had shown barely five months ago, he now voiced only one concern. He and Beulah had been looking forward to a vacation in July. He sure hoped his grand jury appearance wouldn't interfere with their trip.

The grand jury was going to be managed by Andy Reich, a Brooklyn-born, twenty-five-year-old lawyer from the Justice Department's public integrity section. It was Reich's first case of any importance. Hillin had sized him up as dedicated but awfully green. Another public integrity attorney with more experience, Steve Pitt, had been sent along to monitor Reich. Pitt was from Kentucky, and that at least gave him a regional feel for the case. But the thought of the lines running back to Washington continued to nag at Hillin. He wished Hal Hardin were handling it. Hardin had been confirmed as U.S. attorney for the Middle District of Tennessee on June 30 and promptly declared himself out of the investigation because of the Justice Department's involvement. Privately, though, he said he was available for any help Hillin wanted.

Hillin had an immediate, touchy problem. In Dalton, after Tommy Prater had apparently disappeared into federal hands and Special Prosecutor Erwin Mitchell contacted the governor of Georgia to find out what was what, Mitchell had been told not to worry. Prater would be produced in a matter of weeks. The weeks, however, had turned into months, and the pressure from Georgia couldn't be ignored by Hillin any longer.

A classic agent/informant relationship had developed between Hillin and Prater. In effect, they'd become partners. Hillin felt an obligation to Prater. He had gotten Prater accepted into the federal witness protection program. All Prater had to do was sign the waivers. While this wouldn't eliminate the robbery charges Prater faced in Dalton, it would buy him time, and you never knew what could happen. Time was always a mitigating factor. Prater's role in the pardons and paroles investigation would become a matter of record. Hillin would testify on his behalf. "You go back now, they'll burn you in Georgia," he told Prater. "Sign up. The restrictions aren't so bad."

But Prater was unwilling to forgo Chattanooga and Market Street. Hillin was probably right, he said. The idea, however, of living in some strange part of the country was too much for him. The same as being in jail without getting credit for it. So he'd take his chances. Bobby Lee Cook, one of the best criminal lawyers in Georgia, had agreed to represent him. They say, said Prater, that if the devil needed an attorney, he'd hire Mr. Cook.

Still, there was Prater's expectation that Hillin would go to bat for him, and the agent tried. He had reviewed the Dalton robberies and was convinced that although Prater might have fenced the stolen property, he hadn't actually entered any of the houses and manhandled people. All the descriptions of the robbers had them over six feet tall, and Prater was five six.

Hillin asked Andy Reich to sound out Mitchell about making some sort of deal for Prater. Reich reported that Mitchell wasn't buying. He had waited long enough. Said his job was to prosecute Prater for the Dalton robberies. Didn't give a damn about Governor Ray Blanton, Eddie Sisk or anybody else in Tennessee.

Then Hillin requested a meeting with Mitchell. He took Reich with him. When he arrived at Mitchell's office, he found present not only Mitchell but all of the victims, along with GBI agent Bill Dodd. It was the most difficult encounter Hillin had ever had. He told the assemblage that he had spent his entire adult life in law enforcement. He personally had sent many, many people to the penitentiary. "I understand where you all are coming from," he said. "I understand your frustration. I know how you feel."

It was in this context, he went on, that he was appealing to them. He spoke of corruption at the highest level in the pardons and paroles case, how it struck at the heart of the criminal justice system, how Tommy Prater was a key witness. Never, said Hillin, had he been involved in an investigation of such importance. Sometimes you had to weigh things out. That was why he was asking consideration for Prater.

In the middle of Hillin's pitch, George Stafford, who'd been Maced in the third break-in, got up and paused at the door before leaving. "I don't know how the rest of you are going to vote, but I'm voting this way," he said, jerking both thumbs down. Hillin remembered Dodd staring at him from a corner of the office, fisheyed. "Mr. Hillin," Sims Lambert said, "how would you like it if someone came into your house and tied you up and tied your children up and then ransacked your belongings?"

Driving away from Dalton, Reich said, "What do you think?"

"I think," said Hillin, "we better get out of here before they ride us out on a rail."

· 3 ·

Virginia started getting concerned. "You're losing weight, Ree. You've got those big rings under your eyes. You've got to slow down."

Marie knew her mother was right. She was frazzled out. She'd been operating on nerves for so long. A flat-out, eight-cylinder, high-octane trip. But she couldn't stop. There was so little time. Just the other day she was leaving the main prison in Nashville when a young inmate came up to her, saying he'd mailed in a letter for clemency and had gotten back a form reply.

"I'm really sorry," she said. "I hate those form letters. I'm trying to do away with them."

The inmate said he was serving a ten-year sentence for murder two. He'd been in an automobile accident, and somebody had been killed as a result. He had three children, and his wife was supporting them. He had never broken the law before, he said. It had been an accident. But nevertheless he had been convicted of second-degree murder. Marie thought of Larkin Bibbs. Bibbs also had been serving time for murder two. Except it wasn't because of a car accident. Bibbs had gunned down people. And Bibbs was out in only three months. Had paid his way out. Marie took the inmate's name. She'd look into it, she said. Oh God, she thought.

For the first time she snapped at Hank Hillin. He had called to tell her she would have to testify again before the July grand jury. She demanded to know why. She'd already testified to everything. Well, there was this new Justice Department attorney from Washington, he said, and the grand jury was a different one.

In a corner of her mind Marie was aware that she was losing hold. Not thinking as keenly as she should. Yet she seemed unable to do anything about it. She bought the ticket during this craziness. The ticket was for a mammoth state Democratic fund-raiser a month off, on July 30. The star attraction was Vice-President Mondale. At the moment she couldn't have given two hoots about hearing Mondale speak, much less spending $150 for the dinner. But she clung to the idea that it would somehow demonstrate that she remained a loyal Democrat despite her battle with Blanton. In retrospect, she would wonder how she ever could have imagined that.

At least she'd have a respite. The boys were home from Morris, and Marie was taking them and Therese and Rosie to what was becoming their annual Fourth of July week in Daytona Beach. And instead of a motel, she rented a cottage. They'd have a grand time.

But for once, Daytona didn't work. She spent all her days restlessly pacing the beach, fretting about what was going on in Nashville. What new plots were being hatched against her.

On the way back, Marie's BMW broke down and was towed to Atlanta for repairs. She borrowed a car from Dr. Espy.

In July the moves to break Marie mounted. In an executive session of the board, Traughber and Mitchell voted against seeking accreditation with the American Correctional Association, voted to disagree with the opinion of the attorney general's office that probation and parole officers were to report to the board, voted against even participating in the selection of these officers and voted against controlling its own budget at the present time. Marie kind of expected the last three votes. They were close to home and politically hot. But to vote against meeting national parole standards left her stunned. If she had sponsored a resolution in favor of saluting the flag, the vote would be two to one against it. Marie remembered how Joe Mitchell, a couple of months earlier, had taken her aside and said that all he wanted was to get through the next year or so without any big fights, get his pension and get out. Now, on the accreditation issue, Traughber was saying he didn't think they should be doing anything like that, and there was Mitchell going along with him.

She needed to fight back harder, she thought, and Bill Leech wasn't helping. It wasn't her nature to take this lying down, but all Bill counseled was caution. Kept telling her that her visibility was too high. She was sick of it. She was annoyed that he hadn't been aggressive enough in defense of her reckless-driving arrest, which was still pending. "It's better," he had said, "to inject a little air in the situation."

Marie began to think Leech had a built-in conflict of interest, one perhaps he wasn't conscious of. Bill was going to be a delegate at the state constitutional convention in August. Wanted to be a power at it, and representing her wouldn't help him in the slightest. Around the time of the Murray subcommittee, Leech himself had given her an opening. "If you don't like what you're hearing from me, you should get another attorney," he said. "If you don't want my advice, don't take it."

So now Marie considered contacting Jim Neal, who was about the biggest legal name in Nashville. As a special prosecutor hired by Robert F. Kennedy, Neal had sent Jimmy Hoffa to prison. He'd also been a special prosecutor in the Watergate trials. But suddenly, as a lifelong Democrat, she found herself worrying about Neal being a Democrat. It was so intertwined at the top. Jim Neal had impeccable credentials. Yet for all she knew, he might be best friends with Ray Blanton's third cousin. She couldn't afford to entertain the tiniest notion that anyone representing her was cozy with the administration.

On that score, though, there was another lawyer in Nashville she wouldn't have to be concerned about. If you scratched Fred Thompson, all you discovered was more Republican. Thompson, an imposing six foot five, was from Lawrenceburg in rural Lawrence County, part of Blanton's old congressional district. When Blanton ran for his third term in 1968, Thompson, barely out of Vanderbilt Law School, had managed the losing Republican effort to unseat him. Then in '72 he had been Howard Baker's Middle Tennessee reelection campaign director when Blanton had tried for the U.S. Senate. And Thompson was getting right up in Jim Neal's league. Marie had been lying in Columbia-Presbyterian Medical Center, recovering from her lung biopsy, when she first saw him in action day after day during the televised inquiry into the Watergate break-in. Even though he was only thirty, Thompson had been handpicked by Baker to be the chief minority counsel for the Senate Select Committee on Watergate.

But that was all out in public. What was the real Fred Thompson? One of her friends, Kay Johnson, had worked as a secretary for him, so Marie called Kay and told her that it was terribly confidential, but she was thinking of changing attorneys. Thinking about Thompson. Was he hardworking? Driven? Or were his cases just cases to him?

"Oh, Ree," Kay said, "don't you remember? I quit because he always was keeping me working nights, and he wanted me there Saturdays and Sundays. And every now and then he'd storm all over the office if he felt some client was being mistreated, and yell at me about it."

Exactly what Marie wanted to hear, and after the board's vote on accreditation, she put in a call to Thompson. He was back to her within the hour. "What can I do for you?"

"Mr. Thompson, I would like to meet with you as soon as possible. I want to talk to you about representing me."

"Representing you?"

"Yes, you may have noticed that I've been having some problems, and I need advice."

"Well, I'll confess you're not an unfamiliar name. But I thought Bill Leech was representing you. Have you talked to him about this?"

"No. I wanted to find out your feelings."

"You talk to Bill first. This has to be done in a proper way."

Calling Leech was hard. For once, Marie prayed she wouldn't be able to reach him. Not getting through to Bill when she wanted to was one of her biggest gripes. Maybe she could take the coward's way out and just leave a message. This time, naturally, he was on the line in a matter of seconds. In a small voice she said, "Bill, I don't know how to say this —it's very difficult for me because I appreciate so much what you've done—but I know you're running for the presidency of the constitutional convention, and representing me places you in an impossible position."

"No, not at all, Marie."

She gulped on that. "I'll never be able to express my gratitude, but I truly believe I'm doing you a favor. I want you to know that I've spoken to Fred Thompson today about representing me."

There was an agonizing pause before Leech said, "You tell Fred to call me, and I'll help you any way I can."

Afterward, she could only hope she'd done the right thing.

· 4 ·

July 21

What a day! Am exhausted. After talking to Fred last night, drove to Monteagle to spend a few hrs in sleep, Chatt. hearings this morning.

Visited Gary. Drove to Murf. for wasted office call to Judge Holloway, who wasn't there. Arrived home to blaring news reports that Clayton Dawson had pled guilty today to his 15th rape. I am incensed, because it's inexcusable!

She'd been hanging around Holloway's office in Murfreesboro on the chance he might show up when she decided to check in with her own office. Ernestine told her there'd been calls from the *Tennessean*, the *Banner*, AP, all the television stations and she didn't know who else.

"What in the world for?"

"They said Clayton Dawson pleaded guilty here to rape, and they want to know why you all let him out."

Marie ran to her car, seeing red. Dawson had been given the death penalty in 1960 for raping a teenage girl and her mother, although Governor Frank Clement subsequently commuted his sentence to ninety-nine years. In 1976, five months before Marie became chairman, the board had recommended clemency, and Blanton commuted him to time served, and now he'd been arrested again for raping a college student. The man should never have been let loose. And driving toward Nashville, listening to the radio reports, Marie remained livid. Traughber and Mitchell had voted to free Dawson. The same two who had voted against adopting parole procedures that would measure up to nationally accepted standards. By God, she thought, even though the accreditation vote had been in executive session, people were going to know about it. She'd see to that.

The phone was ringing when she got home. A reporter from Memphis. The kids said the phone had been ringing constantly. She was kept busy all evening taking calls from across the state, trying to explain the process by which Dawson had been allowed to walk. She sounded so defensive, and the coverage reflected it. As if she'd been a party to Dawson's release. Marie could hear people everywhere in Tennessee saying, Hell, *she's* the one who put him on the street.

In the morning she pulled Dawson's file. Right on top was a letter from the Shelby County DA protesting clemency. *Our records show that he was convicted and received a death penalty for these offenses. Governor Clement commuted this to ninety-nine (99) years. I would suspect without benefit of parole, but I am not sure. In addition, we dismissed twelve (12) other cases of Rape against this individual, believing the death penalty was sufficient punishment. Therefore, I must in good conscience oppose the granting of such clemency against this individual. These cases were serious, and of a horrible nature.*

That wasn't all. An evaluation report requested by the board four months before he was set free described him as *highly rebellious and nonconforming, worrisome and apprehensive, experiencing dissatisfaction with social relationships.* The words leaped at her. Dawson was *impulsive . . . unpredictable . . . easily upset and changeable.* This psychological profile of the Shelby County rapist, dated October 31, 1975, had been ignored in the clemency recommendation forwarded by the board while Traughber was its chairman.

That afternoon Marie gave a television interview. There was a lot of trial and error in paroles, she said. You did the best you could. She'd been trying to upgrade the board's guidelines. That's why she was so baffled by the vote of her fellow members not to seek accreditation. Other states were doing it. She had hoped Tennessee would be leading the way.

The media jumped on the accreditation story, tying it in with the Dawson clemency. Then, to Marie's amazement, Traughber denied that a vote had been taken. And Mitchell backed him up, although a little less flatly. "I think maybe she misunderstood, but there was no vote taken on the matter at all," his quote went. "I only expressed my opinion." Traughber was pretty cute, she thought. Since the board was in executive session, only the three members were present—and Kevin McCormack. From now on, she swore to herself, she would have every session taped.

Marie said to Kevin, "Did you see that s.o.b. Traughber on the tube last night? Can you believe his gall? How can he lie like that, Kevin?" She noticed Kevin wasn't responding. "You were there," she said. "You heard the vote. Can you believe this?" Marie looked at Kevin. Not a word. "Kevin, you were there, weren't you?" He still didn't speak, didn't nod. It took a moment, but she got the message, and the message was that Kevin wasn't remembering anything, Kevin had chosen sides, and that time last March flashed back to her when Kevin had said she was finished unless she went along with the administration.

This was on a Saturday, July 23. Marie returned to her office. She thought of all the Saturdays they'd been there together, the Saturday they'd first met and he got her a hamburger, the Saturdays they'd spent drafting the criminal justice legislation, the Saturdays at the Judge's Chambers drinking beer and devouring too many potato chips, gossiping and laughing and having such a good time. Mechanically she started shuffling papers, set up her Dictaphone and tried to catch up on her work. Finally she gave up and left.

Marie was at the penitentiary in Nashville early the morning of July 25 when she got word that Commissioner Henderson was holding a 10 A.M. press conference to discuss the parole system. She arrived late on purpose. Henderson had barely finished saying that the state's prison population was becoming unmanageable and that the rate of recidivism for Tennessee parolees was much lower than the national average. As soon as Marie entered the room, all the cameras and reporters turned to her. Question after question about the accreditation vote and Traughber's denial. What was the story? Was there a personality conflict between her and the other board members? Had there really been a vote?

Yes, there had been a vote, she said. To say otherwise would be untruthful. As for any personality conflict, there wasn't one as far as she was concerned. Perhaps they should ask the other members of the board how they felt. Her sole goal was to raise the board's professionalism.

A television reporter, Virg Jacques, and Dwight Lewis of the *Tennessean*, who had written about her reckless-driving arrest, stayed with her on the accreditation issue. Jacques demanded to know why Traughber and Mitchell were denying it. She couldn't say, Marie replied. He'd have to talk to them. Just then she spotted Kevin trying to get out of the room. Marie grabbed him by the sleeve. "Mr. McCormack was also at the meeting," she said. "Why don't you ask him?"

The TV lights swung on Kevin. He was white-faced. Marie could see his panic. Under the best of circumstances, those lights were intimidating. "Please turn off the lights," Kevin said. He'd speak to them, but he didn't want to be on camera. So the lights went off, and Jacques said, "Okay, what happened at the meeting?" Marie remembered Lewis standing next to Jacques, scribbling away. She didn't like Lewis. Lewis was too tight with Traughber. She felt the tension. Clayton Dawson was black. Traughber was black. Both Jacques and Lewis were black.

Marie's eyes met Kevin's. There was a long silence. At last, in a low voice, Kevin said, "I left the meeting with the distinct impression that a vote had been taken opposing accreditation."

That evening on the six o'clock news Virg Jacques reported Kevin's quote verbatim. So at least it was on the record. In his front-page story in the *Tennessean*, Lewis didn't mention it.

· 5 ·

All during July while the grand jury was in session on pardons, paroles and extraditions, the Blanton administration had been on the attack. Eddie Sisk got the first headline. There had been no improprieties. The whole thing was a "witch-hunt" orchestrated by Hillin. Then Chattanooga Democratic boss Ward Crutchfield, whose law firm had been involved in the Georgia extraditions and the Cole and Bibbs clemencies, claimed he was the victim of systematic federal harassment launched by the Republicans before they left office. Even the IRS, he said, was after him. But the biggest headlines were created by a local

TV personality and political commentator named Floyd Kephart.

Prater had told Hillin that Kephart had made the arrangements for Billy Gene Cole's polygraph test. Prater also said he'd been with Eddie Sisk and Bill Thompson at a Nashville restaurant, the Captain's Table, waiting for Kephart but he hadn't shown. Hillin had wanted to know from Kephart what that was all about, and Kephart replied he was a politically active, unabashed Democrat and did plenty of things for people. Bill Thompson might have asked him to set up the polygraph. So what? Kephart said he couldn't recall Thompson asking him to meet with Sisk at the Captain's Table. He said he once had dinner with Thompson and Prater in another restaurant, but that was about a coal deal Thompson was promoting.

Kephart's appearance before the grand jury got enormous media coverage. Afterward on the courthouse steps he conveyed the administration's pitch. The FBI was out to get Eddie Sisk. He picked up on the witch-hunt theme. "A witch-hunt? Sure, that's all it is," said Kephart. "This investigation of the grand jury has been going on almost a year. If they have proved anybody involved did anything wrong, they should indict him and not keep parading us up there." For good measure, Kephart characterized Andy Reich as an "arrogant fellow."

Let them spout off, Hank Hillin thought. There were some items that neither the administration nor the press was aware of. Nobody knew that Billy Gene Cole had been turned. Both Prater and Cole had been slipped into the courthouse without being seen.

Critical backup had been obtained in the Larkin Bibbs payoff as well. Hillin had gone to see big, jovial Sam Pettyjohn a couple of times since his last grand jury testimony, but Sam kept insisting that he didn't know anything about any fifteen thousand to get Bibbs out. Pettyjohn's instinct was to accommodate himself out of trouble. Hillin knew, though, that he was petrified of the drug traffickers Bibbs had worked for. That was the key. And now, in July, in a grand jury waiting room, Hillin caught up with Pettyjohn and told him how bad it looked. He surely was going to be indicted. Perjury was a grave offense. Suddenly Pettyjohn was saying he just wished he didn't have to go in front of that grand jury, things had a way of getting out, and Hillin said he'd fix it so Sam wouldn't have to, and Pettyjohn said, "You serious, Mr. Hillin?" He didn't make promises he couldn't keep, Hillin said. So right then and there Sam Pettyjohn confirmed the substance of what Prater had sworn to.

Nobody knew about Charles Traughber either. While the grand jury was still in session, Hillin had arranged a meeting with Traughber on a blazing hot day in Shelby Park on the east side of Nashville. Hillin often used the park for interviews because of its seclusion. What he needed was to work Sisk a little more into the Cole clemency. He got right to it with Traughber. Unless Traughber did a lot better, the chances were he would also be indicted as part of the conspiracy. Traughber's story, especially regarding Cole, wasn't adding up.

All at once Traughber, who had constantly maintained that he hadn't felt the slightest pressure from the Governor's office on any commutation, announced that he'd kept a diary on the Cole case in the fall of '75. He'd done so, he said, because it might prove embarrassing and he'd better keep a record of what happened.

Oct. 3. Telephone call to Mr. Sisk. During conversation, he instructed me to have commutation papers prepared on William G. Cole, No. 73060, for time served with parole supervision to maximum expiration date of sentence.

A) Mr. Sisk had given instruction based on what he said was Gov. Blanton's interest, the Cole case be given positive consideration. My understanding is that the Governor has a personal friend (name not mentioned).

B) The problem in the Cole case, that TBCI is investigating his possible involvement in two murders. He asked to take lie detector test. He did and failed. Now TBCI has reactivated the case.

Oct. 4. Informed Board member Mitchell that Mr. Sisk had asked that papers be drawn up on Cole.

Oct. 6. Informed Board member Greer.

Note: all Board members reluctant and agreed that our Governor wants papers to submit report for consideration by Governor to time served with parole supervision, expiration date of sentence.

Oct. 7. Mr. Sisk called me and said, "Prepare the papers. I'll be by the next morning to pick them up."

Oct. 8. 8:15 A.M. Mr. Sisk called and says he will pick up commutation papers this morning before going to court. At approximately 8:30 A.M. Mr. Sisk arrived, and I gave him commutation papers on Cole. While he reads, I ask whether or not this Cole matter is going to embarrass anyone. He states, "No, that the only person that will proba-

bly be in trouble is Cole if he violates, because he was given extra consideration."

Traughber said he had made his October 8 entry because it was odd that Sisk would come for the commutation papers himself. Usually they'd go over by messenger from the board to the legal counsel's office. Also the hour. Sisk never got in that early. Not so odd, Hillin thought. October 8 was the day Bill Thompson, Tommy Prater and Cole's wife had gone out to the penitentiary to tell Cole his papers had gone through, that he hadn't wasted his money.

· 6 ·

The evening of July 27, the last day the grand jury met, Marie was home reading in the *Banner* about the testimony of Erwin Mitchell and former Dalton DA Sam Brantley. Both had told reporters that they'd never encountered such foot-dragging on what should have been routine extraditions.

Buried in the story was a note that Bernard Weinthal, reputedly a key witness against Prater, Barnes, McBryar and Bekovich, had been found dead on the outskirts of Dalton, an apparent suicide.

The chill went straight to Marie's bones. She just knew it wasn't a suicide.

She had some company. For several days anxiety had been curdling Bill Dodd's stomach. Dodd still got steamed up every time he thought of that FBI agent coming down trying to make a case for Prater, but the four wanted men were going to be returned any time now. Then Dodd got disturbing news. A confidential informant had said there was a contract out on Weinthal. Dodd tried to persuade Weinthal to go into protective custody. Weinthal, however, didn't want to be put in jail. Like Prater, he couldn't stand being locked up.

Finally Dodd made arrangements to move Weinthal to another county, where he wouldn't have to be incarcerated. But Weinthal didn't want to leave his young wife. On the night of July 25 Dodd made a last attempt at getting Weinthal to change his mind, and this time Weinthal at least said he'd think it over. He sounded nervous to Dodd.

The next morning Dodd arrived at the Dalton correctional center about eight-thirty. That was when he learned that Weinthal had been found dead in his green Oldsmobile an hour earlier. Furious that he had not been contacted immediately, Dodd sped to the scene. But it was too late. The car and the body had already been removed. The immediate area where the car had been parked was trampled over, obliterating any physical clues.

Dodd blamed it all on a city detective who had taken one look and automatically decided it was a suicide. A passing motorist had spotted Weinthal slumped over in the Olds on the shoulder of a paved city road not far from the trailer where he and his wife lived. A garden hose ran from the exhaust pipe into the car. Clothing had been stuffed around the exhaust-pipe connection and also around the window through which the other end of the hose went.

His wife identified the clothing and the hose as belonging to Weinthal. She said her husband had driven her to work that morning, and neither the hose nor the clothes were in the car then, so obviously he had gone back to the trailer. She described his mood as anxious and depressed.

The trailer was situated on property owned by Weinthal's mother-in-law, whose house was about thirty-five yards from the trailer. There was an intervening rise that obscured the view, and besides, the mother-in-law said, she'd been sleeping.

The autopsy showed that Weinthal had a lethal level of carbon monoxide in his system—and also traces of a barbiturate. The rear entrance to the trailer was very accessible without anyone being able to see who was going in or out. Bill Dodd kept thinking about the contract on Weinthal. It wasn't hard for him to imagine people waiting for Weinthal, doping him up and rigging the suicide. Maybe the crime scene would have provided the answers if the case had been properly worked. Officially, local authorities ruled it a suicide. For Dodd, there'd always be a huge doubt. He couldn't prove it was a suicide, or that it wasn't.

All he knew for certain was that his star witness in the Dalton robberies wouldn't be testifying.

· 7 ·

On Thursday afternoon, July 28, Kevin came into Marie's office. Said he wanted to speak to her privately. Could they go somewhere? He seemed extra tense.

They went to a mezzanine lounge at the Hyatt Regency called the

Window Box. At that hour it was deserted. Marie had a Tab. Kevin ordered a Bloody Mary. He'd redeemed himself somewhat by backing her up on the accreditation vote, and she was so fond of him. Marie wondered what he had to say that was so important. Kevin squirmed. He said what he was about to tell her wasn't easy for him, but she had to know that she was being secretly audited by Arnold Hurst, an accountant in the corrections department.

"So what?" she snapped.

She didn't understand, he said. She wasn't thinking it through. The worst was yet to come if she didn't resign.

That brought her right up. "Resign?" she said, barely able to keep the incredulity out of her voice.

"*Yes.* They're going to drag you through the mud if you don't. You haven't seen anything yet, and I think you need to think about your children."

It's always the children, she thought, they always bring up the children. Never right and wrong. She looked at Kevin carefully. Was he doing this on his own, or had he been dispatched as their agent? "Let them do their audit," she said. "I don't have anything to hide."

"Marie, *I* know you haven't done anything. But don't you see? It doesn't make any difference. They're going to get you, and they don't care how. There's no way you can win. *They will win,*" and she remembered how he had spaced out the words, underscoring them. "I don't think you realize how bad it could be."

She almost welcomed the spasm of rage in her. "Look," she said, "you should know me well enough to know I will *not* resign, ever! If they want me gone, they can fire me. Let them show cause."

Marie could see this was not proceeding the way Kevin wanted. He ordered another Bloody Mary, and hesitated, then bent forward, lowering his voice, and stammered that he'd been doing some poking around about her audit. "I think you need to know," he said, "that they've found eighteen exceptions."

Exceptions! What in the world were exceptions? It was a term accountants and lawyers used, he said, when they were questioning something.

My God, she thought, is this what it has come to? With everything that was happening to her, was that the word they were hurling at her? *Exceptions!*

"Listen," she said, "give them a little message for me. Tell them to take their eighteen exceptions to the DA's office. In fact, the more I think about it, they should call the U.S. attorney. No, wait," she said, pausing, fastening her eyes wide open on him. "I have a better idea. Tell them to turn it all over to the Justice Department."

Kevin stared at her for a second in amazement. He started to grin. The grin became a laugh. He leaned back in his chair and roared uncontrollably, taking off his glasses and wiping his eyes, shaking his head all the while. "Marie, you're really something," he said. Then he looked at her again and stopped laughing.

On the sidewalk he spoke to her once more, soberly, waving at the state capitol with its green cupola, said to have been fashioned after the lamp of Diogenes, and told her, "Those people are hell-bent to get you, Marie. You know that, but I've got to tell you something, and *please* don't tell anybody. About two months ago, they tried to get me to sign an affidavit against you. That you weren't doing your job. Being disruptive, demoralizing everyone. Of course I didn't, after all we've been through, but I had to tell you, that's all."

Friday morning the garage in Atlanta called to say her BMW had finally been repaired, and Marie said she would drive down and pick it up the next day.

SEVENTEEN

It wasn't until after she had spoken to the garage and phoned Dr. Espy to tell him she'd be returning his car that Marie remembered the Saturday night fund-raiser featuring Mondale.

Then she thought, Well, it wouldn't be so bad. She'd leave for Atlanta in the evening, get the BMW first thing Saturday morning and be on her way back. Nashville was in the central time zone, so that would give her an extra hour, and she ought to be able to make the dinner easily.

Driving had become a form of therapy. She'd get on the road, turn on the tape deck and let Fleetwood Mac, the Eagles, Billy Joel wash over her. Sometimes, as she cruised alone along an Interstate, an image of the meetings about her, up at the capitol, at the executive mansion, would come to Marie, all of those men sitting around dissecting her, trying to get to the bottom of her, deciding she must be a psycho. And she would begin to laugh, and the laughter would get mixed up with the music, and she'd think if they could only see her, they would be convinced that she had gone around the bend. Sometimes, though, in the car, the laughter would abruptly turn to tears.

That Friday, June 29, she never was able to get away early as she had planned. One little thing after another. Still another reporter came in to see her about Clayton Dawson. More than anything, it was the Dawson case that had gotten to her. The unprofessionalism. The laziness and cynicism. That's how corruption burrowed in. She got out some statistics for the reporter. During the year before Marie became chairman, there had been two hundred eleven commutation recommendations. In the comparable period after her appointment, fifty-eight. That had been her answer to a query about whether the board had been judicious enough in its deliberations.

It was past 7 P.M. before she arrived home. The sitter Marie had arranged for called to say there'd been a last-minute family emergency and she couldn't make it. Marie tried other sitters to no avail. Rosie had already gone out for the evening, and to saddle Virginia with the kids was out of the question. She decided to take them with her. The car she'd borrowed from Dr. Espy, a Chevrolet Caprice, was large enough to let them sleep during the drive.

So at ten, instead of being in bed in Atlanta, she was just starting on the road. After better than a year of stupefying overloads, Marie's circuitry was finally shorting out. The trip was no big deal, she remembered thinking. She could do anything. She was unbreakable.

About 3 A.M. she stopped at a motel in Cartersville, Georgia. She rousted everyone early, but by the time breakfast for the kids was over, Marie's schedule was irretrievably off. Greater Atlanta sprawled all over. The garage with the BMW was on one side of the city; the place where she was supposed to leave the Caprice was as far as could be in the opposite direction. It was midafternoon before she headed back to Nashville. The fund-raiser began at 7 P.M., and even with the time-zone difference, she knew she couldn't make it by then. The children were clamoring for something to eat, and she pulled in at a McDonald's. She'd forgotten to bring enough cash and barely had the money to feed them. Therese gave Marie a bite of her hamburger.

Getting home took nearly five hours. For a second she considered skipping the dinner, but a new thought was drumming through her. By God, she was going to show everyone she wasn't beaten down. Wasn't off in some corner licking her wounds. Therese could cook for herself and her brothers. Marie told Dante and Ricky to be sure to help Therese clean up. She'd be home before midnight, she said.

She showered and took special care in making up her face. She put on a floor-length navy-blue gown and rushed to the Municipal Auditorium. The dinner part was over when she arrived, the speeches in progress. But as she made her way to her table she was conscious of the eyes on her. She'd been seen, which was the main thing.

At the motel in Cartersville that morning, she'd had only coffee, and except for the bite of Therese's hamburger, Marie hadn't eaten all day.

A waiter brought her a plate of food. It was cold and unappetizing, and she left it untouched. She did have a couple of glasses of wine. The people at her table were from corrections. Sam Lipford and his wife were there. So were Kevin and his date, and Martha Bernard, a research analyst, and Ramon. Arnold Hurst, the accountant who Kevin said was auditing her, was also at the table. What a creep Hurst was, she thought, and then she said to Kevin in a voice loud enough for Hurst to hear, "I was wondering something. Can you audit tickets? I mean traffic tickets." She tried to keep her voice as demure as she could and was delighted to see Hurst give her a startled, sideways glance. She thought it was kind of comical. Let them audit her forever.

To her surprise, she was having a good time. Never felt better, in fact, despite the occasional hostile stare she received from around the auditorium. It had been the right decision to come, to let them know she was still in one piece. Kevin brought her a vodka and tonic, and then as the fund-raiser began to break up, he suggested they all walk to the Hyatt Regency for a nightcap. Sam and his wife came along. So did Ramon and Martha. Kevin ordered his favorite drink, Old Charter bourbon on the rocks with a twist, and one for her. She had another. She was having fun, chatting about nothing special. For once, no pardons and paroles, no extraditions, no Clayton Dawsons.

Kevin nudged her. Eddie Sisk was at a nearby table, huddled with, of all people, Representative Roger Murray. She couldn't help thinking about the old days when she and Eddie had joked and kidded around. Now, as their eyes met, his face went blank. Deadly cold. He got up and walked away. She tried to shrug it off. But whatever gaiety had been bubbling in her fizzled out. Marie picked up her purse, excusing herself as if she were going to the rest room, and went to the parking complex where she had left her BMW. Later, Martha Bernard would tell her that Sisk had boasted about calling the police.

For the first time Marie realized how completely she'd been operating on nerves the past twenty-four hours, the past week even. She was so truly drained. On Harding Road, as she passed Vanderbilt University, she cautioned herself to drive extra carefully. She kept glancing at the speedometer. She wasn't close to the limit.

Incredulous, she saw the flashing blue lights of a motorcycle cop again. What confused her was that the lights were in front of her, and she needed a couple of seconds to figure out they were for her. Where had the cop come from? And then she thought, why was she worrying about that now? Had she lost all touch with reality?

In that instant, in the flashing lights, she saw the headlines about her firing. This time she didn't bother with the thought that her taillight might be out. She sat with her head bowed, overwhelmed by nausea and unbearable grief. After all she had tried to do, this was how it would end.

The cop asked to see her license, and she wanted to ask why they had to go through this charade. Why not just arrest her and get it over with? They both knew who she was.

Had she had anything to drink? Yes, she said, a little. He told her he was sending for the Batmobile, and this time she didn't argue. When it arrived, she climbed in, sat down and blew into the bag. The digital numbers on the computer blinked rapidly—.04, .05, .06. They slowed: .08 took a while, .09 longer. She watched as the numbers registered .10 percent and stopped. Although it was the bare minimum for a DUI, it was enough, and Marie was booked on that charge. The combination of the drinks on top of an empty stomach was all it had taken.

When one of the cops in the Batmobile asked her occupation, she replied, "I used to be chairman of the Board of Pardons and Paroles."

This time she used her allotted call to phone Toni Greer, a neighbor she had become friendly with at the Valley Ridge development. She asked Toni to look in on the children. She didn't know quite when she would be home.

"Marie, where are you?"

"I'm at police headquarters."

"What's wrong?"

"I think you heard where I am."

"They haven't arrested you again, have they?"

"Yes."

"Have you called Fred Thompson?"

"No."

"You're going to, though, aren't you?"

"How can I?" Marie said.

The shame came at her once more. The bottom line, she had always thought, was you lived your life in such a way that if, at any given moment the veil was pulled away for all the world to see, you were seen doing your best. And this night she had failed, and she could not forgive herself.

Marie was sitting on a bench in some corridor when she looked up and saw Fred Thompson looming over her, and she felt a flicker of hope.

· 2 ·

The afternoon Marie called to retain him, Thompson had agreed to see her mostly out of curiosity. Never dreamed anything would come of it. He'd enjoyed seeing Blanton get some flack in the media and hadn't been surprised at all that there were rumbles of corruption in the administration. But Thompson had figured it was basically penny ante. Never thought for a moment that any of it would reach Blanton himself, or even Sisk. Most of what Thompson knew came from the papers. He was too busy building up a practice that had been interrupted by eighteen months in Washington on Watergate to think of much else. And the little he'd heard about Marie was standard gossip. She'd had a romantic falling-out with Sisk. Also he'd been surprised and skeptical that she was coming to him, a high-profile Republican. Who knew what was in her head? Some people might think he was into raising hell with Democrats for his own amusement. Well, there were no bucks in that.

Even after their first meeting, Thompson's attitude didn't really change. Marie was just another person caught up in a messy situation, about to get canned because she'd rocked the boat. And being a female undoubtedly exacerbated the situation. While women appointees were sprinkled throughout the administration, they were expected to know their place. His counsel was much the same as Leech's. Lie low. Make her peace with Blanton as a way to hang on to her job. After all, Blanton had won the election and had the right to run things as he saw fit. If you didn't like it, you went after him the next time out. It seemed to Thompson more a political than a criminal matter. If she kept her mouth shut, this would blow over. A few days later, however, Thompson had a chat with Hank Hillin about Marie and began having some second thoughts.

When Toni Greer woke up Thompson in the middle of the night and told him Marie had been arrested, he dressed immediately and drove to headquarters.

He remembered thinking Marie looked like a bedraggled Cinderella, all dressed up in a gown, dazed, blank disbelief on her face. He tried a wisecrack. "Hey, come on," he said. "With time off for good behavior, we'll have you out of here in a couple of years."

It fell flat. He got her a Coke. Told her he'd be back in a minute, went in to see the night-court judge and arranged for her release without bail.

Afterward, Thompson chewed her out. How could she have been so stupid? She was the one who kept insisting the administration was out to get her. She should have known she was being watched. She had to be more careful. She listened without saying anything. He regretted having been so harsh and told her not to worry. He meant it. He didn't think Ray Blanton would use this incident to get rid of her. Blanton had the reputation of being a pretty good drinker himself.

The arrest had been too late to make Sunday's *Tennessean.* The first broadcasts were in the afternoon on radio. Then came the early- and late-evening TV news.

When Larry Brinton called and said they had stuck it to her again, she knew Larry was looking for a story, especially something about the FBI investigation, but she sensed genuine commiseration in his voice. He seemed to know none of this was right. Maybe other people would as well.

What she wasn't able to escape was that she had ruined everything. Then around 11 P.M. Fred Thompson called. He couldn't have been gentler. "A lawyer friend of mine told me a while ago he'd seen the ten-o'clock news," he said, "and I knew you must be having a hard time. Don't let this get you down." He said she had absolutely nothing to feel bad about. She'd been fighting against so much for so long. They'd tired her out this once. Worn her to a nub. It wasn't the end of the world.

She was so grateful. Afterward, Marie fell into a deep sleep, the first she'd had in she didn't know how long.

On Monday, when Blanton held a press conference, the arrest got big play. The Governor had said not only that he wasn't going to take any action on Marie's DUI until the courts decided her guilt or innocence, but also that he hadn't yet discussed her future with any of his advisers. In fact, he'd been getting progress reports on her audit, and then on Sunday night after her arrest he instructed C. Murray Henderson to demand her resignation. When Henderson notified him that she wouldn't quit, Blanton told Jack Strickland, Marie's old friend and confidant, to get together with Henderson on a letter terminating her. They were finally going to teach this damn bitch a lesson.

Hank Hillin groaned when he heard the news. His one spotless witness tarnished. Why had she left herself open for this? In any trial with Marie as a prosecution witness, it was certain to come up, and that afternoon in Thompson's office Hillin took a lengthy statement from her about the arrest and the circumstances surrounding it. At least there'd been Henderson's offer to find her another job at an equivalent salary if she resigned, so long as it wasn't in the criminal justice area. That might make a jury wonder. Hillin hoped he wasn't whistling past the graveyard.

· 3 ·

Someone told her that Blanton had been a model of restraint during his press conference. As she watched him on the news, however, all Marie saw was a cat licking its chops after a hearty meal. *Her.* They had the guillotine in place, despite what Fred was saying. And even Fred had backed off some when she told him about her meeting with Henderson and his constant references to her audit and how she should quit. Then she had to watch more on her arrest. Silent film clips of her in past interviews while a voice-over said she had declined comment. Film of where she'd been stopped Saturday night. More film of the May 10 arrest site. Film of police headquarters.

First thing in the morning she was at the penitentiary for hearings. Any doubts about what lay in store for her vanished when she saw the reaction of the inmates to her presence. Normally they vied to snatch a moment with her, trying to get a word in on their behalf. Now she might as well have been invisible. The inmates knew. She was through. Going out the main gate, she was certain that it was her last visit as chairman.

Home after work she told the children she was tired and wanted to be alone. If anyone called, except for Mr. Thompson or Mr. Hillin, she wasn't in. Even though it was still daylight, she went into her room, pulled the drapes, put on a nightgown and got into bed. There was a tentative knock on the door, and Ricky came in.

"Momma, what's wrong?"

"Nothing, honey."

"Please, Momma, talk to me about it."

"Honey, there are just some things we can't talk about."

"Are you worried about your job?"

"Well, yes, honey, a little. You go on out and play, though. You don't need to worry about it."

Perhaps twenty minutes later, as she lay there despondent, Ricky was back in the room. He lay on the other twin bed. "You know," he said, "I'm tired too."

"Honey, are you sure you're tired?"

"Real tired, Momma." He got up and came to her and threw his arms around her. "You know what?" he said. "When you get up for mass tomorrow, I'd like to go with you. Will you wake me?"

It was so incredibly sensitive of him, she thought. She'd long since given up trying to get any of the kids to go to early weekday mass with her. Rousing them for Sunday mass was tough enough.

All that night she wondered how Blanton was going to fire her. What would he have his people say, and who would say it? Would she find out the next day? She rehashed all the threats and the ultimatums and remembered Sisk's warning that they were building a file on her. She felt outnumbered. Traughber and Mitchell could be counted on to say absolutely anything. Now that it was at the point of no return, she was frightened again.

The morning of August 3 Marie was at work when Henderson told her this was her last chance. He could still stop the letter if she'd resign. She said her position was the same. She had done nothing to warrant resigning. So it was going to be a letter, she thought.

The final draft of the letter firing Marie was composed in the law office of George Barrett, the Nashville Democratic leader, a pillar of the local Catholic community, the same George Barrett whom she'd bumped into when she was a Young Democrat at Vanderbilt, who had said to Marie that if he ever could do anything for her, why, just come see him. Henderson was there, and so was Jack Strickland. Arnold Hurst was also on hand to supply the statistical evidence of Marie's malfeasance. Hurst was reeling off the figures from hastily compiled work sheets. When it had been typed, Strickland took the letter to the capitol to get it signed. Then he sent it by messenger to Henderson. Copies went to the Governor's press office.

Shortly after noon Marie spoke to Fred Thompson. By then he was aware of the letter. "There's still time for you to resign if you want to," he said, and she replied, "Oh, no." Thompson decided not to tell Marie she was going to be more alone than she might think. He'd been calling around, and was getting very negative responses about her, even from those who despised Blanton. This chick had messed herself up. She had thrown in with Blanton in the beginning, so whose fault was it? You lived by the sword and you died by the sword, they said. Anyway, how did she get the job in the first place? It was essentially the same story from people who one way or another had been pro-Marie. The consensus on her second arrest was that perhaps she'd been set up, but boy, she was awful dumb to have allowed it to work. Larry Brinton subscribed to this theory, and Brinton had been the friendliest of any reporter to Marie.

There was a great irony in all of this, Thompson thought. From the first Marie had constantly warned Sisk and Blanton that somebody would discover everything that was going on, and although she didn't know it at the time, she was the "somebody."

A half-dozen media calls had come in on her firing, none of which she accepted, before Henderson finally, officially, presented Marie with her letter of termination. She didn't want to read it alone, so she hurried up to Thompson's offices in the First American Center, three floors above the space the corrections department occupied. Then, when she looked at the letter with him, she didn't know whether to laugh or cry. Did a little of both.

Right off, Fred Thompson saw that he was dealing with a Marie far different from the forlorn figure he'd seen at Metro police headquarters the early hours of July 31. She was one angry woman as they continued to review her transgressions—the thirteen board meetings she hadn't attended for which she allegedly billed expenses to the state, the six meetings she had charged the state for that weren't scheduled, the simultaneous charges for the correctional conference in Denver and a board hearing at the Nashville penitentiary, the $7,584.94 in overtime she'd tried to bilk out of Tennessee taxpayers.

At the moment she couldn't answer for every single item, she said. It was ludicrous, though, to equate the Denver meeting and the Nashville hearing. She'd been in Denver, and it had cost money. But going to the penitentiary was no more than a couple of dollars in gas mileage.

Yet they'd made it sound like a great fraud. And as for trying to steal more than $7,500! It just wasn't so. Departmental regulations required keeping monthly time sheets. She'd been especially careful about that in case she was charged with being a no-show after her relations with the administration started deteriorating, but she had never billed the state a penny for overtime. She could prove it, she said. Thompson hoped so. Somehow, he was thinking, the letter was the key to Marie's salvation. The letter was overkill. And it had come so fast, without warning almost. Made Thompson smell that the administration was worried about something else.

In going over the financial charges in the letter, Marie jumped from sarcasm to derision. But the other parts—about her administrative failings, demoralizing the corrections department, crippling the board's effectiveness, acting criminally while she was supposed to be rehabilitating criminals, being an embarrassment not only to the state but to Blanton personally—really hurt. "How could they say that?" she beseeched Thompson.

Listen, he told her, he had an idea for a statement. *The people of Tennessee will have to concede that my client has accomplished one thing. She alone has been able to accomplish what no other individual or set of circumstances has been able to do—which is to embarrass the Governor.*

She burst out laughing. "Oh, Fred, that's marvelous."

Thompson's face turned mock solemn. No, that wasn't the right tone, he said. Too flip. What about a formal reply? *Dear Governor Blanton: I represent Marie Ragghianti in this matter. I can certainly understand your chagrin and dismay over the dire offenses that she has committed, and thus your desire to terminate her. But please be advised that it is my considered opinion that she will soon be indicted, at which time we expect that you will immediately reinstate her.*

Watching the news in Thompson's office, listening to the laundry list of charges against her, cut the merriment. Thompson asked her what she wanted to do. Fight, she said. Get her job back. Sue for it. They were trying to run her out of town. He couldn't guarantee a thing, he said. The chances weren't good. Not even fifty-fifty. The Governor, when you got down to it, had an inherent right to hire and fire members of his administration. She replied that she didn't care. What

Blanton had done was wrong. Think about it overnight, Thompson said.

She went back to the corrections department floor. To her surprise, Henderson hadn't gone yet. Undoubtedly he'd been taking a lot of press calls too. He followed Marie into her office and stood in front of her desk, groping for something to say. She saved him the trouble. "That's okay, Murray," she said. "I know you don't have any choice in this. It's not your doing." Marie could see that made him even more uncomfortable.

When she was alone, she got to work, pulling out every paper and document she could think of, hearing dockets, travel and expense records, correspondence to judges and DAs, copies of key clemency files, memos pertaining to the board's work, memoranda of the previous board, communications to Sisk and Benson, memos to herself—anything and everything that reflected her chairmanship, that would give the lie to Blanton's letter. In the frenzy to fire her they had forgotten to lock up her files. Any time, though, they would think of it, but she'd beat them to it. She had thought about it in Fred's office when she was telling him she could prove the charges in the letter were baseless. All told, there must have been a couple of feet of folders. She peeked out of her office. Nobody seemed to be around. Clutching the stack, the top tucked under her chin, she was trying to puzzle out how to ring for an elevator without dropping all the papers when she heard footsteps and froze. It was her famous auditor, Arnold Hurst. Suppose he demanded to know what she was doing with the folders? But she realized he was so disconcerted at running into her now that all he wanted was to be somewhere else. "Hello, Arnold," she said, "could you get the button for me?"

"Oh, yes, ma'am, sure thing."

"Tell me, Arnold," Marie said, "do you suppose you'll be seeing Jack Strickland?"

"Uh, it's possible."

"Well, if you do, I want you to give Jack a message for me. Tell him I forgive him."

The elevator door slid open. "See you, Arnold," she said. She knew he wouldn't dare get in with her, and he didn't.

When Marie arrived home, the kids were waiting on the steps going up to her section of Valley Ridge. They'd heard something, for sure.

"Come on, you all," she said. "I've got a bunch of papers here you can help carry in. But be careful."

"Momma!" Dante shouted. "Are you going to sue?"
"You bet," Marie said.

· 4 ·

NASHVILLE BANNER, *August 4, 1977*

RAGGHIANTI, ATTORNEY CONTEST CHARGES
By Larry Brinton

The firing of State Board of Pardons and Paroles
Chairman Marie Ragghianti followed a year of
"close scrutiny" and came nine months after Gov.
Ray Blanton personally asked her to resign, her attorney said today.

Fred Thompson, Mrs. Ragghianti's lawyer, had
taken issue with allegations lodged against his client,
saying most were either untrue or exaggerated.

The attorney met with Mrs. Ragghianti this
morning to discuss if the firing will be appealed in
chancery court.

Thompson said the board chairman, appointed by
Blanton in June of 1976, was offered another job
within the state government earlier this week if she
would resign.

That morning, after telling Fred she was adamant about fighting
back, they had met with Brinton. The story ran the full six columns
across the *Banner*'s front page. In the afternoon she held a jammed
press conference in Thompson's office. He had been hesitant about it,
but Marie handled herself expertly. Sincere, just a touch bewildered.
Got everyone to thinking about why she was really fired. "Maybe I
haven't played the game right," she said. "You know, maybe I'm a little
too outspoken. Certainly, I've attempted to be open at all times, and
this has, ah, created considerable embarrassment at times for other
people."

She was going to make a hell of a witness, Thompson thought.

The letter from Blanton had been expressly designed to crush Marie.
Drive her away once and for all. Eddie Sisk had been kept out of it,
so nobody could link up her firing with the federal investigation. When
Sisk saw a copy the afternoon of August 3, he thought it was heavy-
handed. But like everyone else around Blanton, he didn't expect for a

moment that she'd seriously contest the charges. It was inconceivable
that she'd put herself and her children through any more humiliation.
He figured the press reports that Marie was contemplating a lawsuit
had to be a bluff. She was going through the motions to save face. Her
last hurrah, Sisk thought.

The original idea had been to use managerial incompetence as good
cause to fire Marie. Show how she couldn't get along with the other
board members. How she'd gone through three administrative aides in
a year. Suddenly the auditing theme became dominant. Blanton had
seized on it. Everybody cheated on expenses, he said. That was the way
to get her. So Henderson had turned Arnold Hurst loose on Marie the
middle of July. Hurst was from McNairy County, Blanton's home
county. Had been in college with Ray Blanton. Knew brother Gene.
Hurst didn't have to be told what to search for.

When Henderson met with Blanton and Strickland at the executive
mansion on July 27, four days before Marie's DUI bust, all the Governor wanted to hear was how the audit was coming, and Henderson said
it was looking good. Blanton got especially titillated by the six hundred
hours of overtime for Marie worth more than $7,500, according to
Hurst's calculations. Anxious to keep the Governor happy, Henderson
downplayed that the audit was only in its preliminary stages, that there
was a lot yet to check out. He reasoned there'd be plenty of time to
get everything in place. But there wasn't. Henderson was as astonished
as anyone else at Blanton's order to move on Marie less than twenty-
four hours after her arrest. Use the audit, the Governor said.

The administration tried hustling more details to demonstrate her sorry
performance. Out of a hundred and thirteen board sessions the past
year she had missed forty-one. But Marie's press conference had stalled
the assault against her in the media. Why had the administration
offered her another job at the same salary in state government if she'd
committed such terrible transgressions? Then Thompson announced
that if Marie had indeed mistakenly charged expenses for thirteen
board meetings she hadn't attended, which he wasn't about to concede,
the grand total of the money involved would be less than sixty dollars
—$59.05, to be exact.

The source for that was the stack of folders Marie had lugged into
Thompson's office and dumped on his desk, the ones she had filched
from her office the night she bumped into Hurst. Thompson didn't ask
where the documentation came from, but he was flabbergasted at the

extent of it. For someone as slipshod as Marie was being portrayed, she
appeared to have it all quite together. Even to the forty-one missed
board meetings the administration was now trumpeting. Aside from
illness, she had ample proof that she was engaged in other board
business in each instance, mostly conferring with judges and DAs. And
at no time did the board lack a quorum to carry on hearings because
of her absence.

Jousting on the specifics of where she'd been on such and such a date
was seductive, but Thompson decided this would mire him in minutiae
that in the end nobody gave a damn about. What counted was the
overall picture. That riled Marie, and Fred had to sit on her some. She
demanded to know why they couldn't answer back. It was *her* reputation. She was the one being pilloried in public. Was she supposed to
just sit still and take it?

Yes, he said. At this stage it was pointless to start trading more
charges in the press. And the fact was there had been some billing
mistakes, however minor. She'd been careless. Had left herself open to
attack. She had to face up to it.

Marie didn't give up easily. He didn't realize, she said, how hard
she'd worked during her chairmanship. She didn't have time to fill out
those forms. She was too busy. Her secretary, Sherry Lomax, was
responsible.

Look, Thompson told her, she was going to have to concede certain
errors. That was all there was to it. To win in the end she didn't have
to win every point. The final fight would be in court, and if Marie lost
there, people would assume she was guilty of all the allegations in the
letter anyway. She was taking a big chance going into court as it was,
and she had to play it smart. Still, Thompson was a little awed by her
gumption, her fierce conviction that right would out. Fred couldn't
recall ever having a client like Marie. As a matter of fact, if she hadn't
been the kind of client she was, he never would have gone this far. At
best, it would be a long, hard, dubious haul.

Marie might get a hundred percent on morality, but Thompson had
to deal with the legal considerations—a difference she always had
trouble accepting. From the first, it was apparent to Fred that he had
to prove Marie was not only *not* fired for good cause but that there was
much more involved. The good-cause aspect was nebulous, treacherous.
The Governor, after all, was the Governor. Where did you draw the
line between sixty bucks and six hundred, or even six thousand, in
expenses that couldn't be backed up? If the argument got down to just
how good "good cause" had to be, Blanton was a sure victor. For

instance, regardless of what the excuse was, Marie had missed some board meetings.

Obviously, the state would try to limit the trial issues to Marie's performance as chairman. Did she fail to carry out particular functions expected of her, and did the Governor therefore have the right to fire her? So Thompson had to show that it wasn't a question of good cause or bad cause, but what the real cause was. Marie had been thrown out because she hadn't played the game. It was academic whether there'd been payoffs in clemency cases or whether it came down to merely doing favors for friends. She hadn't gone along. She'd been independent, in accordance with the statutes setting up the pardons and paroles board. That was all she was guilty of.

To pull this off, Thompson knew he had to shift the focus of the lawsuit entirely, greatly widen its scope. Proving that Marie was not a crook wasn't enough. He had to try the administration. And to do that, he had to hurdle a huge, immediate problem. He needed to have a jury make the findings of fact. Were the allegations contained in the letter true or false? Technically, though, Marie would be suing for reinstatement. That made it an equity case. And equity cases were almost always heard by judges alone. Of Nashville's three chancery courtrooms, only one had a jury box. But a judge would look at the issues narrowly, and given the political realities, Thompson had few illusions about the outcome.

Thank God for the letter, Thompson thought. It gave him the opening to move for a jury. If Blanton had just written a sentence or so saying he was dissatisfied with Marie's management of the board, that she'd been a disruptive influence, and let it go at that, she would be dead in the water. Thompson wondered what had possessed the Governor. An intriguing notion began noodling around in Fred's mind. Instead of Marie cracking under the strain of pardons and paroles, maybe it was Ray Blanton.

In Marie's brief against Blanton, Thompson claimed that selected individuals in the Governor's office had sought improperly to influence board decisions and proceedings. *Plaintiff further states that she resisted this attempted influence and thereby incurred the enmity of defendant Blanton and members of his staff. . . . The plaintiff alleges that her employment was not terminated for good cause but on the contrary because she carried out her duties in a forthright and honest manner and*

because she would not participate or succumb to improper pressure from
the Governor's office.

Thompson also asked that Blanton be enjoined from replacing Marie
on the board. Chancery Court Judge C. Allen High denied the request
because she failed to show irreparable harm. Marie was distressed to
read that Sheriff Fate Thomas was being touted as the leading candidate to fill the board vacancy.

On August 12, the day after Marie's suit was filed, Thompson was in
general sessions court with her on the traffic arrests. The reckless-
driving charge was dismissed outright, and the DUI was held for review
when she agreed to take an alcohol safety course.

A fellow student in the course asked her what her score was, and
Marie said she didn't understand.

"You know, on the drunkometer."

"Point one-oh."

"That's crazy," the man said. "I've never seen anyone here who
scored one-oh, and I've been here twice. I was point two-three. The
lowest I ever heard of was point one-seven, one-eight. Most of these
people are twos, even threes. They must have really been on you."

"I suppose," said Marie. "But I even know of a point oh-seven."

"It can't be. Who?"

"Me," she said.

"I'll be damned," he replied. "That's sure one for the books."

Toward the end of August, Virginia called to ask if Marie had read the
letter in the *Tennessean.*

"No, Mom. What did it say?"

"You better read it yourself."

The letter was from a Mrs. Faye Rambo. Mrs. Rambo, after identifying herself as not being a "women's libber," wrote that she had met
Marie at the annual dinner of a volunteer group working with inmates
at the Nashville penitentiary. Mrs. Ragghianti had been the principal
speaker and addressed the audience eloquently on pardons and paroles.

I wonder if the men who attended the party along with Mrs. Rag-
ghianti had been stopped and given the alcohol test as Mrs. Ragghianti
was and barely failed as Mrs. Ragghianti did, would they have been

arrested? I also wonder if Commissioner Shaw of the Tennessee Depart-
ment of Transportation and Mr. Eddie Sisk were stopped and given the
test and failed it, would Governor Blanton have asked for their resigna-
tions as he did Mrs. Ragghianti's?

Commissioner Shaw, even though under indictment, remains on the
state payroll while Mrs. Marie Ragghianti was never indicted and no
longer is on the payroll.

Well, Marie thought, somebody out there likes me. But she had to
get away from Nashville for a while. And she would, as soon as the kids
were back in school.

PART IV

EIGHTEEN

In the winter of '77 Marie's sister Mary Therese joined Madonna House, an organization of Catholic laity and priests, a sort of Catholic peace corps working among the poor, and also a place for retreat and spiritual restoration. Madonna prayer houses and shelters were scattered across Canada and the United States and in the West Indies. Its members, after a lengthy apprenticeship, took vows of poverty, chastity and obedience. Mary Therese had gone to the Madonna House headquarters and training center in rural northeast Ontario. Marie couldn't get over the transformation in her sister. Mary Therese had been floundering around so unhappily after she graduated from college. Within weeks, though, whenever she called to see how Marie was, she came through as a completely different person, at peace with herself, so full of joy. Madonna House was a self-sustaining apostolate, and visitors were welcome so long as they participated in daily communal labor in the fields, in the barns, the kitchen and laundry, wherever they were needed, in accordance with their capabilities.

In September, Marie drove to Canada, to the hamlet of Combermere, to escape Nashville, to spend some time with her sister, to learn what the magic of Madonna House was. Almost instantly she discovered it—a sense of pervasive love of human beings for one another. The loneliness and isolation she'd been experiencing for so many months evaporated in the purity of community life she found there.

· 2 ·

Dick Pectol had been the first to mention Roger Humphreys to Marie. At lunch soon after she was appointed chairman. Pectol was an attorney from Johnson City, in Washington County, in the northeast corner of Tennessee. She'd met him when she was extradition officer, and they had become friendly.

Pectol asked if Humphreys had been proposed for executive clemency yet, and Marie said not that she was aware of. Who was he? And Pectol said Humphreys was a young Johnson City fellow serving twenty to forty years. In 1973 he had pumped a total of eighteen bullets into his ex-wife and her lover, twelve in her and six more in the boyfriend. Roger had to reload quite a bit, Pectol dryly remarked, as he had used a two-shot derringer pistol. Humphreys failed to get off on an insanity defense. Pectol had been a special prosecutor during the trial.

"Well, don't worry," he told Marie. "Humphreys will be up for a recommendation soon enough."

"That's ridiculous. What possible merits could there be?" she asked.

There weren't any, Pectol said, laughing, but it didn't matter. Humphreys' father was one of Ray Blanton's money men, and it was a sure bet Marie was going to have to recommend Humphreys for clemency or a pardon or something. She remembered how irritated she was when Pectol continued to laugh about it, as if it were a given.

Lee Smith, the editor of the weekly political tipsheet, the *Tennessee Journal*, was also from Johnson City and had gone to school with Humphreys. While Marie was headed toward Madonna House, Smith happened to be in the office of Ned Ray McWherter, the speaker of the House of Representatives, to interview him about some pending legislation. McWherter was getting ready to leave on a trip to Europe. His press aide interrupted to say that a state photographer was outside to snap McWherter's passport picture. "Do you mind?" McWherter said, and the next thing Smith knew, the photographer walked in, and it was Roger Humphreys. Smith barely managed to croak, "Hello, Roger, how you doing?" and Humphreys replied, "Oh, under the circumstances, all right."

Smith raced back to his own office. He had only an hour before that week's issue closed. He phoned the corrections department's press officer, Becca Cottrill, and said he wanted to know the status of an inmate, Roger Humphreys. Becca called back in a few minutes and said that although Humphreys was originally assigned to the Nashville penitentiary, he had been made a trusty and was out working as a state photographer. "How could that be?" Smith asked. What with his appeals and all, Humphreys hadn't been in the state penal system a year. Cottrill said Smith couldn't quote her, but according to the file she was looking at, the arrangements for Humphreys had been done at the Governor's personal direction. Then Smith recalled that Humphreys' father had raised a lot of money in East Tennessee for Blanton's gubernatorial race.

THE TENNESSEE JOURNAL, *September 5, 1977*

TENNESSEE NOTES

> On Oct. 10, 1975, the Department of Correction received custody of Roger Humphreys of Johnson City on a 20- to 40-year sentence for two murders. Only two months later the department, acting on direct orders of the office of Gov. Ray Blanton, placed Humphreys at the Correctional Rehabilitation Center, a facility for minimum security prisoners outside the walls of the Main Prison. He was subsequently given a job as a state photographer in downtown Nashville. Humphreys is the son of Frank Humphreys Jr., the chairman of Blanton's Washington County patronage committee.

Blanton at the time was in Detroit attending a national conference of governors. Gassing it up with reporters, he didn't seem to have a care in the world. There was every indication the state constitutional convention would adopt a measure allowing the governor to succeed himself, but, of course, he couldn't comment on that until it actually occurred. The federal probe into pardons and paroles was getting to be a bad joke. And he'd rectified the one big mistake his administration had made by ridding the state of that thieving broad who'd been in bed with everybody, Marie Ragghianti. Meanwhile, at the end of the month he'd be off to Europe and the Far East to close several deals on his foreign industrial-development program for Tennessee. Blanton was riding high in more ways than one. At a press availability session at the Detroit Plaza hotel, Doug Hall, a reporter for the *Tennessean*, noticed the Governor working on his second double martini—at ten-thirty in the morning. *Tennessean* editors had spotted Smith's item and asked Hall to query Blanton. Hall caught up with the Governor in a hotel corridor. Lee Smith, said Blanton, was a pimple on the ass of mankind.

Blanton was still in Detroit when Robin Beard, a Republican congressman, picked up on the Humphreys case and held a press conference in which he demanded a legislative investigation of the Governor's flagrant political meddling in the state correctional system. On his return to Nashville, Blanton lambasted Beard for having his picture plastered all over the state first with Richard Nixon and then Gerald Ford, even though Ford had pardoned Nixon before a trial could be held on all the crimes the former President had committed. Who the hell was Beard to be telling him what to do? As for Roger Humphreys, he said it was all a lot about nothing. There was nothing unusual about Humphreys being a trusty. He had, Blanton declared, full confidence in the corrections department in such matters.

That just brought more heat. The circumstances of the double murder and the relationship of Humphreys' father to Blanton were too much. Reporters began digging into the trusty situation. It was discovered that a convicted murderer, Carl Burmeister, who had killed a Memphis man and wounded the man's wife and son, was serving as C. Murray Henderson's official driver. New attention was focused on a corrections department scheme of early furlough, whereby inmates were being administratively released months before their parole eligibility in order to ease overcrowding in the prisons.

Ramon Sanchez-Viñas convinced Henderson that the Governor had to go on television to explain. There was a real case to be made for what the administration was doing, Sanchez-Viñas argued, and the Roger Humphreys business had obscured everything. You had to deal with convicts on a selective basis. The size of the prison population had become an immense problem. You had to break down the percentages on different offender classes and show that the minor ones were clogging the system. Show, too, that it was murderers like Roger Humphreys who in fact had the best rehabilitation records. Finally, you had to drive home to the public exactly how much it was costing the taxpayers to put people away. Things had gotten out of hand, said Sanchez-Viñas. Only the Governor could put them right. Henderson agreed, and Blanton bought the strategy. From being a minus, Roger

Humphreys would turn into a mighty plus. Sanchez-Viñas was instructed to prepare charts and statistics to get the message across. The
news show with the largest audience in Nashville was Channel 4's
Scene at Six. Jim Gilchrist in Blanton's press office phoned Channel
4's news director, Mike Kettenring, and told him the Governor wanted
to come on live to clarify correctional procedures, especially in light of
a critical report co-anchor Carol Marin had done on the Humphreys
case earlier in the week. A date was set. Thursday, September 15.

Around five-thirty on Wednesday John Seigenthaler had just concluded his afternoon editorial meeting when the *Tennessean*'s principal owner, Amon Evans, called and said, "Come on over. Ray's here
visiting." From the tone of Amon's voice, Seigenthaler could tell he
needed help.

In Evans' office, Seigenthaler found the Governor slumped in a club
chair, arm dangling over the side, clutching a glass of Scotch, clearly
drunk. "John," Evans said, "Ray has been telling me how he's going
on Channel Four tomorrow night and pardon Roger Humphreys and
five or six other inmates to show how it's done."

"You're kidding," Seigenthaler said.

"No, it's true," said Blanton. "Humphreys doesn't belong in prison.
He's rehabilitated himself." Blanton lurched up and poured another
drink. "I'm going down there and show them how it's done," he said.
"I'm going to change that commercial station into an educational
station."

"Well, if you're going on TV, maybe you should have Humphreys
right there, and Murray Henderson too. Humphreys is a good-looking
boy, and you can talk about how he's straightened himself out, and
Henderson can talk about how crowded the prisons are and what could
happen to a boy like Humphreys."

To Seigenthaler's astonishment, Blanton said he thought that was a
great idea. By God, he might do it.

Seigenthaler figured nothing would come of this. To be on the safe side,
though, he made sure a *Tennessean* reporter, Jimmy Carnahan, spent
the next day with the Governor. On the agenda was West Tennessee
agriculture. First lunch and the inspection of a research station and pig
farm in Bolivar, then on to Jackson for a look at a University of
Tennessee farm and dairy operation. Aboard the four-passenger twin-

engine King Air turbojet were Carnahan, Blanton, Gilchrist and a security man. Blanton appeared to be in excellent spirits. At the pig farm he demonstrated the way to scratch a hog's back so it'd lie down. Carnahan remembered how after a couple of grunts under Blanton's ministrations, the hog looked up gratefully at the Governor and rolled right over.

They were late coming back to Nashville because of thunderstorms. Had to detour around Paducah, Kentucky. Blanton knocked off a couple of Styrofoam cups of Scotch, but with the turbulence neither cup was full.

During the landing approach, Carnahan asked, "How are you going to resolve the Humphreys situation?"

"Well, let me tell you about Roger Humphreys," Blanton said. "He's the best photographer the State of Tennessee has got. His pictures are clearer and have more life than the pictures any of the other photographers take. My wife, Betty, always requests Roger Humphreys."

"Yes, sir. But how are you going to resolve it?"

"I'm going to pardon him."

Carnahan recalled glancing at Gilchrist. The press aide was staring at Blanton popeyed, as if it was the first time he'd ever heard of this.

The pilot called out that there were TV crews on the ground. They were from Channels 2 and 5. Word of Blanton's Channel 4 appearance had leaked.

Carnahan wanted to pin down what Blanton had said. "Are you going to tell them that?"

Blanton smirked and said, "You speaking as an expert adviser or authority on what I should do?"

On the ground, cameras trailed the Governor. Wasn't it against prison regulations for Humphreys to be out so early? They were just guidelines, not the law, Blanton said. As chief executive officer, he could do a number of things. One of them, he allowed, was consideration of a pardon for Humphreys. The same went for some other deserving inmates.

Sanchez-Viñas and Henderson were waiting at the executive mansion to give Blanton a final briefing. Ramon had all his statistical charts ready, on sheets in big, bold print. Blanton went over them. He appeared to be crisp, alert, in command of the figures. They were exactly what he wanted, he said. Sanchez-Viñas felt good. It was going to work out as planned.

For his daylong trip, Blanton had worn a sport shirt and jacket. He went upstairs to change. "You all have yourselves a drink," he said. Ramon sipped a gin and tonic, feeling even better. It was exciting to be part of this.

Blanton was gone about half an hour. When he came back down, Ramon had a vague sense that something was different, but he couldn't put his finger on it at first. Blanton called for his car, and they piled in. It was a ten-minute ride to the station. Sanchez-Viñas got out his charts again to go over the facts and figures a last time. Blanton shunted them aside. Without warning, he started ranting about Carol Marin, who would be conducting the interview. How much damage she'd done to the corrections department, to the administration, because of her one-sided commentary. "I'm going to show her ass," he said.

Sanchez-Viñas tried once more to get the Governor to review his material. He didn't need it, Blanton said. He knew what to do. My God, Ramon thought. He must have had two or three belts when he was upstairs changing.

The expectation was that Marin might begin with the Humphreys case, and the plan was to shift the emphasis to correctional problems generally. Place Humphreys in perspective.

But when Marin started out saying that Humphreys had been in prison less than a year, Blanton jumped on her. "Wrong," he said. Humphreys had already spent two years in jail. In the ensuing wrangle about how long Humphreys had been behind bars, it turned out Blanton was referring to his county-jail time while his appeal was being heard.

At any rate, Marin said, he was now out of prison working as a state photographer. Wrong again, said Blanton, leaning forward, eyes squinting more than usual, his words slurring, saying he wanted to get something straight, except it came out "state." Humphreys was still incarcerated, and he was a bargain for Tennessee. Blanton had saved the taxpayers money by hiring Humphreys. Even he hadn't realized what a crackerjack photographer Humphreys was.

What does this have to do with anything? Sanchez-Viñas thought. The interview was being held in a large studio, separate from the one used for the rest of the show. Bleachers had been set up as though for a softball game. They were packed with media people. All around him, Ramon saw reporters gaping in amazement.

Blanton kept rattling off Humphreys' photographic qualifications. How he'd gone to photography school. The long hours he'd spent perfecting his art.

Maybe so, Marin said, but there was nothing in his prison file to indicate any photographic experience, and yet Humphreys had been reclassified at the request of the Governor's office only two months after he'd been put "behind the walls."

If she would just stop making statements and ask some questions, Blanton said, he'd be glad to respond.

Had the fact that Humphreys' father was a close Blanton political ally given him an edge?

"His own conduct gave him the edge."

Was politics involved at all?

"Everything I do is political," replied Ray Blanton. "I have the authority and the trust of the people who elected me. It's all part of the political process."

But wasn't Humphreys in for murder?

The question here, Blanton said, was his judgment of the case. Then he delivered his bombshell. Humphreys was a fine young man. "Before I go out of office, he is going to be pardoned," he announced.

You could hear a pin drop in the studio, Sanchez-Viñas remembered thinking. The idea of a pardon had never come up with him. He could hardly trust his ears.

The Governor, however, kept right on. It had been a crime of passion, he explained, turning philosophical. You know, he confided, he and his wife requested murderers to work for them out at the mansion because they weren't repeaters.

Marin persisted. "He was put on work release only two months after being behind the walls. Why?"

Out of the blue, Blanton replied, "I haven't sold a single pardon."

In his office, viewing Blanton's performance on TV, John Seigenthaler was mesmerized. It was like Nixon saying he wasn't a crook, he thought. The image came to him of a man sitting in a warm bath, slitting his wrists.

"That's not what we're talking about," Carol Marin said.

"Ask me a question."

"What information did you have to put him on work release?"

Almost as if Blanton had suddenly recalled the statistics that had been compiled for him, he began talking about how marvelous the Tennessee prison system was. Number one in the South. One of the

top ten in the nation. There had been a huge prison-population increase, and yet the state's pardon, parole and release programs had
remained constant.

And again apropos of nothing, he said, "I haven't sold a single
pardon or parole, and none of my people have." Blanton gazed at
Marin, daring her to challenge him.

While she was trying to figure out what to say next, the Governor
continued in a burst of free association. He was proud of his administration's accomplishments in the field of corrections. "I am not proud of
what you and your station have done," said Blanton. "I don't see why
your license should be renewed." He didn't mind if attacks on him were
clearly editorial in nature, but he did when they were disguised as news.
It was Channel 4 and the Republicans who were bent on getting him,
he said. He was thinking of going to the Federal Communications
Commission regarding Channel 4's license.

That was his prerogative, Marin replied. What about Humphreys?

He'd try to put it as simply as he could, Blanton sneered. So even
she could understand. Humphreys was currently on work release, first,
because of his vocational aptitude; second, because of his ability; third,
because of his trustworthiness; fourth, because he had performed. At
that very moment, Blanton wanted Marin to know, Roger Humphreys
was out at the mansion to take pictures of a party the Governor and
his wife were hosting that evening.

In all, the interview lasted sixteen minutes. For Doug Hall, covering
it for the *Tennessean,* it had been bad enough watching in the studio.
Looking at a monitor replay, seeing Blanton's arrogance close up, it was
even worse. Hall couldn't believe it when Blanton's chief spokesman,
Brooks Parker, like the manager for a punch-drunk fighter, ran around
telling everybody how tremendous the Governor had been. The whole
administration was loony, Hall decided.

Ramon Sanchez-Viñas felt the same way. Murray Henderson had
come up to him afterward and asked if he didn't think Blanton had
straightened everything out. It was as though Henderson were pleading
with him to say yes.

The party Blanton had mentioned was for a group of road contractors.
Since the Belle Meade establishment wasn't coming through, the Governor was soliciting funds elsewhere for some restoration work at the
mansion. The contractors and their wives were still reeling from his

performance when Blanton walked in, face flushed, and loudly proclaimed he'd shown that TV station, hadn't he?

Betty Blanton, who was rarely outspoken, at least in public, was heard to whisper, "You made a complete fool of yourself."

On the afternoon of September 16 in Combermere, Ontario, Marie was in the Madonna House kitchen, up to her elbows mashing tomatoes for catsup. Nashville never seemed farther away. Then she was called to the phone. Over the crackling line a man identifying himself as a reporter for Channel 2 wanted her comments on the Blanton interview. Later Virginia would confess that she had given him the number. Everyone had been calling, Virginia said, but Channel 2 news had been so nice to Marie in the past that she couldn't help herself.

When Marie told the reporter she didn't know what he was talking about, he explained what had happened the night before with Blanton and Roger Humphreys, and she said, well, all she could say was that she wasn't surprised.

Good Lord, she thought, here she'd been fighting Blanton for a year now, and she goes away for a couple of weeks and he does himself in.

· 3 ·

THE TENNESSEAN, *September 16, 1977*

BLANTON: HE'LL PARDON
MURDERER HUMPHREYS

NASHVILLE BANNER, *September 19, 1977*

PARDON-PRONE
BLANTON CALLED
'HILLBILLY NIXON'

NASHVILLE BANNER, *September 20, 1977*

HUMPHREYS CONSIDERED
KILLING HIS OWN FATHER

THE TENNESSEAN, *September 20, 1977*

Gov. Ray Blanton apologized to former Gov. Winfield Dunn yesterday after it was disclosed Blanton erroneously declared Saturday that his predecessor granted more pardons and paroles.

THE TENNESSEAN, *September 23, 1977*

> Gov. Ray Blanton's scheduled appearance to-
> night in Johnson City was canceled late yesterday
> after reports the governor might be met by protes-
> tors angry about his proposed pardon of double
> murderer Roger Humphreys.

NASHVILLE BANNER, *September 26, 1977*

BLANTON LEAVES WOES, FLIES OVERSEAS

At the state constitutional convention, after three hours of floor debate, an amendment aimed at preventing Blanton from running again was defeated 75–15. A delegate from Nashville, Mary Pruitt, said it would be "a personal affront against one individual." A resolution allowing a Tennessee governor to serve two consecutive four-year terms was then approved 85–2.

· 4 ·

On Marie's return from Madonna House, Fred Thompson won a crucial legal decision. She would get a jury trial. The factual issues surrounding her dismissal, Thompson had argued, were so sharply drawn that they could be resolved only on the basis of dramatically contradictory testimony. The state attorney general's office, on the Governor's behalf, had responded that her complaint was entirely equitable in nature, and thus triable by the court without the interven-tion of a jury. The state's brief had been perfunctory. Good, Thompson thought. Let them keep thinking it was Marie's performance that was going to be on trial, not the administration's. Somehow they still appeared to embrace the notion that Marie's lawsuit would never actually materialize.

Her DUI charge was dropped after she informed a general sessions judge that she'd completed her alcohol safety course. It was done so routinely, in less than a minute. She thought of her long night of shame, the flashing blue lights, Blanton's press conference. The letter!

Sheriff Fate Thomas turned down the board post. Considering the explosion over Humphreys and the ongoing investigation into pardons

and paroles, that came as no surprise. For the record, Thomas said he
was afraid some hack might succeed him as sheriff.

After getting several more turndowns, Blanton appointed a United
Methodist minister, the Reverend J. Richard Allison, to the board. "I
think his integrity is beyond question, and I think he will be interested
in protecting the public and, at the same time, seeing that all offenders
are treated fairly," said C. Murray Henderson.

Charles Traughber replaced Marie as chairman.

· 5 ·

When Corbett Hart of the FBI's Memphis field office called Hank
Hillin about Sammye Lynn McGrory, Hillin said, "Damn, here I've
been working on this for a year, and you hit bingo right off the bat."

Sammye Lynn had a boyfriend named Jerry Cook whom she wanted
to help get out of prison. Cook had been serving a murder sentence,
had escaped and was convicted of committing another murder while
he was on the lam. Sammye Lynn met Cook during the time he was
a fugitive and fell in love with him. She claimed Cook had been with
her the entire night of the second murder, and she even retained a
private investigator to prove his innocence.

One day the investigator, according to Sammye Lynn, suggested that
a Tennessee Alcoholic Beverage Commission agent, Ernest Withers,
could arrange clemency for Cook—for a price. The investigator introduced her to Withers, who told her that a down payment of $2,000
plus air fare to and from Nashville to see "some people" would be
required to get things started. Sammye Lynn discussed the offer with
one of Cook's lawyers, and the lawyer sent her to see Corbett Hart.
Since she had spent practically every cent she had on Cook's case, going
to the FBI might end up the best way to help him.

What excited Hillin was this wasn't the first he'd heard of Jerry Cook.
Cook had been Billy Gene Cole's cell mate in the Nashville penitentiary. After Cole got out and was living in his trailer, a woman had come
to see him and Bill Thompson about clemency for Cook. At the time
Cook hadn't gone on trial for the second murder. Cole told Hillin that
Thompson had taken the woman into another room in the trailer for
a few minutes, and then the woman had left. That was the last Cole

saw of her. He said he couldn't recall her name. He remembered the
incident only because he couldn't believe a woman could be so in love
with a convict in Cook's predicament.

Sammye Lynn confirmed to Hart that she was the female visitor. She
identified mug shots of Billy Gene Cole and Bill Thompson. She said
that when Thompson took her into the back room of the trailer, he had
told her it would cost twenty-five thousand to spring Cook. That kind
of money was out of the question, so she hadn't pursued it. Besides,
there was always the hope that Cook would beat the second murder
rap.

But now she was desperate. Even agreed to record conversations with
Withers. And in mid-September, just as the Roger Humphreys case
began making headlines, Sammye Lynn McGrory had three telephone
contacts with Withers. After the first one, on September 14, everybody
was hopping up and down. Hart had wanted her to get into a money
conversation with Withers to show how serious she was. How much
would it cost? Six or seven thousand? Something in that area?

WITHERS   The difference is that what it really takes—now, I don't
    have no figure—but I would think that if they gave a figure, they
    would give a figure much more than what we have talked about,
    based on he—who he is.
MCGRORY   Are you talking about to get him on the street now?
WITHERS   Right.
MCGRORY   You think it will take much more than six or seven thou-
    sand?
WITHERS   Well, I mean, I don't— I would think that you—you
    couldn't even expect to get him on the street for less than twelve to
    fifteen thousand dollars.

The next conversation, under Hart's guidance, was designed to draw
out Withers more. Try to get the names of his Nashville "people." Tell
Withers that she loved Jerry so much she'd pay anything to see him
free, but she'd like some sense of how it would be done. Suddenly
Withers turned leery. Maybe they'd better table the idea. "I mean
maybe you have, I don't know, I get the feeling that maybe, maybe you
should just deal with a lawyer and not with me. Because I don't want
to get in no hassle about trying to do a favor," he said.

Hart was sure he had botched it. Sammye Lynn didn't have enough guile to pull this off. He'd crowded her too hard and Withers had gotten suspicious. Then Hart learned that he had been spotted at Sammye Lynn's home by the private investigator who'd introduced her to Withers. The investigator warned the ABC agent something was up. She made one more try at talking to Withers, but now he wasn't having any of it. Another breakthrough shut off.

Well, Hillin thought, it wasn't a total loss. Sammye Lynn testified before the grand jury on October 4. In all the uproar over Roger Humphreys, the reconvening of the grand jury that fall hadn't received much attention. Hillin was just as glad. He hoped it would be the final session before indictments were handed down. Bill Thompson was subpoenaed. There was a squabble over whether he had to provide copies of his handwriting, specifically a copy of the note the FBI had seized asking Eddie Sisk to speak to Blanton about Cole's clemency. The Governor's appointments secretary, Ken Lavender, acknowledged that Thompson had met privately with Blanton before the note was written. Nobody else was present, said Lavender, and he had no idea what subjects were discussed.

The best part of Sammye Lynn McGrory's testimony was that a completely independent source had connected Billy Gene Cole with Bill Thompson on clemency payoffs. Verified what Cole had admitted to, what Tommy Prater had said. With the addition of Withers, who could say how far the conspiracy extended? But at least the Georgia extraditions and the Cole and Bibbs cases had been nailed down. And Prater, eyewitness to the envelope of money passing from Thompson to Sisk at the Capitol Park Inn, had tied in Sisk.

With some indictments, Hank Hillin thought, you never knew what else could happen.

· 6 ·

In the phalanx of lawyers serving the corporate, financial and political interests of Nashville, William Willis was first-rank. Eddie Sisk had been briefly associated with his firm. Willis was counsel to the *Tennessean.* From time to time Blanton sought his advice.

And now, in early October, Willis visited the Justice Department on Sisk's behalf. Among those he saw were Thomas Henderson, chief of the public integrity section, and Andy Reich and Steve Pitt, the two federal attorneys assigned to the case.

The pitch Willis made was simple and strongly worded. The pardons and paroles investigation had no merit. It was a personal vendetta coming out of the FBI's Nashville office. Grand jury hearings had been going on for a year. Sisk's standing in the community was being slashed to pieces. Willis pulled out all the stops. Even passed around photographs of Eddie with his wife, daughter and infant son. There had to be an end to it. Enough was enough.

With Sisk at his side, the Governor had also been calling the U.S. attorney general, Griffin Bell—three times in one week alone in September. The words were the same. Vendetta. Witch-hunt. How long was Bell going to countenance this? All it was doing was giving ammunition to the Republicans. If there was anything to these charges, said Blanton, he'd be the first to root out the culprits. The Governor, Bell remarked in exasperation, was ringing his phone off the wall.

At the same time Tennessee's Democratic congressional delegation was being buttonholed. The harassment had to cease. Elections were coming up in '78. U.S. Senator Jim Sasser was contacted. Party loyalty was at stake. Blanton personally complained at the White House. His support was being sought for President Carter's bitterly debated Panama Canal treaty.

For Steve Pitt, monitoring the pardons and paroles probe, the politics of the case wasn't his problem.

Pitt had no doubt there was a massive conspiracy in Blanton's administration to sell clemencies. His worry was proving it in court. Marie Ragghianti had provided vital intelligence, but with her DUI arrest and firing, a lot of her impact had gone down the drain. Besides, she had no direct evidence of a payoff. What it got down to was Tommy Prater. Prater was the link to Sisk, to the Governor's office. And despite the backup Hillin had gathered to support Prater's story, Pitt couldn't see him as a creditable witness on which you hung everything. Prater was naturally shifty. He came across as a con artist. Pitt shuddered when he thought of Prater testifying before a jury that had to weigh reasonable doubt.

They needed somebody else to make it all stick, and the person Pitt had in mind was Bill Thompson. In the grand jury Thompson had been defiant, taking the Fifth. Offering him immunity at this stage would have been useless. But in a parallel action the Internal Revenue Service had worked up a hell of an income tax case against Thompson. Get him on tax fraud, and maybe he'd be more inclined to cooperate on pardons and paroles.

On this basis, Pitt was more than willing to continue with the investigation. But he had another problem. His role as a mentor to Andy Reich was becoming increasingly awkward. Andy was a good kid, but if Pitt stayed on, he wanted full responsibility for the case. He intended to tell this to his section chief, Tom Henderson. Toward the end of October, however, a Louisville law firm, considered to be the best in the city, offered Pitt a partnership, and he decided he couldn't turn it down.

The first inkling Hillin had that anything was amiss was on October 18, when Reich told him that before the case got too far along, "We're going to have to do some reviewing."

"We're already far along," Hillin replied curtly. "What in the world are you talking about?" All of Hillin's old fears about Washington flooded back. He pressed Reich about what was behind the review but couldn't get a straight answer out of him. He started hoping that perhaps it was because Reich was young and inexperienced, extra cautious.

Critical to the review was giving Prater another polygraph test, specifically about seeing money go from Thompson to Sisk. That really got Hillin concerned. Prater had passed a test months ago. It was only routine, Reich said. How could Reich use a word like routine? Hillin began to wonder if Reich knew what was at stake. That the Democratic party in Tennessee could be blown up.

Tommy Prater by then was in Dalton, in jail awaiting trial. U.S. marshals brought him back to Nashville for the test.

QUESTION   Did you give Thompson an envelope containing money like you said?
PRATER   Yes, I did.
QUESTION   In Chattanooga, did you give Thompson an envelope containing money?
PRATER   Yes.
QUESTION   Did Thompson put an envelope containing any money in his pocket like you said?
PRATER   Yes.
QUESTION   Did you see an envelope passed between Thompson and Sisk like you said?

PRATER Yes, I did.
QUESTION Did Thompson give Sisk an envelope like you said?
PRATER Yes.

Well, that should do it, Hillin said, and Reich agreed. He started preparing the indictments with Andy, and that made him feel a lot more relaxed.

· 7 ·

In November the showstopper at the annual Gridiron Show put on by the press was a reporter impersonating Blanton singing to the melody of "Camelot."

> "It seems like only yesterday we came here.
> The mansion is a fascinating spot."

And the stand-in for Betty Blanton trilled—

> "Why should the FBI share our domain here
> In Camelot?"

Marie, though, had come to realize that the federal investigation, for so long the focus of her life, wasn't going to help her or hurt her, however it turned out. What counted now for her was the lawsuit against Blanton.

She spent all her spare time going over in detail with Fred Thompson the documents she had brought to him, discussing the witnesses she needed to call to testify for her. Her paychecks as chairman had lagged about a month behind, so she had that, plus some vacation time coming and what she'd saved. Yet she had to have a job, and she went to work in sales for a local real estate agency. The most attractive feature was that she could determine her own hours and would be free to meet with Fred at his availability. She hated real estate, although she was actually quite good at it. She didn't lack clients. Seemed that an awful lot of people wanted to view the notorious Marie Ragghianti up close.

One evening Kevin McCormack called her. She could tell he'd been drinking. And he was beside himself. He just wanted to tell her what a terrible mistake he had made, being party to what they'd done to her, how he'd tried to convince Marie to knuckle under to them.

Life with Traughber as board chairman had become intolerable, he said. She knew how he liked to work in the office on weekends, catching up on things. Anyway, Traughber had demanded that Kevin turn in his office key, saying he didn't want him in the office after hours or on weekends. Traughber had been jabbing at him one way or another ever since Marie was fired, Kevin said, and this was about the last straw. It'd been such a direct insult.

Kevin had gone to Sisk and Benson, and after some kidding around about why he wanted to work on weekends, they got serious on the topic of his relations with Traughber. You know, they'd both said, there was this lawsuit of Marie's coming up, and he could be very helpful to the administration. Sisk had looked at him and said that maybe they all could work something out. It was just possible that he could help out with Traughber, and Kevin could help out with Marie. You know how it is, Sisk had said. One hand washes the other.

He'd had it, Kevin told Marie. He was looking around for another job. She could visualize Kevin stewing in some bar and exploding. She'd never been able to work up much anger at the way he'd switched on her. She had seen the fear in his face, confronted with the administration's power. Had felt sorry for him more than anything else.

"Listen," she said, "I believe I have a little of that Old Charter here. Why don't you come by sometime? I missed your birthday. I was up in Canada. We'll have a birthday drink."

About a week later Kevin called again and said, "You still have that Old Charter handy?" and she replied, "Absolutely. It's right over the shelf. I'm looking at it."

When Kevin arrived, he appeared uncomfortable, and Marie did her best to put him at ease. She told him she was truly happy to see him. Therese helped. Therese was genuinely fond of Kevin, and her face lit up when she saw him. "Hey," he said, "I've missed those freckles. Still love those curls."

After Therese went to bed, they stayed up talking. Kevin said he was about to quit the board. He'd gotten an interesting job in city government up in nearby Clarksville. He wanted her to know that he would do anything to aid her lawsuit. Would testify about what the administration had tried to do to her. He also had plenty of papers and notes he'd made that would be helpful. Then he said he had to tell her something important. Right after she was fired, he had written a letter to Murray Henderson, applauding her dismissal. He said he was so ashamed even thinking about what he had done. Must have been out of his head.

Marie was extraordinarily moved. She touched his hand. It didn't matter, she said. It was what he was doing now that mattered.

At the approach of Christmas she found an official-looking envelope from American Express. Oh God, she thought, they found out she'd been fired and they were canceling her credit. But when she opened it, she found a new card for the coming year.

Although Marie was doing well in her embryonic real estate career, her income didn't yet compare with what it had been. From the time of Ricky's terrible illness, possessions meant practically nothing to her, and she was determined to drastically curtail the list of presents the kids had asked for. Then at the last minute she changed her mind. She'd use the American Express card and worry later. She didn't want the children at such an impressionable age equating a moral stand with material deprivation. Thinking that it didn't pay to put yourself on the line for what you believed in.

NINETEEN

When Tommy Prater went on trial in Dalton on January 23, 1978, Bill Thompson was on hand to help put him away.

A couple of weeks earlier Thompson had shown up at Erwin Mitchell's office, offering to be a prosecution witness. And on the stand Thompson swore that Prater told him he had gone into the home of Mr. and Mrs. Odell Edwards with a gun, accompanied by one of his men, and robbed them. Thompson said he had not come forward until Prater was locked up because he was afraid the defendant would have him killed. "That's his reputation for having things done," said Thompson. The image of Bernard Weinthal, dead in an Oldsmobile sedan by the side of a road, wasn't lost in the courtroom. Prater's attorney immediately demanded a mistrial. The judge instructed the jury to ignore the characterization and denied the motion.

Prater was being tried on one count of burglary and two counts of armed robbery in the Edwards break-in. Mitchell fought successfully to have Weinthal speak, as he put it, from beyond the grave, and excerpts of Prater's taped conversations with Bernie were admitted. Barnes and McBryar pleaded guilty to lesser charges and testified against Prater. Testimony was also allowed that the Edwards case was only one of several robberies Prater had masterminded in and around Dalton. Although there was conflicting evidence about whether Prater had been inside the Edwards house, Tommy was paying for the rage that mounted during those months he'd avoided extradition, and in Nashville Hank Hillin learned that his main witness had been convicted and sentenced to twenty years on each count.

· 2 ·

Federal indictments against Sisk and Thompson had been written up, yet nothing was being handed down. Hillin started getting uneasy all over again. First Andy Reich said it would be worked out in a month or so. Then he called and said, "We have a real problem."

Personally, said Reich, he was for going ahead, but he'd been outvoted. As it stood, getting to the Governor's office rested on Prater and Prater's credibility. The feeling was that Prater wouldn't be a good witness. "My section chief isn't going with it," Reich said.

There wasn't a thing Prater had told them that hadn't been corroborated, Hillin replied. And as for the envelope, he'd taken a polygraph twice and passed without a hitch. What more could anyone want?

"I can't believe what you're saying," Hillin said.

"Look," Reich said, "it isn't over. There's still the tax thing on Thompson. That keeps it alive."

"You know, Andy, I want to tell you something. They're just jacking you around. And me too."

Hillin was wiped out by the news. He rarely discussed his work with his wife, Frances. This time he did. It was such a total miscarriage of justice, he said. How could this be happening? Were they really afraid of Prater's credibility or was there more to it than that?

If he felt so strongly, Frances Hillin said, he should do something about it. Hillin talked over the situation with Irvin Wells, the Chattanooga agent who had predicted that Prater would crack. Wells reminded him that there was a bureau policy allowing an agent to ask for the review of a case. So for the first time in his entire FBI career, Hillin questioned a decision from on high. It was unconscionable to call off the investigation now after all the work that had gone into it. Nothing was a sure thing, but in this instance the evidence was there. Implicit in Hillin's protest was that the public integrity section was trying to hang its hat on any negative hook it could find. Acting like defense lawyers instead of prosecutors. Joe Trimbach, Hillin's field superior, backed him. So did the agent in charge of the Knoxville field office, which covered East Tennessee. In Washington Dave Malarney, who worked in FBI liaison with the Department of Justice, spoke directly with Hillin several times and caught some of his emotion. Although it never appeared in writing in any internal memos, the political fallout hung over everyone, like fog on a dark road. A Democratic administration. A Democratic governor in a weather-vane state. It was already clear that in 1980 Jimmy Carter would need every electoral vote he could scrape up. The President might not like the Governor, but he was stuck with him.

The pardons and paroles case had begun with one woman's misgivings about an obscure, apparently ordinary extradition. As it became a bit more complicated, she'd been cautioned that she was, after all, just one little girl. She should think of herself. Her children. What could *she* do? Now it was being contested at the highest levels in Washington, D.C. America, at its best and worst.

There was a built-in hostility between the FBI and the public integrity section. Public integrity was not noted for its aggressiveness. FBI agents, as well as Justice Department attorneys in the organized crime section, called it "piss."

On January 30 Benjamin Civiletti, the assistant attorney general in charge of the criminal division, which included public integrity, officially notified the director of the FBI that the division desired no further investigation into the case.

Dave Malarney immediately started to yell.

John Dowd's office was away from the Justice Department, in a back corner on the sixth floor of the old Triangle Building at Ninth and D streets, overlooking Lansburgh's dilapidated department store. Hardly Washington's most imposing view.

The neighborhood's seediness, however, was an ideal metaphor for the documents that passed across Dowd's desk every day. Dowd was in charge of Strike Force 18, an elite law-enforcement group composed of more than a hundred Justice Department lawyers and FBI agents, specializing in long-range organized crime and complex malfeasance cases, augmenting regional strike forces and local U.S. attorneys.

Dowd was also the chief architect of the four-year-old RICO statute —the Racketeering Influenced and Corrupt Organizations Act. RICO had been originally designed to combat the infiltration of organized crime into legitimate business enterprises. Its dimensions had since widened, and some twenty times so far its use had been upheld on appeal. One appeal contended that the business being infiltrated was illegitimate to begin with, and thus wasn't in RICO's purview.

The package to Dowd came by messenger from Civiletti. Civiletti's covering letter said he was enclosing material on a possible RICO case involving the sale of pardons and paroles in Tennessee. Inside were several memos prepared by the public integrity section summarizing the case and giving the reasons why it had decided not to prosecute. Without going into details, Civiletti indicated that some questions had been raised about this decision, and he wanted to know what Dowd thought. Was there a case or not?

For the record, public integrity was declining the case because there was a grave doubt about whether a governor's office fit the RICO definition of an enterprise. There was, moreover, a serious lack of witness credibility. Almost without exception, the principal witnesses had long criminal histories. There was no direct physical evidence— no marked money, no tapes, no proof on paper. It was all circumstantial.

Dowd didn't buy the circumstantial evidence putdown. Obviously, direct evidence was preferable, but circumstantial evidence was nothing to sneeze at. Dowd subscribed to the "snow theory." If you walked into a courthouse and there was no snow on the ground, and you came out of the courthouse a couple of hours later and there was six inches of snow, it was reasonable to conclude that it had snowed while you were inside, even though you didn't actually see it fall. It was a fair inference that not only had it snowed, but the snow had come from the sky.

Dowd wasn't sympathetic to the witness-credibility problem either. He'd worked on too many organized crime cases, where you rarely got good guys testifying for you. Dowd's rule, the one he conveyed to a jury, was that you couldn't believe any witness unless there was independent corroboration for what he was saying. Every witness had a credibility problem when you got down to it. There were all kinds of motivations swirling around inside anybody who was on the stand.

Then there was RICO. In Dowd's opinion, unless a prosecutor was being frivolous, it was up to the courts to rule on applicability. That's the way law was shaped, defined, accepted. Besides, if public integrity didn't want to go with RICO, there was always the long-established Hobbs Act, which dealt with extortion under official color. In this instance the extortion would be exacting payments from inmates to get clemency.

Based on his reading of the public integrity memos, Dowd wrote his own memo to Civiletti recommending prosecution, and thought that was the end of it.

· 3 ·

2/7/78

Saw Hank today. He was very anxious about a trip to Washington tomorrow. He told me it would possibly be the finale with regard to the case, & he seemed extremely apprehensive. He said, "Marie, I know you believe in prayer. I want to ask you to pray for me while I'm in Washington." I assured him, earnestly, that I would—& I did. I never prayed more intensely.

To Dowd's surprise, there had been a countermemo from Tom Henderson in public integrity challenging his recommendation. Usually when Dowd was brought in to review a case, it was to rein in some overly eager prosecutor. He couldn't recall when it had been the other way around. Now Henderson was questioning whether there had been enough interstate commerce for federal intervention under the Hobbs Act.

I-24, the main route between Chattanooga and Nashville, on which Thompson, Prater and Sisk had made multiple trips in furtherance of the alleged conspiracy, dipped for several miles into Georgia, just west of Chattanooga. As a matter of fact, according to Prater, Thompson had become aware of this and started directing him to take a bypass that kept them in Tennessee. There were, in addition, a number of acts where the U.S. mail had been used regarding suspect clemencies. Offhand, Dowd could think of a dozen cases with less of a federal hook that had been sustained in court. As chief of Strike Force 18, Dowd worked closely with FBI agents, and by then he knew that Malarney had pushed the controversy to the attorney general's office, that FBI Director Clarence Kelly was into it. He also learned that Blanton had gone to see Bell, complaining of FBI harassment, and that the bureau was very upset about this.

Dowd asked to examine the FBI 302 interviews and the grand jury testimony. He wanted to see the case agent, Hillin, as well, In poring over the 302s, Dowd found more factual information to support his recommendation. How tenacious the investigation had been. Far more impressive, indeed, than the manner in which the grand jury hearings had been conducted.

From his reading, Dowd thought that the agents, especially Hillin, had done superb work. It was the kind of case that ate your guts out. It was like a big jigsaw puzzle. You had to find a piece here and a piece there. You had to think about it constantly. Why was this guy giving you half a loaf? What more did he have to say? What about the other guys? How could so-and-so be shoved a little more? Dowd admired agents who stuck with it. Fine job, fine job, he kept thinking.

Hank Hillin, on February 9, was just as convincing in the flesh. While it was clear he had dug in his heels, Hillin was no wild-eyed zealot. Dowd was persuaded more than ever that the case not only was prosecutable but also should be pursued vigorously. This was a case, Dowd noted, where you could put witnesses on in an orderly fashion, spelling out what had happened, and a jury would get the picture. Granted, the chain was intricate. But the key was that the witnesses did back up one another.

There needed to be more witnesses. More probing. That was important. A great deal of what was occurring had become a media football. Word was out that the case was being dropped, that the grand jury would be asked to hand down a no true bill. This alone allowed for devastating consequences. Momentum was so important. A case could get stale. The people involved would start questioning themselves about whether something was really there or not.

Dowd made it plain that he considered Tennessee pardons and paroles one of the most egregious cases he'd ever come across. Absolutely repugnant. The idea of cutting murderers loose for cash was dumbfounding.

Hillin, with Malarney, also met with Henderson, Henderson's deputy and Andy Reich. He pleaded for better than an hour. He couldn't understand why the investigation was being called off just as they had it in their grasp. He echoed what he'd said down in Dalton, in Erwin Mitchell's office. The case hit at the heart of the criminal justice system. It had to be followed through. Hillin expected the worst, but Tom Henderson was cool, diplomatic. Told Hillin that if he went back and got a little more substantiation, he'd see. Perhaps two or three additional interviews. Clear up some of the details Prater and Barnes had related about the extradition payoff to Thompson and Sisk. Check over the Jimmy Pendleton clemency sequence and Sisk's explanation to Marie about why it hadn't gone through. Really minor stuff, Hillin thought.

He left feeling he'd won his point, and on February 15 there seemed
to be confirmation of this. Civiletti wrote to the director of the FBI.

> Re: T. Edward Sisk, Legal Counsel to the
> Governor of the State of Tennessee;
> and William Aubrey Thompson

> . . . On February 9, 1978, Attorneys from the Public Integrity Section
> of the Criminal Division met with representatives of the Federal Bureau
> of Investigation (FBI) to discuss this matter. As a result of that meeting,
> we have determined that additional investigation is warranted.
> We therefore request that certain witnesses be interviewed, and that
> a flow chart be prepared, in order to focus on the acts and statements
> made by Sisk concerning the commutations of sentences and extradi-
> tions. The details of this request were discussed at the aforementioned
> meeting of February 9, 1978.

Hillin got a scrawled note from Malarney on February 28. *Chalk one
up for us!* it said.

But the whole thing was a shabby bureaucratic shell game. Three
weeks later, after Hillin had fulfilled the requests made at the February
9 meeting, Reich told him that the case was being dropped. There was
still the IRS investigation of Thompson, Reich said.

"Yeah, sure, Andy," Hillin said, too dispirited to argue.

A letter was going out, said Reich, that no more testimony would
be taken.

> *11 April 1978*

> *William R. Willis Jr.*
> *Willis and Knight*
> *700 Union Street*
> *Nashville, Tennessee 37219*

> > Re: Thomas Edward Sisk, Legal Counsel to the
> > Governor of the State of Tennessee

> *Dear Mr. Willis:*
> *As you know, an investigation has been conducted by the Department
> of Justice and the Federal Grand Jury in Nashville, Tennessee, into
> allegations that there have been violations of extraditions, paroles and*

commutations in the State of Tennessee. Your client, Thomas Edward Sisk . . . has been one of the subjects of that investigation.

Please be advised that this matter is no longer under active investigation. Absent the receipt of additional information, we have determined that no further evidence will be presented to the grand jury.

> *Sincerely,*
> *Thomas H. Henderson Jr.*
> *Chief, Public Integrity Section*
> *Criminal Division*

THE TENNESSEAN, *April 18, 1978*

Was Jury Probe Worth Cost?

A 17-month federal grand jury investigation of state pardons and paroles practices appears to be ending without any indication that indictments will be returned.

. . . more than 100 witnesses have testified and perhaps millions of words have been taken down and stored.

All of this would be justified if someone had good reason at the start to believe that laws had been violated. But if it was just a political fishing trip, the taxpayers have been taken for a ride.

Now that the investigation had been called off, Hillin got a letter of his own from Henderson, commending him for his splendid job. A final karate chop, he thought.

U.S. Attorney Hal Hardin asked if Hillin wanted him to get the case back from Washington. Without much enthusiasm, Hillin said okay. Public integrity was only too happy to oblige. Hillin perked up a little after that. Somehow, something would happen. Occasionally he delivered a talk at his local Church of Christ, and he found himself slipping into a homily about faith bringing you through just when things looked darkest. Even he had to laugh. Probably nobody in the congregation had a clue to what was on his mind.

· 5 ·

In Memphis, agent Corbett Hart didn't know anything about the letter canceling the pardons and paroles case. He'd brooded a lot about how the business with Sammye Lynn McGrory and Ernest Withers hadn't panned out last fall. Hart couldn't help thinking that it was partly his fault for not running Sammye better.

Hart had some familiarity with electronic equipment, and on April 23 he was asked by another agent to put a Nagra body recorder on an FBI informer named Arthur Baldwin, an ex-convict who operated several topless clubs in Memphis. In order to stave off federal drug charges pending against him, Baldwin had agreed to cooperate in the ongoing FBI look at corruption in Tennessee's Alcoholic Beverage Commission.

It wasn't Hart's investigation. At first he didn't even know whom Baldwin would be secretly recording. But when he learned it was none other than his old friend, ABC agent Withers, Hart got very interested. Listen, Hart said, if Baldwin got a chance, could he mention to Withers that he had a friend in prison he'd like to get out, and did Withers know anybody who could help?

No sweat, said Baldwin. He was tight with Withers. Withers was always chasing money.

The next day Baldwin said it'd been a piece of cake. Said he told Withers he had these friends whose son was in jail, and that the boy's mother was terrified he would be raped. Withers wanted to know the kid's name. Steve Hamilton, Baldwin had said, and Withers promised to get right on it.

This time, Hart thought, maybe his luck would change.

THE TENNESSEAN, *April 23, 1978*

ERIN, Tenn.—Gov. Ray Blanton said at an Ireland Day luncheon here yesterday that his family will help him decide whether to run for reelection.

The governor also made a reference to the federal pardons and paroles investigation. "I've stood the test," he said.

· 6 ·

May 11, 1978

Just returned from Hank's office, & going through files—so many, so old! Picked up the Jack Lowery report & a couple of other items, & Hank will be dropping the rest off at Fred's later. He objected (gently), as I expected, to some of the files, esp Larkin Bibbs—fortunately, I don't think it's essential to my case. Also, although he wouldn't allow me to remove Geo. Edwards file material, he did let me look at it, & even made the suggestion that I subpoena anything I wanted for my lawsuit. Well, once again we sat back, looked at one another like 2 friends who have been through a lot together, smiled & commiserated, etc.

. . . He said all that is really needed is a "courageous U.S. Attorney who'll sign the dotted line." Since this seemed to shed an unflattering light on Andy Reich, I withheld comment. Hank said in some ways he had to hand it to the Administration, they really knew how to fight. I said, "Yes, & they know how to wield power, too." He hesitated slightly, & then said, "You know the problem is that Blanton is close to Carter." We talked politics for a few minutes, mostly about the impending gubernatorial elections. Everyone up there expects Blanton to run, & Hank even thinks he could win.

He talked about the lies Blanton has told about him. Hank irritates me somewhat—in that my firing was such a monstrous, libelous act— yet one which he has expressed little anxiety over—though evidently expecting sympathy from me when the Governor utters some half-truth against him.

At one point he took me out to meet a new agent from Clarksville, introducing me as a good friend who helped break the pardons & paroles probe (or words to that effect). I added, demurely but with a touch of sarcasm, "Yes, I was the sacrificial lamb."

He keeps forgetting what I endured "for the cause." Sometimes I wonder exactly what I might have to do to be taken seriously. These men —Hank included—continue to see me as a female first—even the Governor called me "pretty Marie." Perhaps maturity will change all that. (We'll see!)

For sure, Fred Thompson thought, the apparent closing out of the pardons and paroles case wasn't going to help Marie's lawsuit. Especially the *Tennessean's* editorial about what a waste of taxpayer money the investigation had been. Although it wasn't in any of the court papers, her identification with the probe, that she in fact had been at the bottom of it, was by now hardly the best-kept secret in town.

Over the winter the state had been foot-dragging on Marie, and Thompson wondered if the reason was connected to the grand jury hearings. Ostensibly, the delay was to permit a complete review of

Marie's performance as chairman by both the state comptroller's and the state auditor's offices. Thompson continued to be amazed at the amount of documentation Marie brought him, and as they went over it together, he had no worries about the preliminary audit that led to her being fired. Almost every allegation could be met head on. And the few that couldn't were laughable. Take her famous double-billing of August 24 and 25 about being at the Nashville penitentiary and in Denver at the same time. The charges for each day in Nashville were $1.80 for mileage and $1.25 for parking—a total of $6.10. Not quite grand larceny.

What the final state audit would find was still up in the air. In February Thompson was angered to learn that inmates were being quizzed about whether Marie was at a particular hearing. He stormed into the office of the auditor, Frank Greathouse. At six five, his voice booming, Thompson could leave an impression, and he had the whole auditing staff quaking. How dare they interview inmates? Weakly, Greathouse said the attorney general's office had told him to.

Thompson sent off a blistering letter to the attorney general, Brooks McLemore. The attorney general's office was representing the Governor, yet it was directing what supposedly was an independent audit.

Even more shocking, the Auditor has been asked to interview state prisoners in an attempt to gather evidence against Mrs. Ragghianti. Every man, woman and child in the State of Tennessee must know of the Governor's power to put prisoners back on the street and his great proclivity for doing so. In a dispute between Mrs. Ragghianti and the Governor, how can anyone expect these prisoners to do anything but support the Governor's position?

Toward the end of April, Thompson at last received a draft of the state audit findings. If this was their best shot, he thought as he prepared his response, they're in trouble.

. . . the first page of your audit reflects that this is supposedly an audit of the entire Board of Pardons and Paroles and not just Marie Ragghianti. In reading the audit, I see that ninety-five percent (95%) of it deals with the Governor's allegations against Marie Ragghianti. We do not object to this since ninety-five percent (95%) of the Governor's letter

is false. However, I must ask why the other two board members are spared this treatment.

After all the hoopla about Marie missing board meetings, the audit could find only eight of them when she was not engaged in other board business. But even in each of these instances, she could prove that she was, including a meeting with Eddie Sisk at his request. What Thompson didn't like was the way the audit's language was framed.

Contained in this section is the most damaging and most unfair finding in the entire audit. That is a statement that Mrs. Ragghianti was "less than diligent." As I recall, this is the only subjective conclusion of this nature in the entire report (either with regard to Mrs. Ragghianti or with regard to the libelous and false statements in the Governor's letter) . . . We readily agree that Mrs. Ragghianti missed some board meetings as did the other board members, but as T.C.A. 40-3601 (3) plainly states, Mrs. Ragghianti has the duty not only to attend meetings but to "perform all other duties and functions of the chairman."

The audit challenged claims Marie had made for travel to see Bill Leech. Thompson decided he'd wait for the trial and put David Raybin on the stand.

With regard to trips to see a private attorney . . . we do not wish to get into the nature of these meetings. I will say that an assistant attorney general did, in fact, advise her to seek private counsel. This matter will be discussed in another forum.

Nothing angered Thompson more than the way the audit dodged around Marie's alleged cash claims for extra work, noting only that she'd logged in 688.6 hours of compensatory time.

Mrs. Ragghianti never "claimed" 688.6 hours of comp time. The time was simply recorded. The Governor accused her of costing the taxpayers $7,500 and stated that she had "charged the state" this amount, an obvious lie. Nowhere do I find this kind of conclusion in the Ragghianti

audit . . . The fact of the matter is that Mrs. Ragghianti gave the state
over 600 hours of her own time.

The draft also had a new, unexpected charge. From July 1 through July 6, 1976, right after Marie was sworn in as chairman, she'd been on vacation in Daytona Beach. Yet her time sheets reflected that she was on the job July 1 and 2, as well as July 6. These three days, worth $301.68 according to the audit, should have been credited to annual leave. When Thompson asked her about this, Marie explained it was the first time sheet she'd ever been asked to sign. Sherry Lomax had prepared it. Marie hadn't even looked at it. My God, she said, could they get her on that?

Don't worry, Thompson said. It was something they'd just stumbled on. An obvious oversight on her part. The money could be paid back to the state. It had nothing to do with compensatory time. Hadn't even been included in the Governor's letter firing her.

The deal with the Tennessee comptroller, William Snodgrass, was that the state's final audit wouldn't be released until Thompson had a chance to discuss all the allegations in the draft version.

But early on May 19 Kevin McCormack called Marie at home and told her that the audit was out.

"That's impossible. They promised Fred."

"I'm telling you, Marie. Corrections has it."

By the time she reached Thompson it was too late. When he phoned back, he said he'd been informed the audit was on its way to him by messenger. And the *Banner* already had called him.

The news reports picked up most of the audit's language. Some of the Governor's charges were true. She *failed to attend, preside and administer the business of the board at a number of board meetings.* She'd billed the state for travel expenses for four meetings with a private attorney—in reality, car mileage amounting to less than $25. The annual-leave error was couched in such a way as to make it appear Marie had put in for compensatory time.

Thompson tried to calm her down. She'd have to bite the bullet on this one. Actually, he told her, when you got through all the packaging, the facts in the audit were just what he needed for her lawsuit.

· 7 ·

On June 6 the attorney general's office took a last stab at trying to get Marie's suit dismissed, claiming that a state court couldn't interfere with the Governor's official, discretionary powers. The Tennessee Supreme Court refused to consider, and a trial date was set for June 28.

In Memphis, Arthur Baldwin advised Corbett Hart that Ernest Withers had gotten back to him about young Steve Hamilton. Withers said he'd been in touch with his people, but there was a problem. Hamilton was being held for sentencing in the Shelby County Penal Farm. Nothing could be done about getting him out until he was transferred into the state prison system, sometime in August.

Baldwin said he had thought about giving Withers another inmate's name. He was afraid, though, it might make the ABC agent suspicious. Hart agreed. They'd have to wait it out.

Hart didn't inform Hank Hillin about any of this. He wanted to be sure it wasn't another blind alley.

It was the weirdest experience Fred Thompson had ever encountered in his legal career. He had driven out to the executive mansion to take Blanton's deposition, in lieu of the Governor's appearance in court. What Blanton said would be for the purpose of evidence.

The Governor received Thompson in the mansion's sun-room. He was ensconced on a sofa. Behind him was a sweeping vista of the mansion's grounds. Thompson could see a couple of inmates from the Nashville penitentiary clipping hedges. C. Hayes Cooney, the deputy attorney general, and Claudius Smith, the assistant AG, were with the Governor.

Blanton's demeanor was distinctly hostile. He barely nodded at Thompson. He said that he'd just like to know if there were any secret electronic recording or sending devices in the room. "And I ask that for you, Mr. Thompson, first."

"Governor," said Thompson, not sure he was hearing correctly, "are you asking me if I've got a recording device on me?"

"Or sending device," Blanton said.

"Or sending device?" Thompson repeated, still bemused. "The answer to that is no."

"I have none, no such equipment," said Deputy Attorney General Cooney. Thompson remembered thinking that Cooney looked as if he'd just been hit with an electric prod.

Then the assistant AG, Smith, chimed in. "No, sir!"

The hell with this, Thompson thought. "May I ask the same question of you, Governor?"

"You sure can, and I can answer you that no, there are not any devices either here or on the person of me, sending or recording."

"I don't have any," Cooney repeated plaintively.

"That's the only question I have to ask," Blanton declared.

For Thompson, it was one of Ray Blanton's grandstand plays. Put everybody on the defensive, show who the boss is. But what made it so eerie was that as Blanton had prattled on about hidden electronic devices, a legal stenographer sat not ten feet away from him, taking down every word being uttered in the room. And the idea again flickered in Thompson's head that the Governor was losing some of his buttons.

The deposition went on for nearly two hours. Blanton grew increasingly peevish. Thompson could practically hear him thinking, Why is this happening? Why hadn't Marie gone away?

THOMPSON So at the time you thought she was stealing?

BLANTON In simple country terms, yes.

And finally—

THOMPSON Did you tell Commissioner Henderson to deliver the letter of August 3rd to Mrs. Ragghianti?

BLANTON I think it was hand-delivered, yes.

THOMPSON Did you tell him to offer her another job in some other department if she wanted it?

BLANTON I did not.

THOMPSON That's all. Thank you.

On the way back to his office, Thompson whistled a little to himself. Couldn't help daydreaming about bringing perjury charges against Blanton. Fred Thompson was feeling fine. But then he bumped into a very knowledgeable judge. The judge said, "You know what you're up against, don't you? I'd say it's pretty much a hopeless battle."

· 8 ·

On Friday, June 16, twelve days before her lawsuit would start, Marie was still recovering from surgery on an infected right eyelid. A growth had been removed. The doctor said it might have come from tension. As a result, she had begun jogging regularly. That morning, after jogging and then attending mass, she had stopped by the doctor's to have the eyelid checked. It continued to drain annoyingly.

By the time she got to the real estate office, it was around noon. In the afternoon she had appointments to show two houses. She never kept them.

The phone call came from Mike Pigott of the *Banner*. "Marie, how are you?" he said.

"Okay," she replied, thinking of the upcoming trial, "all things considered."

Pigott hesitated. "You haven't heard?"

"Heard what?"

That's when Marie found out that Kevin McCormack, who was going to be her only eyewitness to the day-to-day pressure the administration had brought to bear against her, had been found dead in a motel room. Murdered.

TWENTY

Have just returned from being deposed at State Atty Gen'ls Ofc. Waiting on call from John Bryant (Kevin's friend). We are supposed to be going to dinner.

I still have difficulty committing my thoughts re Kevin's death to paper. I cannot, even as I write the words—believe that Kevin is dead. . . .

"Marie, Kevin's been murdered."

It wasn't like all the movies, as they say. I didn't say "it can't be true." Not even for an instant did I doubt it. Instead, the enormity of what Mike Pigott said struck me with its total impact—instantly—the horror, the sorrow, the loss—all came crushing down on me. I don't believe I even spoke—instead, I sobbed spontaneously, & I remember clasping my hand over my mouth in a half-conscious attempt to suppress my sobbing. I remember Mike saying, "I'm sorry, Marie, will you call me back," & something about information about Kevin. I remember telling him I was going home. I remember walking out, coming back, and walking out again. I stood at the top of the stairwell alone, & sobbed aloud. Unseeing, I walked down the stairs, out to my car, & the uncaring, unknowing world. I remember driving home, thinking I don't even know how it happened, or who did it—& all the while I knew who'd done it, & that

it didn't matter how—murder is always brutal, unjust, horrible—I knew
they'd gotten him at last, just like they wished they had gotten me so
very long ago—long before I caused them all the trouble, all the public-
ity, all the controversy.

And I came in, & the phone was ringing, & for some reason I was
reminded of the night so long ago when I'd come home to a ringing
telephone, & it was Jack Lowery, telling me about the extortion attempt.

· 2 ·

All during May she'd either seen Kevin when he came down from
Clarksville or talked with him on the phone.

He was going to make one fantastic witness for her, he had said.
Don't forget he'd been a probation officer. Knew what it was like to
be on the stand. How to relate to judges. People.

He was putting all his papers together in his apartment. He'd made
tapes of phone conversations with Benson. Had stuff on Traughber. He
was going to hang them all, he said. She'd see. Fred Thompson had
been especially interested in Kevin's meeting with Sisk and Benson
when they told him they'd help him with Traughber if he helped them
with Marie. Fred had planned on deposing Kevin the week before the
trial.

"Listen, Kevin," Marie had said. "I want you to wear that navy-blue
suit of yours in court, and that's all I'll need. You look very distinguished in it."

"No, no. I'm wearing my seersucker suit."

"Why?"

"Marie," he said, "you haven't spent a lot of time in those courtrooms. They're small and hot, and it's going to be July. I'll be on that
stand at least half a day, and that seersucker is the coolest suit I have.
Don't worry, I'll look terrific. Besides, the important thing is what I'll
say."

So they'd laughed and argued about what he should wear. Marie
remembered, though, wishing Kevin would stop going around saying
how he would hang them all.

McCormack's Clarksville job involved regional planning, and he had
come to Nashville on Thursday, June 15, to attend a one-day housing
conference.

Late in the afternoon he had drinks with Sam Lipford and Martha Bernard at the Capitol Hill Club. Martha was a striking, tawny-haired woman who had been with Marie at the fund-raiser before Marie's DUI arrest. After majoring in criminal psychology at Middle Tennessee State, she'd tried to join the Nashville Metro police but failed the physical by a point. She was about to sue for sexual discrimination when she got a job with the corrections department. Now she was a parole officer.

Lipford hadn't seen Kevin for some time. McCormack filled him in on his Clarksville job. Then he said he'd been subpoenaed for Marie's lawsuit and was going to testify for her. Get them all.

After a couple of drinks, according to Martha Bernard, she walked McCormack to where his car, a 1978 Monte Carlo, was parked. On the way, Kevin kept talking to her about the lawsuit and how he was going to "bury Traughber." Lipford didn't recall McCormack being that specific while they were in the club, but he knew that Kevin detested Traughber. He remembered how Kevin used to say how conniving Traughber was and how much he'd like to get Traughber in a compromising position.

In the parking lot, Martha asked Kevin where he was headed, and he said back to Clarksville. But he didn't go to Clarksville. Instead he ended up at a place called the Crow's Nest with two other friends from the corrections department, Larry Boucher and Judy Lambert. They left him around eight-thirty. He was going to Clarksville, he said.

At nine Kevin McCormack checked into the Capitol Park Inn. He had no luggage. He paid $16.50 for his room and left a 6:30 A.M. wake-up call. About twenty minutes later he called the bar, spoke to the bartender, Marilyn Horn, whom he knew, and told her to make sure to stay open. He would be coming down shortly.

At eleven o'clock the next morning, June 16, a motel housekeeper discovered his body in room 216. He'd been strangled.

That afternoon, after Mike Pigott's call, Marie remained home, immobilized. The first person to phone, by accident, was Anita Sheridan, a mother of five whom Marie had met at a *Cursillo* weekend for Catholic women. It had been like a spiritual retreat, except instead of being silent the weekend consisted of lectures as well as group discussions in which you strove to apply your religious experience to daily life. After a *Cursillo* weekend, you usually broke up into smaller groups that continued to meet regularly, and Marie was in one with Anita.

Anita immediately rushed over and tried to console Marie as she explained through her tears about the relationship she'd had with Kevin, how much they'd been through together, how close they were, how in the end they'd survived so much pain and humiliation and trauma—and now this.

There were other calls, of course, from her friends and Kevin's. But after Anita left, she wanted to be alone. Dante and Therese were away on visits. Ricky was out playing, and later, when they'd had dinner and Ricky was in bed, Marie called Toni Greer. Toni knew the assistant police chief, John Sorace, and maybe she could get some details about what had happened to Kevin. But Toni was out.

Marie started to go to bed. All of a sudden, the notion came to her that if they had wanted Kevin dead, how about her? The thought became obsessive. How much more they must want her dead! She looked in on Ricky. He was sleeping peacefully. She looked at his window and thought how easy it would be to get in. The apartment was on the ground floor. She made sure the window was locked. She went back to bed. Then she began thinking she'd better check all the windows, and the doors. She tried the patio door and the front door. The knob on the front door was loose, maybe had been tampered with, and she remembered that she'd meant to have it fixed. As she returned to bed, she thought about the front door some more. They wouldn't have to break a window. They only had to push hard on the door. Marie dashed to a closet and dragged a big trunk out and put the trunk against the door. She went through the apartment to other closets, getting suitcases and piling them on the trunk. She tried to arrange them first one way, and when that didn't work, another. She shoved a chest across the floor to buttress the trunk and suitcases. That should do it, she thought. She was panting from the exertion. In bed again, listening for sounds in the night over her breathing, she began to mock herself. How idiotic it was to think her puny efforts could stop anybody from coming in!

Around midnight she phoned Toni once more, and this time reached her. Toni had moved from Valley Ridge to the Iroquois Apartments, three miles away. "Toni, I'm afraid," she said. "Can I come stay over there? Can I bring Ricky too?" and Toni said of course, and Marie got Ricky out of bed and took her journal and her rosary, and drove to Toni's. Toni had made up two couches, and after Toni retired, Marie tried writing in her journal, but she wasn't able to. The nightmares were next. Kevin had been killed, and Marie was screaming for help, but nobody came. Nobody could help her. It was still dark when she jerked awake. She lay there, waiting for daybreak so she could go to mass. At first light she managed to get Ricky on his feet and went home. With the night gone, she somehow felt safer. She put Ricky in bed in his room and went to mass and prayed for Kevin's soul.

She had asked Toni to find out what she could, and in the morning Toni called and said that, well, it looked as if the murder involved homosexuality.

"What are you saying?"

"Well, you know, Marie, these things happen."

She found herself shrieking into the phone. So that's how they were going to handle it! She supposed they had some homosexual in hand who'd confessed to everything, and everybody would forget why Kevin really was murdered. Kevin wasn't gay, she said, choking with rage. And even granting for a second that he was, what did that have to do with anything?

· 3 ·

Billy Watkins, an investigator for the DA's office, arrived at the Capitol Park Inn about noon. He was there to make sure proper evidentiary procedures were followed. A homicide detective, Charlie Mills, and two uniformed cops were waiting for him.

There was no sign of forcible entry into room 216. There were also several ways to get into the motel, including outside catwalks, without passing the front desk. The body, nude, was lying on the floor between twin beds, arms outstretched, head toward the foot of the beds. Kevin had been throttled from behind with his own belt, pulled through the buckle. It had taken someone with a lot of strength, Watkins thought. *If* it had been one person. There were some broken-skin marks on the right side of the body, as well as severe abrasions on the knees and elbows. There was a spot of blood, about the size of a quarter, on one bed. The mattress on the other bed, by the window, was askew. In an ashtray was a half-smoked joint. There were two beer-can rings and a plastic six-pack holder. But no cans in the room or in the corridor trash bins. A cheap silver-colored metal chain was on the floor. When the room was dusted, only some partial, smeared prints were found. The room appeared to have been wiped clean. Kevin's clothes were strewn all over. His jacket tossed on a bed. His shoes, shirt, tie and shorts scattered about on the floor.

McCormack's wallet was missing. Watkins suggested that people often hid their wallets under mattresses. And there it was, a black billfold with his I.D. and other cards and two one-dollar bills. But missing, and never found, were Kevin's car keys and the keys to his Clarksville apartment.

Considering the general scene in the room, Watkins remembered thinking that there were sexual overtones to the case. Besides the call to the bar, the victim had made two direct-dial local calls. To whom? Nobody in the Capitol Park Inn had seen or heard anything of consequence. No traces of marijuana were found in McCormack's clothes. The medical examiner could not pinpoint the time of death—somewhere between four and twelve hours before the body was discovered.

Martha Bernard made the official identification. She also identified McCormack's car, parked in the motel garage. It still contained his expensive citizens' band radio. Along with finding his wallet, it was another reason to discount robbery as a motive.

Martha introduced the homosexual angle as well. Detective Mills told her that the police were looking to question a tall black hooker wearing a blond wig who'd been hanging around the Capitol Park Inn. Forget it, she said. Kevin didn't like blacks, nor, in her opinion, was he prone to sleeping with women.

By now, other implications were surfacing.

NASHVILLE BANNER, *June 17, 1978*

... McCormack left the Correction department last year amid a controversy between former Parole Board chairman Marie Ragghianti and Gov. Ray Blanton, who accused the former board chairman of falsifying expense accounts.

Sources said McCormack took Mrs. Ragghianti's side, putting him on bad terms with Correction officials.

"I really like working in Correction and I would like to go back there sometime," McCormack told a *Banner* reporter last week. "Maybe I can when a new administration takes over."

McCormack was scheduled to appear as a key witness for Mrs. Ragghianti in a lawsuit she filed against the state in an effort to regain her job.

Charlie Mills, on the job twenty-five years, sixteen as a detective and headed for retirement in less than a year, pursued McCormack's alleged homosexuality. Half the people he questioned who knew Kevin well subscribed to the theory. The rest didn't, or didn't have any opinion. Sam Lipford said, "If he was a fag, he did a hell of a job hiding it from me."

Lipford asked Marie if he could go to the funeral in Lima, Ohio, with her. Kevin's friends saw him as part of the administration—an enemy. Didn't want him there. Certainly, she said. She knew that Sam had liked Kevin. What had occurred was none of his doing. And she was fond of Sam. The only real conflict they'd ever had was whom he should report to as director of the probation and parole officers, and Sam had been very open about where he stood on that and why.

Lipford had already been subpoenaed as an administration witness in Marie's lawsuit. On the way back to Nashville from the funeral, he made up his mind that he would tell the truth no matter what the price was to him, and the truth wasn't going to hurt Marie a bit. The party line was that Marie had torn apart the corrections department. Sisk and Benson, and Cooney in the AG's office, expected everyone to toe the line. Volunteer anything that would tarnish her. Well, Lipford thought, they could count him out. In Nashville, after he got out of the car, Lipford thanked Marie. Said she'd been mighty kind to let him go with her.

That night she moaned with grief. At the funeral, Kevin's identical-twin brother had said the mass, delivered the eulogy. It added a dimension of pain that left her inconsolable.

It was her worst fight with Fred Thompson. Any talk from her, he said, especially to the media, about McCormack's death being connected with the lawsuit could be ruinous. "Marie, if I read or hear anything —*anything*—that I even think *may* have come from you, I'm going to ask for a continuance and drop the case."

John Bryant, a close friend of Kevin's, was the one who got her back on track. Kevin had spoken of John, but she hadn't met him until the funeral. He was in construction work and away a lot.

Then in Nashville he came to see her. To talk about Kevin. Bryant told Marie that he believed Kevin had been in love with her. "You know," he said one evening, "Kevin was really counting on you to win your trial. You've really got to get yourself together. I know you can. From everything Kevin ever said, you can do anything."

"How can I even think about it?" she said.

"You've got to, Marie. For yourself, and for him."

So much of her anguish was directed toward herself. She prayed to understand how this could have happened. It wasn't easy having faith in God's will. Still, if there was one peak she'd managed to climb as far as her relationship with a Supreme Being was concerned, it was her certainty that His judgment was better than hers. A great deal of the pain she'd endured in life which had seemed incomprehensible turned out to have been extraordinarily meaningful. Had given her strengths she hadn't known she possessed. Surely she would come to understand this too, and as she prayed, the commitment at her end was to try to do her personal best.

If it had been a homosexual pickup, Charlie Mills figured to collect some talk off the street. But he didn't, and that was unusual. Nothing from Nashville's gay haunts. One brief lead went nowhere. A kid attempting to get out of a jam by fingering a bigger fish. The suspect, however, came up clean on a polygraph, and there was no other evidence against him.

Several of McCormack's friends said he'd squirreled away pardons and paroles tapes and files in his Clarksville apartment, but the only item of significance Mills found there was the letter McCormack had written to Murray Henderson endorsing Marie's firing, the one Kevin had told her about, the one he'd written for fear of losing his own job. It was dated August 12, 1977.

> . . . *I personally believe that Mrs. Ragghianti's professional ignorance precipitated her misinterpretation of genuine inquiries made by the Governor's Office or the Department regarding parole or possible clemency cases. In fact, I have never observed, nor anticipated, anyone in State government either directly or subtly implying that the Board should accomplish positive case activity for political expediency or gain.*

Mills thought this was a hot new angle until he learned what Kevin's actual role in Marie's lawsuit would have been.

There was something else, however, that got to Charlie Mills and stayed with him. He'd never been in an apartment more fastidiously kept. Particularly the clothes. McCormack's suits were hung in precise order for winter and summer wear. His slacks were hung separately. His sports jackets the same. The shirts in his chest drawers were neatly stacked by color. So were his socks. Dirty laundry was bagged.

Mills thought back to room 216 at the Capitol Park Inn. How McCormack's clothes had been thrown around, his shirt balled up. McCormack had an eight o'clock meeting in Clarksville the following morning. Even if he had time to go home first to change, he would have hung up his clothes in the motel. All you had to do was look at his apartment.

The murder, Mills decided, had been made to look like a sex crime. The door hadn't been forced, and from everything Mills could gather, McCormack wasn't the kind to let a stranger in. There were no physical clues. No street gossip. It was as professional a killing as Mills could recall.

And then there were the missing keys to the Clarksville apartment.

Eddie Sisk could never remember whether it was Benson or Traughber who first told him the cops were asking about the August 12 letter McCormack wrote to Henderson. But he promptly had copies made and sent them anonymously to the *Banner* and WSM-TV, Channel 4. Hey, look at this. Maybe the case wasn't all that simple! Sisk was quite put out when neither the paper nor the station used the letter.

· 4 ·

Fred Thompson's courtroom strategy was to finesse whether or not Blanton had the right to fire Marie and, instead, provide the jury with two other, far more important points to reflect on. First, that Marie was a decent woman, totally devoted to her work. And, second, that she knew more about pardons and paroles than anyone else in Tennessee.

Thompson spent a lot of time with Marie going over potential witnesses for her. She, of course, would be her own best witness. There had to be DA input, though. But who, and how many? Richard Fisher was an obvious choice. Thompson was sure, however, the state would try to imply a romantic tie between Fisher and Marie. Even if they didn't get anywhere, it would tend to cloud things.

Gary Gerbitz was next on the list. But Gerbitz being a Republican would blur things another way. Maybe Gerbitz sensed that too. He didn't appear eager to be called. Thompson came up with the solution

—Bob Gay, the DA for the eleventh judicial circuit, south of Nashville. Socially, Marie hadn't had so much as a drink of water with Gay. Thompson knew Gay. One of Gay's counties was Thompson's home county, Lawrence. When Thompson sounded him out, Gay said he'd be glad to testify. He had considered Marie a first-rate chairman. While more DAs could have been called, Thompson decided against it. A question of too many cooks spoiling the broth. He wanted a portrait of Marie standing almost alone against Blanton, fighting for what was right. He'd try to limit her witnesses wherever possible to one in each area of the criminal justice system.

There would be two judges, however. One, Ernest Pellegrin, a criminal court judge, had first come in contact with Marie when he wrote her a long letter protesting executive clemency for a woman who had "ambushed" her husband and subsequently was convicted of first-degree murder. Marie had written an even longer letter back, explaining that she had looked into the case and felt the woman deserved special consideration. The woman had been brutalized by her husband for some twenty years. Finally she'd separated from him, and he had threatened to come back to beat her once more. She had warned him that if he did, she would kill him, and she did. Pellegrin was amazed by the letter, not so much by its content as by the fact that it was the first letter he'd ever received from the pardons and paroles board that wasn't a form letter. He then came to see Marie in Nashville and, after talking with her, withdrew his objections to clemency. He'd be honored, he now said, to appear for Marie.

The other jurist was Circuit Judge Charles Haston, famous for being tough on the bench. "I don't care what my calendar is," he said to Marie, "I'll be there." Then Haston told Thompson, "I might not agree with every decision she made, but she's the best damn thing that happened to the board."

In addition, there was State Senator Douglas Henry, widely known in Nashville for his fair-mindedness and legislative independence. And Jack Scism, now back to newspapering after his stint on the North Carolina parole commission, would attest to Marie's efforts to upgrade pardons and paroles procedures not only in Tennessee but also across the nation.

David Raybin had left the attorney general's office and was an assistant district attorney in Nashville. Raybin could describe Marie's concern about the Georgia extraditions. And would confirm that, as the board's counsel at the time, he had urged her to confer with a private attorney in her capacity as chairman if the state made an issue of that.

Jim Grisham, Marie's former administrative assistant, agreed to come forward. Grisham was still a parole officer, and it was important for someone within the corrections department to speak for her.

"Jim," Marie said, "I really—if you feel it could cost you your job or something—my God, I know you all have bills to pay, and I'll certainly understand."

"No, I'll be there," he said. "I couldn't live with myself if I wasn't."

Not everyone was so willing. There was Jack Lowery, whose call to Marie had started everything. He was no longer Lebanon's mayor but a politically active lawyer. "Shouldn't I get in touch with Jack?" she asked Thompson, and Fred said, "Well, hell, see what he says."

So she phoned Lowery and said her trial was coming up and she was wondering if he'd testify on her behalf, and Lowery said he'd tell her what he had already told Eddie Sisk. "I'll just tell it like it was," he said. "Well, that's all I would want you to do," she replied, but there was something in his voice that didn't seem too friendly, and Marie thought again about the phrase he'd used. It was as if Lowery were putting her and Eddie in the same boat, so to speak.

"It sounds like Sisk is going to use him," Thompson said.

"But what kind of memory can he have that's going to benefit Eddie?"

"Marie," said Fred Thompson, "Eddie is the legal counsel to the Governor. Who are you?"

The rest of the state's witnesses were predictable. Among them, C. Murray Henderson, Sam Lipford, Sisk, Arnold Hurst, Sherry Lomax, Joe Mitchell and Traughber. The administration had a real hook into Traughber. His term on the board was up June 30, and he hadn't been reappointed yet.

Thompson was pleased with his own lineup. But in the end, he told Marie, she was the one who would make or break the case.

· 5 ·

Thompson had fought hard to have a jury. Now he had to get the right kind. He was looking for law-and-order jurors who'd be offended at the notion of inmates being let loose left and right, a notion Thompson intended to cultivate. Obviously, he didn't want anyone who worked for the state or had relatives who were state employees. Or had relatives or friends in prison. The last part would be tricky. For blacks especially, a direct question would be insulting. He'd just have to work around that. Hope the judge would elicit the information. The same with party affiliation. Nothing direct. He'd put it more gently. Did they have political leanings that might prevent an impartial verdict? In terms of stereotypes, he didn't want matrons who thought a woman had no business being out of the home, and in Nashville there were plenty of them. Other than that, he'd play it by ear. His key question was whether a prospective juror would be reluctant to find against the governor of the State of Tennessee if the facts justified it. "You know," he said, "we all hold that office in high respect." Thompson knew in advance the answer would be no, but he wanted to see how it was said. And subliminally it allowed a juror to make a statement of independence and later to prove it.

There were surprised whispers in the courtroom when Thompson accepted a middle-aged black juror. Many of the controversial clemencies involved blacks. And there was Traughber. But for Fred Thompson, there wasn't a better law-and-order fellow than a solid, black businessman who'd made his own way. He'd see right through Traughber. Thompson thought the man would make his best juror, along with a young data processor who he figured would be put off by the shoddy auditing that had led to Marie's firing.

There would be six jurors in all. Thompson used his last challenge on a garden-club lady. Just the kind he didn't want passing judgment on Marie. Then he realized he'd made a mistake. Next in line was one he wanted even less. A young black woman, hostile, not too intelligent. He was still cursing himself when she blurted out that she had a husband in the state penitentiary, and the judge, Chancellor High, dismissed her on his own. Thompson ended up with a lieutenant in the Nashville fire department, which didn't make him all that happy either, mostly because the job was only a step removed from being a state worker.

Otherwise, though, the panel looked pretty good. All holding responsible jobs or retired from them. Of course, the quickest way to go broke was betting on what a particular jury would do.

There was a time, Fred Thompson said in his opening statement, when a governor of Tennessee could fire someone for little or no reason. But the legislature in its wisdom had changed this concept for certain appointments where independence was required, and now he had to have "good cause." That was the situation in this case, Thompson said.

He asked the jury to look at the totality of Marie's performance as chairman. See it in context of what she had to do. Her job entailed much more than that of the other board members, more than simply attending board meetings. She had tremendous administrative responsibilities. And from the first, she was faced with the problem of repairing deteriorating relations between the board and many judges and district attorneys.

A large part of the case, he said, involved executive clemency. He explained that the Governor didn't need the board's okay to grant a clemency, but it sure was nice to have if there was any heat afterward. This was the area where conflicts began to rise between Marie and the Governor's office and the other board members. This was why she was fired. Marie wouldn't go along. "Her problem was she took her job seriously," said Thompson. "That was the reason for her downfall."

So they started looking for anything they could use to get rid of her, he continued. "They launched a midnight investigation, day and night, for about a week, and they came up with an incomplete and largely inaccurate preliminary audit. On the basis of that, they terminated her."

They sent her a letter, he said. "The letter was not a letter saying, you know, it'd be better for the board if you left. The letter equated her conduct with that of the criminal element she was supposed to be supervising. The letter said she was an embarrassment to Tennessee. Before the letter was sent, nobody ever came to her and said, 'What about this, or what about that?' "

It was all political, Thompson said. He told the jury to pay special attention to where the letter had been written, in whose office. That would come out during the trial. "The proof will show there was no good cause in firing Marie Ragghianti," he said. "It wasn't done in good faith. It wasn't done for the reasons set forth. But for other reasons."

Deputy Attorney General Hayes Cooney responded that it was the Governor who had appointed Marie. And as soon as he did, "she assumed the role of chairman to be one in which she could do whatever she pleased, whenever she pleased, whether it was related to her job or not."

She was expressly charged by law to preside over board meetings, yet she wasn't there to vote on cases "time after time." She filed travel claims that were not correct. She took overtime "at a cost the state valued at $7,500." It was for these and other reasons that the Governor dismissed her. "We'll show," said Cooney, "that her problem was stated in the Governor's letter of termination."

Thompson couldn't believe that Cooney was going with the letter. The letter was Thompson's whole case. Thompson had anticipated the state would hang its hat on the Governor's inherent right to hire and fire people in his administration, and would contend that was cause enough. But it seemed that Cooney had gotten a little unhinged by Thompson's remark to the jury about where the letter had been written —that Thompson was going to make an issue of the fact that it had been drafted in the office of the Nashville Democratic leader.

Don't be diverted by Mr. Thompson, Cooney exhorted the jurors. What difference did it make what lawyer's office it was written in? There was only one issue, Cooney said, "Was the letter right or wrong? Were the allegations in it right or wrong?" Cooney wouldn't let go of it, as if transfixed by the unassailable logic of what he was saying. He spoke of a framed quotation on the wall of a friend's office. *If it's the truth, what matter does it make who said it?*

"That's what this case is about," Cooney declared. "The truth!"

Amen, Marie thought.

· 6 ·

The trial began on June 28. The night before, in Fred's office, she had looked at him knee-deep in papers, sleeves rolled up, and she realized how hard he'd worked on her case. And now, at the eleventh hour, after having felt such certainty for so long, she wondered if she was actually deranged. Had lost contact with reality in even imagining she could pull this off. If she lost, how could she possibly pay this man?

All three kids were in the courtroom. At first she hadn't wanted them there. She had planned on sending them to Daytona Beach to stay with a good friend from her high school days. She'd worried about what the state's witnesses might say about her. What the message might be to them if they saw her defeated. That it didn't pay to buck the system.

"Look," she argued, "a courtroom is not the place for children. You never see children in a courtroom." They immediately set up a yowl. So Marie relented. They'd already been through her DUI arrest. What could be worse than that? And suppose she did win, and they weren't there?

A friend from St. Henry's parish, Eva Campbell, volunteered to drive the kids in. Roque was in court every day. So was Virginia, although she was pretty much confined to a wheelchair now. Rosie would bring her, and then Ricky would wheel her inside.

Almost at once, after Marie took the stand, wrangling commenced between Thompson and Cooney over the admissibility of her first speech to the state district attorneys outlining her program and goals as chairman and her subsequent correspondence with various DAs and judges. It was all hearsay, Cooney objected.

THOMPSON   Mr. Cooney doesn't mind us testifying to a point, he just doesn't want us to prove it.
CHANCELLOR HIGH   Mr. Thompson, the fact that she wrote the letters and received letters, which was part of her duties that she carried out, is properly admissible. But the contents of the letters and the details of the letters—I'm going to sustain the objection.

Outside the courtroom, during a brief recess, a woman said to Marie, "Well, the Governor's got *his* judge. Where's yours?"

There was another break in Marie's testimony when DA Gay and State Senator Henry were sworn in. Thompson questioned Gay closely about her cooperation with his office.

THOMPSON   You said that Mrs. Ragghianti called you on the telephone.
GAY   Yes.
THOMPSON   Had you ever before received a personal telephone call from a chairman of the Board of Pardons and Paroles?
GAY   I had never received a telephone call from any member or the chairman.

THOMPSON   Senator Henry, in your dealings with Mrs. Ragghianti, how did you find her to be, her expressed attitude concerning her work on the board?

HENRY   . . . My impression of Mrs. Ragghianti was that she was one of the relatively few number of people who had a genuine desire to change the system in which she was involved, so as to make it function better. She made a distinct impression on me in that regard.

But the best part of the day for Thompson was when he managed to get in, without an objection from Cooney, that Marie also had been the president of the Southern Paroling Authority.

THOMPSON   How did it make a contribution to the Board of Pardons and Paroles?
MARIE   Well, it enabled me to see that—what some of the differences in Tennessee's board and other boards or commissions were. Some of those differences were cause for pride, some of those differences were cause for grave concern.

By the time he'd finished, Thompson felt he had achieved a primary objective. To establish Marie's credentials. To let the jury know that it couldn't want a better expert in the field of pardons and paroles.

· 7 ·

On the second day Judges Pellegrin and Haston testified.

THOMPSON   [to Pellegrin] All right, sir. How would you describe Mrs. Ragghianti's responsiveness as far as your desire to have input was concerned?
PELLEGRIN   She was very courteous, very conscientious, very dedicated. I was very much impressed with her.

With Judge Haston, Thompson pursued the degree of sensitivity Marie had exhibited regarding parole and clemency petitions in cases he'd presided over.

THOMPSON   Would you say that she was always receptive and considerate to your inquiries and opinions?
HASTON   Without exception.

THOMPSON   Have you ever been visited or your opinion solicited or
responded to in that manner by a previous board member?
HASTON   No.

When Marie was recalled, Fred Thompson began leading her all
through her forebodings about the Georgia extraditions, followed by
the $20,000 clemency bribe offer reported by Lowery, and how that
had been the beginning of her troubles with Sisk and Benson. Next
more concern, more conflicts with them, in the Rose Lee Cooper
clemency. And then how her executive secretary, Sherry Lomax, had
rewritten the Gary Keene clemency and signed Marie's name to it, and
how Marie had fired Sherry as a result. How she subsequently discovered that Sherry had taken the pardons and paroles card file. How the
pressures continued to increase in the George Edwards pardon petition,
and how this caused major problems with her two fellow board members. How the Governor himself summoned her to his office and informed her that she was on "probation," that he was keeping tabs on
her performance. How Eddie Sisk threatened to have her fired if she
didn't support the administration version of a new criminal justice bill.
How her fellow board members voted against national accreditation,
and how, right afterward, she learned that Clayton Dawson had been
convicted again of rape. And how, at the end, C. Murray Henderson
told her the Governor would give her another job with the state at the
same salary if she would only resign as chairman.

THOMPSON   Mrs. Ragghianti, just a couple of more questions and I'll
turn it over to Mr. Cooney. They are general in nature. Did you
claim overtime costing the taxpayers $7,500?
MARIE   No, I did not.
THOMPSON   Did you claim to attend board meetings when in fact you
did not attend those meetings?
MARIE   No, I did not. The meetings to which they referred in almost
every instance were meetings that I had with various officials that we
brought out today and yesterday. Judges and district attorneys.
THOMPSON   When you were having those meetings, on your travel
vouchers were you claiming to be at board meetings?
MARIE   No.
THOMPSON   With regard to . . . charging you with missing some
thirteen board meetings but claiming compensation for attending

those meetings. If all those charges were true, how much are we talking about in terms of money?

MARIE   I think around thirty-six or forty some-odd dollars, to the best of my recollection.

THOMPSON   Are all those charges true?

MARIE   No, they are not. In a few instances it was true that I had planned to be at some board meetings when I wasn't. Those were honest mistakes that I overlooked when signing expense vouchers.

THOMPSON   Who prepared those vouchers?

MARIE   My secretary, Mrs. Lomax, whom I later had to fire.

Assistant State Attorney General Claudius Smith cross-examined her. Smith went right to the error in Marie's annual leave. Hadn't she been in Florida on July 1 through July 6, 1976, and didn't her attendance and leave record show she had worked July 1, 2 and 6?

SMITH   Mrs. Ragghianti, didn't you also sign the official records kept by the state that you were at work on those dates?

MARIE   I did sign the time sheet. I think it's pertinent to say that—

SMITH   I just want your answer. Did you sign the time sheets, Mrs. Ragghianti?

MARIE   I did.

On the objection of Thompson's partner, John Rodgers, she was allowed to explain that while she had signed the forms, often weeks after the fact, she had not filled them out. It had been the first time she'd been asked to submit any such forms. Prior to that, Eddie Sisk had told her that the hours she kept as extradition officer were of no interest to him as long as she did her work.

Caustically, Smith kept up his attack.

SMITH   Is it your testimony, then, that filling out and filing expense claims which involves state money is just something insignificant?

MARIE   No.

SMITH   Is it your testimony that there are many other things more important than filling out and filing expense claims in which you claim money from the state?

MARIE   I wouldn't want to make a value judgment about which is more important. I think that every aspect of my job was important.

SMITH   Let me ask you again. Is the filling out and filing of an expense
claim insignificant?
MARIE   No, it's not. It's important.

Smith hammered at her absences from board meetings. By her own
admission, she'd missed meetings, although by law she was required to
preside over them.

MARIE   Sir, it is obvious that I am charged to be all things to all people,
and that I'm charged at being with—it does say all meetings, but I
think it's apparent that it is impossible for the board chairman to
attend all meetings. . . . I believe that I am authorized to conduct
other activities. However, I would also point out that the same
statute provides for the absence of the chairman. It provides for the
presiding of another board member in the absence of the chairman.
And I think it does this to enable the chairman to conduct the proper
administration of the other duties the chairman has.

Marie, said Smith, seemed to have problems with the corrections
commissioner, with other board members, with the Governor's office.

SMITH   Did you have problems with everyone with whom you came
in contact officially?
MARIE   No, I didn't. I didn't have problems with the prisoners, I
didn't have problems with officials I had to deal with, many of whom
have been here in this room.
SMITH   Mrs. Ragghianti, some of those gentlemen whom I have just
enumerated are in the large sense state officials.
MARIE   Yes, that's true. I did have problems with some of the people
you have enumerated.

Then, Fred Thompson thought, Smith made a big mistake. In trying
to show that Marie was motivated by an insatiable appetite for power,
he brought up the corrections department's extended-furlough program whereby an inmate could be administratively released six months
before coming up for parole. Hadn't Marie objected to that simply
because it impinged on her authority? No, she replied, it was because
she feared that a sex offender might be inadvertently let loose in some

community. She wouldn't be legally liable as the board chairman, Smith persisted. True, Marie said, but she bore other responsibilities as well—as a citizen.

Thompson marveled at her composure on the stand. As the day wore on, Smith's cross-examination got increasingly churlish. Thompson thought about objecting, but he decided Smith's badgering was getting through to the jury.

SMITH I would like to speak to you about the card file which you mentioned in your direct testimony.

MARIE Which card file, sir? The first one or the second one?

SMITH I'm speaking of the card file in which you said that you fired Mrs. Lomax because of the card file. . . . Were these files that you kept yourself?

MARIE No, sir, they were files that Mrs. Lomax was in charge of.

SMITH . . . Then it was Mrs. Lomax's card file and you got Mrs. Lomax's card file back?

MARIE No, sir, it was the board's card file and I got the board's card file back.

SMITH Then it was your card file?

MARIE No, it was the board's card file.

SMITH . . . I believe that testimony has been introduced that your salary was, during your period as chairman, something above $26,000 a year?

MARIE Yes.

SMITH What I'm asking you, then, your official salary is slightly in excess of $100 a day, is that correct?

MARIE It is.

SMITH I return to July 1, 2 and 6 of 1976. If you put three days down as having worked when you were, in fact, in Florida, this would be a matter of some $300, would it not?

MARIE Yes.

SMITH Your Honor, I have no further questions.

It had gone well, Fred Thompson thought. Smith had made some picayune points. But the image of Marie as an able, concerned, beleaguered chairman trying to do her job had remained intact.

Still, you never knew.

If that was the lead in the *Tennessean*, Thompson had to wonder
if that was the message the jury had gotten as well.

· 8 ·

On July 3, the third day of the trial, the state put on its initial witness,
C. Murray Henderson. From the start, he was shaky. Couldn't remember board member Mitchell's name. Couldn't remember Arnold
Hurst's first name either. He testified that Hurst's audit, which culminated in Marie's discharge, had been triggered by information from
Kevin McCormack and Sherry Lomax. Henderson couldn't recall who
else might have been responsible. Then he managed to remember that
Charles Traughber had also complained about Marie missing some
board meetings.

Under cross-examination by Thompson, Henderson admitted that
he knew that Lomax had already been fired by Marie. And why,
Thompson demanded, hadn't Henderson mentioned anything about
Kevin McCormack in his deposition? Why was he bringing his name
into the case only now? Well, replied Henderson, it was because he had
gotten the most damaging statements against Marie from McCormack.

For the first time, Thompson's voice thundered in the courtroom.

THOMPSON   Are you aware of pressure from the Governor's office that
if he didn't testify according to the way that they thought should be
testified—
HENDERSON   Absolutely not.
COONEY   Objection, Your Honor.

THOMPSON Was Kevin McCormack the young man who was found murdered a couple of weeks ago?

HENDERSON That's correct.

CHANCELLOR HIGH Did you have an objection, General Cooney?

COONEY Yes, Your Honor. I would also object to the question of murder, the term murder about Mr. McCormack. I don't think the authorities have announced the official statement.

CHANCELLOR HIGH All right. Sustain the objection.

THOMPSON I'll ask him whether or not he is aware Mr. McCormack was found with his own belt wrapped around his neck, found dead.

HENDERSON Yes.

Then Thompson got to the matter of where the letter terminating Marie had been drafted and typed—in George Barrett's office.

THOMPSON George Barrett, correct me again if I'm wrong, is the chairman of the Democratic Executive Committee for Davidson County, is that right?

HENDERSON I don't know whether he is or not. He's a Democrat, I know that.

But for all his evasiveness, his claims of faulty recollection, Henderson would not commit perjury.

THOMPSON Commissioner . . . you told her that if she resigned that she could be given another job with the state in any department except the Department of Correction and the Department of Safety?

HENDERSON Yes, sir.

THOMPSON Was that done with the knowledge and consent of the Governor?

HENDERSON Yes.

THOMPSON And if the Governor testified under oath that no such offer was given her, or option was given her, he would be incorrect, so far as you recall?

HENDERSON Yes, as far as I recall, he would be, because I think he indicated a willingness for that.

Sam Lipford was next. Questioned by Cooney, Lipford described his relationship with Marie as cordial until the problem of authority over the probation and parole officers arose. After that, it became somewhat strained. Essentially, he said, the fight was between his boss, Henderson, and Marie. "I was caught in the middle," Lipford said. He could see Cooney was waiting for him to say how disruptive Marie had been, but he wouldn't. Cooney couldn't wait to get him off the stand.

Once Eddie Sisk was sworn in, Marie immediately noticed the nervous clicking in his voice, even under Cooney's gentle guidance. Squirming in the witness chair, reaching for endless glasses of water. This is going to be interesting, Marie thought. Then Cooney got to the clemency guarantee made to Lowery for his client, Will Midgett.

COONEY   There has been some testimony here by Mrs. Ragghianti about a matter in Lebanon. . . . Involved Mr. Jack Lowery and several other persons?

SISK   That's correct.

COONEY   Do you recall having any discussions with Mrs. Ragghianti about the Lebanon matter?

SISK   . . . I discussed it with Mr. Lowery, and I discussed it with Mrs. Ragghianti.

COONEY   As a lawyer and having been involved in these matters, did you reach any conclusions at that time and so advise her about whether any crime was involved, if you recall?

SISK   I reached a conclusion. I don't know whether that's relevant or not.

THOMPSON   I have no objection.

SISK   Okay. Mr. Lowery and I discussed it. And it was, you know, our opinion as lawyers that there had not been—

THOMPSON   Now, I would object to Mr. Lowery's testimony.

SISK   But it was my opinion based upon my discussion with Mr. Lowery that no crime had occurred and—but I did ask Mr. Lowery to the best of my recollection if he had notified the law-enforcement authorities in Lebanon, and he had.

COONEY   Did she ever complain to you or anyone else in the Governor's office about pressuring her?

SISK   The first time I ever heard Marie Ragghianti say that anyone

pressured her or gave her any directives is right here from this witness
stand last week.

COONEY   Did you ever receive complaints about her from other state
employees that you recall?
SISK   Well, I had complaints from Commissioner Henderson. I had
complaints from Sherry Lomax. I had several discussions with Kevin
McCormack.

Thompson let his partner, John Rodgers, a Democrat who had supported Blanton, handle the cross-examination. Fred was worried about
the impact Marie's three days of leave-taking in Florida might have on
the jury. That was when Sisk's clicking got worse.

RODGERS   In connection with your position, what is the policy as far
as leave is concerned? Do you earn leave, or what's the situation as
far as leave is concerned on your job?
SISK   In our position, the Governor really considers us to work 24
hours a day if he calls, so there is no real policy in regard to our
job.
RODGERS   You testified that you took a vacation and went to Florida.
. . . Is there any formality in your doing that?
SISK   Well, you accumulate so many days a year, and I work within
that framework. I don't know exactly what it is, 22 days or something
of sick leave, whatever . . .
RODGERS   I gather from that answer, then, that you really keep no
records of how much leave you do take, is that correct?
SISK   That is correct.

RODGERS   I have been told you are quite an outstanding golfer. . . .
Was there a time when they were having a tournament down at the
public course toward Chapel Hill, whatever that course is, the state
park, what's the name of that course down there?
SISK   Henry Horton.
RODGERS   Henry Horton. Was there a time when you were playing a
tournament down there and got caught on television, and the Gover-
nor had a discussion with you about your playing golf?
SISK   He laughed about it.
RODGERS   He did?

SISK   Yes, he did.

RODGERS   But needless to say, there are no records of your leave or anything of that sort. You go and come when you so desire, right?

SISK   That's correct.

When Rodgers got into the Lebanon extortion and Bill Thompson, Eddie's body movement became almost spastic. He kept throwing looks at Chancellor High, as if pleading with him to put a halt to this.

RODGERS   Now, you know Bill Thompson. . . . How long have you known him?

SISK   I've known him about six years.

RODGERS   About how old is he?

SISK   I don't know. I think he's in his forties.

RODGERS   He is a white male, is that right?

SISK   That's correct.

RODGERS   Is he kind of dark-complected?

SISK   I don't know. I don't know if he's dark-complected or light-complected.

RODGERS   Would you give me your best estimate as to his complexion?

SISK   I don't pay much attention to people's complexion.

RODGERS   Would you say he'd weigh around, say, two hundred pounds?

SISK   I think he probably weighs two hundred pounds.

RODGERS   Is he about five feet eleven?

SISK   Probably somewhere in that neighborhood.

RODGERS   Would you say his hair is kind of dark, maybe a little gray in it, kind of curly?

SISK   His hair is dark. Yeah, I guess you would say it was curly.

Now Rodgers paused to contemplate Sisk.

RODGERS   Would it not be true to say that Mr. Lowery reported that he was contacted in his office by a white male?

SISK   To the best of my recollection, that's correct.

RODGERS   And that time, was it not called to your attention that the description of that white male coincided with the description of Bill Thompson?

SISK   Absolutely not.

RODGERS   Are you saying that Mr. Lowery . . . and Marie Ragghianti
   never stated anything like this?
SISK   Mr. Lowery definitely never stated anything like that. Mrs.
   Ragghianti may have said that she thought the description was that
   of Bill Thompson. I don't recall.
RODGERS   Well, all right. So Mr. Lowery reports that a white male,
   dark complexion, 200 pounds, five feet eleven, dark, graying curly
   hair, approached his office. Would that be correct, sir?
SISK   I don't recall the exact facts.
RODGERS   . . . And that this individual told him that he could get a
   commutation for Will Midgett for $20,000?
SISK   I don't recall exactly what was said.

So much for Eddie's credibility, Fred Thompson thought when court
adjourned. Fred puffed contentedly on a big Montecristo as he watched
the evening news play up Sisk's apparent lack of interest in getting to
the bottom of a $20,000 clemency bribe attempt—a "solicitation," it
was called—that Marie had told him about. For certain, the jury had
gotten that.

· 9 ·

The next day Marie listened in disbelief as Jack Lowery did his best
to bail Sisk out. In direct testimony, he said he agreed with Sisk that
no crime had been committed concerning the commutation-for-pay
pitch for Will Midgett. Under Thompson's cross, though, Lowery
allowed that if it hadn't been a violation of criminal law, "it was a very
good beginning to a violation." He said he'd done all he could. He'd
reported it.

Charles Traughber was a much tougher customer. According to his
direct testimony, he was never aware of any pressure from the Governor's office regarding clemency or parole matters. Under Marie, he said,
the board's efficiency dropped precipitously. Marie maintained an erratic office schedule. Often she simply disappeared. Nobody knew
where she was. Just went off on her own. She not only missed board
hearings consistently but was often late for them. She instituted procedures without consulting the other board members, such as logging all

incoming and outgoing phone calls. She decreed that no clemency recommendation would be valid without her signature. She had multiple staff problems. She failed to communicate with the other board members. It got so that he couldn't trust her. "It got to the point where I was more than reluctant to mention anything around Mrs. Ragghianti," Traughber said. He denied voting against national accreditation for Tennessee's pardons and paroles board.

Traughber also denied getting a phone call from Sisk right after George Edwards had been refused a pardon the first time out.

Then, in his cross-examination, Thompson brought up the Billy Gene Cole clemency.

THOMPSON   Do you recall the matter of Bill Cole?

TRAUGHBER   Bill Cole?

THOMPSON   Yes.

TRAUGHBER   If I'm not mistaken, this is a matter that was asked about some months ago by the federal government.

THOMPSON   Now, I'm not asking about that. Do you recall the individual Bill Cole?

TRAUGHBER   No, I don't recall him.

COONEY   Objection, Your Honor. I don't see that that has any relationship to her chairmanship and I object to any more questions at this time unless it's explained.

THOMPSON   I promise I'll make it directly pertinent to the line of questioning Your Honor has allowed so far.

CHANCELLOR HIGH   He's answered he doesn't recall who Bill Cole is. You don't know who Bill Cole is, do you?

TRAUGHBER   No.

CHANCELLOR HIGH   All right. He already said he doesn't know.

Ten months before, however, Traughber had remembered Bill Cole very well when he met with Hank Hillin in a Nashville park. Had given Hillin a detailed written summary of the pressures Sisk had exerted to obtain a clemency recommendation for Cole. Had testified under oath about it in front of a federal grand jury. At the time, of course, there'd been the shadow of an indictment over Traughber. Now, as far as anyone could tell, the federal probe was dead and buried.

Now, it would seem, Traughber had more pressing matters on his

mind. Like his reappointment to the board. Thompson jumped right
on that.

THOMPSON   Mr. Traughber, when does your term expire?
TRAUGHBER   June 30, 1978.
THOMPSON   So it's already expired.
TRAUGHBER   It expired except for the fact the Governor has asked me
  to continue in this capacity and the law requires unless you are
  discharged by the Governor, you can continue to serve in the capac-
  ity until someone is qualified to fill the job.
THOMPSON   . . . So as of this moment, the Governor can reappoint you
  or he can choose not to reappoint you?
TRAUGHBER   Correct.

· 10 ·

On July 6 Thompson called three rebuttal witnesses: David Raybin,
Mike Rothwell, a parole officer from Knoxville who had phoned on his
own to testify that Marie had been doing a splendid job, and Jim
Grisham. They barely had time to identify themselves before their
presence was objected to.

THOMPSON   What was your relationship with Mrs. Ragghianti when
  you left?
GRISHAM   I felt friendship toward her.
THOMPSON   When you worked for her, did you have any problem
  getting along with her?
COONEY   Objection, Your Honor. He's trying to get his opinion.
CHANCELLOR HIGH   Sustained.

Then, after five days, the testimony was over.
    In his closing argument for Blanton, Cooney likened Marie to a
railroad train run amok. "The Ragghianti railroad and road show," he
said. Going wherever she wanted, doing whatever she felt like. Being
all things to all people. Showing off all the way, choosing to "travel
around and meet everybody and give speeches" instead of tending to
business at the office. No wonder the Governor had gotten rid of her.
Her lawsuit, Cooney said, was motivated by spite. Political revenge.

Fred Thompson singled out Traughber's testimony. The administration had left him twisting in the wind until it saw how well he did on the stand. He asked the jurors to consider that if they had right on their side, and all the power was on the other side, wouldn't they want to do something about it? That's what motivated Marie to bring the lawsuit. Why, he asked, had the Governor offered Marie another job that wouldn't cost her a dime in salary if the allegations in his letter were true? The truth was that Marie hadn't been thrown out for good cause. She wasn't fired because she didn't do her job. "No," he said softly, "it was because she did do her job." The letter terminating her had been brutal and cowardly, "designed to cripple and humiliate her."

Thompson had expected one issue of fact to be presented to the jury. Had Marie been fired for good cause? In the jury selection, Chancellor High had explained repeatedly that this was what the case was about. And in High's charge to the jury now, Thompson was pleased that good cause was defined as something substantial. It couldn't be trivial or inconsequential.

But to Thompson's consternation, instead of a single issue of fact, there were seven of them. The first five were specific. Did the plaintiff fail to perform her statutory duties by being absent from parole board meetings? Did the plaintiff improperly charge the state for travel expenses? Did the plaintiff fail to perform her statutory duty of coordinating the activities of the parole board members? Did the plaintiff wrongfully violate the rules by publicly discussing board votes? Did the plaintiff wrongfully charge the state for overtime pay?

Not until the sixth factual issue was the question of good cause raised. And the seventh gave Blanton yet another shot. Had he acted "arbitrarily and capriciously" in firing Marie?

The big question, of course, remained good cause. But the fact was that Marie had missed board meetings. A few of her travel-expense vouchers were incorrect. The jury could answer yes to those issues and still find for her on the issue of good cause. The jury could also decide that the Governor lacked good cause but that he hadn't acted arbitrarily and capriciously considering the information he had at his disposal.

What worried Thompson was that if all this happened, if Marie didn't win on every count, High could set aside a good-cause verdict for Marie as being legally inconsistent. Thompson had to make a snap decision. If he protested now and failed, he might be giving High or Cooney an idea they hadn't entertained. Thompson could hear High saying, well, old Fred over there was right—it is legally inconsistent. So Thompson elected to say nothing. If his worst fears were realized, he'd just have to find arguments that it was legally consistent.

Marie didn't need Fred to tell her what all those questions could mean. And in the corridor outside the courtroom, while the jury met, she felt so detached. In a vacuum. A reporter put a mike in front of her and asked if she had it to do over again, would she? Unhesitatingly she said, "Yes."

Suddenly she had to get away from everyone, and she walked to the far end of the corridor—away from her kids, her mother and father, Fred, friends, the press. People somehow sensed to let her be. Marie kept thinking about what she'd said to the reporter. Her answer had slipped out so easily, as though it had been expected of her. But alone now, she was asking herself, would she really? *Why* had she done what she did? Was she a masochist? Someone who refused to give up in the face of overwhelming reasons to do so? Her motive hadn't been vindictiveness, she knew, or self-vindication. It wasn't the back pay. Or even her being right and their being wrong.

And then it came to her, this deep abiding belief she had in the democratic process, in the system, akin to her religious faith. She had to find out if she was right. Had to hold the system under her personal microscope. She couldn't bear the thought of looking back years later, tortured by *what if?* And if she lost, she'd find a way to deal with that. At least she'd fought her best fight, her dignity was in one piece.

In relief, she rejoined the others milling around. She was thirsty and went for a Tab. Someone said, "Well, they say it's a good sign if they don't take a long time," and she replied, "I guess so. I hope we're not here all night, for sure."

Virginia had to go to the rest room, and Marie wheeled her in. In their relationship, her mother had never been the sort to get emotional, but by themselves at that moment Marie saw the tears glisten in Virginia's eyes. "Ree," she said, "regardless of what happens, I admire you so much. I'm so proud of you. I never could have done what you're doing."

The court stenographer walked in. All through the trial, she had sat in front of Marie, blank-faced, registering not the slightest reaction. "Mrs. Ragghianti," she said, "I'm hoping—I'm praying so hard for you to win. You've just got to win! I'm not supposed to say anything, but I've been rooting for you all the way."

Back in the corridor, Fred was saying, "Come on, let's go. The jury's coming in." It seemed so fast. The jury had been out fifty minutes.

She was almost the last one in, and all at once High was asking the jury if it had reached a verdict, and the foreman was saying, "Yes, we have, Your Honor," and he started reading the first question, the one about her being derelict in attending board meetings. Marie, fingering her rosary, holding her breath, hadn't counted on that, the suspense of it, and then there was the answer, "No." She let out her breath a little. But she realized that one no didn't mean a thing. In all, she would need six nos and, at the end, a yes. There was a second no, another, and another. By the fifth no—had she wrongfully charged for over-time?—she thought, well, anyway, she had that many, and that was something they could never take from her.

Had she been fired for good cause? "No," the foreman said for the sixth time. He said that one a lot louder, she noticed. Her temples throbbed. And, finally, had Blanton acted capriciously? The foreman boomed out, "Yes!" He was looking right at her when he said it, and he was beaming.

In the uproar, she grabbed Thompson's sleeve. "We won! We won!" she cried. "We did win, didn't we?" "Yes," he said. He didn't turn toward her when he answered. She remembered how he stood there, surveying the courtroom, with this look of intense satisfaction. "Remarkable," he said, as if to himself.

· 11 ·

July 10, '78

... Well, not surprisingly, Hank's esteem for me is at a new high now that I've won my lawsuit. I now have all the trappings of an essential witness—including prestige & credibility, & we will overlook the fact that I am the same person I would have been if I had <u>lost.</u>

TWENTY-ONE

Blanton had waited till the last minute before the filing deadline for the August primary to announce that he would not seek reelection. Two thousand people, about half of them from his county patronage committees, gathered on the executive-mansion lawn to hear him. The Governor was quite emotional. "You that are here today have the distinction of being accused, of being reprimanded, of being part of the Blanton administration. . . . You've been tested, tried, investigated and interrogated. But I worship all of you, because you've stood through thick and thin," he said.

He cited no specific reasons for his withdrawal. But after firing Marie and declaring his intention to pardon Roger Humphreys, his popularity in the polls had continued to slip. It was just like Ray, Eddie Sisk thought. Canny till the end. He'd step aside in the interests of party unity. When things settled down, he'd be back. There was still plenty of grass-roots support out there for Blanton. Probably he'd go for the U.S. Senate. That's where Blanton always wanted to be, Sisk remembered. In Washington, D.C. He had a real case of Potomac fever.

On July 28 Chancellor C. Allen High ruled that Marie not only was to be reinstated but also had a year's back pay coming. The state immediately declared it would appeal, a process certain to consume

many months. With nearly half a year to go in office, the last thing
Blanton wanted was to have Marie around.

· 2 ·

Hank Hillin began to despair that he would ever have the breakthrough
he'd once so grandly envisioned. But though Hillin wasn't aware of it,
the breakthrough was at last taking place with unexpected swiftness.

In Memphis ex-con Arthur Baldwin contacted Ernest Withers again
about buying clemency for young Steve Hamilton, who had finally been
moved into the state prison system. Withers had told Baldwin it would
cost fifteen thousand. He wanted to know if the money was still there.
You bet, Baldwin said. That boy's people would do anything to free
him. Okay, said Withers, he'd get on it. Said his man from Nashville
would be in Memphis shortly, and they'd talk.

Baldwin passed the news to agent Corbett Hart, and Hart told him
not to fool around with Withers. Find out who was who in Nashville.
"Just ask him if you can meet the man," Hart said. The odds were that
Withers wouldn't bite, but they had to chance it. Otherwise this thing
could drag on and on, and end up nowhere.

Hey, don't worry, Arthur Baldwin replied. He'd handle Withers.
Baldwin had all the credentials. Had done time for income tax evasion,
and upon his return to Memphis, where he started up a series of topless
bars, he further enhanced his underworld reputation by his supposed
connection with New Orleans Mafia boss Carlos Marcello. He'd also
served six months in the Shelby County Penal Farm for attempting to
bribe a Memphis cop and was currently under indictment for possess-
ing and selling cocaine, at which point he had become an FBI informant. Baldwin favored open-necked shirts that showed off his gold
chains. He flashed hundred-dollar bills the way other people showed
fives. To Ernest Withers, Baldwin looked like the mother lode.

"Listen, Withers," he told the ABC agent, "you say that man's
going to be here in three or four days. I'd like to shake his hand and
call him by his name." This Hamilton kid was only the beginning,
Baldwin said. He represented big bucks. There were plenty of others,
heavy cases, that wanted out. Withers would sort of be his silent
partner. Withers went for it at once, the thought of all pay and no work
irresistible. His Nashville contact, he said, was Fred Taylor—the highway patrolman on the Governor's security staff, driver for Blanton's

brother Gene, the same Fred Taylor who had recommended Charlie Benson for his job in the legal counsel's office assisting Marie. Taylor, said Withers, worked directly with Eddie Sisk.

The U.S. attorney in Memphis, Mike Cody, decided it was time to coordinate the operation with Nashville, and he called Hardin and informed him of the latest turn in the case. That's when Hillin learned about Taylor. It was unbelievable, he remembered thinking. With Marie now out of the picture, at least for the remainder of Blanton's term, together with the Justice Department letter advising Sisk that the federal probe was off, here these guys were all back at the same old stand, selling clemencies.

Baldwin and Taylor hit it right off. Unlike Sammye Lynn McGrory, Baldwin knew exactly which buttons to push. Indeed, the fact was that if Arthur Baldwin wasn't working for the FBI, he'd have jumped at the chance to be in the pardons and paroles scheme himself. Practically the first thing Baldwin told Taylor was that there was no deal on the fifteen thousand for Steve Hamilton unless Baldwin got to keep five for himself, and Taylor said fine, as long as there was ten for his "man" in Nashville. Then, in a subsequent conversation, Baldwin brought up another inmate he wanted released, Larry Gillespie, but from now on he wanted Withers kept out of it. You could just hear Taylor salivating, agent Hart thought. Baldwin was Taylor's kind of guy. No use splitting up any more than you had to.

Throughout the fall of '78 Baldwin and Taylor were on the phone constantly or meeting in Memphis, at the Hilton, the Executive Plaza, mostly in rooms at the Holiday Inn. All of it being taped and video-taped. Baldwin would hold Taylor entranced for hours about his life in crime, his big-time mob pals. As he monitored the conversations in an adjoining room, Hart, pretending to be a hotel employee, would occasionally phone Baldwin to tell him to watch his language. This was all going to be evidence in court.

After Taylor left these meetings with Baldwin, he was placed under surveillance. Charlie Benson would be seen picking him up at the Nashville airport.

On October 9 Baldwin gave Taylor $2,000 as a good-faith payment for Hamilton, and on October 12, three thousand more. Taylor explained that a decision had been made to lie low on clemencies until after the gubernatorial election. Then, said Taylor, there was a new plan. They'd wait until around Christmas to hand out a whole bunch of clemencies. Another batch, especially hot, would be held until January 15—just before Blanton vacated his office.

Corbett Hart decided he had to get things moving faster. He had Baldwin advise Taylor there could be a $100,000 deal to free Larry Ed Hacker, then in Tennessee's maximum-security penitentiary, Brushy Mountain. Next to James Earl Ray, Hacker, with a long history of armed robbery, was the state's most notorious inmate. He'd been with Ray during Ray's abortive escape from Brushy Mountain in 1977, and was suspected by prison officials of masterminding the breakout.

Hart was afraid that Taylor would walk away from it. But Taylor never blinked. For that kind of money, he said, if he couldn't get clemency papers cut for the guy, he'd arrange an escape himself.

· 3 ·

On November 7, Republican Lamar Alexander, whom Blanton had trounced four years before largely on the issue of Watergate, was elected Tennessee's next governor. Alexander won handily.

Even though Hal Hardin had gotten the pardons and paroles case back from Washington, the U.S. attorney's office required Justice Department approval before indictments could be pursued. And on November 15, the day after Baldwin first broached a release for Larry Hacker, Thomas Henderson, the public integrity section chief, came to Memphis to see the videotapes.

Hillin couldn't restrain himself. "Do you think we've got a case now?"

Henderson tried to make the best of it. "You're pretty close," he said.

"I thought you might think that," Hillin replied.

On November 28, in a room in the Executive Plaza, Baldwin let Taylor have a look at $50,000 of the cash he had for Hacker's freedom.

On December 13 Baldwin gave Taylor a $10,000 advance. The serial numbers of the bills, all hundreds, had been recorded by Hart. Baldwin said there wouldn't be any more money unless all three commutation papers, especially Hacker's, were signed. Taylor assured Baldwin they were in the works. Then the next day Taylor told Baldwin that the papers, along with many others, wouldn't be issued until January 19, Blanton's final day in office. "Had a meeting in there with the Governor this morning," Taylor said in a taped call. "It's gonna have to be the nineteenth."

Hillin and Hart discussed the situation. Obviously, Blanton himself would be the prize catch. But the way it was going, this whole thing could dribble away. On the other hand, if they moved in now, maybe Taylor would break. Besides, Hillin still had the administration's sale of liquor-store franchises as another possibility.

So in Memphis, on December 15, Baldwin peeled off six thousand more for Taylor. It was now or never, Baldwin said. His man financing the Hacker commutation had said if he didn't have the papers with Blanton's signature on them by three o'clock that afternoon, the deal was off. Taylor started making calls. It was all set, he then told Baldwin. The signed commutations for Steve Hamilton, Larry Gillespie—and Larry Hacker—would be brought on a plane leaving Nashville at two-fifteen, landing in Memphis at 2:57 P.M.

Fred Taylor thereupon was placed under arrest by Hart, who confiscated the six thousand Taylor had just received.

About 2 P.M. at the Nashville airport, Hillin arrested Charlie Benson. Benson had in his possession an air ticket to Memphis, the clemency papers and $3,300 in marked bills from the ten thousand Baldwin had given Taylor on December 13.

Shortly afterward, Eddie Sisk was arrested in his office at the capitol. Sisk had $1,200, out of the same ten thousand, in his wallet.

Dec 15

I came in, & the children were watching TV. On seeing me, they jumped up saying Guess what, Momma, Charlie & Eddie were arrested! I responded by saying that I was tired & not in the mood for jokes. No kidding, Mom, they've arrested both of them—the F.B.I. did! Look, I said w/irritation, I don't *think this is funny, & I'm not going to joke about it. At that moment there was a bulletin on TV, & Chris Clark flashed on, saying how Eddie had been picked up at his Capitol Hill office, & Charlie at the airport w/a briefcase full of clemency forms, money, etc.*

I was ASTOUNDED. I couldn't believe it, yet I knew it was true. My heart leapt with joy & triumph—then fell into sorrow for Eddie— somehow, I have always had difficulty w/blaming him. Somehow, I always blamed the others for sucking him into their scheme, & leading him down the primrose path. I guess I've never credited Eddie with being his own person.

But I didn't have time to dwell at length on these kinds of thoughts —almost instantly, my phone started ringing—for hours—people calling from all over the state—mostly reporters, wanting statements, mingled with friends, corrections people (Sam, Ramon), etc.

And in the midst of all the calls, I said hello & there was that old familiar voice—"Marie, I just had to call you—I just had to share this moment with you." It was Hank—"Marie, guess who just left my office —Eddie and Charlie. They're on their way to the Federal Magistrate. Marie, I wanted to share this with you. Without you, it never would have been possible."

I was profoundly moved.

· 5 ·

Voices notably silent throughout the pardons and paroles scandal were heard. House Speaker Ned McWherter and Lieutenant Governor John Wilder, after demanding the firing of all three Blanton aides, called for "an in-depth look at the entire pardons and paroles procedure."

On December 19 Sisk and Benson resigned. Taylor was under suspension.

John Jay Hooker Jr., the publisher of the *Banner,* went to court in an attempt to enjoin Blanton from signing any more commutations. Hooker wanted to know where everyone had been all this time.

Called before the federal grand jury on December 22, Blanton retained Jim Neal, the Nashville attorney whose counsel he'd once rejected because everybody in the state would think he was guilty of something. There were more headlines when it was discovered that Blanton's appointments secretary, Ken Lavender, had actually been signing the commutations. A chancery court judge prohibited Lavender from signing any more but said nothing could be done about Blanton himself putting his name to them. A question remained, however, about the legality of more than six hundred pardons and clemencies issued during Blanton's reign.

In Nashville's tightly knit power structure, you sometimes met yourself coming through the door. And now Bill Leech, who had first represented Marie on pardons and paroles, was advising the Governor. Right after Marie's lawsuit, the Tennessee Supreme Court had appointed him state attorney general. To be on the safe side, Leech told Blanton that he should review and personally sign all the commutations handed out while he was in office. Leech also said that if there were any he didn't want to sign, he didn't have to. Don't worry, he'd sign them, Blanton retorted.

The state secretary, Gentry Crowell, had to sign as well. Crowell confided to Leech that every so often Blanton would pause at a former inmate's name, excuse himself and make a phone call. Leech wondered to whom. To brother Gene? Sisk?

· 6 ·

As a piece of black comedy, the drama continued to outdo itself, unveiling dazzling new scenes. Leech was away in Washington while Blanton worked through the night of January 15 in an orgy of more executive clemencies. Fifty-two of them, only fourteen of which had board recommendations. They included twenty-four murderers, among them Roger Humphreys. Asked by a reporter if there were clouds over any of the commutation papers he'd signed, Blanton replied, "If I signed my own commutation, there'd be a cloud over it because the FBI said I'm a target of their investigation."

After Leech rushed back to Nashville, Gentry Crowell told him there had been the same business of Blanton coming to a name and getting up and making a call.

January 17 was a day Hal Hardin—and most of Tennessee—would not soon forget. Early that morning the FBI told Hardin it had learned that Blanton was secretly readying commutations for yet another batch of convicts who would go out on the Governor's last day.

Hardin was sickened by the list of names. Among them was Eddie Dallas (Rusty) Denton, a triple-murderer serving sixty years. In their videotaped conversations, Taylor told Arthur Baldwin that $85,000 had already passed hands on Denton. Denton was from xenophobic Cocke County in the East Tennessee mountains—Benson's and Taylor's county.

Hardin agonized over what to do. Blanton had to be out of his mind drunk, Hardin thought, and that was giving him the benefit of the doubt. Finally he decided Blanton had to be blocked no matter what.

During the afternoon in a room at the Sheraton Inn, not far from the federal courthouse, Hardin reviewed with Bill Leech the possibility of an early swearing-in of Alexander. According to the state constitution, a new governor's term officially began at midnight, January 15. The tradition had been that the inauguration took place the following Saturday. But then again, a governor was supposed to be in office a full four years. Leech's opinion was that Alexander was eligible to take over anytime after the fifteenth, since the legislature had certified his election.

So at 5:55 P.M. on Wednesday, January 17, in a hastily arranged ceremony at the Tennessee Supreme Court, Lamar Alexander was sworn in, three days ahead of schedule. Federal and state guards were stationed around the capitol. Blanton's office suite was sealed. About two hours after Alexander had taken his oath, Robert Lillard, Blanton's new legal counsel, was prevented from taking out of the capitol thirty sets of executive clemency papers he had prepared for Blanton's signature.

Tennessee's pardons and paroles troubles had become a national story. Following Alexander's sudden swearing-in, Blanton said on the CBS evening news with Walter Cronkite, "I'm saddened and hurt for the State of Tennessee that this clandestine action has taken place."

(Wed) Jan 17, 1979
11:30 pm

. . . *I am overwhelmed, looking back over the past 2 1/2 yrs. What will happen to me now?*

I find myself praying—for this state & its new governor—for the men behind the walls—and for myself.

Jan 18

Dinner with Rep. Roger Murray.
One might say I was primed for it, after all that had transpired, but the fact is, I wasn't.

Roger advised me that I will forever be doomed politically as being "unpredictable & uncontrollable." It took me a brief period to absorb the impact of his words. When I did I could barely contain my anger —anger at the certainty that what he said was true, & anger at our chauvinistic society which attributes courage to a man who does what I did, but "female unpredictability" to me.

· 7 ·

At approximately 2 A.M. on February 1, 1979, Sam Pettyjohn, Hillin's key corroborative witness in the Larkin H. Bibbs clemency payoff, was found dead on the floor of his Chattanooga beer store, one .45-caliber bullet hole in his chest, three more in his head. His glittering diamond rings were untouched. A couple of months before, Pettyjohn had been charged with arson to collect insurance on some property, and in a preliminary hearing it was divulged that he would be a party to the government's pardons and paroles case. Friends of Pettyjohn said he'd not been himself recently. Police described the killing as very professional.

Another break in the case developed. A list of thirteen convicts up for clemency had been discovered in Sisk's office immediately after his arrest. One of the inmates was James Webb Anglin of Columbia, Tennessee. The resident FBI agent in Columbia reported to Hillin that a confidential informant was saying that Anglin's brother Ernest had paid cash for his release. The go-between was Arthur Brandon, the capitol custodian. Brandon was the one person Marie had neglected to mention in her interviews with Hillin. Brandon had been exceedingly considerate in helping her settle in as extradition officer. And when she became chairman, he had come to her on behalf of a prisoner, a God-fearing man, he'd said, a member of his church, who really wasn't bad. Marie had promptly looked at his file and had been stunned to find how extensive the man's criminal record was. She'd told Brandon there was nothing she could do. If she showed him the man's record, he'd understand. Marie had thought no more about it. Brandon was just a nice elderly, misguided black gentleman trying to do someone a favor.

Under questioning, Brandon cracked almost at once. Yes, he'd been dealing on Anglin's behalf with Sisk and Benson. Said sixty-five hundred against thirteen thousand had already been paid. He had given Benson fifty-five hundred, while keeping a thousand for himself.

On March 15 conspiracy indictments involving bribery and extortion were returned under the Racketeering Influenced and Corrupt Organizations Act against Sisk, Benson, Taylor and William Aubrey Thompson.

Named as unindicted co-conspirators were Tommy Prater, Arthur Brandon and Ernest Withers. Withers was also a link between the pardons and paroles scheme and the illegal sale of liquor-store franchises, about which he was testifying before another grand jury.

Thompson entered a general denial.

Sisk's explanation of the $1,200 in marked bills in his possession was that it was a loan repayment from Benson. In all, Benson owed him $1,500. Sisk happened to have the bills on his person that day because he was waiting for Taylor to fly in from Memphis. Taylor, he said, was going to buy him some television equipment through a discount contact. To get the full discount, Taylor needed to have all cash.

Benson said that Taylor had asked him to hold $5,000 for him and he had used some of it to repay Sisk.

Taylor claimed entrapment.

In Columbia, Ernest Anglin had just about corroborated Arthur Brandon's story but had yet to make a formal statement before his grand jury appearance. In return for his cooperation, he was still trying to make a deal to get his brother out of prison.

On the evening of April 14 Anglin was at his girl friend's house. Around 9 P.M. two masked men entered, one with a pistol, the other with a shotgun. Anglin was a bookmaker. "If it's my money you want, you can have it," he said, and handed one of the men approximately $8,000. The man took the cash but then ordered Anglin outside. He was taken across the street and was shot in the back with two blasts from a Remington 12-gauge automatic. Anglin's girl friend was unable to say whether the two men had been black or white. There were no other witnesses.

In June an FBI informant reported rumors of a contract on Marie's life. That possibility had been with her ever since the federal investigation became known. During her lawsuit, Traughber had complained that the board never knew where she was. There'd been a reason for that. She had felt most vulnerable crisscrossing the state alone in her BMW. She could recall the dark nights on deserted roads, going over Lookout Mountain near Chattanooga, say, seeing headlights coming up fast behind her, a car trying to pass, and wondering if this was the time she'd be nudged over the edge and sent careening into the blackness below. This was why she would announce she was on her way to Memphis, and would go to Knoxville. Why she'd say she would be at the Holiday Inn, and stay at a Sheraton instead. Sometimes she'd think she was letting her imagination run wild, but then Marie had read about Bernard Weinthal's "suicide" in Dalton and nothing seemed too farfetched after that.

Hillin said U.S. marshals could be assigned to guard her. Marie was living with Therese in a town house she had bought while working in real estate. The boys were on a trip out of state. She was more concerned about Therese than herself, but the idea of marshals constantly underfoot was upsetting. So she and Therese moved in with a friend. After a week, though, Marie decided she'd had enough. She wasn't going to spend her days in hiding. It might be a different story if the investigation were just beginning. But she already had testified before one grand jury after another. And had testified in public as well. Hillin agreed. Marie's high profile in the case was probably her best insurance now.

· 8 ·

In the Tennessee legislature, an Alexander-backed bill was passed creating a new pardons and paroles board. Almost everything Marie had striven for two years ago finally came into being. The board would be autonomous. Would have its own budget, its own budget director. Its staff would be enlarged, with an executive director reporting to the chairman. It would have its own attorney. It also would have five board members, four appointed by the governor, one by the legislature. The expectation was that Alexander would install Marie again as chairman.

Marie couldn't help fantasizing about going back. How nice it'd be to have a little hour of triumph. Have Traughber move his things out of *her* office. But despite Alexander's victory, both the state Senate and House remained in Democratic control, and the Democratic leadership was seething at Marie. She more than anyone else had caused the loss of the executive branch. While House Speaker McWherter was publicly wringing his hands over the pardons and paroles disgrace, he was privately drawing the line on Marie. There was no way she was returning to the board, and Alexander backed off, declaring that he now wanted a fresh start for the board. With a completely new membership.

But that wasn't to be, either. The legislative black caucus went into action for Traughber, arguing that no specific instance of wrongdoing on his part had been demonstrated. Alexander seemed ready to fight it. "Mr. Traughber," he said, "has not shown the kind of character and independence we have to have on the pardons and paroles board." In the end, however, what was called the political realities won out. If Alexander wanted a legislative package for a restructured board, he'd have to accept Traughber along with it, and he caved in. She could just hear Alexander rationalizing his decision on her.

At first Marie was angry, then hurt. It wasn't as if she wanted to be on the board forever, but she would have liked to oversee its new directions. The darned board was like a lover she couldn't get out of her system, she thought. Every time she almost succeeded, the phone would ring, and it'd be a prisoner, or a relative of a prisoner, or a student researching an aspect of the criminal justice system, or a reporter.

Finally she arrived at a reality of her own. She never would have been able to bring herself to sit on the board with Traughber.

Maybe she wasn't cut out to be in politics after all—the gap between personal ideals and political reality too much for her to bridge. She'd have to think more about it. But even if she herself was not returning to the board, most of the reforms she'd worked so hard for were in place at last. Wasn't that a more important reality?

And still far more important was the day she'd won her lawsuit against Blanton. It had been the biggest moment of her life, so definitive in its truth. Marie couldn't conceive of another event ever equaling it. She would always remember turning away from Fred Thompson after the verdict and hugging each of her children in turn, looking at their young faces with big, slightly bewildered grins, and telling them never, never to forget this moment. When justice triumphed over injustice. She knew they didn't quite comprehend it then, but she wanted to fix this moment in their minds so they would in years to come. She remembered her father standing there smiling through his tears. And Fred Thompson's parents spontaneously embracing her. She remembered seeing the mix of astonishment and pleasure on the faces of so many strangers in the jammed courtroom and suddenly realizing that the message of the verdict had reached them as well—that no matter what anyone said, it did pay to fight for what was right. She remembered, too, thinking about all those other, unseen faces outside the courtroom.

Paying the tuition herself, Marie had completed her requirements for a master's degree in the management of human services at Peabody College, part of the Vanderbilt complex. Her thesis was based on her own experience—personal responsibility in the crunch of institutional power. She came across a passage in *The Meditations of Marcus Aurelius* in her research.

> *Have I done something for the general interest? Well, then, I have had my reward.*

Marie figured she could look Marcus Aurelius right in the eye.

EPILOGUE

Jury selection in the instance of the *United States of America* v. *Thomas Edward Sisk et al.* commenced on July 16, 1980. As the government's star witness, Marie was on the stand for more than two days.

Charles Traughber, now testifying for the prosecution, was able to recall Billy Gene Cole and the efforts for clemency on Cole's behalf in great detail. This contradiction with his previous testimony during Marie's lawsuit escaped notice.

Just before the videotapes between Arthur Baldwin and Fred Taylor were to be shown to the jury, the presiding federal judge suffered a heart attack and a mistrial was declared.

On February 6, 1981, as a second trial was about to begin, William Aubrey (Bill) Thompson pleaded guilty to having bribed Sisk to obtain freedom for Billy Gene Cole and was sentenced to two and a half years.

Sisk and Taylor subsequently confessed to conspiring to sell clemencies to state inmates. Each received five years in prison, the maximum allowed in their plea bargaining.

Charlie Benson still went to trial. The U.S. attorney's office, caught off base, found itself prosecuting Benson in a conspiracy case where for days at a stretch Benson's name wasn't mentioned. He claimed that he was only an errand boy, and on May 1 he was acquitted. One of the jurors, quoted in the *Tennessean,* said, "We all believed he was involved in what was going on but felt the government didn't lock him into the proof."

As an outgrowth of the pardons and paroles investigation, Ray Blanton was indicted and convicted of conspiring to take kickbacks for liquor-store licenses. On June 10, 1981, he was sentenced to three years and fined $11,000. On February 11, 1983, the U.S. Sixth Circuit Court of Appeals "reluctantly" reversed Blanton's conviction—not because of any flawed evidence against him, but because the trial judge didn't sufficiently question jurors about hidden opinions they might have formed concerning the case. The government announced that it would appeal.

Meanwhile, Marie moved with her kids back to Daytona Beach. She had to get out of the pressure cooker of Nashville. She began teaching courses in criminal justice at Daytona Beach Community College. A number of inmates in Tennessee continued to correspond with her. One of them wrote that he was sure she must be glad that *those worms were getting theirs.* No, she replied, that wasn't the way she felt at all. *I get no pleasure out of the suffering of these people. I only feel great sadness. None of this had to be.*

AUTHOR'S NOTE

The book was thirteen months in the writing, preceded by nineteen months of research and interviewing.

I was not on the scene until the last court trials. The events described, therefore, the quoted and paraphrased dialogue of the participants, their thoughts at the time, were taken from their own recollections, from television tapes and from official and private papers approximating ten thousand pages.

These included the 49-page indictment and 1,692-page transcript of the first, aborted trial of Sisk and his confederates; 1,135 pages of trial transcript and depositions in Marie's lawsuit against Governor Blanton; 469 transcript pages of the secretly videotaped conversations between Arthur Baldwin and Fred Taylor; dozens of investigative reports—federal, state and local—most of which were unofficially obtained; grand jury testimony used with witness approval; and eighty-five file folders covering activities of the Tennessee Board of Pardons and Paroles from 1975 through 1978.

Also, two hundred eleven letters from Marie to her sons written between January 1975 and February 1978, additional personal and professional correspondence during and beyond that period, and four hundred pages of her private journal.

· 2 ·

This book could not have been written the way it was without the cooperation of Marie. However, she had no editorial control over the book's content.

Her nature is to look forward, not back, and it wasn't easy for her to relive painful intimacies of her marriage, or those long nights in the hospital with Ricky. Neither was presented here gratuituously. Both of these shattering episodes were pivotal in forging her character and strengthening her resolve against the Blanton administration's efforts to humiliate and crush her.

At this writing, Marie's focus is entirely on her children, and until they've finished their education, her own life is in flux. She thinks about a law degree. And she thinks about being alone. It is fourteen years since her divorce. There's another, deeper loneliness. With her contemporaries, there is not that much shared experience. Still, she feels good about herself. Given the same circumstances, she would not have done things differently.

The recorded interviews with her add up to 4,200 pages. I thank her for her trust. I wish to acknowledge, as well, the openness and forbearance of her mother and father, her children, her brothers Chris and Bobby Fajardo, and her sister Rose Ellen.

· 3 ·

Besides Marie, I interviewed seventy-six people in 310 sessions, with repeated follow-ups by phone. While not all of these people appear in the book, each made a valuable contribution. I was struck by their candor, as if they too wanted to piece together what really happened, even those who might have misread Marie as various incidents unfolded.

I especially want to thank Henderson Hillin Jr., retired from the FBI and now head of a Nashville security and investigative agency bearing his name; John and Dolores Seigenthaler; Larry Brinton, who continues his investigative reporting on Nashville's WTVF; Fred Thompson; Richard Fisher; Bill Dodd and his wife, Bette; Hal Hardin; George Haynes; Monsignor Leo Siener; Dr. G. B. Espy III; *Tennessean* reporter Adell Crowe; and, in what assuredly were difficult moments for him, Eddie Sisk.

Sandra Roberts, chief librarian of the *Tennessean*, was unstinting in seeking out more than three thousand pertinent news clips dating back to 1964 from the *Tennessean*, the Nashville *Banner*, the *Commercial Appeal* in Memphis, the Chattanooga *Times*, the Chattanooga *News-Free Press*, the Dalton *Citizen-News*, the New York *Times*, the Washington *Post* and *Time* magazine. I also thank Mike Kettenring and Anne Woodmore for making WSM-TV's videotape news library available.

Generous with their time in recalling their roles in the story were Sam Lipford; Ramon Sanchez-Viñas; David Raybin; Bill Leech; Erwin Mitchell; Corbett Hart; State Senator Ed Blank; Maribeth Blank; Joe Brown, then the chief assistant U.S. attorney in Nashville; Lee Smith of the *Tennessee Journal*; John Dowd, Steve Pitt; Charlie Mills; Billy Watkins; Jack Scism; and former TBCI agent Charles Lee.

Kay Johnson, who befriended Marie during the last stages of her marriage, provided indispensable insights. The help of two other of Marie's friends, Linda Goodman and Toni Greer, was much appreciated. So was that of Charles Weathers and Martha Bernard.

My thanks also to William Beaver, special agent in charge of the Memphis field office of the FBI; Georgia Bureau of Investigation director Phil Peters; Cynthia Trainor, who was unswervingly loyal to Marie on the pardons and paroles board; Chief of Police Paul Griffin of Rossville, Georgia; Judge Charles Pannell of Dalton; attorney Bobby Lee Cook; and Judge Gilbert Merritt of the U.S. Sixth Circuit Court of Appeals. The director of the newly independent Tennessee Bureau of Investigation, Arzo Carson, and his deputy, Steve Watson, supplied a vivid picture of the agency under the Blanton regime, as did Joe Hannah, who has left the bureau.

In addition, there was Dick Ferrando, who employed Marie at the Villa; Paul Corbin; Fred Chappell of Columbia, Tennessee; John Jay Hooker Jr.; and Carol Marin, now with WGM-TV in Chicago. Wendell Rawls Jr. of the New York *Times* opened an essential door. Present and past members of the *Tennessean*'s staff were particularly informative. They include Doug Hall, Jimmy Carnahan, Larry Daughtrey, Frank Sutherland, Robert Sherborne, Joel Kaplan and Carol Clurman. Acknowledgments are also due FBI Director William H. Webster, Assistant Director Lee Colwell, and Roger Young and David Divan of the FBI's public affairs office.

I am grateful for the hospitality and other courtesies extended by Father Albert Siener during my many trips to Nashville.

· 4 ·

The book could never have been completed on schedule without the expert organizing of vast quantities of raw material by my research assistant, Joan Spano, who always seemed to know where everything was and who kept a sharp editorial eye on the manuscript. Rita Lynch had the unenviable task of transcribing dozens of hours of recorded interviews.

Among those asked to read the work in progress were Sam Cohn, Arlene Donovan, Gloria Steinem, Helen Doctorow, Julia Miles, Lisa Miles, Susan Braudy, Vivienne Jaffe, Alan Gelb and Suzanne Jones. I am indebted to them all for their detailed, thoughtful comments.

An appreciation here, too, for my editor, Jason Epstein, a man of care and discernment, who always kept me on track.

Lastly, a personal word. My late wife, Audrey Gellen Maas, would have been pleased to know that the film she nurtured and co-produced, *Alice Doesn't Live Here Anymore*, had such an impact on Marie.